Second Edition

Introduction to
Emergency Management

Second Edition

Introduction to
Emergency
Management

Brenda D. Phillips
David M. Neal
Gary R. Webb

CRC Press
Taylor & Francis Group
Boca Raton London New York

CRC Press is an imprint of the
Taylor & Francis Group, an **informa** business

CRC Press
Taylor & Francis Group
6000 Broken Sound Parkway NW, Suite 300
Boca Raton, FL 33487-2742

Library of Congress Cataloging-in-Publication Data

Names: Phillips, Brenda D., author. | Neal, David M., author. | Webb, Gary R., author. Title: Introduction to emergency management / Brenda D. Phillips, David M. Neal, and Gary R. Webb. Description: 2nd edition. | New York : CRC Press, 2016. | Revised edition of the authors's Introduction to emergency management, 2012. | Includes bibliographical references and index. Identifiers: LCCN 2016025578| ISBN 9781482245066 (hbk) | ISBN 9781315394701 (ebk) Subjects: LCSH: Emergency management. Classification: LCC HV551.2 .P45 2016 | DDC 363.34/8--dc23 LC record available at https://lccn.loc.gov/2016025578

Visit the Taylor & Francis Web site at
http://www.taylorandfrancis.com

and the CRC Press Web site at
http://www.crcpress.com

We dedicate this book to William A. Anderson (1937–2013)—a friend, mentor, and pioneer who devoted his life to building and diversifying the hazards and disasters research community and advancing the profession of emergency management; Joseph B. Perry, Jr. (1930–2010), a scholar of the field, mentor, and force for social justice; and Henry Quarantelli—a mentor and cofounder of this field whose direct and indirect influence is seen throughout this book.

Contents

Preface

Despite their potential for causing severe damage and disruption, significant financial losses, and tragic human suffering, disasters can and do have a brighter side. In their wakes, citizens often engage in extraordinary feats of heroism, first responders rush to the scene, volunteers give selflessly, and emergency management professionals work tirelessly to navigate and solve the complex challenges brought on by disasters. In a word, people and communities often exhibit remarkable *resilience* in the face of disaster. While we are certainly mindful of and deeply impacted by the devastating effects disasters can have, we also recognize that these tragic events can provide important learning opportunities. Thus, we have written and revised this book to highlight the valuable lessons that have been learned as communities all around the world have dealt with devastating disasters and to enhance future societal resilience by providing students and the next generation of emergency management professionals with a solid foundation on which to build.

Our appreciation extends to the entire Taylor & Francis team, especially editor Mark Listewnik, Jen Abbott, Natalja Mortensen, Stephanie Morkert, and Prudence Taylor Board. Their efforts and professionalism were instrumental in producing the first edition and have made the task of preparing a second edition much easier. For many years, faculty teaching emergency management courses had to cobble sparse and disparate resources together, but that has all changed because of the vision that they have had for the CRC Press series of books in emergency management. On behalf of the many faculty now teaching in this emerging discipline of emergency management, we acknowledge and express our sincere appreciation for their efforts. In addition to the Taylor & Francis team, special thanks are owed to Brandi Weaver, the director of Quinn Library at Ohio University, Chillicothe.

We also express our sincere gratitude to family members who care about what we do and have provided unwavering support over the years: Frank and Mary Jane Phillips, Robert Neal, and Joyce Stanley; Lisa Dalton-Webb and Spencer Webb. In addition, we would be remiss if we did not mention Scarlet, Graycie, Krissy, Lucy, Roxie, and Goldie, special family members who inspired the sections on pets and disasters.

Our professors and mentors, E.L. Quarantelli, Russell R. Dynes, Joseph B. Perry, Jr., Kathleen Tierney, Gary Kreps, and Bill Anderson, taught us what they know about the social aspects of disasters and how best to manage them, and for that we are all grateful. Their impact can be seen throughout this book, and we are proud to pass that knowledge on to the next generation.

Throughout our careers, we have stressed the importance of empirical research in terms of enhancing our understanding of disasters and improving the practice of emergency management. This book was inspired by that research, and we have done our best to include references to the most important studies, from the classics published many years ago to the most recently published, cutting-edge studies that have come out in recent months. We are fortunate to work in a relatively small—albeit growing—field of study, and we are thankful to our many friends and colleagues who have shared their work with us over the years at conferences, through journals, and in great conversations. The research literature on hazards, disasters, crises, and emergency management is diverse and constantly expanding, and we hope that we have honored the work of our colleagues without overlooking anyone unintentionally.

While we have emphasized the value of research throughout this book, we recognize that experience also matters. Indeed, one of the many challenges the profession of emergency management faces today is bridging the gap between research and practice. Thus, in addition to citing research studies, we have also integrated our many years of experience—gained through extensive fieldwork, volunteering, consulting, and serving as federal subject matter experts — throughout this book, and so in places where references are not indicated, content originates from those experiences. While this textbook is based primarily on our cumulative years of experience, conducting research and teaching in the field, we have benefitted from the constructive feedback of many who adopted the first edition for their courses and anonymous reviewers for the second edition. We have incorporated many of their suggestions by including more coverage of federal-level disaster policies, addressing international issues throughout this book, and providing up-to-date examples of recent disasters.

As we have finalized the revisions of this second edition over the past few months, we have witnessed several major disasters: another round of massive flooding in Houston, Texas; a devastating earthquake in Ecuador; and tragic terrorist attacks in Paris, Brussels, Pakistan, and San Bernardino. While each of these disasters is unique, there are also many important commonalities among them. In this book, you will be introduced to the principles of effective emergency management that are essential to understanding those commonalities, enhancing societal resilience, and improving our ability to effectively manage future disasters.

Brenda D. Phillips
Ohio University-Chillicothe

David M. Neal
Oklahoma State University

Gary R. Webb
University of North Texas

Authors

Brenda D. Phillips, PhD, is the associate dean and professor of sociology at Ohio University in Chillicothe. She is the author of *Disaster Recovery*, *Introduction to Emergency Management*, *Qualitative Disaster Research*, and *Mennonite Disaster Service*. She has coedited *Social Vulnerability to Disasters* and *Women and Disasters: From Theory to Practice*. Dr. Phillips is the recipient of the Blanchard Award for excellence in emergency management education and the Myers Award for work on the effects of disasters on women. She was inducted into the International Women's Hall of Fame for Emergency Management and Homeland Security in 2013. She has been funded multiple times by the National Science Foundation with publications in multiple peer-reviewed journals. Dr. Phillips has been invited to teach, consult, or present in New Zealand, Australia, Germany, India, Peru, Costa Rica, Mexico, Canada, Sweden, and the People's Republic of China. She is a graduate of Bluffton University (Ohio) and The Ohio State University, Columbus, Ohio. Locally, Dr. Phillips is a member of the Ross County Local Emergency Planning Committee, the Ross County Safety Council Board of Directors, and the Chillicothe Rotary. She recently led efforts to re-establish the OUC Emergency Response Training Center for widespread and affordable local use by emergency responders.

David M. Neal, PhD, is a sociologist serving as a professor with the Fire and Emergency Management Program in the Department of Political Science at

Oklahoma State University, Stillwater, Oklahoma. He has studied a wide range of events (e.g., blizzards, tornadoes, floods, hurricanes, earthquakes, hazardous materials, and tsunamis) throughout the United States, and also in Sweden and India. Organizations such as FEMA, NASA, the National Science Foundation, and the American Red Cross have funded his research. He taught his first class on disasters in 1979 at the University of Evansville, Indiana. In 1989, he joined the Institute of Emergency Administration Planning at the University of North Texas, Denton, Texas, where he became the first full time PhD faculty member with the first emergency management degree program and later served as its director. He has published academic articles on developing emergency management degree programs and using virtual teaching environments for teaching emergency management. He has also served as a consultant for universities starting undergraduate and graduate degrees in emergency management and fire administration. In 2015, he received the Blanchard Award for excellence in emergency management education. He has also served as a Red Cross disaster volunteer and as Chapter Chair of the Denton County Red Cross. He earned his bachelor's and master's degrees at Bowling Green State University, Ohio, and his PhD in sociology at The Ohio State University, where he also served as a research assistant with the Disaster Research Center. His current interests focus on crisis and disaster research in Sweden, and writing on the sociology of science of disaster research.

Gary R. Webb, PhD, is professor and chair of Emergency Management and Disaster Science at the University of North Texas, Denton, Texas. Previously he was a faculty member in the sociology department at Oklahoma State University, Stillwater, Oklahoma, where he received the Regents Distinguished Teaching Award. He holds a PhD from the University of Delaware, Newark, Delaware, where he worked at the Disaster Research Center, and he specializes in the study of organizational preparedness for and response to extreme events. His research has been supported by various agencies, including the U.S. National Science Foundation, and it has appeared in a variety of professional journals, including the *International Journal of Mass Emergencies and Disasters*, *International Journal of Emergency Management*, *Journal of Contingencies and Crisis Management*, *Natural Hazards Review*, and *Environmental Hazards*. His research has also been featured in national media, including the *Los Angeles Times*, *Newsday*, and *Christian Science Monitor*. He has been invited to teach or present his research to international audiences in Denmark, France, South Korea, the Netherlands, and Turkey.

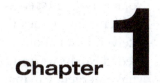

Chapter **1**

History and Current Status of Emergency Management

Objectives

Upon completing this chapter, readers should be able to:

- Describe the development of emergency management in the United States.
- Understand FEMA's central role in emergency management since 1979.
- Describe the reasons behind the successes and failures of FEMA during its existence.
- Comprehend the importance and growth of research centers focusing on disasters.
- Realize that important disaster research is also occurring outside of the United States.

Key Terms

- Civil Defense
- Disaster Research
- Dual Track
- Emergency Management
- Emergency Support Function
- Federal Emergency Management Agency (FEMA)
- Federal Response Plan
- Homeland Security
- National Response Framework
- Natural Disasters
- Project Impact
- Technological Hazards
- Terrorist Threats

1.1 Introduction

Noah was the first emergency manager (Dynes 2003), and he faced the same problems and issues that emergency managers face today. Although Noah received news about a major flood from an impeccable source, only a few heeded Noah's warning and helped him to prepare. The story of Noah reflects what emergency managers may experience today. For example, people continue to live in disaster-prone areas (e.g., earthquakes and hurricanes) but take few steps to lessen the impact of these events. Indeed, annual loss of life or economic losses from disasters continue to increase both in the United States and worldwide. Although emergency managers work diligently to lessen the impacts of disasters, people may not pay attention and politicians may hold different priorities. Emergency management thus represents a challenging field, albeit one in which you can make a difference professionally and personally.

The field of emergency management has grown dramatically, particularly over the past 50 years. A wide range of events, including floods, hurricanes, tornados, tsunamis, earthquakes, volcanoes, massive explosions, large hazardous waste sites, and terrorist attacks, highlights the importance of understanding how people and organizations behave when confronted by disasters. To deal with existing and new types of threats that we will prepare for, respond to, recover from, and mitigate against, we need professional, well-educated emergency managers. Education, coupled with relevant experience, can play a role in creating a more effective approach to disasters.

For example, imagine that without warning you are told you cannot drink your water. No walking to the tap to pour a quick glass of water to quench your thirst. No filling your pot with water to prepare spaghetti or other food. The water is so contaminated that you cannot even make a cup of coffee. The widespread water contamination makes trips to local restaurants for food or coffee fruitless, as they have the same water issues. By the time you head to grocery stores to buy water, you find that others have already bought the existing supply. An official message you read on Twitter or Facebook states that you may not be able to drink your local water for at least a week—maybe longer. Officials warn to not even shower or bathe in the water. Suddenly, you are in the mid of a crisis. And remember, humans must have water to survive.

As this event evolves into a crisis and even disaster, local and state emergency management officials coordinate with each other and with businesses and volunteer organizations in order to provide a temporary supply of water. Suddenly, people from even 40 miles away show up with trucks full of donated water. While officials tackle these issues, other groups focus on trying to find the source of the problem and ways to make the water safe again. Once water specialists discover the source of the problem and find a solution, working with local governments and the media, they will provide information about when the water will be safe again.

Although this scenario may sound unlikely, this event recently occurred. In early August 2014, officials from Toledo, Ohio warned regional citizens that their drinking water became unsafe as water taken from Lake Erie contained a fungus. Water treatment processes could not make the water safe. As a result, city and county officials in Northwestern Ohio warned over 400,000 people not to drink, cook, bathe, or shower in with the water. Officials warned that boiling the water would only make the toxins in the water more concentrated (Henry 2015a, b; Seewer 2015). In 2016, the city of Flint, Michigan, faced a similar threat when reports of lead-contaminated drinking water surfaced. Lead exposure can cause serious health problems including brain damage in children.

A look at any media outlet punctuates the constant threat and impact of such disasters. For example, we continue to see a relentless parade of tornadoes, floods, earthquakes, hurricanes and typhoons, chemical releases, and explosions worldwide. Occasionally, catastrophic events occur. For example, on April 25, 2015, a massive earthquake (Richter 7.8) and major aftershocks struck the country of Nepal. Extreme damage occurred southwest of the epicenter at the nation's capital, Kathmandu. Initial estimates suggested almost 9,000 died with almost 22,000 more sustaining injuries (USAID 2015; USGS 2015). In addition to much of the nation's capital of Kathmandu being damaged or destroyed, the earthquakes devastated rural villages. Overall, the earthquake destroyed over 500,000 homes and damaged about 270,000 other homes. At least 2.8 million people needed food, water, shelter, and other basic supplies for survival (USAID 2015).

New types of disasters also occur, about which we will read further in Chapter 2. To illustrate, cyber terrorists (perhaps from North Korea) infiltrated e-mail inside of Sony, a major media company. Under the potential of more e-mails being revealed, Sony at first decided not to release a movie titled *The Interview* that many assumed to be about the leader of North Korea. The economic impacts of such Internet intrusions can be significant.

In short, events related to hazards, disasters, risks, and crises continue to occur. Some are more typical (e.g., floods and tornadoes), some are new in nature (e.g., cyber-attacks), and others are catastrophic. As a result, a continuing need exists to have professionals involved in emergency management with a wide and deep scope of knowledge. Your journey toward a career in emergency management begins with this chapter that describes the field of emergency management. As our primary audience for this text is in the United States, we concentrate on that historical evolution of the field (for an example from the United Kingdom, please view Box 1.1). We focus on the field's roots in civil defense and natural disasters. Next, we discuss the creation and role of the Federal Emergency Management Agency (FEMA) and later the Department of Homeland Security (DHS). Although FEMA coordinates most disaster issues at the federal level in the United States, we also show how other organizations play a role in disasters. Finally, we look at the emergence and value of research centers that study disasters worldwide. These centers generate much of the research we use to make policy, to teach from, and to generate new ideas on how to deal with disasters, a topic that we will expand upon in Chapter 3.

BOX 1.1   EMERGENCY MANAGEMENT IN ENGLAND AND WALES

Eve Coles

In 2015, Eve Coles took up a temporary 1-year post at Auckland University of Technology (AUT), New Zealand, where she is a senior lecturer in emergency management. She is also a visiting research fellow to the Cabinet Office Emergency Planning College in the United Kingdom and a founder member of the Future City and Community Resilience network

(Continued)

BOX 1.1 (*Continued*)   EMERGENCY MANAGEMENT IN ENGLAND AND WALES

(www.FCCRNet.org). Her research interests include emergency management policy in the United Kingdom, learning the lessons from emergencies, resilient cities, and business continuity management, particularly for public sector organizations.

Emergency management in the United Kingdom is based on the twin principles of subsidiarity and localism. Essentially the principles aim to give communities the power to make their own decisions regarding their own problems: defer responsibility and decision making to the lowest level while coordinating at the highest necessary level and allow each responder service to retain command authority over their own resources, while activities are coordinated by multiagency groups such as Local Resilience Forums for planning, risk assessment and preparedness, and strategic/tactical groups for response and recovery (HM Government 2013).

Drivers for change in the United Kingdom, which had previously been governed by the 1948 Civil Defence Act and subsequent *ad hoc* civil protection legislation, were the chaos of the fuel crisis and severe flooding experienced during 2000 and the foot & mouth crisis of 2001 (collectively known as the 3 Fs). These events exposed a serious weakness in the capability to deal with wide area emergencies in the United Kingdom. The terrorist attacks of 9/11 in the United States further emphasized the *ad hoc* nature of the UK system and added impetus to the need to restructure.

Restructuring began in November 2001 when responsibility for emergency management moved from the Home Office to the Cabinet Office; under the auspices of the Civil Contingencies Secretariat (CCS) with the aim … *to improve the UK's resilience to disruptive challenges at every level* (Home Office 2001:1). The "resilience agenda" sought to do three things:

1. Build a comprehensive capability for anticipating major incidents and where possible prevent them or take action in advance that will mitigate their effects
2. Ensure that planning for response and recovery is geared to the risk therefore ensuring preparedness
3. Promote a "culture of resilience" including business continuity thus helping to reduce the disruptive effects of disaster

Arguably, the two foundation building blocks of the agenda are the National Resilience Capabilities Programme (NRCP) and the Civil Contingencies Act 2004. One of the first measures put in place post the 3 Fs and 9/11 was the NRCP that has grown and evolved in the years since 2002. It is a cyclical auditing program, the purpose of which is to identify, challenge, and monitor the current levels of capability in each of the areas covered by the 22 work streams described in detail below. The information gathered on how

(*Continued*)

BOX 1.1 (*Continued*) EMERGENCY MANAGEMENT IN ENGLAND AND WALES

much capability each work stream has delivered is then used to provide assurance on how ready the United Kingdom is to respond to civil emergencies. The 22 work streams consist of the following:

- Two work streams that are structural, dealing with the central (national), and local response capabilities
- Five that are concerned with the maintenance of essential services (food, water, fuel, transport, health, and financial services)
- Eight functional work streams, dealing with chemical, biological, radiological, and nuclear (CBRN) resilience; infectious diseases—human; infectious diseases—animal and plant; mass casualties; mass fatalities; mass evacuation/shelter; site clearance; and flooding
- Six supporting work streams: warning and informing the public; humanitarian assistance; community and corporate resilience, recovery, resilient telecommunications, and interoperability

Since 2005*, emergency management provisions and legislation in the United Kingdom have been governed by the Civil Contingencies Act (2004), and the Civil Contingencies Act 2004 (Contingency Planning) Regulations 2012, together with statutory (*Emergency Preparedness*) and nonstatutory (*Emergency Response and Recovery*) guidance. The Act along with its accompanying measures provides a single framework for civil protection in the United Kingdom and for the first time placed a statutory duty on local responders to plan for emergencies through the concept of integrated emergency management.

Work on the Civil Contingencies Act (2004) began in 2002, but it did not receive its royal assent until November 2004 and pass into law until April 2005. It is an enabling Act in two parts that encompassed and repealed the 1948 Civil Defence Act and subsequent *ad hoc* civil protection legislation and the 1920s Emergency Powers Act. Part 1 of the Act includes the following:

- A working definition of an emergency
- Provision for a Local Resilience Forum of Category 1 responders (and Category 2 responders when relevant)
- Provision for identification of risks and the development of a community risk register
- A duty to plan for civil emergencies
- A duty for responders to share information

---

* Before 2005, emergency management was subject to the 1948 Civil Defence Act and subsequent civil protection regulations and *ad hoc* measures.

(*Continued*)

BOX 1.1 (*Continued*)   EMERGENCY MANAGEMENT IN ENGLAND AND WALES

- A duty for first responders to have business continuity plans in place
- A duty on local authorities to provide advice and support to the business community
- A categorization of responders
- A duty to warn and inform the public

Part 2 of the Act includes the following:

- Provision to declare a state of emergency on a regional basis (previously it was only on a national basis)
- Provision for the appointment of regional coordinators and regional resilience forums
- Provision for the Minister of State to draw a regulatory framework for dealing with emergencies

The Act also categorizes responders into the following two groups:

- Category 1 Responders
  - Local government
  - Emergency services
    - Police forces
    - Fire and rescue authorities
    - Ambulance services
  - NHS and health bodies
    - Primary care trusts, acute trusts (hospitals), foundation trusts, port health authorities, Welsh local health boards
  - Government agencies
    - The Environment Agency and Scottish Environment Agency
    - The Maritime and Coastguard Agency
    - Public Health England
- Category 2 Responders
  - Utilities (water, sewerage, gas, and electricity)
  - Telephone service providers
  - Railway operators
  - Airport operators
  - Harbor authorities
  - The Highways Agency
  - The health and safety executive
  - Strategic health authorities

The regulations also make provision for the establishment of Local Resilience Forums (LRFs) based on Police Force areas. There are 42 LRFs in England and Wales. Although not a legal entity or with powers to direct its members,

(Continued)

**BOX 1.1 (*Continued*) EMERGENCY
MANAGEMENT IN ENGLAND AND WALES**

they provide Category 1 and Category 2 responders with the collective responsibility to plan, prepare and communicate in a multi-agency environment (HM Government 2013).

In 2011/2012, the statutory guidelines, *Emergency Preparedness,* and nonstatutory guidelines, *Emergency Response and Recovery,* were reviewed and revised to bring them in line with new thinking and changing current practices.

Additionally, the developing resilience policy agenda has been supported over the past 15 years by a growing raft of on-going measures including the following:

- National Risk Register
- The Fire and Rescue Services Act (2004)
- Anti-Terrorism Act (2005)
- National Flood Risk Policy
- Information to the public on how to prepare for emergencies
- Increased funding mainly for "blue light" services
- National Security Strategy
- Government Concept of Operations (CONOPS)
- Strategic Framework for the Resilience of Critical Infrastructure, 2010
- Community Resilience Programme
- Flood & Water Management Act 2010 (direct result of the Pitt Review 2008)
- Corporate Resilience work stream (including government sponsored British standards such as BS:11200 in Crisis Management and BS:6500 in Organizational Resilience along with ISO 3200 in Business Continuity Management)
- National Recovery Guidance
- Sector Resilience Plans (2014)
- Joint Emergency Services Interoperability Programme (JESIP)

More recently, the Pitt Inquiry into the 2007 Floods and the Rule 43 Inquest Report from Lady Justice Hallet into the deaths from the 7/7 bombings in London both identified a number of key problems with the way in which responders worked together to manage the emergencies and the way they perceived and shared information. As a result, in 2012, the Home Secretary initiated the Joint Emergency Services Interoperability Programme (JESIP) to address the issues raised by both reports with the aim of developing and promoting joint working in emergencies and complex situations as the norm rather than the exception. The programme has since developed Principles for Joint Working, Joint Doctrine for the Emergency Services, and Joint Standard Operating Procedures (SOPs).

(Continued)

BOX 1.1 (*Continued*)   EMERGENCY MANAGEMENT IN ENGLAND AND WALES

Quite clearly in the UK emergency management legislation, systems and frameworks as well as practice have evolved and grown considerably since the beginning of the millennium. There has also been what May (1992) would describe as considerable *instrumental policy change* (cited Coles 2014) to meet new and emerging threats and hazards. The aspiration made by the Home Office in 2001 ... *to improve the UK's resilience to disruptive challenges at every level* (Home Office 2001:1) has been taken seriously by successive governments, considered and worked on to provide a resilience framework that is robust and preparing for what may come in the future.

References

Coles E. L. 2014. *Learning the Lessons from Major Incidents; A Short Review of the Literature.* Emergency Planning College Occasional Papers No.10, Easingwold, York.
HM Government. 2013. *The Role of Local Resilience Forums: A Reference Document.* England: Cabinet Office Civil Contingencies Secretariat.
Home Office. 2001. *The CCS: What It Means.* England: Home Office.
May P. 1992. Policy Learning and Failure. *Journal of Public Policy.* 12(4): 331–354.

Links to UK Government Documents

Civil Contingencies Act (2004): https://www.gov.uk/government/policies/emergency-planning?keywords=Civil+Contingencies+Act+2004&public_timestamp%5Bfrom%5D=&public_timestamp%5Bto%5D.
Emergency Preparedness: https://www.gov.uk/government/publications/emergency-preparedness
Emergency Response and Recovery: https://www.gov.uk/government/publications/emergency-response-and-recovery.
National Recovery Guidance: https://www.gov.uk/government/uploads/system/uploads/attachment_data/file/419549/20150331_2015-NRR-WA_Final.pdf.
Joint Emergency Services Interoperability Programme (JESIP): http://www.jesip.org.uk/home].

1.2 The Evolution of Emergency Management in the United States

Almost 60 years ago, the profession named emergency management did not exist. Within the federal government in the United States, disasters offices were scattered throughout the federal bureaucracy. Some local governments had offices of civil defense to help protect the nation against a possible attack from the Soviet Union. Typically, civil defense positions were part time, low paying, and required little if any training or education. The American National Red Cross and Salvation Army were the most common volunteer organizations available to assist disaster victims. Businesses typically did not have disaster planners. Only a few organizations throughout the world provided international disaster relief. No university offered a major or minor in emergency management, nor was any individual course available.

However, emergency management has slowly risen to become a full-fledged profession. Today, those in FEMA, as a part of DHS, coordinate most national disaster efforts. All states and most local governments have disaster managers throughout the United States. All major businesses have individuals in charge of disaster planning. In addition to the Red Cross and Salvation Army, a large number of volunteer organizations stand ready to assist both victims and responders. A wide range of organizations throughout the world offer disaster relief across national borders. Many professionals in the field today have college degrees, and about 150 universities in the United States alone offer bachelor's or master's degrees, and several offer PhDs in emergency management. In short, the field of emergency management has grown dramatically over the past 60 years. This section provides an overview of this extraordinary growth and describes some of the key organizations today that play major roles in emergency management.

1.2.1 Civil Defense

The federal government in the United States has played a large role in protecting the nation from a foreign attack through the idea of civil defense. During World War II, civil defense activities gave members of the public a chance to contribute to the war effort. For example, civilians were trained to spot enemy aircraft. Cities practiced evening blackouts, turning out all lights, so enemy bombers could not find their targets. Others watched coastal waters for enemy submarines. However, these activities did not really enhance the nation's defense, except for giving civilians a feeling that they were contributing to the war effort.

Civil defense became even more prominent starting in the early 1950s with the arrival of the Cold War. With both the Soviet Union and the United States becoming bitter ideological enemies and each having nuclear weapons, potential existed for a nuclear war. In the United States, the federal government created various offices of civil defense (i.e., Federal Civil Defense Agency 1953–1958; Office of Civil Defense Mobilization 1958–1961; and the Office of Civil Defense 1968–1979) to lead and coordinate efforts to protect U.S. residents from chemical and nuclear attacks. Well-known activities supported by civil defense included "duck and cover" protective actions and encouraging nuclear bomb shelters in people's homes. In addition, some public buildings were designated as "civil defense shelters." In case of a nuclear war, citizens would seek shelter in these buildings, while also being provided food and water (Sylves 2008; Task Force 2010). Often buildings such as schools or county courthouses served as civil defense shelters. Today, we can often still find civil defense shelter signs on public buildings.

Local civil defense directors were more likely than not to be part time employees, with offices often located in county courthouse basements.

Many such employees had retired from the military. These retirees often had a military pension, so local governments could get by with paying a minimal salary. In addition, officials assumed that civil defense military backgrounds would be useful during a nuclear attack. Known as "air raid wardens," their job was ultimately to blow the signs in the case of imminent nuclear attack (Waugh 2000). Though this focus on civil defense—and today on terrorism—has reappeared throughout the history of emergency management, other types of disasters have compelled significant changes in the field. In the next section, we discuss how certain natural and technological disasters have influenced disaster management.

1.2.2 Managing Natural and Technological Disasters in the United States

Until the 1950s, disaster management had been primarily a matter for local and state governments. Only in case-by-case situations did the federal government, primarily through specific legislation, become involved. For example, the U.S. Congress would provide specific funding to provide aid or assistance to a community. Voluntary organizations, such as the American National Red Cross or the Salvation Army, were the main consistent national sources of peacetime relief efforts. In 1950, following severe flooding in the upper Midwest, Congress passed the Disaster Relief Act. This legislation allowed the federal government to become involved in any future disaster relief efforts without additional Congressional approval. Although this act provided only a narrow scope of disaster assistance, it created a foundation for Congress to later expand the role of the federal government in disaster. In addition, this act gave the President a means to provide disaster assistance without Congressional approval (Kreps 1990; Sylves 2008).

Through the Disaster Relief Act of 1974 and later the Stafford Act of 1988, the federal government could provide aid for communities and later directly to disaster victims. Most importantly, these acts describe how the President declares an event a disaster (e.g., a Presidential Declaration) and outlines what kinds of aid can be delivered (Sylves 2008). In addition, political outcomes from other big disasters (e.g., Hurricane Camille, 1969; San Fernando Earthquake, 1971; and Hurricane Agnes, 1972) further broadened the federal government's role during disaster (Kreps 1990) as well as the involvement of many voluntary organizations.

Thus, the federal government supported civil defense initiatives, and it also provided a different set of programs for other types of disasters. One track focused on civil defense, while the other track primarily focused on natural disasters (and to a lesser extent technological disasters). Although this unintended dual track may have made sense at the time, it also created problems. First, some redundancy existed between the civil defense and natural disaster efforts. Second, emergency management offices were scattered all over the federal bureaucracies. Since these disaster offices were not centralized, problems of communication and inefficiency developed (National Governor's Association 1979). In addition, in both the civil defense and peace-time focused organizations, occasional reorganization seemed to be the norm. For many, the dual tracks (rather than having one centralized federal agency) and constant reorganization hurt the nation's ability to deal with disasters (Kreps 1990). As we describe in more detail later in this chapter, President Jimmy Carter centralized most of the nation's disaster efforts under one organization by creating FEMA.

1.2.3 The Development of the U.S. FEMA

Since 1979, FEMA has served as the key federal agency for coordinating disaster activities in the United States. This section discusses the factors leading to the creation of FEMA, events impacting FEMA during its inception and up to the terrorist attacks of September 11, 2001, and FEMA's role and activities since that pivotal date. Keep in mind that until 1979, the federal government had no true centralized department to deal with emergency management issues.

FEMA is now close to being 40 years old. During this time, it often experienced dramatic changes coupled with varying degrees of public support. FEMA has been recognized during these decades as both the best federal agency in the nation (during the Clinton Administration in the mid and late 1990s) to one of the worst run agencies (e.g., following its responses to Hurricane Andrew in 1992 and Hurricane Katrina in 2005, see The White House 2006 and U.S. Congress 2006). The Clinton Administration elevated FEMA to a cabinet level post with its administrator reporting directly to the President. The Bush Administration subsequently retracted that position and then subsumed FEMA under a new bureaucracy called DHS in response to the terrorist attacks of September 11. To understand the dynamic evolution of FEMA, the next section briefly describes FEMA's creation in 1979 and some of its main activities since that time.

1.2.3.1 Creation of FEMA

Several events and actions have influenced the creation of FEMA (see Figure 1.1). As noted earlier, a dual track of emergency management organizations existed in the United States. One focused on civil defense issues, whereas the other focused generally on natural and technical disasters. Many, but not all, civil defense programs operated under the U.S. Department of Defense (DOD), while the natural and technological disaster programs were scattered throughout the federal bureaucracy. The dual tracks and lack of any centralized disaster agency created tension and inefficiency within

FIGURE 1.1   Factors influencing the development of FEMA.

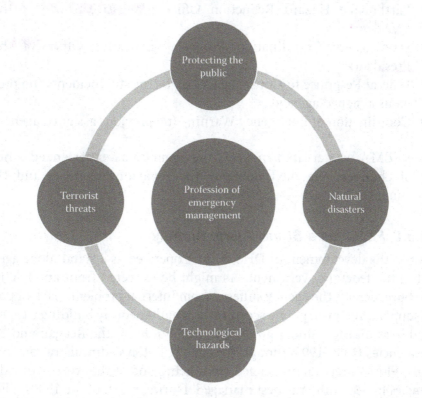

FIGURE 1.2   FEMA responsibilities.

the federal government (Kreps 1990; NGA 1979; Sylves 2008). To improve the overall effectiveness of emergency management in the United States, President Carter in 1978 initiated Reorganization Plan #3 to consolidate almost all emergency management under one federal agency to perform centralized roles (see Figure 1.2). This agency became known as FEMA. The following list shows which federal departments became part of FEMA.

The organization in parentheses shows which department or agency the department came from (NGA 1979, p. 3):

- Federal Insurance Administration (Department of Housing and Urban Development)
- National Fire Prevention and Control Administration (Department of Commerce)
- Federal Broadcast System (Executive Office of the President)
- Defense Civil Preparedness Agency (DOD)
- Federal Disaster Assistance Administration (Department of Housing and Urban Development)
- Federal Preparedness Agency (General Services Administration)
- National Weather Service Community Preparedness Program (Department of Commerce)
- Earthquake Hazard Reduction Office (Executive Office of the President)
- Dam Safety Coordination Program (Executive Office of the President)
- Federal Response to Consequences of Terroristic Incidents (no previous assigned agency)
- Coordination of Emergency Warning (no previous assigned agency)

Since FEMA was created in 1979, the agency has experienced a number of changes. We next describe these various changes and their consequences.

1.2.3.2 FEMA as a Stand-Alone Agency

Prior to the development of DHS, FEMA operated as a stand-alone agency within the federal government. As might be expected from any relatively new bureaucracy, the agency suffered from internal problems, lack of political support, and even public scorn while simultaneously building a capacity to address disasters under guiding legislation. From the Reagan and Bush presidencies (1981–1993) though President Clinton's administration (1993–2001), FEMA's reputation ranged from being one of the worst run federal agencies to becoming the best managed. During much of the 1980s, FEMA moved through the process of defining itself and its role in the federal government (Daniels and Clark-Daniels 2000).

During President George H. Bush's administration (1989–1993), criticism over ineffective internal leadership and poor disaster responses led to further questions about FEMA's value. For example, the federal government seemed incapable of providing the needed assistance to state and local governments following the "dual disasters" (Hurricane Hugo and the Loma Prieta/California Earthquake) during the late summer and early fall of 1989.

Politicians, the media, and the public leveled similar criticisms following Hurricane Andrew in 1992 (Daniels and Clark-Daniels 2000).

Following the dual disasters of 1989, concerns grew over the nation's capabilities to manage large-scale disasters and catastrophes. To address this gap in federal planning, FEMA coordinated a major effort among federal agencies and the Red Cross to create the Federal Response Plan (FRP). The FRP detailed how a large-scale disaster response should be managed, including jurisdictional issues, and which federal agency should coordinate specific tasks (FEMA 1992; Neal 1993). The structure of the FRP outlined Emergency Support Functions (ESFs). The original FRP listed 12 functions or tasks that would be needed to enhance disaster response. These tasks included (FEMA 1992, p. 14) the following:

- ESF #1 Transportation
- ESF #2 Communications
- ESF #3 Public works and engineering
- ESF #4 Firefighting
- ESF #5 Information and (disaster) planning
- ESF #6 Mass care
- ESF #7 Resource support
- ESF #8 Health and medical services
- ESF #9 Urban search and rescue
- ESF #10 Hazardous materials
- ESF #11 Food
- ESF #12 Energy

At the time of the FRP's creation, each ESF was coordinated by a federal agency (except ESF #6, Mass Care, which was headed by the Red Cross). The logic behind the ESF format was quite simple. A federal agency related to a specific function would coordinate the overall efforts with other federal agencies to mobilize key resources toward the overall response. Let us take the 1992 version of ESF #8, Health and Medical Services as a brief example. The Primary Agency coordinating the ESF #8 efforts would be the Department of Human Services (specifically through the U.S. Public Health Service). Examples of tasks coordinated by the Department of Human Services in ESF #8 would include (FEMA 1992, pp. 8-1 to 8-2):

- Assessment of health/medical needs
- Health surveillance
- Medical care personnel
- Health/medical equipment and supplies
- Patient evacuation
- In-hospital care

- Food/drug/medical device safety
- Worker health/safety
- Radiological, chemical, and biological hazards
- Mental health
- Water issues
- Victim identification and mortuary services

Certainly, the Department of Human Services does not have all the resources or capabilities to accomplish all of these tasks alone. To do so, they would draw upon the support agencies to assist. Examples of some of the support agencies for ESF #8 included the Department of Agriculture, DOD, Department of Justice, Department of Transportation, and Department of Veterans Affairs among many others (FEMA 1992).

Soon after the federal government completed the final version of the FRP in August 1991, Hurricane Andrew struck the Dade County, particularly the Miami, Florida area. Although final data vary, losses were large. Recent data suggest that hurricane Andrew damaged or destroyed about 125,000 residences, killed at least 61, and caused $27 billion (or $40 billion in 2007 dollars) in economic losses (NOAA 2011). Since the hurricane was considered close to being catastrophic, government officials quickly shipped hundreds of copies of the FRP to provide help and direction with the overall response (Neal 1993). However, observers generally considered the overall response as an abysmal failure. Federal assistance arrived slowly to disaster areas, in some cases taking over 10 days due to poor initial reconnaissance and damage assessment. Congressional hearings following Hurricane Andrew questioned why FEMA directors and those in top management possessed little if any background in disaster management (NAPA 1993, pp. 1–3; Neal 1993). Senator Barbara Mikulski of Maryland, in a letter to the Comptroller General of the United States, stated that the response to Hurricane Andrew was "pathetically sluggish and ill-planned" (NAPA 1993, p. 1).

Through the years, the name of the FRP has changed (i.e., National Response Plan to the current National Response Framework). Some general management issues have changed through the years with these documents. However, the main idea and format of the ESF structure remains in place. Consequently, over the past two decades, local emergency coordinators have written their disaster plans based on the ESF format with some local Emergency Operating Centers designs relying upon the ESF framework as well. In short, the ESF format as outlined in the original FRP in 1992 has become an important component of disaster planning and response.

After winning the 1992 presidential election, President Bill Clinton appointed James Lee Witt as the new FEMA director. Clinton's appointment set the stage for a number of improvements that FEMA would experience. For the first time in FEMA's history, a person with disaster management experience held the post of FEMA director. As a County Judge in Arkansas, Witt also had served as the county emergency manager. Later, Witt became the state's director of emergency management when Clinton was elected as governor. Witt arrived at FEMA well-grounded in disaster terminology and issues while also understanding the roles of the local, state, and federal government during disasters. In addition, other appointed FEMA officials at the federal and regional offices brought extensive emergency management experience (Daniels and Clark-Daniels 2000; FEMA 2010b). Second, Clinton made FEMA a cabinet level post, ensuring that disasters became a top priority in his administration, and that the FEMA director would have direct access to the President (Daniels and Clark-Daniels 2000).

During his tenure as FEMA director, Witt and his associate director Kay Goss (the first woman in such a high-level position) emphasized mitigation or efforts to reduce disaster impacts. Seeing the millions of dollars spent on response and recovery, Witt realized that steps taken to minimize the impact of a disaster could ultimately save millions of dollars. He initiated a number of programs designed to reduce physical, human, and financial impacts of disasters. One key initial program was Project Impact, a citizen-based communitywide effort that involved individuals, community, and business leaders (Witt and Morgan 2002, pp. 4–7). By 1999, nearly 200 communities and more than 1,000 business partners nationwide became involved in Project Impact. For example, residents in the City of Chesapeake, Virginia, initiated projects to install storm shutters in their homes. Local governments in the area invested in public buildings to strengthen them against hurricane winds. Current statistics show that for every dollar spent on prevention, at least two dollars are saved on disaster repairs (FEMA 1999).

Witt's actions went beyond mitigation or the four phases of emergency management. As a manager, he held informal discussions with his employees, noting that many of the FEMA staff had never met the FEMA director. He searched for new ways to solve old problems. Witt and his colleagues found ways to streamline the bureaucratic process such as the development and use of a National Teleregistration Center located in Denton, Texas to quickly and effectively provide aid. Also, for the first time, FEMA developed a strategic plan, which gave the organization a better sense of direction and purpose (Witt and Morgan 2002).

1.2.3.3 FEMA, Terrorism, and the DHS

Upon his inauguration in 2001, President Bush named one of his top political aides, Joe Allbaugh, as the new FEMA director. Similar to most previous FEMA directors, he lacked a background in emergency management. President Bush also eliminated Project Impact (Holderman 2005, p. A17). Ironically, on the same day of the announcement regarding Project Impact, a magnitude 6.8 earthquake rattled the Seattle area (Freitag 2001). Project Impact initiatives in the area, such as retrofitting homes and schools to absorb shaking, showed its value. Thus, it appeared to some in the profession, emergency management was not an initial top priority for the new administration (Holderman 2005, p. A17).

The terrorist attacks of September 11, 2001 moved emergency management back into view. An analysis following the attacks showed that the federal government had developed various problems related to disaster preparedness and response, including security issues. In addition, various government agencies were not sharing information that could have been useful for stopping a terrorist attack (9/11 Commission Report 2004). After much public debate and through a number of steps, President Bush and the U.S. Congress authorized and financed the DHS, which became a formal part of the U.S. government on January 24, 2003, with Tom Ridge serving as its first director (DHS 2008a). In order to protect the homeland in a unified fashion, DHS would focus on four major tasks (DHS 2002, p. 3):

- Border and transportation security
- Emergency preparedness and response
- Chemical, biological, radiological, and nuclear countermeasures
- Information analysis and infrastructure protection

To pursue these tasks, the new federal department would integrate 22 federal agencies. FEMA lost its cabinet-level status under DHS. In short, DHS would coordinate activities among government to improve the security of the United States.

Although the creation of DHS was intended to improve FEMA, Hurricane Katrina proved otherwise (Waugh 2006). Striking the U.S. Gulf Coast on August 29, 2005, Hurricane Katrina damaged levees in New Orleans and sent a massive storm surge six to twelve miles inland across Mississippi. The storm killed over 1200 and injured thousands more while causing some of the largest economic and infrastructural damage in U.S. disaster history. For example, areas around New Orleans and the Mississippi coast sustained about $75 billion worth of damage (NOAA 2011.). Critics again pointed fingers, charging FEMA, DHS, state, and local governments with a slow response that claimed lives. FEMA Director Michael Brown was relieved of his duties. In subsequent investigations by the U.S. Congress and the White House, concerns generated a context for change. As written in the U.S. Congressional investigation report, *A Failure of Initiative* (2006, p. 1):

The Select Committee identified failures at all levels of government that significantly undermined and detracted from the heroic efforts of first responders, private individuals and organizations, faith-based groups and others. The institutional and individual failures we have identified became all the more clear when compared to the heroic efforts of those who acted decisively. Those who didn't flinch, who took matters into their own hands when bureaucratic inertia was causing death, injury and suffering. Those whose exceptional initiative saved time and money and lives.

The massive hurricane generated numerous changes in FEMA besides a change of personnel. New attention emerged concerning those at the highest risk including people with disabilities, medical conditions, and inadequate resources that would influence one's ability to evacuate. States commenced extensive efforts to revise evacuation and shelter plans. Drills and exercises increased to build stronger relationships between involved agencies, particularly across state lines. Those efforts paid off in 2008 when Hurricane Ike slammed into Texas. Well in advance, a massive transportation effort took thousands of people to safety. Public shelters opened to serve nursing home and medically fragile patients. Even pets and livestock were accommodated in special shelters and locations. Hurricane Gustav also prompted evacuation away from New Orleans and into the neighboring states of Mississippi and Alabama. Ready to help, the host states absorbed tens of thousands of evacuees.

Today, emergency management continues as one of the many functions assigned to DHS (see Figure 1.3). Other tasks include U.S. Customs and Border Protection, U.S. Citizenship and Immigration Services, U.S. Coast Guard, U.S. Immigration and Customs Enforcement, U.S. Secret Service, and Transportation Security Administration. DHS is the second largest department in the federal government, with only the DOD having more employees. Furthermore, Figure 1.3 also highlights other administrative functions and tasks for DHS. As a result, those in the emergency management field still express concern that the important tasks of FEMA will be less visible in a large bureaucracy.

Following his inauguration, President Barack Obama named Craig Fugate as the new director of FEMA. With extensive experience as a fire fighter and paramedic, later becoming a county emergency manager and director of the Florida Division of Emergency Management, Fugate quelled concerns about lack of experience in the agency leadership. Speaking to the FEMA Higher Education Conference in 2009, Fugate supported the value of social science research, and encouraged those at the conference to listen to the social scientists and their findings. Many efforts that emerged after Hurricane Katrina, particularly planning initiatives, gained additional momentum. A National Disaster Housing Strategy developed along with new guidelines to make emergency shelters accessible to people with disabilities (visit http://www.fema.gov/housing-resources/).

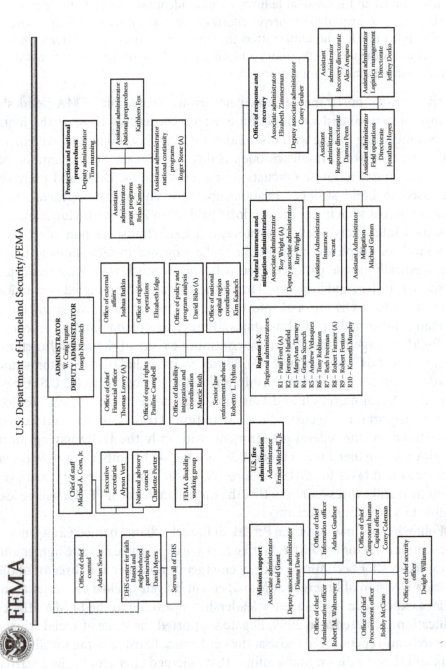

FIGURE 1.3 Organizational chart of FEMA.

As of 2014, FEMA employs over 15,000 personnel (this includes full and part time). Many of these employees serve as reservists, ready to travel to a disaster site to help those in need following an event. FEMA's offices include its main location in Washington, D.C., 10 regional offices throughout the United States, the Mount Weather Emergency Operations Center, and Center for Domestic Preparedness and Noble Training Center in Anniston, Alabama, and the National Emergency Training Center in Emmitsburg, Maryland. Since coordination of activities is a key task of the agency, FEMA works with 27 different federal agencies and the Red Cross, in addition to the many state governments and local jurisdictions throughout the country (FEMA 2015b).

To understand visually the many activities of FEMA, look at the organizational chart of FEMA (2015c, see Figure 1.3). In addition to the different activities noted above at different physical locations, FEMA also oversees Protection and National Preparedness, the United States Fire Administration, Federal Insurance and Mitigation Administration, and the Office of Response and Recovery. Before DHS, the creation of these or similar tasks were just two steps away from the President (i.e., head of FEMA and the President). Now, FEMA representatives must work through the bureaucracy of DHS before getting the attention of the President, which highlights the concerns of those who desire a more nimble emergency management agency.

Looking back over the past 60 years, we see that major steps have been taken in policy and professionalism related to emergency management. A new generation of thinking about and doing disaster management is upon us. Trained, experienced, and educated professionals lead the way in hazards and disasters. Yet, with so many steps forward in the field as noted earlier, we still see significant challenges ahead. Certainly, terrorism continues to be a major concern worldwide. Many disaster-related issues continue to be driven by the terror threat (whether internal or external). As a result, resources may be drawn from more common risks such as tornadoes, floods, hurricanes, earthquakes, and many other related hazards. In many ways, this focus resembles what we described during the 1950s and 1960s. At that time, government officials poured resources into civil defense to protect the American public. By comparison, officials directed few resources toward natural and technological resources. We can even see this with funded research during this same time period. Major efforts such as the National Opinion Research Center's funding during the 1950s and the Disaster Research Center's (now at the University of Delaware) initial research funding during the 1960s came from military sources. Their work focused on human response amid the proliferation of nuclear and chemical weapons (Quarantelli 1987). Only later did policy makers use the research to manage hazards and disasters. We will discuss research centers more in an upcoming chapter. For an international example, though, see Box 1.2.

BOX 1.2 AFRICAN CENTRE FOR DISASTER STUDIES, NORTH-WEST UNIVERSITY, SOUTH AFRICA

Dewald Van Niekerk

Dewald Van Niekerk is the founder and current director of the African Centre for Disaster Studies (ACDS). In his tenure at the ACDS, he founded the international peer review journal Jamba: Journal of Disaster Risk Studies, and the ACDS has grown to the biggest of its kind on the continent with the most PhDs in its program. He initiated, and is a founding member of the Southern Africa Society for Disaster Reduction. Dewald is a National Research Foundation C2 rated researcher. He is happily married to Liezel and has three wonderful children, Tumé, Ruan and Zander, and shares a home with four dachshunds.

Leandri Kruger

Leandri Kruger is a researcher and lecturer at the African Centre for Disaster Studies. She is the program manager for the postgraduate diploma in disaster risk reduction. In 2014, Leandri received the campus award for the best

(Continued)

BOX 1.2 (*Continued*)   AFRICAN CENTRE FOR DISASTER STUDIES, NORTH-WEST UNIVERSITY, SOUTH AFRICA

master's degree student in the Faculty of Natural Sciences for her thesis on social impact assessments. This topic still dominates her reading toward a PhD. She is married to Le Roux and both recently became the proud parents of a dapple dachshund: Geneva.

The African Centre for Disaster Studies (ACDS—see www.acds.co.za) was established in 2002 within the Faculty of Arts at North-West University, South Africa. The Centre was created due to a growing need within South Africa and the wider Africa context for capacity development in disaster risk management. The staff component (full time, faculty, and associates) comes from a variety of different disciplines spanning the natural and social sciences.

Initially, the focus of the ACDS was on the development and implementation of practice-based projects. Such projects also generated additional funding for the university and were seen as part of the university's commercialization drive. The development of various capacities through short learning programs created a need for more formal qualifications aligned with research needs.

In 2007, a research program (named Water and Disaster Studies) was created under the research entity Sustainable Social Development (subsequently in 2010, the research program was changed to Disaster Risk Studies). The ACDS also established the first academic peer reviewed disaster risk reduction journal in Africa, the *Journal of Disaster Risk Studies* (see www.jamba.org.za).

One year later, the ACDS implemented master's and PhD degrees in development and management (disaster studies). A number of students have graduated from the master's program, and the PhD program is currently one of the biggest, if not the biggest, programs in Africa.

The ACDS has also been instrumental in the creation of the Southern Africa Society for Disaster Reduction (SASDiR—see www.sasdir.org)—an organization designed to bring practice and academia together in the SADC region. To bridge the gap between undergraduate and postgraduate studies, the ACDS started a postgraduate diploma in disaster risk reduction in 2014 (which gives students entry to the master's degree). All of the postgraduate offerings are uniquely transdisciplinary focused, attracting students from more than 10 disciplines annually.

The centre aims to find synergy between its practice-based projects, staff and student research, and research outputs. To this end, an alignment of postgraduate research projects, contract and other research, capacity development, and community outreach is emphasized. Due to

(Continued)

BOX 1.2 (*Continued*)   AFRICAN CENTRE FOR DISASTER STUDIES, NORTH-WEST UNIVERSITY, SOUTH AFRICA

PHOTO 1.1   Field research. Conducting field research on small farmer agriculture resilience in Malawi.

its direct link to practice through research, the ACDS has been involved in the drafting and amendment of the policies and legislation of a number of Southern Africa countries, and its staff is regularly consulted by regional and international organizations on disaster risk reduction matters. Since 2015, the ACDS is focusing its research on the broader theme of socio-ecological resilience (Photo 1.1).

1.3 Other Federal Organizations

FEMA certainly is the main federal organization that drives disaster issues in the United States, but it does not have sole responsibility for disasters. For historical reasons, Native American tribes have their own emergency management offices, and they coordinate their efforts with the federal government. Any nuclear accident or disaster falls under the jurisdiction of the Department of Energy (DOE). Finally, the Centers for Disease Control (CDC) plays a role when potential or actual epidemics break out. Below, we briefly discuss their unique positions in emergency management.

1.3.1 Native American Tribes

Native American tribes represent an important population regarding disasters in the public sector. Tribes have their own designated political jurisdictions and, as a result, have a wide range of public safety (e.g., fire, police, and emergency management) related responsibilities. They typically coordinate their activities with surrounding local governments. However, by law, tribes can bypass state governments and work directly with the federal government on disaster issues. FEMA has made working with Native American tribes a top priority in recent years:

> In the spirit of community, FEMA commits itself to building a strong and lasting partnership with American Indians and Alaska Natives to assist them in preparing for the hazards they face, reducing their disaster vulnerabilities, responding quickly and effectively when disasters strike, and recovering in their aftermath. (FEMA 2010c, p. 2)

In addition, soon after taking office, FEMA Director Craig Fugate contacted all 564 federally recognized tribes asking for feedback on current existing policy on tribal matters and emergency management (FEMA 2010a).

FEMA has also been working with Native American tribes on historical preservation issues. A wide range of disasters can do great damage to sacred areas. To assist with this issue, FEMA has published specific recommendations on how to mitigate sacred or historical sites from disasters. Simply stated, the federal, state, or local governments should not and legally cannot take Native American lands in an effort to "help" mitigate historical sites from disasters. Rather, FEMA recommends a series of steps so that all parties can work together. For example, some historical or sacred sites demand varying degrees of secrecy, such as archeological sites. Thus, workers must consider the sensitivity of the situation (FEMA 2005).

Additionally, any attempt to mitigate for a disaster or recover from a disaster on tribal lands must consider minimizing dramatic changes to the landscape. In areas open to the public, simple plaques, or relatively unobtrusive markers, should be used. Pathways to historical areas, or within floodplains, for example, must blend well with the local surroundings (FEMA 2005). Finally, saving or protecting archeological or burial sites from disaster, involves many people and regulations. Before work begins, good faith efforts must be made by all parties to include all relevant groups for their input and perspective. Involving tribal leaders, local, state, and federal agencies along with historians, archeologists, and others related to any mitigation project is essential. Finally, tribal representatives and others must continue to work together, such as updating disaster plans and other related agreements (FEMA 2005).

Sensitivity to cultural contexts underlies FEMA efforts to address tribal concerns. The diversity among the tribes represents a particular challenge in that each tribe has values, norms, and customs specific to their ancestry and beliefs. By understanding that diversity and working within a culturally appropriate framework, emergency managers can be more effective in safeguarding the public.

1.3.2 Department of Energy

Since the development of nuclear weapons and power, DOE has become the lead agency for any radiological or nuclear accident or disaster in the United States. Within DOE, the National Nuclear Security Administration (NNSA) Office of Emergency Operations (OEO) oversees emergency planning and response capabilities for all radiological and nuclear events. Such events may occur through natural disasters, technological accidents, or terrorist attacks. The OEO has three main tasks regarding radiological or nuclear safety. The first is radiological search. Here, trained experts seek out any materials or devices that could be detonated or cause harm. The second task is to render safe any materials found. In this case, if an explosive device is found, team members will disarm the device before a nuclear explosion occurs or a conventional device explodes and spreads radiation (or radiation waste) throughout an area. Finally, OEO coordinates efforts to mitigate the spread of radiological materials following any type of explosion (DOE 2015b). In addition, the Counterterrorism branch of NNSA focuses specifically on terrorism and counterterrorism issues (DOE 2015a).

Although most people may not have heard of the NNSA, it plays an active role in readiness. At least a 100 times a year, teams travel to events such as major professional sports (e.g., the Superbowl), political activities (e.g., political conventions and Presidential inaugurations), and other large gatherings to detect potential radiological or nuclear devices and respond if an explosion occurs. Within this context, NNSA and OEO are quite busy with coordinating, planning, training, responding to radiological and nuclear events, and ensuring the continuation of the U.S. government if a major event occurs. In addition, due to their expertise, they work with representatives of other countries if such incidents occur outside the United States.

1.3.3 The Centers for Disease Control and Prevention

Over the past few decades, the CDC has taken an active central role with health issues related to emergencies and disasters. In fact, the broader issue of public health has emerged as a key emergency management topic. Generally CDC plays two roles related to disasters. First, they investigate and provide advice on disaster-generated health issues. A short example of such health problems that could emerge during or following a disaster include the consequences of drinking unsafe water after a disaster, exposure to mold while re-entering a home, environmental contamination that might impact health, the occurrence of chainsaw accidents, or injuries during a disaster cleanup such as a tornado (CDC 2015).

Their most important and probably most visible role, however, relates to pandemic disease. We are all familiar with stories of the "black death" or the bubonic plague during the Dark Ages. CDC monitors and provides extensive advice on how to prevent, mitigate, and treat patients if similar outbreaks occur today. Recently, it played the central role with coordination and information regarding the summer and fall 2015 Ebola cases, including those few cases that reached the United States. The central location of the outbreak was in West Africa, primarily in the countries of Guinea, Liberia, and Sierra Leone. Along with the World Health Organization, CDC estimated that over 27,000 people contracted the disease, and more than 11,000 people died. CDC confirmed four cases in the United States. Three were health workers who contracted the disease either by providing health services in West Africa or by being exposed to a patient in the United States. All survived. A fourth person arrived in the United States (Dallas, Texas) from Liberia already having the virus and died. A nurse who worked on this case contracted the Ebola virus from a work-related exposure. Before showing symptoms, she traveled to Akron, Ohio to plan her wedding. Upon returning to Dallas she discovered that she had contracted the subsequently virus upon receiving treatment, she survived. Despite great concern, especially for those in the Akron area and on her flights, nobody caught the Ebola virus from her. Others were watched or even quarantined if they were exposed to the virus (CDC 2015b). Although major concerns developed about CDC and its capabilities to manage the Ebola crisis in the United States, the data show that health care workers contained the virus well.

1.4 Research Centers

Research centers that focus on disasters, hazards, risks, and crises all help provide a means for systematically studying disasters. Findings from these centers help emergency managers prepare, respond, recover, and mitigate disaster events. The centers' research findings can also assist policy makers to create new and better plans and guidance for emergency managers.

In 1963, sociologists E. L. Quarantelli, Russell Dynes, and J. Eugene Haas created the first center devoted to disasters, the Disaster Research Center, at The Ohio State University (now located at the University of Delaware). A decade later, geographer Gilbert White formed the Natural Hazard Research and Applications Information Center at the University of Colorado—Boulder. Since then, scholars initiated research centers at Texas A&M University, University of South Carolina, Colorado State University, Millersville University, Louisiana State University, and other locations. Such research centers are not limited today to the United States. Internationally, various research centers exist in Europe, Africa, Asia, and Australia.

In summary, research centers are an important part of understanding how people behave before, during, and following disasters. Findings help guide disaster professionals and policy makers, and help direct further research projects. We provide a more detailed overview of research centers in Chapter 4.

Summary

Noah was the first emergency manager. Similar to emergency managers today, he faced skepticism on a number of issues related to disasters despite having a great source of information. Today, throughout the world, emergency managers face both traditional risks such as tornadoes, floods, earthquakes, and explosions and new risks including water problems, cascading disasters that create multiple impacts, and large-scale or catastrophic events. The job of the emergency manager continues to be more complex.

Following World War II and during the start of the Cold War, emergency management evolved in two different paths. One path was oriented toward civil defense, aimed at protecting the nation from primarily a nuclear war with the Soviet Union. The other path focused primarily on natural disasters. As time progressed, emergency management functions spread throughout the federal bureaucracy, impacting the effectiveness of both civil defense and civil preparedness. In an effort to improve the nation's disaster capabilities, in 1979 President Carter consolidated most emergency management tasks and functions under a new federal organization—FEMA. FEMA had its share of successes and failures. The terrorist attacks of 9/11 led to FEMA being placed under a new large federal bureaucracy, DHS. Although FEMA continues to be the nation's lead emergency disaster organization, others also have key roles under specific circumstances. Native American tribes have jurisdiction over their reservations and work with FEMA. The DOE oversees any nuclear or radiological event. CDC plays a central role in planning for and responding to any health or pandemic situation.

The Cold War also played a key role in initiating disaster research and related centers. Initial disaster work by NORC at the University of Chicago and the formation of the Disaster Research Center at The Ohio State University led the way for the creation of many other centers. Later, such research centers were formed on other continents. Today, disaster research worldwide helps policy makers and others understand human behavior before, during, and after disaster, and how we can better prepare, plan, recover, and mitigate events. Much of the research today is interdisciplinary in order to support emergency management practice.

Discussion Questions

1. Can you think of any recent examples of citizens, government officials, or others ignoring warnings about possible disasters from credible sources? What are the possible disasters and from whom do these warnings come from?

2. In contrast to the lack of a nuclear war during the 1950s and 1960s and hundreds of natural disasters in the United States during the same time period, explain why most resources were directed toward civil defense rather than civil preparedness during this time.

3. What advantages do you see in putting FEMA under the direction of DHS? What connections exist between FEMA and DHS? Please provide some good examples. Pg 18 , Pg 13

4. What disadvantages do you see in putting FEMA under the direction of DHS? What are some of the problems that have developed from putting FEMA under DHS? Please provide some good examples.

5. Discuss and provide examples how social science and interdisciplinary research can help improve emergency management today.

6. Think about why disaster research should take place in as many different countries as possible rather than just in the United States. Provide some good illustrations for your answers.

Resources

A number of websites provide good information on topics related to emergency management, disasters, and hazards. Since this is the first chapter of the text, consider these resources as starting points or overviews. As we explore other topics throughout the text, we will provide resources with deeper information.

- The websites sponsored by the federal government provide plenty of good and relevant information on disasters. Both FEMA and DHS websites are excellent starting points for general information. FEMA can be found at www.fema.gov and DHS can be located at www.dhs.gov.
- Other federal agencies noted in this chapter include DOE (www.energy.gov) and CDC (www.cdc.gov).
- The National Emergency Management Association (NEMA) represents the state emergency management directors' perspective on emergency management. Their link is www.nemaweb.org.

- Although discussed in more detail in later chapters, The International Association of Emergency Managers (IAEM) represents primarily the interests of local emergency managers. You can find information on IAEM at www.ieam.org.

References and Recommended Readings

Centers for Disease Control and Prevention (CDC). 2015a. "Emergency Preparedness and Response." Available at http://emergency.cdc.gov/disasters/index.asp, last accessed June 12, 2015.

Centers for Disease Control and Prevention (CDC). 2015b. "Cases of Ebola Diagnosed in the United States." Available at http://www.cdc.gov/vhf/ebola/outbreaks/2014-west-africa/united-states-imported-case.html, last accessed June 12, 2015.

Daniels, Steven R. and Carolyn L. Clark-Daniels. 2000. *Transforming Government: The Renewal and Revitalization of the Federal Emergency Management Agency.* 2000 Presidential Transition Series. Birmingham, AL: University of Alabama.

Department of Energy (DOE). 2015a. "National Nuclear Security Agency: Counterterrorism." Available at http://nnsa.energy.gov/ourmission/counterterrorism, last accessed June 12, 2015.

Department of Energy (DOE). 2015b. "National Nuclear Security Agency: Emergency Response." Available at http://nnsa.energy.gov/aboutus/ourprograms/emergency-operationscounterterrorism, last accessed June 12, 2015.

Department of Homeland Security (DHS). 2002. "The Department of Homeland Security." Available at http://www.dhs.gov/xlibrary/assets/book.pdf, last accessed February 15, 2011.

Department of Homeland Security (DHS). 2008a. *Brief Documentary History of the Department of Homeland Security: 2001–2008.* Available at http://www.dhs.gov/xlibrary/assets/brief_documentary_history_of_dhs_2001_2008.pdf, last accessed February 15, 2011.

Department of Homeland Security (DHS). 2008b. "Federal Response Framework." Available at http://www.fema.gov/pdf/emergency/nrf/nrf-core.pdf, last assessed February 22, 2011.

Department of Homeland Security (DHS). 2013. "U.S. Department of Homeland Security Organizational Chart." Available at http://www.dhs.gov/organizational-chart, last accessed June 10, 2015.

Dynes, Russell R. 2003. "Noah and Disaster Planning." *Journal of Contingencies and Crisis Management* 11(4): 170–177.

Federal Emergency Management Agency (FEMA). 1992. *Federal Response Plan.* Washington, D.C.: U.S. Government Printing Office.

Federal Emergency Management Agency (FEMA). 1999. "Project Impact: Building a Disaster Resistant Community." Available at http://www.fema.gov/news/newsrelease.fema?id=8895, last accessed December 11, 2010.

Federal Emergency Management Agency (FEMA). 2005. *Historic Properties and Cultural Resources.* Available at http://www.fema.gov/pdf/fima/386-6_Phase_4.pdf, last accessed February 23, 2011.

Federal Emergency Management Agency (FEMA). 2010a. Emergency Management Guide for Business and Industry. Available at http://www.fema.gov/business/guide/index.shtm, last accessed on February 24, 2011.

Federal Emergency Management Agency (FEMA). 2010b. "FEMA History." Available at http://www.fema.gov/about/history.shtm, last accessed February 15, 20110.

Federal Emergency Management Agency (FEMA). 2010c. "FEMA Tribal Policy." Available at http://www.fema.gov/government/tribal/natamerpolcy.shtm, last accessed January 7, 2011.

Federal Emergency Management Agency (FEMA). 2010d. "Tribal Information." Available at http://www.fema.gov/government/tribal/index.shtm, last accessed February 23, 2011.

Federal Emergency Management Agency (FEMA). 2015a. "About the Agency." Available at https://www.fema.gov/about-agency, last accessed on June 14, 2015.

Federal Emergency Management Agency (FEMA). 2015b. "Organizational Chart." Available at https://www.fema.gov/media-library/assets/documents/28183, last accessed on June 10, 2015.

Freitag, Robert. 2001. "The Impact of Project Impact on the Nisqually Earthquake." Natural Hazards Observer XXV (1): 1–6.

Hazard Reduction and Recovery Center (HRRC). 2015. "About." Available at http://hrrc.arch.tamu.edu/about/, last accessed June 13, 2015.

Hazards & Vulnerability Research Institute (HVRI). 2015. "Hazards & Vulnerability Research Institute." Available at http://artsandsciences.sc.edu/geog/hvri/front-page, last accessed June 13, 2015.

Henry, Tom. 2015a. "Toledo Water Test Results are Improving but Region Still Has a Long Way, Mayor Says." *The Toledo Blade.* Available at http://www.toledo-blade.com/local/2014/08/03/Toledo-water-test-results-face-extended-delay.html#kXvJrSXldfL2WDW0.99, last accessed August 3, 2014.

Henry, Tom. 2015b. "Water Crisis Grips Hundreds of Thousands in Toledo Area, State of Emergency Declared." Available at http://www.toledoblade.com/local/2014/08/03/Water-crisis-grips-area.html#UUjuPlQmtbcXbR7i.99, last accessed August 3, 2015.

Holderman, Eric. 2005. "Destroying FEMA." *The Washington Post.* Available at http://www.radixonline.org/resources/destroying_fema.doc, last accessed February 15, 2011.

Kreps, Gary. 1990. "The Federal Emergency Management System in the United States: Past and Present." *International Journal of Mass Emergencies and Disasters* 8(3): 275–300.

Meyers, Mary Fran. 1993. Bridging the Gap between Research and Practice. *International Journal of Mass Emergencies and Disasters* 11(1): 41–54.

National Academy of Public Administration (NAPA). 1993. *Coping with Catastrophe: Building an Emergency Management System to Meet People's Needs in Natural and Manmade Disasters.* Washington, D.C.: National Academy of Public Administration.

National Governor's Association (NGA). 1979. *1978 Emergency Preparedness Project: Final Report.* Washington, D.C.: Defense Civil Preparedness Agency.

Natural Hazards Center. 2015. "Natural Hazards Center." Available at http://www.colorado.edu/hazards/, last accessed June 12, 2015.

Neal, David M. 1993. "Emergency Response Philosophy of the Federal Response Plan: Implications in the Case of a Catastrophic Disaster." *Proceedings of the 1993 National Earthquake Conference,* 511–518.

NOAA Economics. 2011. "Extreme Events: Hurricane and Tropical Storm." Available at http://www.economics.noaa.gov/?goal=weather&file=events/hurricane&view=costs, last accessed February 9, 2011.

Quarantelli, Henry L. 1987. "Disaster Studies: An Analysis of the Social Historical Factors Affecting the Development of Research in the Area." *International Journal of Mass Emergencies and Disasters* 5(3): 285–310.

Seewer, John. 2015. "More Tests Needed before Ohio City Gets Water Back." *The Toledo Blade.* Available at http://www.toledoblade.com/local/2014/08/03/Toledo-water-test-results-face-extended-delay.html, last Accessed August 3, 2014.

Sylves, Richard. 2008. *Disaster Policy and Politics: Emergency Management and Homeland Security.* Washington, D.C.: CQ Press.

Task Force. 2010. *Perspective on Preparedness: Taking Stock since 9/11.* Available at http://www.fema.gov/pdf/preparednesstaskforce/perspective_on_preparedness.pdf, last accessed February 9, 2011.

United States Agency for International Development (USAID). 2015. "Nepal—Earthquake: Fact Sheet #17." Washington, D.C.: USAID.

United States Army Corps of Engineers. 2007a. "The U.S. Army Corps of Engineers: A Brief History." Available at http://www.usace.army.mil/History/Documents/Brief/index.html, last accessed February 23, 2011.

United States Congress. 2006. *A Failure of Initiative.* Washington, D.C.: U.S. Congress. Available at http://www.gpoaccess.gov/serialset/creports/katrina.html, last accessed January 7, 2011.

United States Geological Survey (USGS). 2015. Available at http://earthquake.usgs.gov/earthquakes/eventpage/us20002926#general_summary, last accessed June 15, 2015.

Waugh, William. 2000. *Living with Hazards, Dealing with Disasters: Introduction to Emergency Management.* Armonk, NY: M.E. Sharpe.

Waugh, William. 2006. *Shelter from the Storm: Repairing the National Emergency Management System after Katrina.* The ANNALS of the American Academy of Political and Social Science Series.

White House, The. 2006. *The Federal Response to Hurricane Katrina: Lessons Learned.* Washington, D.C.: The White House. Available at http://georgewbush-whitehouse.archives.gov/reports/katrina-lessons-learned/letter.html, last accessed January 7, 2011.

Witt, James Lee and James Morgan. 2002. *Stronger in the Broken Places.* New York: Times Books.

Chapter **2**

Working in Emergency Management

Objectives

Upon completing this chapter, readers should be able to:

- Describe the work of an emergency manager in the United States and globally.
- Identify and begin to pursue core competencies in emergency management practice.
- Discuss the types of jobs in which emergency managers typically work.
- Observe differences between emergency management in the United States and globally.
- Appreciate the value and explain the process of becoming a Certified Emergency Manager.

Key Terms

- Associate Emergency Manager (AEM)
- Certified Emergency Manager (CEM)
- Compounding natural disaster
- Core competencies
- Cyberterrorism
- Disaster
- Emergency manager
- Emergency Support Function (ESF)
- Hazards
- International Association of Emergency Managers (IAEM)
- Life cycle of emergency management
- Local emergency management agency (LEMA)
- Local Emergency Planning Committee (LEPC)

- Mitigation
- National Response Framework (NRF)
- National Voluntary Organizations Active in Disaster (NVOAD)
- NaTech
- NFPA 1600
- Nongovernmental organization
- Preparedness
- Private sector
- Recovery
- Response
- Space weather
- Terrorism
- Voluntary organization
- Wildland–urban interface (WUI)

2.1 Introduction

People enjoy living where hazards exist. We settle along coastlines (hurricanes), rivers (floods), cold weather areas (blizzards), mountains (earthquakes, volcanoes), extreme climate locales (heat waves and droughts), and areas with sudden and violent weather changes (tornadoes and hail). In short, we do not and probably cannot avoid disasters. Consequently, we need to live in, interact with, and understand the natural environment that will continue to evolve and change (Quarantelli 1996, 2001). In addition to the natural environment, people will need to coexist with an array of technological hazards related to various industries (from paint factories to farms, and from chemical companies to art studios). Presently, significant threats also imperil people and places deemed as "soft targets" for terrorists.

The job of the emergency manager is to alert the endangered public and reduce potential injuries and deaths. For example, meteorologists may issue "watches" that means that conditions are suitable for a disaster to occur. A "warning" means that a disaster is going to happen and people need to take appropriate actions to protect themselves, family members, coworkers, pets, and livestock. Emergency managers use such information to help protect the public. For a tornado, a warning from the National Weather Service may result in the emergency manager turning on sirens and sending social media alerts. In the case of a terrorist threat considered "imminent," emergency managers will likely help to inform the public. These and other comprise the work of the emergency manager, which is the focus of this chapter including a consideration of the types of events they may face as practitioners.

2.2 The Profession of Emergency Management

Emergency management has evolved considerably over the years, but it essentially involves people working to reduce risks, prepare for and respond to emergencies and disasters, and foster postevent recovery. To do the work of emergency management, the U.S. National Governor's Association (1979) first organized the activities of emergency managers into four phases that they called preparedness, response, recovery, and mitigation—a set of phases that we will return to throughout this text.

Preparedness includes efforts to educate the public, to plan with responding partners, and to encourage readiness across communities likely to be affected by disaster. Even more importantly, emergency managers will prepare their staff and partners by learning, exercising, and revising their plans. By walking through table top scenarios and then conducting full-scale field exercises, emergency managers and their partners will build relationships usable in an actual event. Emergency managers also use the preparedness period to assess their assets and acquire necessary resources. They design and test warning systems to alert the public. Doing so requires public education, which occurs during the preparedness phase as well.

The *response* phase of disasters involves a wide range of partners activating warning systems, supporting evacuations, opening shelters, conducting search and rescue, and taking action to limit damage, injuries, or deaths. Partners in response may include public works who place barricades around a hazardous area. Firefighters and emergency medical services, along with airborne and water-based rescue teams will try to help those who did not or could not adhere to warning and protective action recommendations. Waste management may then initiate debris removal so that emergency response vehicles can be deployed to help survivors. Voluntary organizations and medical teams will set up shelters to serve displaced residents. Experienced voluntary organizations then arrive to help with clean-up and repairs. If damages warrant, outside aid will be set up from both governmental and nongovernmental organizations (NGOs) that provide immediate relief to longer-term reconstruction efforts.

The line between response and recovery is fairly blurred (Neal 1997), but once the roads are cleared and utilities restored, recovery usually begins. *Recovery* involves many partners to assess and determine local needs, and may require many years to complete. Organizations are often mission-specific in what they do. Government may deploy agencies and organizations to erect temporary housing sites, repair bridges, and roads, and support private utilities in restoring communications, power and other utilities. NGOs like Mennonite Disaster Services offer cleanup, repairs, and complete house rebuilding (Phillips 2014). The American Red Cross may offer mental health services for traumatized survivors along with vouchers for clothing and other resources.

Ideally, an emergency management agency will have conducted *mitigation* planning prior to disaster and put into place measures that reduced the impacts of a disaster. Mitigation actions can be organized into structural or nonstructural mitigation measures. A structural or built mitigation measure might include a seawall, a dam, a levee, or a building retrofitted for earthquakes or terrorist attack. Nonstructural mitigation measures include buying insurance to offset the expenses of rebuilding, zoning that sets aside floodplains as nonbuilding areas, creating codes that require hurricane clamps on roofs or preserving coastal wetlands, barrier islands, and sand dunes that break storm surge. The remaining chapters in this book will walk you through these phases in detail, providing evidence-based best practices for each.

2.3 Working in the Profession of Emergency Management

Within the field of emergency management, a number of work locations and career opportunities exist (Edwards and Daniel 2007). Emergency managers may find work in several sectors: government or public sector work, voluntary organizations (paid or service work), international or humanitarian care, and private companies that require a range of knowledge, skills, and abilities (see Box 2.1). In this section, we look briefly at each of these prior to learning more in the following chapters.

BOX 2.1   CORE COMPETENCIES AND PRACTICE STANDARDS IN EMERGENCY MANAGEMENT

Dr. Wayne Blanchard (2005), the first Director of the FEMA Higher Education Project in the United States, compiled a list of core competencies from a wide set of academics and practitioners for the practice of emergency management. They include the following:

1. *Comprehensive Emergency Management Framework or Philosophy.* Emergency managers must embrace an all-hazards perspective to be efficient. To illustrate, writing an emergency operations plan for many hazards would require considerable amount of time, training and exercising. Writing a function-based plan that spans all hazards streamlines common elements such as communication, sheltering, or recovery. Elements of hazards that require unique attention can then be planned for specifically, such as hazardous materials or terrorism.
2. *Leadership and Team-Building.* Working together in a collaborative manner helps emergency managers meet the demands of disasters. Indeed, "leadership is needed—not just an ability to provide a command presence, but the demonstration of vision, compassion, flexibility, imagination, resolve and courage" (Blanchard 2010). Flexibility may be the most important quality of all, as disasters do not know the plan, tend to span jurisdictions and usually require improvisation.
3. *Management.* What is the difference between a leader and a manager? Managers take on tasks and direct activities to accomplish a particular job or mission. For example, good managers ensure that the best warning system has been identified and purchased, implemented, tested, and explained fully to the public. Leaders provide inspiration and direction, managers ensure that teams get things done.
4. *Networking and Coordination.* Working together leverages resources toward a greater good. Emergency managers should always be working with and educating their partners on procedures and plans.
5. *Integrated Emergency Management.* In a disaster, you might be surprised at how many organizations and agencies become involved. For example, transportation agencies support evacuation of those without cars. People in nursing homes or hospitals may require advanced medical support that will involve public health agencies, medical volunteers, air ambulances, the military, and animal care providers. Integrated emergency management means that emergency managers plan and coordinate with a variety of offices and agencies to be effective.
6. *Key Emergency Management Functions.* The main functions of emergency management involve professionals in:
   a. *Risk Assessment.* To identify the local hazards and assess the potential impact on the area's population, infrastructure, and utilities.

(Continued)

BOX 2.1 (*Continued*) CORE COMPETENCIES AND PRACTICE STANDARDS IN EMERGENCY MANAGEMENT

b. *Planning.* To write plans and standard operational procedures (SOPs) for response, recovery, and mitigation.

c. *Training and Exercising.* To train people on the plan, particularly specific roles and responsibilities. To offer a table top or full-scale exercise to test the plan.

d. *Emergency Operations Centers.* To design, organize, and resource a site supporting the functional areas of an emergency operations plan in a fixed, mobile, or virtual site.

7. *Interoperable Communications.* Interoperability is defined as the capacity to communicate across organizations with the help of radio communication frequencies. Interoperability also means being able to communicate within and across organizational cultures. Because emergency management emanates from multiple disciplines, learning to speak across those disciplinary bodies of jargon is necessary too.

8. *Applying Lessons Learned and Research Findings.* By looking actively for lessons from experience and evidence-based best practices, an emergency manager can increase effectiveness.

9. *Political, Bureaucratic, and Social Contexts.* Context refers to time, place and circumstances. The New Zealand context, for example, requires an understanding of the diverse populations and cultures on the islands as well as its geographic risks: earthquakes, volcanoes and tsunamis. Within India, an emerging emergency response framework tapped administrative professionals to handle debris removal, establish temporary shelters, provide food and water and deal with over 10,000 fatalities. The 2010 earthquake in Haiti destroyed critical emergency response facilities and killed both responders and officials. Assisting the badly damaged capital city of Port-au-Prince required extensive, multinational collaboration for search and rescue, mass care (shelter, food and water), emergency surgeries, continuing health care, rebuilding and debris removal. An emergency manager who is politically savvy and able to work within a culturally diverse context can increase effectiveness.

10. *Technical Systems and Standards.* Practitioners of emergency management would be well advised to learn about emergency communication systems, warning technologies, social media, software packages from Geographic Information Systems (GIS) to WebEOC, a virtual platform that can record critical event data in real time. But, because technologies can fail, and because all people may not access social media, backup systems are needed.

11. *Social Vulnerability Reduction Approach.* The sheer diversity of any given community means that someone may not get a warning or be able to respond as desired unless we design warning systems to reach

(Continued)

BOX 2.1 (*Continued*)   CORE COMPETENCIES AND PRACTICE STANDARDS IN EMERGENCY MANAGEMENT

them (Bennett et al. 2016). Telling people to evacuate, and making that happen for a community with dozens of nursing homes, recent immigrants who may not speak the language, and visitors/tourists takes sensitivity to a community's diversity (Phillips et al. 2010).

12. *Experience.* While understanding can inform principles and practices for how one approaches a disaster, being in the trenches helps you to apply textbook knowledge to practical experience. New York City, for example, was well-prepared for emergencies. Yet, when the September 11 attack occurred, the collapse destroyed a state-of-the-art emergency operations center. Emergency managers rebuilt a new EOC in a warehouse down the street within 48 hours and led the city through relief efforts and trauma. Doing so in the context of losing one's fellow citizens, as well as the damage to the infrastructure surrounding Ground Zero—took experience, strong interorganizational relationships, good leaders and effective managers—all of the core competencies contained in this list.

In addition to the core competencies addressed here, the National Fire Protection Association (NFPA 2007) established the NFPA 1600 Standard on Disaster/Emergency Management and Business Continuity Programs. The NFPA 1600 standard embraces the four phases of preparedness, response, recovery and mitigation and in 2007 added prevention (NFPA 2007).

Certain activities and behaviors serve as the foundation for NFPA 1600 (see *italics* next). The starting point is a *risk analysis* to identify local hazards. Understanding local hazards forms a base for *preventing incidents* through *mitigation*. Response to incidents requires effective *resource management and logistical coordination* of facilities, services, equipment and personnel. When needed, emergency managers rely on *mutual aid agreements* that have been negotiated with local partners. Doing so requires careful *planning* across all of the phases of disaster and must involve key stakeholders. During the response and recovery phases, *incident management* requires attention to inter- and intraorganizational *communication, crisis communication, warning dissemination and informing the public*. *Operational procedures* will include standard operations for life safety matters as well as situational analyses of the unfolding event, and subsequent damage assessment. *Facilities* need to include development, maintenance, and operational functionality of the EOC. Carrying out all of these tasks means involving critical personnel in *training, education, and exercises*. Finally, because most emergency managers report to a public, corporate, or nongovernmental structure, an agency must ensure *financial accountability*.

2.3.1 Public Sector Emergency Management in the United States

In the United States, the first line of defense against disasters is local. Emergency management begins with city, county, or parish employees working with state, regional, and national counterparts as needed. Because disasters are usually experienced locally, the local emergency management agency (LEMA; Lindell 1994) takes responsibility for organizing preparedness, response, recovery, and mitigation activities. LEMAs can vary widely from a small office in the basement of city hall, staffed mostly by volunteers, to major urban areas with personnel employed in specialized areas.

In addition, emergency management agencies (EMAs) may develop structurally in several different ways (Labadie 1984). Probably the two most common forms are the departmental structure or the embedded structure. In the departmental structure, an emergency manager serves as the head of a department much like a department of public works or parks and recreation. As such, she or he then serves under the city manager or elected official responsible for the departments. Such a model implies competition with other departments for personnel, budget, and resources. This intra-organizational department structure may not work effectively in a disaster when rapidly changing conditions require immediate, adaptable management rather than a standardized, bureaucratic response (Neal and Phillips 1995). Another matter to consider within an EMA is the number of personnel that should be hired. In 2007, one published set of guidelines in the United States suggested that a LEMA should have at least one professional emergency manager for every 100,000 persons in the population. Most countries remain far below that benchmark, including the United States, although emergency management does continue to hire new people while other professions report downsizing.

It is unlikely, though, that a LEMA will act alone as disasters rarely recognize jurisdictional boundaries. Tornadoes, hurricanes, and earthquakes occur across city, county, and state boundaries. In addition, an area may be so affected that it will require assistance from outside their jurisdiction. Within the United States, the Emergency Management Association Compact (EMAC, Public Law 104-321 in 1996) facilitates partnerships across state lines (Kapucu, Augustin, and Garayev 2009). EMAC functions as a mutual aid agreement and spells out standard operating procedures for reimbursement, equipment, personnel, liability, and related matters. All 50 U.S. states as well as the District of Columbia, Puerto Rico and the U.S. Virgin Islands participate in EMAC. How useful can an interstate network be? For Hurricane Katrina, 48 of the 50 states sent equipment and personnel totaling $830 million, as well as 66,000 personnel, an impressive level of assistance.

In the United States, the Federal Emergency Management Agency (FEMA) mission is "to support our citizens and first responders to ensure that as a nation we work together to build, sustain, and improve our capability to prepare for, protect against, respond to, recover from, and mitigate all hazards." FEMA's activities are bounded by legislation called the Stafford Act. When an agency is governed by legislation, there are limits to what it can and cannot do—a true challenge given public expectations that the government can and will show up in times of crisis. In reality, people should expect to be on their own for up to 72 hours after a disaster before outside assistance arrives and commences help in an organized manner.

The National Response Framework (NRF) stresses that various federal agencies must plan, respond, and recover in a coordinated fashion. Participating agencies do so under focused and coordinated Emergency Support Functions (ESFs). For example, if flooding damages roads or bridges, the U.S. Army Corps of Engineers coordinates Emergency Response Function #3—Public Works and Engineering. The Army Corps of Engineers would coordinate with state and local public works departments to determine needs and obtain resources to rebuild the infrastructure of a local community. Other federal organizations assisting the U.S. Army Corps of Engineering might include the Department of Defense (DOD), The Department of Homeland Security (DHS), and FEMA.

As another example of national-level assistance, the Environmental Protection Agency (EPA) would coordinate ESF #10—Oil and Hazardous Response Materials. Representatives from DHS and the United States Coast Guard would support this ESF along with 14 other federal agencies and departments. As we will learn later, EPA monitoring after the attacks of September 11 was needed to safeguard the health of first responders. Their role before, during, and after a disaster is critical to public health and safety including those exposed to potential contaminants.

Under ESF #8, public health partners coordinate. While the Department of Health and Human Services coordinates this function, other partners would collaborate. During the 2015 Ebola crisis, the Centers for Disease Control and Prevention (CDC) helped. In the event of a pandemic, the CDC would play a critical role in monitoring the spread of the disease and by recommending protocol to protect public health (CDC 2006). Tasked with researching health-related issues and gathering data on medical issues including bioterrorism, chemical emergencies, radiation emergencies, mass casualties, natural disasters, and pandemic threats, the CDC is vital to public health interests.

Overall, emergency management in the public sector involves more than emergency management officials. It includes coordinating the efforts of local government (e.g., emergency services organizations, public works, public health, elected officials), state government (state offices of emergency management and homeland security, public health, National Guard, elected officials), the federal government (e.g., DHS, FEMA, CDC, and most other federal agencies, elected officials) and tribal governments. These public partners often work with businesses and volunteer organizations. For some starting points to enter these agencies, see Box 2.2.

BOX 2.2   GETTING STARTED IN THE PROFESSION OF EMERGENCY MANAGEMENT

Historically, emergency managers have come from the fields of emergency response, the military, or through direct experience with disasters. In recent contrast, open positions now call for degrees in emergency management coupled with experience. How can you secure both?

- *Internships.* By securing a student internship in an emergency management or related agency, you can add experience to your resume, obtain academic credit, and secure a letter of recommendation.
- *Research.* Universities expect faculty to produce new knowledge that contributes to their disciplines. Faculty in emergency management, as well as sociology, geography, psychology, business, veterinary medicine, and other disciplines may be able to provide research opportunities for academic credit and as employment.
- *Start at the Beginning.* Entry level positions may open up fastest when a disaster strikes. Being ready and able to deploy to a disaster site can get your "boots on the ground" fastest. FEMA, for example, maintains a list of up to 4,000 Disaster Reservists to be deployed in the event of an emergency (https://www.fema.gov/reservist-program).
- *Volunteer.* Volunteering for local, state, national, or international disaster organizations can provide meaningful and fulfilling work experience. Most volunteer opportunities offer training and credentialing that can be placed on a resume. The experience can also provide insights and skills.
- *Training and Education.* The field of emergency management changes continually. By remaining connected to educational and training opportunities including attending workshops, going to seminars, and continuing your education, you can enhance your potential to experience an upwardly mobile career. Consider starting with the free FEMA Independent Study online courses at http://training.fema.gov/is/.

2.3.2 Private Sector Emergency Management

The private sector includes businesses that need emergency managers as well as consultant companies that work for and with federal, state and local agencies. The Deep Water Horizon Oil Spill that occurred on a British Petroleum (BP) platform in the U.S. Gulf of Mexico in 2010 represents just such a need. In the aftermath of the oil spill, BP worked with local, state, and federal emergency managers from a variety of agencies as well as with elected officials, the military, and private citizens affected by the spill. In addition to its existing staff, BP paid a significant amount of money to hire, supervise, and deploy workers along beaches, in the marshes, and out in the Gulf on both airborne and waterborne units. Other corporations besides the oil industry also hire emergency management professionals including department stores, public malls, banks, and insurance providers. The private sector also includes consultant groups that usually compete for contracts and grants from government agencies or other private groups. These consultants may work on specific tasks such as planning, recovery (e.g., bridge reconstruction, debris removal, or temporary housing parks) or provide expertise on topics such as disability issues during an evacuation. Or consider the business employees themselves. Does the business have a procedure for disaster warnings like tornadoes? What if workers have to "shelter in place," or work at the facility throughout the crisis? How will the business survive if they lose their facility or their personnel?

Interestingly, many businesses fail to prepare for disasters, which can cause considerable losses and lead to business failure. As one example, does the business have a backup plan for their data? Does the business protect such important information from cyber attacks or viruses? Without their accounting receipts, inventory, payroll, customer lists, and other similar sets of information, the business cannot survive. FEMA lists the following general reasons why businesses should be ready to respond to and recover from disaster, visit http://www.fema.gov/media-library/assets/documents/90388:

- Companies have a moral duty to protect their employees, area, and environment.
- Companies need to follow existing local, state, and federal laws related to safety.
- Companies can return to business much more quickly, which not only helps the business, but the community and regions.
- Companies diminish their chance of being sued.
- Companies obtain a positive image from good disaster and crisis planning.
- Companies often have their insurance costs reduced.

Today, both businesses and FEMA recognize the importance of disaster preparedness for the private sector. Companies now hire emergency managers to prepare their workforce and workplaces, to ensure business continuity, and to respond during a crisis. Insurance companies, banks, brokerages, and departmental stores have all found reasons to prepare. On September 11, predisaster evacuation planning and practicing saved thousands of lives.

2.3.3 Voluntary Sector Emergency Management

Voluntary organizations hire paid staff and recruit large cadres of volunteers to alleviate survivor stress by providing food, shelter, housing, debris removal, reconstruction, and health services. Many of these needs fall under ESF #6 Mass Care, so it is not unusual to see many voluntary agencies working out of the FEMA Joint Field Office (JFO). Recovery for many survivors, particularly those at low incomes, would not be possible without the contributions of faith-based, voluntary, and community organizations (Phillips and Jenkins 2009).

For example, the Red Cross and the American Psychological Association provide certified disaster mental health workers to help traumatized survivors. Lutheran Disaster Services offers trained chaplains to assist people. Church of the Brethren sends well-prepared and credentialed disaster child care workers (Peek, Sutton and Gump 2008). The Southern Baptist Men cook food for survivors, which may be delivered by Red Cross volunteers. The Medical Reserve Corps coordinates volunteers with medical and veterinary experience in time of crisis. Mennonite Disaster Service is well known for housing repairs and reconstruction. Catholic Charities often funds specific needs, such as ramps and devices for people with disabilities. The United Methodist Committee on Relief trains case managers to assist survivors through the confusing journey to return home.

In the United States, several volunteer disaster response organizations have been built. The majority support preparedness efforts or response operations such as the Citizen Corps that may include Community Emergency Response Teams (CERTs), Volunteers in Police Service (VIPS), Fire Corps, Neighborhood Watch and Medical Reserve Corps. Citizen Corps emerged after September 11 with a mission "to harness the power of every individual through education, training, and volunteer service to make communities safer, stronger, and better prepared to respond to the threats of terrorism, crime, public health issues, and disasters of all kinds" (see www.citizencorps.gov).

Well-credentialed, trained groups also support emergency management from the volunteer side although some may also receive remuneration for their time (Phillips, Mwarumba and Wagner 2012). Such groups may involve medical professionals from the Disaster Medical Assistance Team (DMAT) that is part of the National Disaster Medical System. Various states, cities, and regions in the United States host DMATs, which are prepared to be deployed on an as-needed basis. They might be involved in triage for injured survivors to help with evacuation, to provide medical care in shelters, or to offer first aid. Specialized DMATs may be able to give even more critical care. Careful training, screening and credentialing is required to become part of a DMAT (see more at www.dmat.org).

Similarly, a Veterinary Medical Assistance Team or VMAT can respond to injured livestock and pets. Associated with the American Veterinary Medical Association (AVMA), the VMAT sends professional veterinarians, veterinary medical students, and animal technicians to locations in need of support. After Hurricane Katrina, volunteer animal teams helped with pet rescues, animal shelters, and emergency medical care (Irvine 2009). The Medical Reserve Corps of Oklahoma activated its County Animal Response Teams after the 2013 tornadoes. Without doubt, they saved the lives of hundreds of pets and livestock through largely volunteer efforts.

2.3.4 International Emergency Management and Humanitarian Aid

Response and recovery capabilities vary dramatically from nation to nation (see Box 2.3). Many nations, especially those facing development challenges, rely upon international disaster relief organizations during crises. In developing nations, such as Haiti or Rwanda, a wider range of disasters exists than what we may experience in the United States. Famines, epidemics, conflicts, and droughts may be more common, prompting people to try and reach refugee camps where humanitarian relief can be secured.

For example, NGOs played a crucial role with response and recovery activities after the Indian Ocean Tsunami struck 13 nations in 2004. Over 400 different NGOs helped impoverished fishermen communities with survival needs such as food, shelter, and health care in the area of Naggapattinam, India. Local NGOs worked with outside organizations to assist the responders and survivors including over 1,000 new orphans. NGOs also obtained materials to bury over 8,000 dead, helped mobilize potable drinking water, provided immunizations to stop the spread of disease such as cholera, and provided new fishing boats to help jump start the local economy (Phillips et al. 2008).

After a 7.8 magnitude earthquake in Nepal in 2015, nongovernmental and governmental agencies provided aid. According to the U.S. Agency for International Development (USAID 2015), dozens of experienced organizations raised money and delivered resources. The USAID itself added $11 million and dispatched search and rescue teams. Military aircraft conducted reconnaissance in remote areas. The USAID Disaster Assistance Response Team, which includes agencies from the United Nations and NGOs, worked collaboratively to provide shelter assistance, water, sanitation, and hygiene. OXFAM, for example, conducted damage assessments to determine needs.

BOX 2.3 INTERNATIONAL EMERGENCY MANAGEMENT

Context influences abilities to respond to disasters and emergencies, particularly the development level of a nation. Along the eastern coast of Australia, Emergency Management Queensland (EMQ) prepares well for cyclone, bushfire, and flooding threats. As a state-level agency, Emergency Management Queensland includes both first responder units like helicopter rescue and Disaster Management Services. New Zealand established the Ministry of Civil Defence and Emergency Management (MCDEM) to manage risks such as earthquakes, flooding, tsunamis and wildfires. MCDEM recognizes the importance of connections to local emergency managers and NGOs, and has designed a series of guidance materials to encourage and foster the development of localized Civil Defence Emergency Management groups (CDEMs). In particular, New Zealand has urged local capacity-building across government, private and community agencies and the integration of utilities, infrastructure managers, and health-care systems. The main principle is partnership at the community level to promote a culture of prevention. In contrast, Pakistan's abilities to respond have always been challenging due to its development status. In 2010, extensive flooding covered the nation of Pakistan, with waters affecting both rural and urban areas (USAID 2010a). Infrastructure, including roads and bridges, failed across the nation, making it difficult to reach and help survivors. The flooding became so severe that it threatened to cut off food reserves and supplies to the major city of Karachi, hosting a population over 18 million.

In Latin America and the Caribbean, an NGO called the Pan American Health Organization (PAHO), provides training, publications, guidance, and relief funds. After the Haitian earthquake, PAHO assisted with health issues including disposal of medical and related hazardous wastes. When disaster strikes, PAHO helps to mobilize Regional Health Disaster Response Teams, support decision making in a nation's emergency operations center, and ensure the delivery of humanitarian supplies (see www.paho.org/disaster). PAHO is only one of dozens of humanitarian organizations worldwide that seek to address human vulnerability by addressing critical needs both before and after disaster strikes.

The Government of Canada's humanitarian team supported sheltering. The United Nations Humanitarian Air Service sent helicopters while the UN World Food Program delivered emergency rations (USAID 2015).

Exceptions do occur of course. When a massive cyclone struck Myanmar (also known as Burma), the military government refused entry to humanitarian organizations. It is widely believed that the Myanmar government denied access to most aid organizations out of fear that the ruling junta would be destabilized. Amid worldwide outcry and accusations of misappropriation of resources, the internal military attempted to deliver assistance while millions suffered. An estimated 100,000 people were believed to have died in the catastrophe.

People living in developed nations tend to fare far better when disaster strikes because of the amount of resources, trained personnel, and number of available volunteers. However, as we will learn in this text, great disparities also exist. Even in a nation as powerful as the United States, when disasters occurred, we could not save some people with disabilities, senior citizens, and single parents due to lack of transportation. Disasters are not equal opportunity events for people in developing nations or for those living in economically marginalized conditions. The purpose of this text, though, is to address such conditions and offer strategies to relieve suffering, build stronger and more disaster resilient communities, and inspire you to become a positive part of that process. Increasingly, emergency managers are professionalizing themselves through the acquisition of college degrees and professional certification (see Box 2.4). The path to a career as an emergency manager will require education, continued training, experience, and the approval of your peers. In order to become an emergency manager, you should pay attention to the annual rhythms of the work which we turn to next.

BOX 2.4   THE CERTIFIED EMERGENCY MANAGER

By the late 1980s and early 1990s, members of The National Coordinating Council for Emergency Management (NCCEM, today the International Association of Emergency Managers or IAEM) in the United States became concerned about the perception of emergency managers and their profession. NCCEM members also wanted to increase salaries as incomes often fell close to the lowest paid positions in local government. As a result, NCCEM established a committee during the early 1990s to offer qualified individuals the title of "Certified Emergency Manager" (CEM). Committee members believed that having a CEM would increase status and pay while simultaneously raising standards and respect for the profession. To assist with the creation of the CEM, NCCEM surveyed local emergency managers and found that half of those surveyed had a high school education or less. Education is one of the three ways to measure socioeconomic status, along with occupation and income. The three measures often interact—along with a low education comes low pay.

In addition, the profession lacked diversity. Given the diversity of the nation along with the very real threat of disaster vulnerability among women, racial and ethnic minorities, and people with disabilities, it was hoped that professionalization would attract a more multicultural set of emergency managers reflective of the larger population.

Today, IAEM offers a Certified Emergency Manager (CEM) or Associate Emergency Manager (AEM) credential. The CEM requires a four-year baccalaureate degree along with experience and additional application materials and testing. The AEM requires contact hours, an essay, and an exam among other materials. For detailed information, visit http://iaem.com/page. cfm?p=certification/getting-started, last accessed May 8, 2015.

2.4 The Seasonal Life of the Emergency Manager

Seasons connote a regular sense of rhythm or activities often in tune with nature. Many disasters come with seasons. In the states of Oklahoma, Texas, Arkansas, Kansas, and Nebraska for example, the "tornado alley" season commences on March 1. Hurricane season, from June 1 through the end of November, alerts coastal residents in the Americas and Caribbean to develop or review evacuation plans and set aside resources to do so. Cyclone season occurs from November 1 through April 30 in the South Pacific. In the United States, Californians are urged to reduce wildfire fuel from May through November while Australians prepare for the onset of such events in August. Depending on where you live, ice storms, blizzards, and spring rains that generate river and flash flooding can be anticipated.

Other disasters do not offer advance warning. Earthquakes can happen any time, although locations of seismic risk and possible magnitude can be identified. Earthquake-prone areas such as the Hayward fault in northern California, or faults along the Indian subcontinent that cause shaking in Pakistan, India, Nepal, and Afghanistan carry significantly higher threats. Similarly, terrorist attacks, gas explosions, transportation accidents, and hazardous materials events usually occur without warning.

Discerning a seasonal pattern or anticipating a threat is the job of the emergency manager. Using that knowledge will reduce the impacts that can cause injuries or deaths as well as economic, environmental, infrastructure, cyber, and psychological harm. Knowing and understanding disaster threats serves as our starting place. This section describes common threats experienced across the United States from natural, technological, and human-generated threats. As you read, reflect on what a professional emergency manager might need to do to protect the public from such risks (see Table 2.1).

2.4.1 Tornadoes

The United States faces an average of 1,200 tornadoes annually, in rapid-onset events that vary in width, length, and intensity. The Enhanced Fujita Scale (EF-Scale) was devised to improve the description of such events. In principal, the EF-Scale compares tornadoes based upon its impacts on various kinds of structures (see Appendix). For example, think about the potential impact of an EF-1 tornado approaching where you live. If your dwelling is a brick house that has a basement shelter, you will be much safer than if you live in a mobile home (NOAA 2009a). However, if an EF-5 impacts the area, catastrophic damage and significant loss of life may occur despite the best levels of protection.

TABLE 2.1 Protective Action from Natural Hazards

Hazard	Immediate Protective Action
Tornado	Underground shelter is best; if above ground put as many walls between yourself and the outside as possible; if outside get as low to the ground as possible while remaining alert for possible flooding.
Hurricane	Evacuation; as a last resort, vertical shelter in a sturdy building may provide some degree of protection.
Earthquake	The best action for an unexpected earthquake is usually to take cover under a sturdy object.
Flood	Evacuate before the flood; do not drive into water of any depth.
Wildfire	The best way to protect yourself from wildfire is to control vegetation around your home, stay alert to "red flag warnings" for wildfire, and obey evacuation orders.
Volcano	Evacuation due to lava, heat, ash/debris, and gas inhalation risks.

An EF-5 tornado struck Joplin, Missouri on 22 May, 2011 with 200 mph winds. The storm generated a one mile wide path of destruction that stretched for a length of 22 miles. The damage trail included a six mile by one mile wide path through the city that ripped apart homes, destroyed a hospital, splintered businesses, and killed 158 people (National Weather Service 2011). A nursing home that lay in the path lost 18 residents and staff. On 20 May, 2013, an EF-5 tornado with a wind of 210 mph killed 24 people in Moore, Oklahoma and injured hundreds more. Fatalities included children at the Plaza Towers Elementary School despite the best efforts of staff to protect them (see Photo 2.1). Emergency managers plan,

PHOTO 2.1   Plaza Towers Elementary School, 2013. Jocelyn Augustino/FEMA. Location: Moore, OK.

warn, and respond to such situations in efforts designed to reduce fatalities, injuries, and property damage.

2.4.2 Hurricanes

Hurricanes also occur during predictable time periods, typically from May through October with a peak in August and September. The Saffir–Simpson scale measures the hurricanes based upon sustained wind speed (see Appendix, Schott et al. 2010). The scale, however, does not capture such factors as how quickly a hurricane moves over land, the amount and intensity of rainfall, or the impacts of floods, tornadoes, and storm surge. Nor does it take into account such factors as the type, quality, and age of buildings in the path of the hurricane.

Hurricane Sandy, which downsized into a "Superstorm," occurred in late October 2012. The storm affected several dozen states but ultimately caused the worst damage in New York and New Jersey. Surge from the storm occurred at the time of a high tide. Significant flooding moved into affected areas causing damage to homes, businesses, commercial sectors, subways, hospitals, airport runways, and more (NOAA 2012). An estimated 147 people died as a result with 72 deaths occurring in eight states. Over 650,000 homes sustained damage and nearly nine million people lost power (NOAA 2012).

2.4.3 Earthquakes

Rather than a seasonal projection, seismologists issue earthquake projections couched as "the probability of a large earthquake on the San Andreas Fault in the next 30 years is about 21%, or about 1 out of 5" (USGS 2008). Although the media and general public still rely on the Richter Scale to measure earthquake intensity, most scientists use the Mercalli scale (USGS n.d., see Appendix for the scales).

The San Andreas fault line in California generated a massive 7.8 Richter Scale San Francisco earthquake in 1906 that devastated the city and caused massive fires. While the United States remains braced for another major earthquake, the worst and most recent events have devastated developing nations.

Five of the ten most fatal earthquakes have happened in the last 35 years. The 1976, Tangshan, China earthquake of Richter magnitude 7.1 killed 255,000 people. An earthquake in Pakistan in 2005 took the lives of 86,000 with a Richter magnitude 7.6 event. The 2010 Haiti earthquake, measuring as a Richter magnitude 7.0, killed at least 222,570 and injured another 300,000. Nepal suffered from an M 7.8 earthquake in 2015 claiming over 7,000 lives (USAID 2015).

2.4.4 Floods

Annually, floods represent the most lethal natural hazard in the United States. In 2014, flooding caused $2,861,426,089 in damage and claimed 38 lives (NOAA 2015). Over the last 10 years, at least 50% of all deaths occur from being trapped in vehicles (NOAA 2009c, 2009d). Over the past 30 years, flood losses averaged $7.96 billion with an average of 82 fatalities a year (NOAA 2015). Worldwide, flooding impacts about 520 million people annually, with 25,000 deaths, and $50–$60 billion in economic damage (United Nations 2007).

River flooding happens when a stream overflows its banks. Major storms can cause significant levels of precipitation causing flooding. Dams and levees may fail, causing water to rush into residential or commercial areas (NOAA 2009a). Flash floods occur when water rises rapidly over a short time period. Since flash floods typically take place with little or no warning, those living next to rivers, streams, or canyons can be in great danger as well as people who drive into flooded areas. In 2014, flooding in Detroit, Michigan accounted for 60% of the flood losses when close to six inches of rain fell in a 4 hour period. The consequence? Nearly two billion dollars of damage to homes and businesses (NOAA 2014).

2.4.5 Wildfires

Wildfires can occur naturally (e.g., lightning strikes) or from human actions (tossing a cigarette out of a car window). Because people choose to live in or adjacent to wooded areas, the "wildland–urban interface" or WUI, can be rapidly overcome by wildfire (National Integrated Fire Agency 2007; Nazzaro 2009). It is anticipated that rising global temperatures will also increase the risk of wildfires (Biello 2006).

Seven of the ten most expensive wildfires in the United States have occurred since 1999 (Nazzaro 2009). The Oakland Hills (CA) fires of 1991 killed 25 people, burned over 3,800 residences, and made about 6,000 victims homeless in just 4 short hours (Hoffman 1998). In July 2013, 19 firefighters lost their lives battling a blaze in Arizona. Known as the Yarnell fire, the tragedy demonstrated a national need to reduce wildfire risks and protect firefighter lives.

Wildfires also occur worldwide. In 2009, hot weather conditions (113°F), drought and high winds created an Australian firestorm. This event killed 200 people, destroyed over 750 homes, and burned 815,000 acres of land. Similar to patterns in the United States, Australian wildfires in the past 30 years have become worse (Lite 2009). In 2015, bushfires burned through South Australia, following extremely high temperatures and dry conditions.

2.4.6 Volcanoes

Volcanoes remain inactive for centuries and then suddenly erupt. The 1980 eruption of Mt. St. Helens in the United States caused over one billion dollars in damage, stranded about 10,000 people, isolated communities, and stopped all forms of transportation. About 900 million tons of white ash caused much of the damage and social disruption (USGS 2005). Mount Eyjafjallajökull in Iceland erupted in 2010. The resulting ash cloud caused airline travel delays around much of the world. The disruption to travelers and resulting losses to businesses were significant. In 2015, scientists reported that magma reservoirs under Yellowstone National Park were larger than believed (USGS 2015). The U.S. Geological Survey maintains a Yellowstone Volcano Observatory to monitor seismic and volcanic activity in the park.

2.4.7 Chemical Hazards

In December, 1985, a pesticide plant in Bhopal, India spewed at least 40 tons of the lethal chemical gas methyl isocyanate, immediately killing at least 2,000 individuals and injuring approximately 170,000 others. The long-term lethal and chronic impacts claimed another 10,000 lives soon after the release, and another 15,000 to 20,000 are believed to have died over the next two decades (Broughton 2005; EPA 2000). Tragically, a few months later another methyl isocyanate leak occurred at a chemical plant in Institute, West Virginia operated by the same company. Although the accident did not take lives, the incident did injure over 100 residents (EPA 2000).

In 1986, Congress passed the Emergency Planning and Community Right to Know Act (EPCRA). Communities formed Local Emergency Planning Committees (LEPCs) to enhance communication and planning among local organizations involved in a hazardous materials response. In addition, EPA regulations require workplaces to keep records about onsite chemicals so that first responders and emergency managers can better handle an accident (EPA 2000). Yet, accidents still occur. On April 17, 2013, an explosion occurred at the West Fertilizer Company in Texas destroying the plant and damaging numerous homes. Fifteen people, including firefighters, died in the accident. According to the U.S. Chemical Safety Board, the event was "preventable. It should never have occurred" (Chemical Safety Board 2014).

2.4.8 Biological Hazards

Some biological hazards develop naturally, such as the Bubonic Plague, the Irish potato blight, and pandemics. Most recently, pandemics have represented one of the most significant threats worldwide. In 2014, multiple nations dealt with the possibility of a global threat from Ebola. Ebola is typically transmitted through direct contact with an infected person's

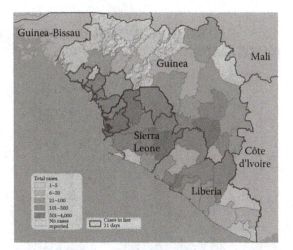

FIGURE 2.1   Ebola West Africa distribution map CDC. (Data from WHO, Ebola response roadmap, April 29, 2015.)

bodily fluids (U.S. CDC, visit http://www.cdc.gov/vhf/ebola/). The most affected countries were in West Africa, particularly Sierra Leone, Liberia and Guinea although Nigeria, Senegal, Spain, the United States, Mali and the United Kingdom also had confirmed cases (see Figure 2.1). A total of 10,995 known deaths occurred from Ebola. Advanced health care is usually needed to save lives at risk from such diseases. In early 2016, the U.S. Centers for Disease Control issued a travel advisory for pregnant women visiting some Central and South American countries in which the Zika virus was being transmitted via mosquito bites. The virus causes birth defects including brain damage (http://wwwnc.cdc.gov/travel/notices/alert/zika-virus-caribbean). In 2015, the World Health Organization alerted the public to the threat of Zika, a mosquito born virus that caused serious birth defects among infected women. Response would take a range of partnerships, something that is central to the practice of emergency management and pandemic planning (see Box 2.5).

2.4.9 Radiological and Nuclear Hazards

Of all technological hazards, perhaps those involving nuclear or radiological threats have the highest "fear factor." In 1986, a meltdown and explosion occurred at the Chernobyl nuclear power plant in the Ukraine. Radiation from the explosion also traveled through the air into Scandinavia and parts of Europe. Hundreds of thousands of people were exposed to radiation, including 350,000 immediate area residents and 200,000 emergency workers. An 18-mile radius around the facility remains closed today (U.S. NRC 2009). In 2013, an earthquake triggered a tsunami off the Japanese coast.

BOX 2.5 PARTNERING WITH PUBLIC HEALTH TO MITIGATE AN INFLUENZA PANDEMIC

Jessica Smartt Gullion

Jessica Smartt Gullion, PhD, is Assistant Professor of Sociology at Texas Woman's University and formerly Chief Epidemiologist at one of the largest health departments in Texas. She is author of the books Fracking the Neighborhood: Reluctant Activists and Natural Gas Drilling and October Birds: A Novel about Pandemic Influenza, Infection Control, and First Responders.

Influenza viruses are masters of evolution. Their components shift, drift, and recombine inside a variety of hosts (humans, pigs, and birds being their favorites). This is why public health officials vaccinate against the flu annually—one year's vaccine is usually different from another year's because of genetic changes in the virus.

We cannot predict how evolving flu viruses will behave in a population. Many flu viruses cause relatively mild illness, except for in the elderly. Some are what is called highly pathogenic, causing severe illness and having a high mortality rate.

A pandemic occurs when a new strain of influenza infects a large number of people worldwide. Public health officials conduct active surveillance for new strains of influenza that could cause a pandemic and they prepare for large-scale disaster response should a pandemic occur. Emergency Managers should ensure that they are included in this planning process.

To facilitate planning, Emergency Managers should build relationships with the following:

1. The Local Health Authority
   This person, usually a physician, holds the public health legal powers to do things like forcibly isolate and/or quarantine people and to otherwise limit population movement in order to control the spread of a disease. This person usually has established legal channels for doing

(Continued)

BOX 2.5 (*Continued*)   PARTNERING WITH PUBLIC HEALTH TO MITIGATE AN INFLUENZA PANDEMIC

this through the District Attorney's office and likely has experience in isolating noncompliant tuberculosis patients and closing restaurants that fail sanitation inspections. The Health Authority also acts as an advisor to healthcare providers throughout their jurisdiction on treatment and prevention of the spread of infectious disease.

2. The Infectious Disease Epidemiologist

   This person may be housed locally or at the state health department. Infectious disease epidemiologists are "disease detectives" whose job is to determine how a disease spreads though a population and what measure should be taken to control the spread. They devise planning scenarios using statistical models to predict the impact of a pandemic on a particular jurisdiction. During a public health disaster, they track the incidence and prevalence of illness and institute control measures. They can also facilitate laboratory testing of specimens.

3. The Strategic National Stockpile Liaison

   Like the Infectious Disease Epidemiologist, this person may be housed either locally or at the state health department. This individual has access to reserve medical supplies, including equipment, medications, and field hospitals. They can help with logistics during a public health disaster.

4. Hospital Emergency Managers

   Hospitals have their own Emergency Managers and incident command systems. Hospitals also have an Infection Control Professional, housed at either the hospital itself or a regional office. Both should be part of the planning for an influenza pandemic. They should already have a plan for their facility; it is important however that the hospitals and other care facilities in the jurisdiction coordinate their efforts.

5. School District Nursing Supervisors

   School districts typically have their own emergency management system just like hospitals. For pandemic planning purposes, it is important that the school nursing supervisor, or head school nurse, is included in discussions. This person should be familiar with district policy and if there is a need to close schools to limit disease spread, this person should be able to facilitate closure.

6. Medical Examiner

   Should a highly pathogenic influenza pandemic occur, the jurisdiction's capacity to store and process the dead may be overwhelmed. The Medical Examiner should have a plan for mass casualties, including storage facilities, and if needed a temporary morgue.

Like any hazard, planning for an influenza pandemic can mitigate the amount of illness and deaths a community experiences. The players in a public health disaster may be slightly different than in other emergencies, so it is important that Emergency Managers connect with them and build relationships before something happens.

The consequences included significant damage at the Fukushima Daiichi nuclear power plant. Massive evacuations ensued with questions lingering about long-term consequences for increased cancer and leukemia risks. At present, cancer risks are believed to have increased by 4%–7% depending on the type of cancer, age, and gender (WHO 2013). An additional concern related to radiological hazards involves using such material to create a "dirty bomb" for use by terrorists.

2.4.10 Terrorism

Terrorism is defined as an intentional or purposeful, goal-oriented act that uses extraordinary violence (Waugh 2007). Terrorists seek out symbolic targets with the goal of causing not only death and destruction but also fear and economic impacts (Waugh 2007). Terrorist attacks have occurred both in the United States and worldwide: a mall in Nairobi, Kenya; a café in Sydney, Australia; a Tunisian art museum; a magazine workplace in Paris; the Pentagon and New York City in the United States; the Boston Marathon; and a holiday party in San Bernardino, California. Attacks have ranged from piloting planes into buildings to the use of improvised explosive devices (IEDs) and violent assaults on workplaces and museums.

Terrorists have historically used resources at their disposal, proving adaptable to new resources and strategies. Generally, explosions and gunfire appear to be the preferred method. Chemicals are relatively easy to obtain and bomb-making information is available on the Internet. Common household materials such as pressure cookers contained explosives used by the Boston Marathon bombers and were hidden in backpacks worn into the site by the attackers.

Radiological threats or "dirty bombs" could spread radiation and contaminate people and property (National Academy of Sciences 2004). An initial blast could kill hundreds of thousands while contaminating the ground in the area of the blast. Fallout (debris made radioactive by the explosion and falling to the ground) could further taint property and perhaps kill more people (National Academy of Sciences 2005). However, while not impossible, the steps involved in getting the needed material, manufacturing a bomb, and transporting it to the proper location would be difficult.

Chemical weapons could also be used. In 1995, domestic terrorists deployed Sarin, a colorless and odorless chemical agent that attacks the nervous system, in a Japanese subway. Twelve people died and another 1,000 sustained injuries. Biological attacks, such as anthrax, have also been used. Following the attacks of September 11, an individual sent anthrax through the U.S. mail. This attack directly exposed 11 people, killing 5 (DHS 2009).

Based on recent attacks, it is clear that terrorists will continue to adapt available resources to their targets (U.S. Department of State 2013). Emergency managers and homeland security professionals must prove similarly flexible in discerning and responding to new and emerging threats such as those described next.

2.4.11 Natechs

Typically, when we consider a hazard or disaster, we think of one type of disaster agent or event. Natech events take matters one step further. The word "Natech" is devised from the first two letters of "natural" disaster and the first four letters of "technological" disaster (Cruz et al. 2004). For example, a hurricane, flood, or other naturally occurring event may spawn a technological disaster such as a chemical release. In 1999, an earthquake in Kocaeli, Turkey killed over 17,000 and injured at least 40,000. At least 21 major hazardous material releases occurred including large amounts of crude oil that spilled into Izmit Bay. Other chemicals were released into the atmosphere and contaminated the ground (Cruz et al. 2004). The problem of natechs illustrates how important it is to plan for both natural and technological events affecting various sectors of the community. When a natech or a "compounding natural disaster" happens, effective response between an array of partners can save lives and property.

This problem became clear in Denton, Texas in May of 2015. During a "bow echo" thunderstorm (a high wind event that may spawn a tornado), lightning struck a gas well. A large explosion resulted with a fire that lingered for some hours. Though no injuries were reported, the site sustained significant damage.

2.4.12 Computer Failures and Cyberterrorism

Computer failures can be accidental or intentional, such as criminal activity or terrorism. Cyberterrorism, in particular, could carry significant impacts. Imagine, for example, if a foreign government infiltrates computer systems and causes weapons to fire or the electrical grid to shut down. The impact of such a power grid failure can be catastrophic given that hospitals, nursing homes, and other sensitive locations rely on power to care for people and respond to emergencies. You may remember the terrorist attack on Charlie Hebdo, a Paris-based satirical magazine. In addition, cyber attacks occurred on over 19,000 French websites and were believed to have been part of the overall attack.

In the United States, the U.S. Computer Emergency Readiness Team (US-CERT) serves as part of the DHS's National Cybersecurity and Communications Integration Center (NCCIC). US-CERT operates round the clock to assess and respond to potential threats. With partners from academia, other federal agencies, government, and private organizations, US-CERT is likely to become one of the nation's most important agencies in the war on international terror. Their concern is real: over 100 foreign intelligence offices attempt to infiltrate military computer installations continuously and the number of attempts over the last 10 years have increased exponentially (Garamone 2010; see also http://www.dhs.gov/cyber-incident-response).

2.4.13 Space Weather

Events that occur outside our atmosphere, called "space weather" represent very real concerns. Meteorologists, emergency managers, and government must plan for these untoward events. Imagine, for example, asteroid alerts or solar flare warnings—how should people react? The U.S. Office of the Federal Coordinator of Meteorology (2010) is working with other federal agencies to address space weather. Three types of space weather represent concerns: electromagnetic emissions (radio blackout), charged particle radiation (solar radiation storm), and magnetized plasma (geomagnetic storm, see Murtagh 2015).

Occasionally, massive solar flares can damage and destroy satellites. Think how much of our life today includes the use of satellites, such as Geographical Positioning Systems (GPS), television, voice and data communications, and weather data. Impacts would be felt on navigation systems for commercial jets, marine traffic, and military aircraft. National security could be compromised with remote sensing satellites out of commission (Murtagh 2010). Some flares could be strong enough to penetrate the Earth's atmosphere. As a result, electronics could be damaged or destroyed. Scientists have found these types dangerous enough that they have devised scales, similar to the EF Scale for tornadoes or the Mercalli Scale for earthquakes (Murtagh 2010; NOAA 2005; USGS 2009, 2010a, 2010b). Scientists today discover and track asteroids and other "near earth objects" through a new satellite (Wide field Infrared Survey Explorer, or WISE) and other means. Data are sent to the Minor Planet Center in Cambridge, Massachusetts to determine if an object presents any danger to the Earth (NASA 2011).

Summary

In this chapter, we have examined the profession of emergency management. The job entails a thorough understanding of the life cycle of disasters, which include activities organized around preparedness, response, recovery, and mitigation. Professional emergency managers conduct activities around these phases in a variety of work settings. The majority work in the public sector, typically in local, state, regional, or national government. The private sector, such as insurance or hazardous materials industries, also offers opportunities to find employment. Emergency management gradu-ates may also find the voluntary sector an exciting place to work, in the service of those affected by disasters. International and humanitarian work also draws people into working events such as genocide, human trafficking, famine, or drought.

The chapter also addressed the range of hazards that an emergency man-ager might face, primarily within the United States. Natural hazards might involve an emergency manager in protecting the public from earthquakes, volcanoes, tornadoes, or similar events. But hazardous materials, biologi-cal threats, and terrorism also present scenarios around which emergency managers must plan and prepare. New and emerging hazards occur as well. Whereas emergency managers rarely concerned themselves with cybersecu-rity a few decades ago, the potential impacts of cyberterrorism and cyber-crime now loom as viable threats. Space weather has also become a concern, with the potential impacts including disruption of power grids, navigational systems, and air travel. Regardless of the threat, it is the job of the emer-gency manager to work collaboratively with an array of partners to protect the public. That work serves as the basis for the remainder of the text. We invite you to join this profession.

Discussion Questions

1. Which of the professional emergency management sectors is of most interest to you and why? What kinds of career opportunities can you find in each of them by searching jobs on the Internet?

2. If you were an emergency manager in Florida, New York, California, or Texas, what seasonal challenges you might face? What could be common hazards that you would have to plan for? How about Australia, Pakistan, or Haiti?

3. How is domestic emergency management different from inter-national locations for emergency managers? Are there other countries or sites that interest you in terms of a professional career? What kinds of hazards may be present in these settings and what kinds of activities would you need to undertake to work in emer-gency management there?

4. Quarantelli wrote decades ago that new and emerging hazards would continually develop. Today, we are discussing cyberwarfare, pandemics, and space weather that were not on the radar for emer-gency management several decades ago. Looking into the future, what kinds of hazards do you foresee?

Resources

- For a radar animation of the Joplin tornado, visit http://www.crh.noaa.gov/sgf/?n=event_2011may22_synopsis, last accessed April 24, 2014.
- FEMA offers free online courses in a range of topics. Consider pursuing the certificate they offer for the Professional Development Series. Go to www.fema.gov and search for Independent Study to start your journey.
- A number of websites provide information on space weather. Start your journey at the Space Weather Prediction Center, found at http://www.swpc.noaa.gov/communities/space-weather-enthusiasts, last accessed July 31, 2015 or the Office of the Federal Coordinator of Meteorology at www.ofcm.gov.

References and Recommended Readings

Barton, Allen. 1970. *Communities in Disaster.* New York: Anchor Books.

Bennett, DeeDee, Brenda D. Phillips and Elizabeth Davis. 2016. The Future of Accessibility in Disaster Conditions: How Wireless Technologies Will Transform the Life Cycle of Emergency Management. *Futures.* Available at http://dx.doi.org/10.1016/j.futures.2016.05.004, last accessed August 26, 2016.

Biello, David. 2006. Warming Climate May Increase Western Wildfire Woes, *Scientific American.* Available at http://www.scientificamerican.com/article.cfm?id=warming-climate-may-incre, last accessed February 4, 2011.

Blanchard, B. Wayne. 2005. Top Ten Competencies for Professional Emergency Management. Available at http://training.fema.gov/EMIWeb/edu/EMCompetencies.asp, last accessed August 31, 2010.

Broughton, Edward. 2005. The Bhopal Disaster and Its Aftermath: A Review. *Environmental Health: A Global Access Science Journal* 4(6). Available at http://www.ehjournal.net/content/pdf/1476-069X-4-6.pdf, last accessed February 27, 2011.

CDC (Center for Disease Control). 2006. Pandemic Influenza Guidance Supplement to the 2006 Public Health Emergency Preparedness Cooperative Agreement Phase II. Atlanta, GA. Available at http://www.cdc.gov/phpr/documents/coopagreement-archive/fy2006/phase2-panflu-guidance.pdf, last accessed August 16, 2016.

Chemical Safety Board. 2014. Statement by CSB Chairperson Rafael Moure-Eraso and Supervisory Investigator Johnnie Banks News Conference, Dallas, TX, West Fertilizer Accident. Available at http://www.csb.gov/assets/1/16/Statement_-_News_Conference_%28Final%29.pdf, last accessed April 24, 2014.

Cruz, Ana Maria, Laura J. Steinbert, Anna Lisa Vetere Arellano, Jean-Pierre Nordvik, and Francesco Pisano. 2004. *State of the Art in Natech Risk Management.* Italy: European Union.

DHS. 2009. Biological Attack: the Danger. Available at http://www.dhs.gov/files/publications/gc_1245183510280.shtm, last accessed January 31, 2011.

Edwards, Frances. L. and Daniel. C Goodrich. 2007. Organizing for Emergency Management. pp. 39 to 56 in *Emergency Management: Principles and Practices* (2nd ed.), edited by W. Waugh and K. Tierney. Washington, D.C.: International City/County Management Association.

EPA/U.S. Environmental Protection Agency. 2000. Methyl Isocyanate. Washington, DC. Available at https://www3.epa.gov/airtoxics/hlthef/methylis.html, last accessed August 16, 2016.

Garamone, Jim, 2010. Lynn Changes Approach to Changes in Warfare. U.S., Department of Defense. Available at http://www.defense.gov/news/newsarticle.aspx?id=58930, last accessed January 30, 2011.

Hoffman, Susanna M. 1998. Eve and Adam among the Embers: Gender Patterns after the Berkeley Firestorm. In *The Gendered Terrain of Disaster*, edited by Elaine Enarson and Betty Hearn Morrow. Westport, CT: Praeger.

Irvine, Leslie. 2009. *Filling the Ark: Animal Welfare in Disasters*. Philadelphia, PA: Temple University Press.

Kapucu, Naim, Maria Elana Augustin and Vener Garayev. 2009. Interstate Partnerships in Emergency Management: Emergency Management Assistance Compact in Response to Catastrophic Disasters. *Public Administration Review* 69: 297–310.

Labadie, John. R. 1984. Problems in Local Emergency Management. *Environmental Management* 8(6), 489–494.

Lindell, Michael. 1994. Are Local Emergency Management Agencies Effective in Developing Community Preparedness? *International Journal of Mass Emergencies and Disasters* 12(2): 159–182.

Lite, Jordan, 2009. Death Toll Climbs in Aussie Wildfires. *Scientific American*. Available at http://www.scientificamerican.com/blog/post.cfm?id=death-toll-climbs-in-aussie-wildfir-2009-02-09, last accessed February 4, 2011.

Murtagh, Bill. 2010. Space Weather Storms: Responding to Global Concerns. Paper Presented to FEMA, Atlanta, GA, November 18.

Murtagh, Bill. 2015. Space Weather Types and Impacts. Presented at the Space Weather Enterprise Forum, Washington, D.C.

NASA. 2011. Near Earth Object Program. Available at http://neo.jpl.nasa.gov/neo/, last accessed February 27, 2011.

National Academy of Sciences. 2004. Radiological Attack: Dirty Bombs and Other Devices. Available at http://www.dhs.gov/xlibrary/assets/prep_radiological_fact_sheet.pdf, last accessed January 31, 2011.

National Academy of Sciences. 2005. Nuclear Attack. Available at http://www.dhs.gov/xlibrary/assets/prep_nuclear_fact_sheet.pdf, last accessed January 31, 2011.

National Fire Protection Association. 2007. *NFPA 1600 Standard on Disaster/Emergency Management and Business Continuity Programs*. Quincy, MA: National Fire Protection Association.

National Governor's Association. 1979. *Comprehensive Emergency Management*. Washington, D.C.: National Governor's Association.

National Integrated Fire Agency. 2007. Fire Information—Wildland Fire Statistics. Available at http://www.nifc.gov/fire_info/fire_stats.htm, last accessed February 6, 2011.

National Weather Service. 2011. Storm Event Reports, May 22, 2011. Available at http://www.crh.noaa.gov/sgf/?n=event_2011may22_reports, last accessed April 24, 2014.

Neal, David M. 1997. Reconsidering the Phases of Disasters. *International Journal of Mass Emergencies and Disasters* 15(2): 239–264.

Neal, David M. and Brenda D. Phillips. 1995. Effective Emergency Management: Reconsidering the Bureaucratic Approach. *Disasters* 19: 327–337.

NOAA. 2005. *Space Weather Scales*. Available at http://www.spc.noaa.gov/faq/tornado/ef-scale.html, last accessed February 27, 2011.

NOAA. 2009a. The Enhanced Fujita Scale. Available at http://www.spc.noaa.gov/efscale/, last accessed January 25, 2011.

NOAA. 2009b. Flood Basics. Available at http://www.nssl.noaa.gov/primer/flood/fld_basics.html, last accessed January 27, 2011.

NOAA. 2009c. Flood Safety. Available at http://www.weather.gov/floodsafety/floodsafe.shtml, last accessed January 27, 2011.

NOAA. 2009d. Flood Fatalities. Available at http://www.nws.noaa.gov/oh/hic/flood_stats/recent_individual_deaths.shtml, last accessed January 27, 2011.

NOAA. 2012. Hurricane/Post-Tropical Cyclone Sandy, October 22–29, 2012. Washington, D.C.: Department of Commerce, National Oceanic and Atmospheric Administration. Available at http://www.nws.noaa.gov/os/assessments/pdfs/Sandy13.pdf, last accessed May 6, 2015.

NOAA. 2014. United States Flood Loss Report Water Year 2014. Washington, D.C.: NOAA. Available at http://www.nws.noaa.gov/hic/summaries/WY2014.pdf, last accessed May 6, 2015.

NOAA. 2015. Hydrologic Information Center—Flood Loss Data. Washington, D.C.: NOAA. Available at http://www.nws.noaa.gov/hic/, last accessed May 6, 2015.

Office of the Federal Coordinator of Meteorology. 2010. 2010 Space Weather Enterprise Forum Summary Report. Available at http://www.ofcm.gov/swef/2010/SWEF_2010_Summary_Report_%28Final%29.pdf, last accessed March 1, 2011.

Peek, Lori, Jeannette Sutton and Judy Gump. 2008. Caring for Children in the Aftermath of Disaster: The Church of the Brethren Children's Disaster Services Program. *Children, Youth and Environments* 18(1): 408–421.

Phillips, Brenda. 2014. *Mennonite Disaster Service: Building a Therapeutic Community after the Gulf Coast Storms.* Lanham, MD: Lexington Books.

Phillips, Brenda and Pam Jenkins. 2009. The Roles of Faith-based Organizations after Hurricane Katrina. pp. 215–238 in *Meeting the Needs of Children, Families, and Communities Post-Disaster: Lessons Learned from Hurricane Katrina and Its Aftermath,* edited by Kilmer, R.P., Gil-Rivas, V., Tedeschi, R.G., & Calhoun, L.G. Washington, D.C.: American Psychological Association.

Phillips, Brenda, Njoki Mwarumba and Debra Wagner. 2012. The Role of the Trained Volunteer. In *Local Planning for Terror and Disasters,* edited by Leonard Cole and Nancy Connell. New York: Wiley and Sons.

Phillips, Brenda, Dave Neal, Tom Wikle, Aswin Subanthore and Shireen Hyrapiet. 2008. Mass Fatality Management after the Indian Ocean Tsunami. *Disaster Prevention and Management* 17(5): 681–697.

Quarantelli, E. L. 1996. The Future Is Not the Past Repeated: Projecting Disasters in the 21st Century from Current Trends. *Journal of Contingencies and Crisis Management* 4(4): 228–240.

Quarantelli, E. L. 2001. Another Selective Look at Future Social Crises: Some Aspects of Which We Can already See in the Present. *Journal of Contingencies and Crisis Management* 9(4): 233–237.

Schott, Timothy et al. 2010. Saffir–Simpson Hurricane Wind Scale. NOAA, National Weather Service. Available at http://www.nhc.noaa.gov/sshws.shtml, last accessed January 25, 2011.

United Nations. 2007. *International Flood Imitative.* Available at http://unesdoc.unesco.org/images/0015/001512/151208e.pdf, last accessed January 27, 2011.

U.S. Agency for International Development. 2015. Nepal Earthquake Fact Sheet #9, May 6, 2015. Available at http://www.usaid.gov/sites/default/files/documents/1866/05.06.15-USAID-DCHANepalEarthquakeFactSheet9.pdf, last accessed May 8, 2015.

U.S. Department of State. 2013. Country Reports on Terrorism. Available at https://www.state.gov/j/ct/rls/crt/2013/, last accessed August 16, 2016.

U.S. Nuclear Regulatory Commission. 2009. Chernobyl Nuclear Power Plant Accident. Washington, DC. Available at https://www.hsdl.org/?view&did=28414, last accessed August 16, 2016.

USGS. n.d. Measuring Earthquakes. Available at http://earthquake.usgs.gov/learn/faq/?faqID=24, last accessed January 25, 2011.

USGS. 2005. Description: Economic Impacts of the May 18, 1980 Eruption. Available at http://pubs.usgs.gov/fs/fs027-00/fs027-00.pdf, last accessed February 27, 2011.

USGS. 2008. 2008 Bay Area Earthquake Probabilities. Available at http://earthquake.usgs.gov/regional/nca/ucerf/, last accessed January 25, 2011.

USGS. 2009. The Modified Mercalli Scale. Available at http://earthquake.usgs.gov/learn/topics/mercalli.php, last accessed January 25, 2011.

USGS. 2010a. Earthquakes with 50,000 or More Deaths. Available at http://earthquake.usgs.gov/earthquakes/world/most_destructive.php, last accessed January 26, 2011.

USGS. 2010b. USGS Earthquake Magnitude Policy. Available at http://earthquake.usgs.gov/aboutus/docs/020204mag_policy.php, last accessed January 26, 2011.

USGS. 2015. Yellowstone Volcano Observatory (multiple pages). Available at http://volcanoes.usgs.gov/observatories/yvo/, last accessed May 6, 2015.

Waugh, William L, Jr. 2007. Terrorism as Disaster. pp. 388–404 in *Handbook of Disaster Research*, edited by H. Rodriguez, E. L. Quarantelli, and Russell R. Dynes. New York: Springer.

World Health Organization (WHO). 2013. Health Risk Assessment from the Nuclear Accident after the 2011 Great East Japan Earthquake and Tsunami. Available at http://www.who.int/ionizing_radiation/pub_meet/fukushima_risk_assessment_2013/en/, last accessed May 6, 2015.

Chapter

Key Concepts, Definitions, and Perspectives

Objectives

Upon completing this chapter, readers should be able to:

- Have a general ability to define disaster.
- Distinguish among emergency, disaster, and catastrophe.
- Understand the importance of the National Governor's Association Report and the contributions it made to the profession.
- Identify the different research traditions in emergency management and be able to distinguish between them.
- Use the main theories often used to describe and explain human behavior in disaster.
- Comprehend current theoretical issues and debates in the field, including the views of professionals and researchers.
- Appreciate the value of a multidisciplinary approach for the practice of emergency management.

Key Terms

- All hazards approach
- Catastrophe
- Comprehensive emergency management
- Crisis
- Disaster
- Emergency
- Emergent norm theory

- Hazard
- Life cycle of disasters (or the four phases)
- Risk
- Sociopolitical ecology theory
- Systems theory
- Theory
- Vulnerability

3.1 Introduction

This chapter will help the reader understand the different definitions of disaster within the field of emergency management. Quarantelli and Dynes (1970) suggest that the word disaster is a "sponge concept," since it soaks up many different meanings. For example, in general conversations, people may refer a traffic ticket, missed appointment, or broken leg as a disaster. Within the context of emergency management, the word disaster may mean the disaster agent (e.g., tornado, flood, and hurricane), the damage and the loss of life caused by the agent, the social definition of the event (e.g., moderate versus very bad) by the various parties involved, or the social disruption generated by the event (Dynes 1974). This chapter will help you understand the concept of disaster, and related terms, in all of its complexity.

Perspective matters. For example, an EF 2 tornado through a suburban neighborhood may be a disaster in the eyes of the victims, but not according to existing government policies that require certain levels of devastation before help can be approved. First responders (police, fire, and ambulance services) will rush to emergencies (traffic accidents and fires). Emergency managers typically organize their efforts around larger events that cause community disruption. To do so, both practitioners and researchers draw upon the "four phases" or the "disaster cycle" (i.e., preparedness, response, recovery, and mitigation) to think about how to manage major events.

And, disasters may not be exclusively natural, technological, or terrorist events. Local leaders may draw upon emergency managers' crisis skills for broader nontraditional events. Such situations include helping to count votes for President, recovering debris from a space shuttle accident, assisting after a riot, or dealing with a pandemic. These broad and wide notions of disaster, which necessarily involve multiple academic disciplines and professions, serve as the foundation for the profession of emergency management and college degree programs. This chapter should help you understand an array of terms such as disaster, provide help when you use the word, and guidance when you become a practitioner.

3.2 Defining Disaster

As we have already seen above and will see further evidence below, people attach a number of different meanings to the word *disaster*. Even those of us who study disaster have different meanings and views on the topic. However, for the purposes of this text, we will draw upon a definition that has guided most researchers. Then, we will explain why we want you to think about disasters on a continuum ranging from emergency, to disaster, to catastrophe. We will deal with some of the other different meanings of the word disaster later in this chapter. Noted scholar Charles Fritz (1961, p. 655) defined disasters as

> … actual or threatened accidental or uncontrollable events that are concentrated in time and space, in which a society, or a relatively self-sufficient subdivision of society undergoes severe danger, and incurs such losses to its members and physical appurtenances that the social structure is disrupted and the fulfillment of all or some of the essential functions of the society, or its subdivision, is prevented.

Notice the main components of this definition. First of all, disasters are social events—unless the event impacts people, it is not a disaster. For example, if a tidal wave totally covered an island not inhabited by people, then the event would not be considered a disaster. Second, the situation must cause social disruption for a specific group of people. For example, if a tornado destroys part of a town of 50,000, life may not change much for those not directly affected. Most actions then focus upon responding to and recovering from the disaster. For an event to be a disaster, significant disruption must occur. For example, businesses, schools, hospitals, and government offices may be closed from the damage.

Third, the area and people impacted will likely need to obtain help from the outside. External help may include search and rescue teams for victims and medical needs, companies with bulldozers and chain saws to assist with clearing debris, or utility specialists to fix power lines. Volunteers and volunteer organizations will also bring in food and water for survivors as well as those assisting with search and rescue, debris removal, and other actions. Another important issue within Fritz's definition is considering that the *situation* may not be an actual physical event, but rather the perception that an event could or is taking place. For example, thousands of people may be evacuated when a hurricane warning is issued. Such an event disrupts the lives of the residents, local, and state government officials, businesses and volunteer organizations. All of these individuals' lives change to varying degrees—even if the hurricane does not strike. But, at least they get to return and resume their day-to-day lives. In short, Fritz's definition suggests that life as we know it dramatically changes when disaster strikes. Next, let's look at the differences among emergencies, disasters, and catastrophes.

3.2.1 A Continuum of Disaster

People may think of an event in simple terms—either something is or is not a disaster. A car wreck is not a disaster. A tornado is a disaster. A house fire is not a disaster. A tornado or large chemical accident is a disaster. Yet, whether an event can be defined as a disaster is not a black and white delineation (Fischer 2003). Rather, think how events occur along a continuum where some events occur as day-to-day emergencies, others as disasters (with some larger than others), and on rare occasions, become catastrophes (See Figure 3.1). In the following sections, we distinguish between the concepts of emergency, disaster, and catastrophe.

3.2.1.1 Emergency

Emergencies are part of everyday life in a community. Emergency response situations may include heart attacks, house fires, or car accidents. Emergency response organizations can generally anticipate their emergency response needs on a yearly basis. For example, in the United States, Independence Day (July 4) and the New Year (December 31 and January 1) are the busiest times of the year for firefighters. The annual July 4 peak in the United States is a result of fireworks and, to a lesser degree, outside grilling. Fires around the New Year also involve firecrackers and flammable Christmas trees (U.S. Fire Administration 2004). Anybody in the medical field knows that weekends generally are busier than weekdays for emergency response organizations. Since these emergency response patterns are predictable, governments and response units can plan accordingly and manage these situations. In addition, except for those primarily directly involved in the emergency, life goes on for everybody else.

Situations do arise where some outside help may be needed. For example, in the case of a large apartment fire, responding fire departments may

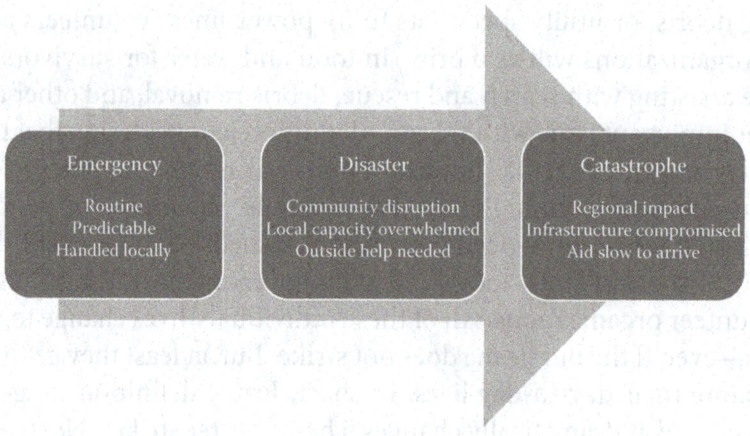

Emergency	Disaster	Catastrophe
Routine	Community disruption	Regional impact
Predictable	Local capacity overwhelmed	Infrastructure compromised
Handled locally	Outside help needed	Aid slow to arrive

FIGURE 3.1   A continuum of disaster.

activate a Memorandum of Understanding (MOU) with nearby fire departments. When a major event occurs, the neighboring fire department will arrive to either aid with the large fire or provide backup if another fire occurs within the city. Thus, although resources may be stretched, local communities can carry on business as usual when the emergency occurs.

3.2.1.2 Disaster

Drawing upon Fritz's (1961) definition noted above, a disaster breaks the local community's ability to respond to an event, even when outside help is drawn upon. For example, response organizations such as fire and police may not be able to respond to all the immediate needs or not able to respond at all. The number of immediate victims may outnumber the availability of emergency response officials. Debris and damage may inhibit emergency responders from quickly entering the disaster site. In addition, the emergency responders may be victims also. But a disaster is much more than the inability of emergency responders to do their duty. The infrastructure may suffer major damage. Most of the community may not have electrical power. Water (including drinking water and sewage) may not be available. Highways and bridges may either be impassable from excessive debris (e.g., from a tornado), inaccessible (e.g., flooded), or destroyed (e.g., earthquake). Family members may be separated from each other, have no food or water, or find their homes may be gone. Businesses, schools, and other organizations will close since the buildings will be damaged or destroyed, and people cannot travel to these locations. In short, everyday life as we know it ceases. Priorities change to focus on the event at hand. The community cannot fend for itself and needs outside help.

3.2.1.3 Catastrophe

Catastrophes are much more than just "larger disasters." Following Hurricane Katrina, Quarantelli (2006) noted that the hurricane's social impact and aftermath included the basic characteristics that distinguish a catastrophe from a disaster. First, in a catastrophe the disaster agent impacts or destroys almost all of an area's buildings and infrastructure. With Hurricane Katrina, over 80% of New Orleans flooded, and much of the area along the Mississippi coast experienced extensive storm surge damage. The floodwaters and wind either directly or indirectly made most of the infrastructure (e.g., electricity, drinking water and sewage, and transportation) inoperable. Police, fire, and other local and even regional emergency response organizations were generally unable to operate since the hurricane's aftermath impacted their buildings and staff. Furthermore, outside assistance organizations (federal, state, volunteer organizations) had difficulty initially helping. Cell phones did not work for most carriers for nearly a week. Transportation was difficult if not impossible into the area. When help did arrive, personnel had trouble finding facilities to use. The sheer magnitude of the event made it difficult to know where to begin.

Second, many local officials could not tend to their jobs after Katrina, even into the initial recovery period. In many cases, these individuals had no place to go to work and/or had lost their homes. This issue also became evident following the Indian Ocean Tsunami in 2004 and the Haitian Earthquake in 2010. With thousands dead, including government officials in some places, response activities became difficult if not impossible to coordinate.

Third, during and following a disaster, help generally arrives rather quickly. In fact, a problem following a disaster is that too much help (e.g., people, food, and supplies) arrives, a problem known as "convergence." However, with the massive nature of a catastrophe, help may be slow in coming. Specifically, large cities may not be able to help nearby smaller cities, and nearby smaller cities cannot help larger cities since the entire region has been impacted. People, food, and other needed supplies initially have no place to go to provide assistance (Quarantelli 2006).

Fourth, catastrophes mean that daily routines of individuals, families, organizations, governments, businesses, schools, and other sites will experience significant disruptions. Consider again the case of hurricane Katrina, with little if any functioning infrastructure, heavily damaged buildings, over one million residents displaced—the routine of life along the Gulf Coast came to a halt. Reflect also on the 2010 Haiti earthquake, where in addition to massive destruction of buildings and infrastructure, approximately 300,000 people died—many of whom carried out important day-to-day tasks for government, businesses, and households (Quarantelli 2006).

Finally, the role of politics emerges as a crucial aspect in the process of managing an event. During a disaster, local and state governments serve as the primary decision makers with the federal government providing some financial aid and resources. During a catastrophe, the federal government's role moves to center stage since it has the resources to provide direct assistance to the impacted region. Following the earthquake in Haiti, issues about who was in charge surfaced quickly. The death of some politicians and possible lack of leadership in other areas created a major political vacuum. In addition, catastrophes such as hurricane Katrina cross local, county (or in this case Parish) and state jurisdictions, so the federal government can help serve under-resources areas (Quarantelli 2006).

In short, a catastrophe varies significantly from a disaster. The disaster agent destroys most if not all of a region's buildings and infrastructure. The lives of individuals and routines of whole communities become totally disrupted. Outside helpers have difficulty in arriving and even setting up operations. Local, state and the federal government must all become increasingly involved to deal with the massive problems generated by a catastrophe.

Now that we have a general understanding of the conceptual continuum from emergency to disaster to catastrophe, we will next discuss some concepts used by both professionals and researchers when trying to understand how emergency managers organize their daily activities to manage disasters.

3.3 The Politics of Disasters

Politics certainly play a role in whether an event is defined a disaster. Political definitions become important in the United States, since the amount and type of aid during and following the event is contingent upon how the event is defined (e.g., hurricane, flood, and landslide) and whether the event becomes a Presidentially declared disaster (PDD).

Through the last few decades, FEMA has established a process and general criteria for a Presidential Declaration of Disaster. Authority for such a declaration comes from a number of related sources. In a general sense, article 2 and section 3 of the U.S. Constitution implicitly gives the President the power to take emergency action to ensure that all laws are followed, and to command the use of the military (as Commander in Chief). The Disaster Relief Act of 1950 and the Disaster Relief Act of 1974 gave the President power to provide relief and assistance to disaster victims. Finally, the Robert T. Stafford Disaster Relief and Emergency Assistance Act (i.e., The Stafford Act; first passed in 1988 and later amended) gave the President further power to declare a disaster more quickly (such as in the case of a terrorist attack). In essence today, with a Presidential Declaration, the federal government through the Executive (i.e., Presidential) branch can provide immediate funds. Through the years, Congress has amended the Stafford Act, including the process and general criteria for the declaration of a disaster (FEMA 2015a; Sylves 2008).

FEMA does not have a set of numerical factors for determining whether an event is a disaster. For example, an event might be declared a disaster if nobody dies, or an event might not be declared a disaster if 150 people die. To illustrate, a slow moving flood may not kill anyone, but it could be declared a disaster. And, cases certainly exist in which a plane crash kills over 100 people, but the President does not declare a disaster. Rather, for an event to qualify for a disaster declaration, FEMA focuses upon the severity, magnitude and impact of the event among other factors. To understand the severity, magnitude and impact of an event, FEMA draws upon the criteria listed below as guidelines for a state's governor to use in making a request for a federal disaster declaration (FEMA 2010c, *verbatim*):

- Amount and type of damage (number of homes destroyed or with major damage)
- Impact on the infrastructure of affected areas or critical facilities

- Imminent threats to public health and safety
- Impacts to essential government services and functions
- Unique capability of the federal Government
- Dispersion or concentration of damage
- Level of insurance coverage in place for homeowners and public facilities.
- Assistance available from other sources (federal, state, local, voluntary organizations)
- State and local resource commitments from previous, undeclared events, and
- Frequency of disaster events over a recent time period.

The Stafford Act also spells out the process local and state governments must follow to apply for a declaration and receive federal resources. Drawing upon the criteria noted above, local and state officials will provide the state's governor with a damage assessment. The state's governor will then submit a formal request to its FEMA regional office (one of ten in the United States). The governor's request should demonstrate that state and local governments do not have the resources to manage and recover from the event. Both the regional and national FEMA offices will assess the report, and then make a recommendation to the President, who will accept or reject FEMA's recommendation (FEMA 2010c). Keep in mind that the process and criteria of a PDD can change and may be different at the time of your reading. A look at FEMA's website (www.fema.gov) can help you determine what if any changes have been made since the time of this writing.

Politics can and at times do enter into the Presidential declaration. During the last few decades, we can certainly argue that we have seen more disasters over the last few decades (Cutter et al. 2015; Mileti 1999; Quarantelli 1986). Additionally, as we have seen that the number of disasters increase, the amount of money spent on federally declared disasters has increased as well.

In a specific analysis on Presidential disaster declarations between May 1953, and January 2007, a distinct pattern emerged (Sylves 2008). First, during this time period, there were 1,674 major disaster declarations. This represents an average of 31 declarations a year or close to 2.5 declarations a month. However, if we look at the time period from January 1993 through September 2005, we see a dramatic rise in disaster declarations. The average increased to 48.2 declarations a year or four a month, with the increase believed to be tied to:

- The public's belief that the federal government's role is to provide aid
- Various politicians' views and use of federalism (or how the state and federal governments interact with each other)
- Presidents being more willing to declare disasters
- Laws allowing more aid to disaster hit communities and victims (Sylves 2008, p. 84)

Interestingly, partisanship does not seem to be part of the political process of major disaster declarations. For example, a request by a Republican governor to a Democratic President will not diminish the chance of an event being declared a disaster. Or, a request by a Republican governor to a Republican President will not enhance the chance of an event being declared a disaster. However, during the same 45-year-time period mentioned earlier, researchers also found that Democratic Presidents accepted a higher proportion of declaration requests than Republican Presidents. In addition, Presidents were more likely to approve a governor's request for natural rather than a technological disasters (Sylves and Buzas 2007). The pace of a disaster may influence a decision as well, for example, when an EF5 tornado devastates an area a Presidential declaration typically occurs more quickly than a slowly developing drought.

3.3.1 Slow- versus Fast-Moving Views of Disaster

Generally we think of disasters as events that quickly strike a population such as an explosion, flood, earthquake, tornado, or similar event. The perspective of looking at sudden or quickly moving events is in part based upon the research and professional roots of the field. Remember that dealing with nuclear and chemical war at the start of the Cold War drove much of our view of emergency management in the United States. To study human behavior in this context, researchers looked at human behavior during sudden or quickly occurring disasters like explosions or tornadoes. Even today, much of our knowledge of disaster behavior, especially in developed nations such as the United States, Canada, Japan, and Western Europe focuses upon the sudden, quick event.

However, not all events occur quickly, suddenly, or without warning. They develop slowly. Long term, slowly changing weather patterns can also create disasters. For example, meteorologists can often predict long-term patterns of drought in Central Africa. Drought can cause crop failure, leading to famine in these countries. In turn, famine often forces large numbers of people to migrate to other areas or even to other countries for survival. Mass migrations then may create civil wars or wars between nations. Human rights violations often occur to those who have fled devastated lands. These patterns are predictable and to a degree can be mitigated (Hoffman and Oliver-Smith 2002).

Environmental disasters can also be slow moving. The neighborhood of Love Canal, part of Niagara Falls, New York, became contaminated due to hazardous waste buried there by Hooker Chemical Company. When Hooker Chemical Company acquired area property in 1942, it started dumping chemical waste. During the early and mid-1950s, the property was sold to a developer to build homes. A school soon followed. By the mid to late 1970s, residents started to notice odd odors and health problems including a higher rate of miscarriages, mental problems, and illnesses. A local newspaper tested the water in the area and found high amounts of hazardous materials. As a result, the local residents formed a protest group in order to help the residents with solving their medical issues, selling their homes, and closing the neighborhood. Overall, as part of an Environmental Protection Agency (EPA) program, over 800 families left the neighborhood with most of the homes then being demolished (Blum 2008; Levine 1982).

In this circumstance, the real issue is "when did the disaster start?" For some, it started the second the hazardous waste was improperly disposed of. For others, it began when the property was sold for development. Perhaps for the residents the event became defined as a disaster when people started to get sick or when residents and others claimed that the hazardous materials were causing the illnesses. By the late 1970s and early 1980s, federal and state government recognized the event as a disaster. Federal assistance and the EPA became involved as people moved out of the area to safer locations. As a slow and long-onset event, it was hard to pinpoint the exact time when the "threshold" was met to call the event a disaster (Blum 2008; Levine 1982).

In short, various types of disasters (e.g., droughts, famines, and hazardous chemicals) do not become immediate disasters. Rather, their impacts, consequences, and even public definition of the event becoming a disaster may occur over years and decades. As a result, emergency managers and others cannot state an exact time when such an event becomes a disaster. These types of events slowly creep upon us, until, perhaps the attributes of disaster suddenly exist, and it becomes too late to mitigate, prepare, or even respond properly. Regardless, it is the job of the emergency manager to take on such challenges, which historically has been characterized as a life cycle of activities organized into four phases.

3.4 The National Governor's Association Report in the United States

For decades, the United States struggled with disasters. The nation had no clear or central vision on how to handle disasters. Consequently, two important steps occurred that continue to impact emergency management today. First, President Carter established FEMA in 1979 to centralize and streamline emergency management responsibilities. During the same time, the National Governor's Association (1979) issued a major report on how to improve emergency management. Almost 40 years since it was published, ideas from this report continue to drive and define emergency management and provide important tools for disaster researchers. These concepts, outlined below, are embedded within the idea of Comprehensive emergency management (CEM) and an "all hazards" approach to disaster that span four phases of emergency management.

CEM encourages a broad holistic approach to managing disasters. First advocated by the National Governor's Association (NGA) report on emergency management, CEM is defined as

> ... a state's responsibility and capability for managing all types of emergencies and disasters by coordinating the actions of numerous agencies. The 'comprehensive' aspect of CEM includes all four phases of disaster or emergency activity: mitigation, preparedness, response, and recovery. It applies to all risks: attack, man-made, and natural, in a federal-state-local partnership. (NGA 1979, p. 11)

The four phases and all hazards approach to disasters continue to serve as the foundation for emergency managers and as important concepts for disaster researchers. We review these two concepts below.

3.4.1 The Disaster Life Cycle

Through the years, researchers and professionals have tried to break the disaster process down into specific categories even beyond the four phases commonly used today. Some have suggested using the terms preimpact, impact, and postimpact. However, the NGA (1979) report of four phases (mitigation, preparedness, response, and recovery) have stayed in place for a long time. Other nations have adopted the same idea. For example, in New Zealand they are known as the four "Rs": readiness, response, recovery, and reduction. Regardless which organization or nation takes on the tasks of emergency management, these four general phases capture the bulk of what typical emergency managers do:

- *Mitigation*: "activities that actually eliminate or reduce the probability of occurrence of a disaster, arms build-up, land-use management, establishing CEM (i.e., comprehensive emergency management) programs, building safety codes" (NGA 1979, p. 13).
- *Preparedness*: "activities [that] are necessary to the extent that mitigation measures have not, or cannot, prevent disasters ... develop plans, mounting training exercises, installing warning systems, stockpiling food and medical supplies, mobilizing emergency personnel" (NGA 1979, p. 13).
- *Response*: "activities [that] follow an emergency or disaster. Generally, they are designed to provide emergency assistance for casualties ... seek to reduce the probability of secondary damage ... and to speed recovery operations" (NGA 1979, pp. 13–14).

- *Recovery*: "activities [that] continue until all systems return to normal or better. Short-term recovery activities return vital life-support systems to minimum operating standards. Long-term recovery activities .... return life to normal or improved levels" (NGA 1979, p. 14).

Both professional emergency managers and researchers have found these categories useful for their work. For professionals, the phases give a unique way to divide their tasks and focus on their work. For example, in many state emergency management agencies and in large cities, offices often have specific sections or jobs related to some of the four phases. Historically, FEMA has had divisions organized around the phases although FEMA's organizational structure today has become even more complex (see Figure 1.3 in Chapter 1). FEMA also provides federal grants related to these categories. As a result, states and local communities can secure funds for preparedness, response, recovery or mitigation activities.

Following the terrorist attacks of 9/11, FEMA and DHS integrated another concept to the life cycle of disasters—prevention. By design, the notion of prevention focuses upon a law enforcement approach to avoid, prevent or even stop a terrorist attack. These actions can occur through the following means (*verbatim*):

- *Intelligence and Information Sharing.* Planning and Direction: Establish the intelligence and information requirements of the consumer.
- *Screening, Search and Detection.* Locate persons and networks associated with imminent terrorist threats.
- *Interdiction and Disruption.* Disrupt terrorist financing or prevent other material support from reaching its target.
- *Forensics and Attribution.* Preserve the crime scene and conduct site exploitation for intelligence collection.
- *Planning.* Initiate a time-sensitive, flexible planning process that builds on existing plans and incorporates real-time intelligence.
- *Public Information and Warning.* Refine and consider options to release preevent information publicly, and take action accordingly.
- *Operational Coordination.* Define and communicate clear roles and responsibilities relative to courses of action (FEMA 2015b).

Although popular among those engaged in anti-terrorism activities, many in the emergency management profession still primarily use the concepts of preparedness, response, recovery, and mitigation. Academic degree programs in disasters and textbooks (including this) draw upon the four phases of emergency management as a way to organize degree programs and courses (Neal 2000). Researchers also use these concepts to categorize the type of studies they do. For example, overviews of research (Drabek 1986; Mileti,

Drabek, and Haas 1975) show that response is the most popular category to study with far less work conducted on recovery (Mileti 1999).

In short, the life cycle or phases approach helps emergency managers to organize their activities although they do overlap to some degree. For example, the removal of disaster debris from roads (response) may still be occurring while people are returning home (recovery). Or, following a flood, people may be rebuilding their homes (recovery) while government officials are building levees to lessen the impact of another flood (mitigation). In addition, certain activities may be hard to distinguish between phases. For example, public education programs for disaster warnings help people know what to do when the alarm is sounded. Yet, the same public education program could be considered mitigation since it can lower the loss of life and injury (Neal 1997).

Rather than occur as discrete sets of phases, the activities may actually occur concurrently or support other activities. Improved preparedness could increase the levels of response when disasters occur. With an effective response, recovery should become easier. Recovery also provides an opportunity, and higher levels of interest, to mitigate disasters. For example, having stricter building codes for earthquakes (i.e., mitigation) means generally that less damage will occur during an earthquake. As a result, less time and money will be needed to repair buildings or the infrastructure (i.e., recovery). In short, all the phases have an important impact on the other phases (Neal 1997).

3.4.2 The Expansion of Emergency Management

Traditionally, emergency managers deal with events such as tornadoes, floods, hurricanes, explosions, and similar events. However, over the last decade or two, those in emergency management have played central roles in events that we often do not think of as disasters. For example, city officials may open the Emergency operations center (EOC) to observe or coordinate activities involving large crowds such as athletic contests, spontaneous outbursts, social protests, and even riots. The EOC is an ideal place to gather information, house decision makers, and coordinate activities. These events and their outcomes involve all facets of local government, including police, fire, paramedics, and public works. Local governments have to organize their activities with businesses, volunteer organizations, and perhaps with some components of state and local government.

When the space shuttle Columbia disintegrated upon reentry on February 1, 2003, emergency management offices played a central role with a number of tasks. Experts determined that a thorough search of an area 240 miles long and 10 miles wide needed to be searched for debris and remains. But this search was not simple, as it involved looking for a wide range of materials including human remains, hazardous materials, and debris. FEMA coordinated the activities among many different organizations including NASA, the U.S. Forest

Service, and the EPA. As the search needs expanded, with hazardous materials being a main concern, the U.S. Coast Guard, the Gulf Strike Team, and a private contracting firm tested for contaminants in the water and atmosphere (none was found). Also included for other reasons in the recovery process included the FBI, the National Guard, search and rescue organizations, and the Texas Department of Public Safety. By February 4th, more organizations became involved, including those from Texas, Louisiana, Oklahoma, and New Mexico (FEMA 2003). Thus, FEMA, state and local emergency management offices played roles in managing (FEMA 2003):

- Over 82,500 pieces of the shuttle.
- A search area over 2.28 million acres.
- Tests across 23 square miles of water for contamination.
- Coordination of over 16,500 people, 130 governmental agencies, and 270 organizations involved in the search.
- Reimbursement of states for costs estimated at about $10 million.

Two other recent cases highlight how emergency managers assist with crises events. In 2014, an Ebola virus scare occurred in the United States. As an exposed victim from Africa and other exposed health-care workers were discovered, EOCs opened in Dallas, Texas and Akron, Ohio. With the Akron case, not only did the local jurisdiction open the EOC, but the local county health office also activated an EOC. These EOCs served as important points of contact between health and emergency management officials, along with politicians and other important decision makers. During the Ebola crisis in the Akron area, the EOCs stayed open for 4 days and the Summit County Department of Health stayed open for 18 days (Schwartz et al. 2015).

In summary, emergency managers can play integral roles in different or extraordinary disasters. A primary daily role of the emergency manager is to help develop connections among people and organizations that may be useful in any type of disaster. So, whether it is an occasional event like a crowd of 40–100,000 people, or a rare event such as a space shuttle accident, emergency managers have many of the resources and the social connections to help coordinate materials and communications among the relevant players. To do so, they rely on an approach that spans a wide array of disasters.

3.4.3 All Hazards Approach

A second idea central to emergency management is what was initially called the "all risks" approach, and is today known as the "all hazards" approach. The National Governor's Report showed that regardless of the event, certain governmental activities have stayed the same across events. Two important points should be mentioned, however, with the all hazards approach. First, hazards must be approached across the four phases of emergency management. Too often, the report noted, people would focus on just "planning" while ignoring the other phases (NGA 1979). Hazards, risks, and disasters must be managed across all four phases and must involve coordination with local, state, and federal government, the public sector, the private sector, volunteers, and others (IAEM 2007).

During the same time researchers also advocated an all hazards approach to disasters, using the phrase "agent generic." Although specific hazards may create specific problems or issues, overall similar issues will arise across disasters. During disasters, communication problems, and organizational coordination issues always arise. Similarly, the process of educating and warning the public follows the same processes across various types of disasters. Or, those more vulnerable to disasters (e.g., the poor, racial and ethnic minorities, women, the elderly, and people with disabilities) are more likely to be affected and require more extensive assistance. In short, the overall similarities of how we respond to disasters are much greater than the differences (Dynes 1974; Quarantelli 1982).

3.5 The Body of Knowledge

As noted earlier, people use the word disaster broadly. In the profession of emergency management, we often draw upon different perspectives to understand hazards, disasters, and risk. Each word represents certain components of emergency management while also reflecting different but important research traditions. We review these differences next.

3.5.1 The Hazard Tradition

In the simplest form, hazards are disasters waiting to happen. People may live, work, or play in the path of floods, tornadoes, hurricanes, or chemical accidents. Simply put, hazards occur when people, nature, and technology interact (Cutter 2001). Mitigation serves as the main step taken by emergency managers to reduce the potential effects of hazards.

Geographer Gilbert White is considered by many to be the father of hazard mitigation. During his long and distinguished career he focused on the value of structural mitigation projects (e.g., levees and dams) that decrease flooding along rivers. Under White's leadership, the Natural Hazards Research and Application Information Center (also known as the Natural Hazards Center) formed at the University of Colorado-Boulder in the mid-1970s (Natural Hazards Center n.d.).

White's work with his colleagues helped to define the hazards perspective that has evolved into a multidisciplinary approach. Geographers, along with psychologists, sociologists, economists, engineers, and geologists now work together on research and practical applications to mitigate hazards. As part of his legacy, the Natural Hazards Center also has a large resource center, and hosts an annual workshop for professionals, researchers, and others interested in the field of hazards (Myers 1993, visit www.colorado.edu/hazards).

As part of the disaster planning process today, emergency managers undertake a "hazard analysis." Typically, they determine the most likely events that could impact their community then work with area stakeholders (businesses, community leaders, residents, schools) to identify and prioritize hazard mitigation projects. Mitigation planning thus involves people to address the potential impacts a hazard may have and foster a more resilient result. Areas subject to flooding may prioritize dams and levees. Tornado alley locations may seek funding for safe rooms. The point is to focus on the hazard and find ways to reduce its human impact.

3.5.2 The Disaster Tradition

The disaster tradition is grounded in disaster preparedness and especially disaster response activities. Much of this goes back to civil defense activities during the start of the Cold War between the United States and the Soviet Union (from the late 1940s until the fall of the Berlin Wall in November, 1989). During the Cold War, each country prepared to respond to potential nuclear strikes. The United States military provided research funding to the University of Chicago in an effort to see how soldiers and civilians would respond to nuclear war or chemical weapons. The National Opinion Research Center (NORC) at the University of Chicago, led by Charles Fritz, initiated much of this research. Obviously researchers could not expose cities and people to nuclear bombs or chemical weapons. So researchers selected to study events similar to war, that is, disasters. To do so, researchers traveled to disaster sites soon after impact and studied how people and organizations responded. Contrary to popular belief, researchers found that disasters did not cause behaviors such as mass panic, looting, or hysteria. Rather, disasters brought out the best of behaviors— altruism abounded (Quarantelli 1987, 1994).

Drawing upon the "quick response" research of the NORC studies, sociologists Henry Quarantelli, Russell Dynes, and Eugene Haas formed the Disaster Research Center (DRC) in 1963 at The Ohio State University. Dynes and Haas both specialized in organizations, and Quarantelli had been a graduate student at the University of Chicago during the 1950s where he served as a research assistant with NORC. Like NORC, much of DRC's initial funding came from the Department of Defense and focused upon the social aspects to disaster response. DRC's earliest research focused on organizational response to disaster.

Today, DRC (now located at the University of Delaware) continues to be a leading international research center studying a wide range of events and topics. Since the center started in 1963, it has studied over 600 events not only in the United States but throughout the world also (e.g., 1964 Alaska earthquake; 1974 Super Outbreak of Tornadoes; 1989 Loma Prieta Earthquake; 2001 Terrorist Attacks; and 2004 Indian Ocean Tsunami). In addition to what could be considered more traditional issues related to disaster research, DRC has focused on new, innovative research topics including handling the dead, sheltering and housing, mental health delivery systems, emergent citizen groups, organizational improvisation, hospitals and medical delivery, and crowds and riots. At the time of publication, DRC has research teams studying the issue of risk during and after the recent Ebola crisis, stakeholder decision in creating disaster policies, resiliency after Hurricane Sandy in New York City, and other projects (DRC 2015, 2016).

DRC has also made a major contribution by training a large number of graduate students. These former graduate students have gone on to further quick response research, provide a clearer understanding of disaster response, and contribute to disaster research. DRC alumni have also helped to design and develop academic programs related to disaster management. More broadly, DRC established a research model over 50 years ago, and today disaster and hazard centers use that model throughout the world. DRC also has the most comprehensive disaster library collection in the world and scholars travel from throughout the world to use the collection and meet with the center's staff (DRC 2015).

The disaster tradition continues today, not only from the Disaster Research Center (now at the University of Delaware), but from many disaster researchers throughout the United States and the world (Dynes, Tierney and Fritz 1994). From a practical view, the disaster research tradition has helped provide emergency managers to plan and prepare and to respond and recover. Recent major federal planning documents, such as Comprehensive Planning Guide (CPG) 101 (see resources), explicitly draw upon the disaster research approach to ground its preparedness and response suggestions.

3.5.3 Risk and Risk Perception Traditions

Another perspective used to understand hazards and disaster is risk and risk perception. In large part, Paul Slovic (the University of Oregon) helped create the study of risk research over 35 years ago (Decision Research 2015a, b; Slovic 1987). Initially, the field of risk analysis grew out of questions of the environment and safety around nuclear power. Such issues and concerns intensified after the Three Mile Island (TMI) nuclear accident in the United States in 1979 and the Chernobyl (in the former Soviet Union) nuclear power plant explosion in 1986. Today, the concept of risk goes beyond issues of nuclear power to consider a range of risk-related topics.

Originally coming from a social psychological perspective, researchers have tried to understand how individuals view and respond to risk.

For example, a risk perspective may focus on why people perceive some activities as more risky than others (e.g., flying a commercial airliner versus driving a car). It may also concern environmental issues, such as how much of a hazardous substance should be allowed into rivers or waste sites. Or, risk can deal with the trade-offs between having offshore oil wells and their potential damage to the environment from a major oil spill occurs vis-a-vis need for oil. Not all activities dealing with the risk perspective may deal with hazards and disasters, such as topic related to "risky activities" (e.g., smoking and skydiving) or other situations (e.g., possible exposure to cancer from environmental threats).

Risk is also defined as the probability of an event occurring. We filter risk through various levels of perception and understanding. The "cone of uncertainty" that is used to describe a projected hurricane path can be very challenging to understand. Public response depends on understanding the way in which the hurricane may move—thus the cone projects a wide path that changes daily if not hourly. Because we cannot know with a high degree of certainty where a hurricane will strike until 24–36 hours before landfall it is hard to inform the public—who must evacuate most areas 48 hours ahead of impact. People may simply take their chances based on an assumption that "it won't happen to me" or previous experience with hurricanes. Coupled with a low degree of concern with disasters for most people (Tierney, Lindell, and Perry 2001), it can be very hard to communicate the message and convince the public of an impending risk. Think, for example, of how likely you think it will be that an area hazard might generate a major disaster in your area—and then think through how many preparations you have taken to be ready. Did you pay attention to risk information and see its relevance to your personal safety?

Understanding risk and risk perception can assist us with understanding why people choose to evacuate or not during a hurricane or chemical explosion, or why people may be willing to live next to a potentially hazardous site such as a chemical company or nuclear power plant. Understanding public perception of risk makes us more capable of helping the public by designing preparedness campaigns and organizing evacuations. Box 3.1 features a new perspective—Crisis.

3.6 Understanding Disasters

In order to understand disasters, we rely upon different perspectives or theories of human behavior (see Box 3.2). No one perspective is right or wrong. Rather, each provides insights into the different types of questions we want to ask and solve. The field of emergency management does not have distinct theoretical perspectives it can call its own. Instead, scholars draw upon

BOX 3.1   THE CRISIS PERSPECTIVE

Scholars from the United States played central roles in developing the hazards, disaster and risk perspectives. Over the last 20 years, European researchers, initially from Sweden and The Netherlands, developed their own approach, known as "Crisis" or "Crisis Management." One can trace these origins of the Crisis Perspective to the Leiden University Center of Crisis Research in the Netherlands, and Crismart, a research arm of the Swedish National Defense College. Generally, the Crisis perspective focuses upon situations where a society's values are threatened, there is a short period of time to act, and decision makers must deal with a high degree of uncertainty (Hansen 2003).

The Crisis Perspective developed during and after the demise of the Soviet Union, during which a sense of the unknown and insecurity developed throughout Europe. Initially, political scientists (including those in public administration) launched the first studies of how former countries of the Soviet Bloc managed their new political situation. As a result, many early crisis studies looked at the causes and outcomes of political events in Eastern Europe. Embedded within this approach, the Crisis approach looks at how leadership and decision making affects political and social outcomes. Through time, Crisis scholars have expanded their research topics to include political assassinations, economic sanctions, dance hall fires, and mad cow disease. In addition, they also broadened their research into more traditional hazard and disaster topics such as earthquakes, floods, and dam breaks. While originally drawing upon the expertise of scholars in political science and public administration, representatives from all the social sciences use the Crisis Perspective today (Neal 2012).

The Crisis Perspective provides a fresh way looking at disasters. First, those from the Crisis perspective look at a much broader range of events. Second, their research focuses upon the decision-making process taking place before, during or after the crisis. They focus upon how leaders make their decisions during times of crisis. From a methodological perspective, researchers generally write systematic case studies to understand the management and decision making process that occurs during a crisis. This approach also allows to do retrospective studies along with studying current unfolding events, and comparing all of these events over time (Boin 2009).

References

Boin, Arjen. 2009. The New World Crises and Crisis Management: Implications for Policymaking and Research. *New Policy Research* 26(4): 367–377.

Hansen, Dan. 2003 (1990). *The Crisis Management of the Murder of Olof Palme*. Stockholm, Sweden: The National Swedish Defense College.

Neal, David M. 2012. The Survivability of Swedish Emergency Management Related Research Centers and Academic Programs: A Preliminary Sociology of Knowledge Analysis. *Sociologiska Forsking* 49(3): 227–242.

BOX 3.2 THEORY AND THE DISCIPLINE OF EMERGENCY MANAGEMENT

Jessica Jensen

Dr. Jessica Jensen is an associate professor in the Department of Emergency Management at North Dakota State University and she is one among the earliest emergency management doctoral degree holders. She studies topics central to the practice of emergency management by examining the existing scholarship and theory, collecting and analyzing the data, and exploring the policy. She works to see theory and research applied by educating students, serving on IAEM committees, facilitating work groups for FEMA Higher Education, publishing in journals, and sharing research findings at conferences.

Scholars often note a lack of attention to the theory development in hazards and disaster research (Drabek 2005; McEntire 2004; National Research Council 2006; Perry 2005; Quarantelli 2005; Tierney 2007; Tierney et al. 2001). There is some truth to the critique. Hazards and disaster theory has received a little attention historically. There are many reasons for this reality which include the applied nature of the work being done (Tierney 2007) and the fragmentation of research on hazards and disasters across many disciplines and their respective outlets (Alexander 1997; Jensen 2010; Mc Entire and Marshall 2003). Yet, acknowledgment of the lack of attention to hazards and disaster theory and theoretical issues ought not to be taken to suggest that such theory is nonexistent or to say that it is not receiving attention somewhere. Hazards and disaster theory exists and it is receiving attention increasingly within the emerging academic discipline of emergency management.

(Continued)

BOX 3.2 (*Continued*) THEORY AND THE DISCIPLINE OF EMERGENCY MANAGEMENT

The discipline studies how humans interact and cope with hazards, vulnerabilities, and the associated events and consequences (Jensen 2014a, 2015). When we use this concept of emergency management as a discipline, it is apparent that the theory related to its purview has been "unrecognized, underused, and underdeveloped" (Jensen 2010, p. 10).

Investigators have produced a significant body of research on hazards and hazard events that is broad in topical coverage and deep with respect to many specific topics. Scholars of anthropology, sociology, political science, public administration, economics, demography, civil engineering, climatology, meteorology, geology, geography, and a variety of other disciplines should continue to contribute to this body of research. The findings of their work now sit in hundreds of edited volumes, more than a thousand case study books, thousands of research center publications, and tens of thousands of scholarly peer-reviewed journal articles.

Reflected within this work are concepts that repeatedly appear, such as hazards, vulnerability, risk, mitigation, recovery, resilience, sustainability, and many others—these same concepts give structure to and appear throughout this introductory textbook. Reflected within this work are other components of theory—components that one can also see in this book. For instance, when post-disaster housing is discussed in Chapter 8, it is based on a known classification of how people move through shelter and into housing. A typology of organized responses is discussed in several chapters. Theoretical frameworks, such as that of sociopolitical ecology or systems, are discussed in Chapter 3, and theories of the middle range, such as those associated with the emergent norm theory also discussed in Chapter 3. Concepts, classifications, typologies, theoretical frameworks, and theories of the middle range are all building blocks, components, or forms, of theory (McEntire 2004).

All of these forms of theory are significant to emergency management both as a discipline and as a profession. Without always being referred to explicitly as a theory, they structure how we approach the topic in study and practice; they help us to understand how various aspects of emergency management work; and, they also help us know what to expect, what we can influence, and the kinds of solutions to emergency management issues that are likely to succeed and fail. And, they are increasingly being identified as theory, communicated to students and discussed with practitioners as such, and further developed through continuing research.

Not only is theory alive and being used, more it awaits discovery and further development. There, among the tens of thousands of pieces of scholarship on hazards and disasters topics, are more of these aforementioned forms of theory that, like those noted above, simply need to be identified, discussed by the students and scholars as important to emergency

(Continued)

BOX 3.2 (*Continued*) THEORY AND THE
DISCIPLINE OF EMERGENCY MANAGEMENT

management, and refined through continuing research. Moreover, the integration and synthesis of the literature being produced on similar topics but by different disciplines holds great potential for additional theoretical development. For instance, while all studying human recovery after disasters, psychologists, sociologists, economists, demographers, and social work scholars do so armed with theoretical frameworks and research questions that differ one to the next. All are conducting important research and must continue to do so. However, without integration and synthesis and a conceptual model based on such activity, it is hard for those learning about or researching human recovery to develop a comprehensive understanding of what is entailed in that process and the factors that drive it. Such an understanding is critical for students, scholars, and practitioners of emergency management. Development of this kind of synthesis-based theory is needed and the conditions ripe for it.

Theoretical development is of critical significance to emergency management and it is the subject of much concern and attention. Emergency management scholars and students are currently working on these issues through coursework and research, but, to get to this point, a few critical issues have to be addressed first. Key among these issues is the need for consensus around the idea that the emergency management could and should be conceived of as an academic discipline and, if such consensus existed, to "identify the components of academic disciplines and to identify, recognize, formalize, and/or otherwise build those components for emergency management" (Jensen 2013a, p. i).

Since 1990s, consensus regarding the need for an emergency management discipline has emerged and the efforts of many individuals have gone in building the critical pieces needed to structure a discipline. Building on the work of many scholars (including the authors of this book), a number of FEMA Higher Education Program convened working groups have considered emergency management's disciplinary domain, the body of knowledge that should inform the discipline, and how the study within the discipline ought to be approached (Jensen 2012a, 2013a). Other FEMA Higher Education sponsored groups have initially suggested some research standards for how contributions of new knowledge and theory are recognized within the emerging discipline (Jensen 2012b, 2013b). Consensus around the ideas from these groups has been built through numerous conference sessions and survey work (Jensen 2014a, b). Further consensus has been developed among an identifiable community of emergency management scholars—individuals who earned or are seeking doctoral degrees at the four institutions offering doctoral degrees in the field—Jacksonville State University, North Dakota State University, Oklahoma State University, University of Delaware (Jensen 2015). It is the job of

(*Continued*)

BOX 3.2 *(Continued)*   THEORY AND THE DISCIPLINE OF EMERGENCY MANAGEMENT

these students and the faculty with whom they work to integrate, to synthesize, and to study the hazards and disaster research to glean from it what is there in terms of theory and expand upon it through their own work. Finally, the formalization of a communication network for the discipline in the form of a theory and research conference was realized in 2014. The conference "creates the opportunity for researchers to receive feedback on their work; exchange new knowledge; and, build on this new knowledge through discourse and debate" (Jensen 2016). This year, 2016, marks the 3rd annual conference and will be held in advance of the FEMA Higher Education Symposium. The emergence of emergency management as a discipline is well underway as is the use of and attention to theory and theoretical issues within it. The theoretical efforts of those associated with the discipline will shape emergency management education and practice increasingly in the future.

References

Alexander, David. 1997. The Study of Natural Disasters, 1977–1997: Some Reflections on a Changing Field of Knowledge. *Disasters* 21(4): 284–304.

Drabek, Thomas. 2005. Theories Relevant to Emergency Management versus a Theory of Emergency Management. *Journal of Emergency Management* 3(4): 49–54.

Jensen, Jessica. 2010. Emergency Management Theory: Unrecognized, Underused, and Underdeveloped. In *Integrating Emergency Management Studies into Higher Education: Ideas, Programs, and Strategies*, pp. 7–24, Jessica Hubbard, (ed.). Fairfax, VA: Public Entity Risk Institute.

Jensen, Jessica. 2012a. Report of the Disciplinary Focus Group: Purview and Core Research Questions for the Academic Discipline of Emergency Management. Report prepared for the FEMA Higher Education Program, available at http://training.fema.gov/emiweb/edu/, last accessed February 11, 2016.

Jensen, Jessica. 2012b. Report of the Focus Group on Research Standards in Emergency Management. Report prepared for the FEMA Higher Education Program, available at http://training.fema.gov/emiweb/edu/, last accessed February 11, 2016.

Jensen, Jessica. 2013a. Report of the Disciplinary Purview Focus Group: Scholarship and Research to Ground the Emerging Discipline of Emergency Management. Report prepared for the FEMA Higher Education Program, available at http://training.fema.gov/emiweb/edu/, last accessed February 11, 2016.

Jensen, Jessica. 2013b. Report of the Research Standards Focus Group: Implementing the Standards within Programs and Across the Emergency Management Higher Education Community. Report prepared for the FEMA Higher Education Program, available at http://training.fema.gov/emiweb/edu/, last accessed February 11, 2016.

Jensen, Jessica. 2014a. Results from a Survey Gauging Emergency Management Higher Education Community Consensus on Key Points Related to the Disciplinary Identity of Emergency. Report prepared for the FEMA Higher Education Program, available at http://training.fema.gov/emiweb/edu/, last accessed February 11, 2016.

Jensen, Jessica. 2014b. Results from a Survey Gauging Emergency Management Higher Education Community Consensus on Key Points Related to Research Standards for the Discipline of Emergency Management. Report prepared for the FEMA Higher Education Program, available at http://training.fema.gov/emiweb/edu/, last accessed February 11, 2016.

Jensen, Jessica. 2015. Statement of the Emergency Management Doctoral Degree Holder/Seeker Focus Group. Report prepared for the FEMA Higher Education Program, available at http://training.fema.gov/emiweb/edu/, last accessed February 11, 2016.

(Continued)

BOX 3.2 (*Continued*)   THEORY AND THE DISCIPLINE OF EMERGENCY MANAGEMENT

Jensen, Jessica. 2016. Call for Abstracts: 3rd Emergency Management Theory and Research Workshop. Available at http://training.fema.gov/emiweb/edu/, last accessed February 11, 2016.

McEntire, David. 2004. The Status of Emergency Management Theory: Issues, Barriers, and Recommendations for Improved Scholarship. Available at http://training.fema.gov/emiweb/edu/, last accessed February 11, 2016.

McEntire, David and Melissa Marshall. 2003. Epistemological Problems in Emergency Management: Theoretical Dilemmas and Implications. *ASPEP Journal* 2003: 119–129.

National Research Council. 2006. *Facing Hazards and Disasters: Understanding Human Dimensions*. Washington, D.C.: National Academies Press.

Perry, Ronald. 2005. Disasters, Definitions, and Theory Construction. In *What is a Disasters? New Answers to Old Questions*, pp. 311–324, Ronald Perry and Enrique Quarantelli (eds.). Philadelphia, PA: Xlibris.

Quarantelli, Enrique. 2005. A Social Science Research Agenda for the Disasters of the 21st Century: Theoretical, Methodological and Empirical Issues and Their Professional Implementation. In *What is a Disasters? New Answers to Old Questions*, pp. 325–396, Ronald Perry and Enrique Quarantelli (eds.). Philadelphia, PA: Xlibris.

Tierney, Kathleen. 2007. From the Margins to the Mainstream? Disaster Research at the Crossroads. *Annual Review of Sociology* 33: 503–525.

Tierney, Kathleen, Lindell, Michael, and Ronald Perry. 2001. *Facing the Unexpected: Disaster Preparedness and Response in the United States*. Washington, D.C.: John Henry Press.

mid-range theories developed from other disciplines to generate research, critique planning, and move the field forward as a discipline. Without concepts, theories, and methods, we cannot claim that emergency management is a discipline (Blanchard 2005; McEntire 2005; Phillips 2005). In this section, we discuss different perspectives and theories used to describe and explain disaster events and behaviors. Practitioners can draw upon these theories to understand events around them, and even anticipate events that may next occur. These perspectives include collective behavior theory (i.e., emergent norm), organizational theory (i.e., loosely coupled systems), systems theory, socio-political ecology theory and vulnerability theory.

3.6.1 Emergent Norm Theory

Early disaster researchers drew upon the study of collective behavior or new types of behavior during unusual or new circumstances. Rapidly moving and fluid events such as crowds, social protests, riots, and disaster behavior can fall under this definition. Early disaster researchers found that collective behavior theory helped to capture the dynamic, changing characteristics of human behavior during disaster. One specific way to study collective behavior events came through the development of emergent norm theory. Emergent norm theory allows researchers to capture the more spontaneous aspects of disaster behavior, especially during the response phase, by focusing upon processes that generate new norms or new social structure. Norms are accepted ways of behavior. Social structure reflects how we organize ourselves, such as knowing who is in charge and who should do specific tasks. Emergent norm theory has shown to be both a popular and successful approach to understand disaster behavior (Dynes and Tierney 1994; Turner and Killian 1987).

Let us provide a few examples where the emergent norm perspective has helped us to understand disaster behavior. For example, research from 50 years ago through today shows that altruism, or significant helping behavior develops following disaster. Neighbor helps neighbor just as emergency responders and volunteers come from surrounding communities to help those in need. Crime rates drop significantly after disaster too, rather than the popular media accounts of looting (Fischer 2008; Fritz and Mathewson 1957). As a current example, consider the outpouring of help, aid, donations, and money following the Haitian Earthquake in January 2010, particularly among international partners. In short, international partners—many that had never worked together before—came together to form rescue, relief, and recovery teams. This new set of relationships demonstrates emergence.

Researchers have also found that disasters can dramatically change the structure of organizations during a disaster. Some organizations must expand in order to take on an influx of new volunteers. Volunteer organizations such as the Red Cross and Salvation Army change and adapt to manage how disasters alter day-to-day operations. In other cases, organizations must change the tasks they do. Often following a disaster, construction companies cease their day-to-day operations to assist with debris removal such as clearing roads and properties. Also, new groups and organizations form to assist with the disaster response. For example, right after a tornado, neighbors quite often spontaneously form search and rescue groups and go door to door to assist others (Dynes 1974). Or, at a broader level, city governments may dramatically change, totally altering their organizational structure, putting new people in charge of new disaster-related activities, and plugging other organizations temporarily into city government (Neal 1985). In summary, the findings noted above all came from researchers drawing upon collective behavior and emergent norm theory.

3.6.2 Loosely Coupled Systems

Organizational theory has provided many perspectives to help us understand effective disaster response by focusing on process and structure. The emergent norm perspective captures the process of organizational changes before, during, or after a disaster. Examples of organizational change include characteristics of a typical bureaucracy, such as a division of labor, hierarchy of authority, having properly trained people in place for a task, and other characteristics. At times, to create an effective organizational response to disaster, changes in structure and process may simultaneously occur (Weller and Quarantelli 1973).

Disaster researchers occasionally use Weik's (1976) notion of "loosely coupled systems" to understand effective organizational response. Weik's idea originated not from disaster, but from studying local school systems. For example, during most times, a large school system of multiple high schools, middle schools, and elementary schools must work as a whole. Yet, at other times, parts of the school must separate themselves to a high degree from the central administration. Elementary and Middle schools often reflect the social and cultural desires and activities of neighborhoods. Thus, a school in an Italian neighborhood may have special activities outside of the school that focus on Italian culture, but it would not be as meaningful in another part of the school system. In this case, the neighborhood school decouples itself to meet the needs of the neighborhood. Such activities also help generate neighborhood support for the broader school system. Everybody wins in this situation. The overall school mission is met (tightly coupled) while neighborhood schools maintain their own identity when necessary (loosely coupled).

The loosely coupled perspective works well to understand disasters (Perrow 1984). Day-to-day operations may rely upon a tightly coupled, rule driven, and hierarchical organization. As a result, tightly coupled organizations run effectively for day-to-day operations. Yet, when disaster occurs, a tightly coupled system may hurt, not help the situation. As a result, the organization must become more loosely coupled. Organizational members may need to alter their organizational structure, improvise new rules, and at times even operate as separate and even isolated units. Perrow's classic book, *Normal Accidents*, provides two examples. Many of you may have seen the movie *Apollo 13* starring Tom Hanks, which documented an actual event. Any spaceflight, including one to the moon, has a very rigid flight plan that both astronauts and mission control must follow. The organizational structure of mission control is tightly coupled—people do not deviate from the flight plan for any reason. Yet, as you may recollect, a side of the spacecraft exploded, with oxygen leaking from tanks. Suddenly the flight plan became useless. On the ground, mission control reorganized itself into a loosely coupled organization (e.g., changing its tight division of labor and hierarchy, eliminating old rules, creating new flight rules) and literally rewrote the flight plan on the fly. If mission control had stayed as a tightly coupled organization, the three astronauts would have died. Instead, by adapting and becoming flexible, the astronauts survived.

Similar to space missions, the operations of nuclear power plants demand a tightly coupled organizational system. During regular operations, managers and staff must follow the rules by the book, including following any and all orders by supervisors and avoiding any improvisation. Engineers design the rules to avoid an accident. Yet, situations occur outside of the control of the operators. The book has no guidance or rules to solve the problem. Suddenly, these highly trained "by the book" managers and operators must improvise, changing their organizational structure and creating their own rules. Those in the operations center may separate themselves from higher-level managers since they are the only ones closest to the data and understand the dynamics of a possible meltdown. Yet, Perrow (1984) fears that in some tightly coupled systems such as nuclear power plants, when events unfold creating a crisis, these highly trained by-the-book managers and operators *will not* be able to change from a tightly coupled to loosely coupled management system. The result? A nuclear power plant meltdown. These lessons are crucial for disaster response. Yet, even today a rigid, some emergency coordinators still advocate a tightly coupled "command and control" model for disaster response. In coming chapters, we show why loosely coupled type management systems are more effective during disaster.

3.6.3 Systems Theory

Systems theory in emergency management refers to looking at how the built environment, physical environment, and human beings interact together (see Figure 3.2; Mileti 1999). When all the parts fit well they work together with minimal problems. However, when one part does not work well, the other parts do not and a disaster may result. As an example, people like to live in beautiful locations like beach communities. However, such areas often experience weather extremes including flooding and hurricanes (the physical environment). Without taking sufficient precautions to elevate or protect the built environment, significant damage or loss of life may occur. To understand systems theory, we define some of the terms used in systems theory, and then provide an example of how systems theory works in emergency management.

The built environment refers to buildings, the infrastructure including utilities (electricity, gas, and water), and transportation (roads, bridges, rail,

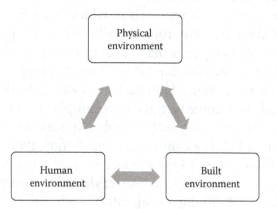

FIGURE 3.2   Systems theory. (Based on Mileti, Dennis, *Disasters by Design*, Joseph Henry Press, Washington, D.C, 1999.; Phillips 2015, with permission).

and ports). The physical environment includes what exists in nature, such as water (e.g., snow, rain, and ice), wind (e.g., tornadoes and hurricanes), or the earth (e.g., earthquakes and landslides). Finally, the human system refers to where and how people may live. Each system interacts with each other. In 2015–2016, for example, a weather event called El Niño produced unusual rains in California and heavy snow in the plains. The impacts disrupted transportation, caused power outages, and loss of life. Rather than a single system being responsible, like the weather, the problems occurred because of the interaction among the systems.

The problem is not likely to go away any time soon. For thousands of years, people have enjoyed settling next to rivers (i.e., physical environment). These waterways provide a source of water, food, and transportation. In short, this location provides a means for people to live, develop an organized culture and create meaningful social relationships (human systems). In putting down roots in such areas, people build highways and bridges, develop water and waste systems, and construct homes and businesses (i.e., the built environment). However, roads may flood preventing transportation to work and school. Fast moving flood waters can destroy bridges when debris builds up behind and cause failures. Flooding can also contaminate water systems and destroy electrical and communication systems. Homes and businesses will also become inundated. As a result, people's lives become totally disrupted (human system). People may drown or become injured. Others may have to be evacuated. Businesses may be lost forever.

After the event, local residents, politicians, and the business community (the human system) may look at ways to lessen the impact through mitigation. They may not allow homes or businesses (the human system) to (re)build (the built environment) in floodplains (i.e., the physical environment). They may build levees or dikes (the built environment) to lessen the impact of future flooding (physical environment) and reduce injuries and economic impacts (human systems).

In summary, the systems approach provides us a means to see how the human, built and physical environment all interact. It can help tell us how certain actions (e.g., living in tornado alley) can impact the residents of an area. In turn, such knowledge can help us mitigate, prepare for, respond to, and recover from such events. Systems theory can also allow us to see how who is more likely to become victims. For example, the poor are more likely to live in inexpensive housing such as mobile homes than any other group. Thus, when a tornado hits a community, much more damage occurs to the mobile homes than to a well-built home. As a result, the poor experience a higher degree of vulnerability to a disaster than those with more economic resources (Mileti 1999; Phillips et al. 2010). Such differential outcomes in human systems have been explained by two theories that we turn to next.

3.6.4 Sociopolitical Ecology Theory

Another popular and effective approach to understanding how disasters impact people is Sociopolitical Ecology Theory. Specifically, this theory looks at competition among various social groups to see who may become victims and who may recover more quickly than others after a disaster (Peacock and Ragsdale 1997, see Figure 3.3). Competition is defined in this theory as the efforts people engage in to secure scarce resources such as food, water, and shelter. When an earthquake occurs, such as the 2005 event in Pakistan, enough tents may not be available for all of the displaced. With winter rapidly approaching, those who fail to secure shelter face increasing danger for their lives.

There will be winners and losers in the process of securing resources, whether they are for mitigation, preparedness, response, or recovery. Single mothers for example, of whom about one-third live below the poverty line, will simply not be able to afford hurricane shutters or tornado safe rooms. Their families will bear disproportionate risk when hazards turn into disasters. The Northridge, California, earthquake of 1994 claimed about 60 lives, injured more than 9,000 and left about 20,000 victims homeless (USGS 1994), while over 200,000 Haitians died in the 2010 earthquake. Even the cost of developing a preparedness kit may be impossible for low-income households, senior citizens, or students like yourself. The 2005 earthquake in Pakistan led to competition over food, health care, and other survival resources. The competition

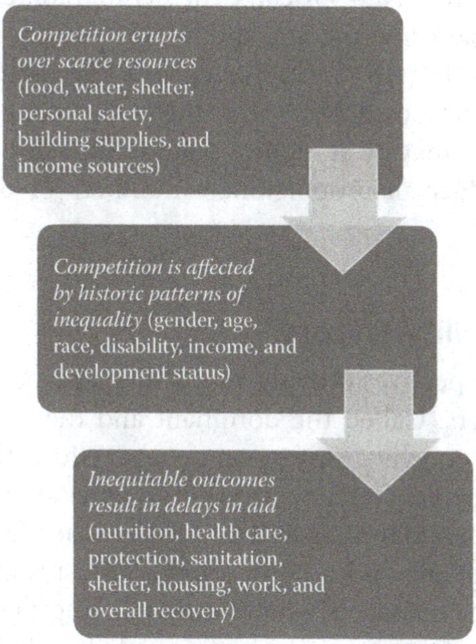

Competition erupts over scarce resources (food, water, shelter, personal safety, building supplies, and income sources)

Competition is affected by historic patterns of inequality (gender, age, race, disability, income, and development status)

Inequitable outcomes result in delays in aid (nutrition, health care, protection, sanitation, shelter, housing, work, and overall recovery)

FIGURE 3.3 Sociopolitical ecology theory explains that when a disaster occurs.

resulted in women and children securing fewer resources than men, which led nongovernmental organizations to provide female-friendly health care sites (Sayeed 2009). Gendered competition in other locations (Sri Lanka after the tsunami, Haiti and Nepal after the earthquakes) has revealed that some women and children face significant, additional threats to their personal safety including human trafficking (Burke 2015).

Recovery is even more difficult. Because lower income households must opt for affordable units, they tend to end up in manufactured housing, apartments closer to floodplains, and buildings that have not been retrofitted for seismic activity. Loss of life is typically higher in such locations. Coupled with loss of personal possessions, clothing, work resources or cars, overcoming the burden of disaster recovery may not be possible. Even in the business community, disparity exists. Smaller businesses fare less well than larger chains with considerably more assets. Smaller businesses are more likely to be owned by women and minorities.

Competition over scarce resources is likely to generate conflict. After Katrina for example, government officials made difficult decisions to destroy public housing units. Local protestors claimed that the units remained livable and decried reconstruction choices that reduced the number of affordable units. Five years after Katrina, uneven rebuilding has taken place across the city of New Orleans. Areas historically populated by racial and ethnic minorities took on high water levels with elderly African American men dying in numbers far higher than their percentage of the city's population (Sharkey 2007). Across New Orleans, the demographics of the community have changed as many low-income and minority residents could not return or afford to rebuild (Kroll-Smith, Baxter, and Jenkins 2015). Sociopolitical ecology theory directs researchers and emergency managers to observe who in their community may be at highest risk for disaster impact and to design measures that reduce disproportionate numbers of deaths, injuries and property losses.

3.6.5 Vulnerability Theory

Two divergent perspectives provide contrasting approaches to explain what happens in disasters. Called the dominant and the vulnerability perspectives, each focuses on why disasters occur, what effects they cause, and what can be done by emergency managers (Fordham et al. 2013). The dominant perspective may sound familiar, as it emphasizes the physical hazard itself— an earthquake happens and a home topples as a result. To care for those affected, emergency managers would move in using a combination of engineering and science to recover. The home would be rebuilt with new seismic bracing standards created within the building code itself. The goal would be to reduce future damage by overcoming the challenge presented by nature.

In contrast, the vulnerability perspective looks at other reasons to explain why the damage occurred. Socioeconomic and political circumstances are considered over the physical hazard itself. For example, if a flood occurs and homes are inundated—why did that occur? Could it be that homes are situated too close to the river or allowed to be built in a floodplain? It could be that policy decisions permit these homes to be built although history and societal relationships also play a role. In some locations, homes are subject to flooding after generations of segregation based on racial and ethnic discrimination (Phillips, Stukes, and Jenkins 2012). Subsequent generations may have lacked the financial means to relocate or may have built strong social ties that provided useful resources, encouraging people to stay. Similarly, places like Haiti or Nepal, which suffered devastating earthquakes in 2010 and 2015, lost hundreds of thousands of people. They died in buildings that collapsed on them, because they could not afford stronger dwellings. Similar outcomes occur after tornadoes strike affordable but less resistant mobile homes, where even an EF1 tornado can destroy a dwelling. In 2004, the Indian Ocean tsunami claimed about 300,000 lives with approximately 80% being women and children. Many perished waiting on the shore for fishermen to return from the sea. Their role? To process and sell the fish as part of a gendered division of labor in places like India and Sri Lanka.

The vulnerability perspective then says that the hazard itself is not the problem. Rather, it is the way in which society marginalizes people by age, disability, gender, race, or income. Overcoming vulnerability requires an approach that empowers those historically marginalized to reduce their vulnerability. Vulnerability reduction also requires that societies address historic patterns of discrimination and marginalization that keep people subject to risk. To illustrate, consider what happened to people with disabilities after hurricane Katrina. A catastrophic event, the federal government lacked sufficient resources to provide accessible temporary housing units—which led to a lawsuit that changed things (*FEMA v. Brou*). Movement through the recovery process meant facing even more barriers, particularly a lack of transportation and access to disability resources and services (Stough et al. 2015).

One common approach is to build bridges between those deemed potentially vulnerable, such as people with disabilities, and those in positions of authority, such as emergency managers. By working together, emergency managers and people with disabilities can identify the potential impacts of disasters and how to reduce impacts. People dependent on mobility devices, for example, may require access to a location with power (such as a fire station) to remain independent. Or, shelter managers will benefit from talking to people with disabilities to design movement pathways, appropriate nutritional options, accessible showers, and advocacy efforts to help people return home (NCD 2009).

3.7 Embracing a Multidisciplinary Approach

As noted earlier in this chapter, defining disaster is not a simple task nor is the decision on which theory—from which discipline—to use. As noted earlier in this chapter, there are several terms important to emergency management: hazards, disasters, risk, and crisis. Initially, geography helped establish the hazards perspective, sociology provided the foundation for disasters, (social) psychology laid the groundwork for risk, and political science established the crisis perspective. The hazards perspective first moved toward a more multidisciplinary approach, drawing upon sociology and social psychology. As more scholars from other social sciences became involved in studying disasters (e.g., psychology, political science, public administration, and anthropology), a broader knowledge base developed to inform the practice of emergency management. Over the last decade, social scientists learned that a multidisciplinary perspective from the social sciences would provide a more robust understanding of disasters.

Of course, those in the natural and physical sciences, such as meteorology, physics, geology, engineering, and other fields made individual contributions by studying the actual agent or how the agent impacted the built environment. Their work has also become more multidisciplinary by involving social scientists. For example, by the early 1980s meteorologists had devised rather sophisticated equipment to detect, show, and predict the strength and paths of tornadoes. Despite setting this equipment up, the number of annual deaths due to tornadoes and severe storms did not decline. However, just hearing a warning does not guarantee that people will take protective action. People must be made aware of the hazard, educated about the warning system and how it works, and given explicit instructions on how to take protective action. Studies also suggested that the warning messages must also be repeated in multiple languages and through multiple modes, and the geographical region must be specified in order to personalize the message to those at risk. Once meteorologists worked with social scientists in devising a social science based tornado warning system, coupled with the sophisticated equipment, deaths from tornadoes and severed storms decreased (Quarantelli 1993, for an example, see the CASA project at the University of Massachusetts, http://www. casa.umass.edu/). In recent years, the Office of the Federal Coordinator of Meteorology has established a working group to integrate social science findings into partnerships with those who detect, predict, and deliver meteorological information. The goal: to reduce deaths among those most vulnerable to weather particularly senior citizens, the poor, people with disabilities, and the traveling public that may be unaware of risks down the road (for more, see the resources section).

Sylves (2008) punctuates the importance of a multidisciplinary approach toward disasters for policy making in governmental settings. Whether at the local, state, or national level, those involved in disaster policy must have a wide range of knowledge. For example, making policy on earthquake preparedness would include geologists (understanding fault lines in an area), planners and geographers (land use), and architects (creating specific building codes), geographers (hazards), and sociologists (public education and risk communication programs). Taking a broad array of courses will serve students well as they pursue a degree in higher education.

3.8 The View from Emergency Management Higher Education

The annual FEMA Higher Education Symposium (which started in 1998), and offshoots from these meetings, has provided a foundation for defining emergency management and what we should teach in the field. Spirited discussion among those who attend have led to some general agreement on what to call "emergency management" and if it constituted a field, a discipline, or a profession (Urby and McEntire 2015). Four common characteristics for a separate field to be named (like sociology or physics) include occupational groups, a body of knowledge, standards of contact, and professional qualifications (Urby and McEntirei 2015). We argue in this text that emergency management has indeed arrived at such a standalone designation.

As the field started, no real consensus existed on what emergency management was and what should be taught. New programs found it difficult to find qualified faculty members who were knowledgeable with the disaster and hazards literature. Since programs were small, administrators placed programs within other academic units, often meaning the emergency management program lost part of its identity or needed resources. Faculty had few quality textbooks to select from. Those within the university did not see emergency management as a sound academic discipline. Many emergency managers saw emergency management programs as just an exercise in "book learning" with little or no practical application (Neal 2000). That has changed with the rapid development of well over 100 degree programs in the United States alone along with programs in Canada, Mexico, New Zealand, India, the United Kingdom, South Africa, and many other locations (see resources for a list).

Today, students graduating from emergency management programs can use a well-developed body of knowledge to secure an occupation. They can pursue additional credentials through graduate degrees and/or certifications. You will be meeting some of them as you read this book. Take the time to read their biographical statement and learn about their journey into the field of emergency management.

As a result of considerable discussions at the FEMA Higher Education Symposium and other conferences, a set of guiding principles has developed for the field of emergency management (FEMA 2008, see Figure 3.4). As we read other statements in the document, similar concepts appear again and again—concepts that we have discussed in this chapter and throughout the book. These concepts include vulnerability, hazards, disasters, risk,

Emergency management

Definition, vision, mission, principles

Definition

Emergency management is the managerial function charged with creating the framework within which communities reduce vulnerability to hazards and cope with disasters.

Vision

Emergency management seeks to promote safer, less vulnerable communities with the capacity to cope with hazards and disasters.

Mission

Emergency management protects communities by coordinating and integrating all activities necessary to build, sustain, and improve the capability to mitigate against, prepare for, respond to, and recover from threatened or actual natural disasters, acts of terrorism, or other man-made disasters.

Principles

Emergency management must be:

1. *Comprehensive* — emergency managers consider and take into account all hazards, all phases, all stakeholders, and all impacts relevant to disasters.

2. *Progressive* — emergency managers anticipate future disasters and take preventive and preparatory measures to build disaster-resistant and disaster-resilient communities.

3. *Risk-driven* — emergency managers use sound risk management principles (hazard identification, risk analysis, and impact analysis) in assigning priorities and resources.

4. *Integrated* — emergency managers ensure unity of effort among all levels of government and all elements of a community.

5. *Collaborative* — emergency managers create and sustain broad and sincere relationships among individuals and organizations to encourage trust, advocate a team atmosphere, build consensus, and facilitate communication.

6. *Coordinated* — emergency managers synchronize the activities of all relevant stakeholders to achieve a common purpose.

7. *Flexible* — emergency managers use creative and innovative approaches in solving disaster challenges.

8. *Professional* — emergency managers value a science and knowledge-based approach based on education, training, experience, ethical practice, public stewardship and continuous improvement.

FEMA   iAEM   EM   NFPA   NEMA   EMAP

FIGURE 3.4 The definition, vision, mission, and principles of emergency management.

preparedness, response, recovery and mitigation. Our journey continues with the next chapter by providing an overview of how the body of knowledge has been produced for the occupation of emergency management.

Summary

The profession of emergency management deals with managing disasters. Yet, among scholars and emergency managers, no firm definition exists. Many today still draw upon Fritz's (1961) definition, defining disasters as a perceived event that occurs rapidly in a specific time and space leading to social disruption. Today, we need to think of disasters in a more sophisticated way—as if it were a variable. During everyday life, emergencies occur (e.g., heart attacks, car accidents, and house fires). But such events are part of the daily fabric. A disaster, such as tornadoes, floods, hurricanes, explosions, among many other events, may damage the infrastructure of a community, disrupt people's lives, and undermine workplaces. A catastrophe may cause total damage and create absolute social disruption within a wide geographical area for a long time. Certainly the impact of Hurricane Katrina or the Fukishima earthquake/tsunami/radiological release would fit in this category. Emergency managers engage in activities to manage disasters and catastrophes.

The NGA (1979) report made such notions as the four phases of emergency management and CEM important tools for the profession. These concepts are still important today for anybody engaged in emergency management. Emergency managers may work across all four phases or may even specialize in one, such as mitigation.

Several different research traditions have emerged within the field: hazards, disasters, risk, and crisis. Although each tradition grew from different academic fields (such as geography, sociology, social psychology), researchers have slowly merged these perspectives in part to create a more multi-disciplinary approach to the field. Researchers also draw upon various theoretical perspectives to understand disasters including organizational theories, emergent norm theory, sociopolitical ecology theory, and vulnerability theory. Finally, emergency management as both an academic field and a profession continues to grow as a multi-disciplinary area.

Discussion Questions

1. Discuss why it is important to be able to distinguish between an emergency and a disaster, and a disaster and catastrophe? Why are these differences important for both the emergency manager and the social scientists studying people's behavior?

2. The National Governor's Association Report (1979) remains a key document today. What are some of the important concepts introduced in this report, and how many of these concepts are still used today by both emergency managers and researchers? How have these concepts influenced emergency management?

3. What specific insights into disaster behavior to each of the three perspectives (i.e., hazards, disasters, risk) provide? Do you see these perspectives becoming more separate from each other, or blending together?

4. How do the broader perspectives or theory on disaster behavior provide unique perspective of what occurs before, during or after disaster? Think about how each perspective gives a unique view to understand behavior during preparedness, response, recovery, or mitigation.

5. Explain why we may have so many different definitions of disaster? This includes different definition among both emergency managers and disaster researchers? Why might different people and different organizational representatives see the same event and (1) define it an emergency rather than a disaster?, (2) have one claim the event is one type of a hazard, whereas another may say the event was a totally different type of hazard (e.g., flood versus a technological failure?)?

6. To what degree to you agree or disagree with the definition of emergency management provided in this chapter? How might you change the definition? Why is it defining emergency management might be a difficult task?

Resources

- Those involved in designing and teaching emergency management courses have also discussed and written extensively on definitions of emergency management. This link will give you access to many other papers and documents that discuss defining emergency management and related concepts to the field: https://training.fema.gov/hiedu/emprinciples.aspx, last accessed February 3, 2016.
- CPG 101 (FEMA), https://www.fema.gov/media-library-data/20130726-1828-25045-0014/cpg_101_comprehensive_preparedness_guide_developing_and_maintaining_emergency_operations_plans_2010.pdf, last accessed February 1, 2016.
- To learn more about Disaster Declarations in the United States, visit https://www.fema.gov/disasters/grid/year/2015?field_disaster_type_term_tid_1=All, last accessed February 2, 2016.
- The FEMA Higher Education College List can be found at https://www.training.fema.gov/hiedu/collegelist/, last accessed February 2, 2016.

References and Recommended Readings

Blanchard, Wayne B. 2005. Top Ten Competencies for Professional Emergency Management. Available at training.fema.gov/EMIWeb/edu/docs/Blanchard%20-%20 Competencies%20EM%20HiEd.doc - 2006-02-13, last accessed February 25, 2011.

Blum, Elizabeth D. 2008. *Love Canal Revisited*. Kansas, MI: University of Kansas Press.

Burke, Jason. 2015. Indian Gangs Found Trafficking Women from Earthquake-hit Nepal. Available at http://www.theguardian.com/law/2015/jul/30/indian-gangs-trafficking-women-nepal-earthquake, last accessed February 2, 2016.

Cutter, Susan L. 2001. The Changing Nature of Risks and Hazards. pp. 1–12 in *American Hazardscapes*, edited by Susan L. Cutter. Washington, D.C.: Joseph Henry Press.

Cutter, Susan L., Alik Ismail-Zadeh, IrasemaAlcantara-Ayala, Orhan Altan, Daniel N. Baker, Salvano Briceno, Harsh Gupta, Ailsa Holloway, David Johnston, Gordono A. McBean, Yujiro Ogawa, Douglas Paton, Emma Porio, Rainer K. Silbereisen, Kuniyoshi Takeuchi, Giovanni B. Valsecchi, Coleen Volgel and Guoxiong Wu. 2015. Global Risks: Pool Knowledge to Stem Losses from Disasters. *Nature* 522(7556): 277–279.

Decision Research. 2015a. Paul Slovic, PhD. Available at http://www.decisionresearch.org/researcher/paul-slovic-ph-d/, last accessed June 17, 2015.

Decision Research. 2015b. About. Available at http://www.decisionresearch.org/about/, last accessed June 17, 2015.

Disaster Research Center (DRC). 2015. Research. Available at http://drc.udel.edu/research/, last accessed June 16, 2015.

Disaster Research Center (DRC). 2016. About DRC. Available at http://www.udel.edu/DRC/aboutus/index.html, last accessed February 3, 2016.

Drabek, Thomas. 1986. *Human Systems Response to Disaster: An Inventory of Sociological Finding*. New York: Springer-Verlag.

Dynes, Russell R. 1974. Organized Behavior in Disaster. Newark, DE: Disaster Research Center.

Dynes, Russell R. and Kathleen J. Tierney. 1994. *Disasters, Collective Behavior, and Social Organization*. Newark, DE: University of Delaware Press.

Dynes, Russell, Kathleen J. Tierney and Charles E. Fritz. 1994. Forward: The Emergence and Importance of Social Organization: The Contributions of E. L. Quarantelli. pp. 9–17 in *Disasters, Collective Behavior, and Social Organization*, edited by Russell R. Dynes and Kathleen J. Tierney. Newark, DE: University of Delaware Press.

FEMA. 2003. Recap of the Search for Columbia Shuttle Material. Available at https://www.fema.gov/news-release/2003/03/18/six-week-look-columbia-recovery-operation-ground-air-crews-top-15-million, last accessed February 3, 2016.

FEMA. 2008. Principles of Emergency Management. Available at https://training.fema.gov/hiedu/emprinciples.aspx, last accessed February 3, 2016.

FEMA. 2015a. *The Declaration Process*. Available at https://www.fema.gov/declaration-process, last accessed February 3, 2016.

FEMA. 2015b. National Prevention Framework. Available at http://www.fema.gov/national-prevention-framework, last Accessed February 2, 2016.

Fischer, Henry W. 2003. The Sociology of Disaster: Definitions, Research Questions and Measurements. *International Journal of Mass Emergencies and Disasters* 21(19): 91–108.

Fischer, Henry W. 2008. *Response to Disaster: Fact versus Fiction and Its Perpetuation: The Sociology of Disaster, 3rd Edition*. New York: University Press of America.

Fordham, Maureen, William E. Lovekamp, Deborah S. K. Thomas, and Brenda D. Phillips. 2013. Understanding Social Vulnerability. pp. 33–56 in *Social Vulnerability to Disaster*, edited by Deborah S. K. Thomas et al. Boca Raton, FL: CRC Press.

Fritz, Charles E. 1961. Disaster. pp. 651–694 in *Contemporary Social Problems*, edited by Robert K. Merton and Robert A. Nisbet. New York: Harcourt Brace Jovanovich.

Fritz, Charles E. and J. H. Mathewson. 1957. *Convergence Behavior in Disasters: A Problem in Social Control*. Washington, D.C.: National Academy of Sciences, National Research Council.

GNOCDC/Greater New Orleans Community Data Center. 2010. *Neighborhood Recovery Rates*. Available at http://www.gnocdc.org/RecoveryByNeighborhood/index.html, last accessed January 18, 2011.

Hoffman, Susanna M. and Anthony Oliver-Smith. 2002. *Catastrophe and Culture: The Anthropology of Disaster*. Sante Fe: School of American Research Press.

International Association of Emergency Managers. 2007. Principles of Emergency Management Supplement. Available at http://www.iaem.com/documents/POEMmonograph.pdf, last accessed February 3, 2016.

Jensen, Jessica. 2010. Emergency Management Theory: Unrecognized, Underused, and Undeveloped, pp. 7–24 in *Integrating Emergency Management Studies into Higher Education*, edited by Jessica A. Hubbard. Fairfax, VA: Public Entity Risk Institute.

Kroll-Smith, Steve, Vern Baxter, and Pam Jenkins. 2015. *Left to Chance: Hurricane Katrina and the story of Two New Orleans Neighborhoods*. Austin, TX: The University of Texas Press.

Levine, Adeline Gordon. 1982. *Love Canal: Science, Politics and People*. New York: D.C. Heath and Company.

McEntire, David M. 2004a. Development, Disaster and Vulnerability. *Disaster Prevention and Management* 13(3): 143–148.

McEntire, David M. 2004b. Status of Emergency Management Theory. *Paper presented at the annual FEMA Higher Education meetings*, June 8.

McEntire, David M. 2005. Emergency Management Theory: Issues, Barriers and Recommendations for Improvement. *Journal of Emergency Management* 3(3): 44–54.

Mileti, Dennis. 1999. *Disasters by Design*. Washington, D.C.: Joseph Henry Press.

Mileti, Dennis S., Thomas E. Drabek, and J. Eugene Haas. 1975. *Human Systems in Extreme Environments: A Sociological Perspective*. Boulder: University of Colorado.

Myers, Mary Fran. 1993. Bridging the Gap between Research and Practice: The Natural Hazards Research and Applications Information Center. *International Journal of Mass Emergencies and Disasters* 11(1): 41–54.

National Council on Disability (NCD). 2009. *Effective Emergency Management*. Washington, DC: National Council on Disability.

National Governor's Association (NGS). 1979. *1978 Emergency Preparedness Project: Final Report*. Washington, D.C.: Defense Civil Preparedness Agency.

Natural Hazards Center. n.d. Gilbert White. Available at http://www.colorado.edu/hazards/gfw/, last accessed February 23, 2011.

Neal, David M. 1985. *A Cross Societal Comparison of Emergent Group Behavior in Disaster: A Look at Sweden and the United States*. Dissertation, Department of Sociology, The Ohio State University, Columbus, OH.

Neal, David M. 2000. Developing Degree Programs in Disaster Management. *International Journal of Mass Emergencies and Disasters* 15(3): 417–437.

Neal, David M. 1997. Reconsidering the Phases of Disaster. *International Journal of Mass Emergencies and Disasters* 15(2): 239–264.

Peacock, W. and A. K. Ragsdale. 1997. Social Systems, Ecological Networks, and Disasters: Toward a Socio-political Ecology of Disasters. pp. 20–35 in *Hurricane Andrew: Ethnicity, Gender and the Sociology of Disasters*, edited by W. G. Peacock, B. H. Morrow and H. Gladwin. London: Routledge.

Perrow, Charles. 1984. *Normal Accidents: Living with High-Risk Technologies*. New York: Basic Books.

Phillips, Brenda. 2005. Disasters as a Discipline: The Status of Emergency Management Education in the U.S. *International Journal of Mass Emergencies and Disasters* 23(1): 85–10.

Phillips, Brenda, Deborah Thomas, Alice Fothergill and Lynn Pike, eds. 2010. *Social Vulnerability to Disaster*. Boca Raton, FL: CRC Press.

Phillips, Brenda, Patricia Stukes and Pam Jenkins. 2012. Freedom Hill Is Not for Sale and Neither Is the Lower Ninth Ward. *Journal of Black Studies* 43(4): 405–426.

Phillips, Brenda D. 2015. *Disaster Recovery, 2nd Edition*. Boca Raton, FL: CRC Press.

Quarantelli, E. L. 1982. What Is a Disaster?: An Agent Specific or an All Disaster Spectrum Approach to Socio-Behavioral Aspects of Earthquakes. pp. 453–478 in *Social and Economic Aspects of Earthquakes*, edited by B. Jones and M. Tomazevic. New York: Cornell University, Program I Urban and Regional Studies.

Quarantelli, E. L. 1986. *Organizational Behavior in Disasters and Implications for Disaster Planning*. Monograph Series 1/2. Emmitsburg, MD: National Emergency Training Center.

Quarantelli, E. L. 1987. Disaster Studies: An Analysis of the Social Historical Factors Affecting the Development of Research in the Area. *International Journal of Mass Emergencies and Disasters* 5(3): 285–310.

Quarantelli, E. L. 1993. Converting Disaster Scholarship into Effective Disaster Planning and Managing. *International Journal of Mass Emergencies and Disasters* 11(1), 15–39.

Quarantelli, E. L. 1994. Disaster Studies: The Consequences of the Historical Use of a Sociological Approach in the Development of Research. *International Journal of Mass Emergencies and Disasters* 12(1): 5–23.

Quarantelli, E. L. 2006. Understanding Katrina: Catastrophes Are Different from Disasters. *Perspectives from the Social Sciences*. Available at http://understandingkatrina.ssrc.org/Quarantelli/, last accessed January 3, 2011.

Quarantelli, E. L., and Russell R. Dynes. 1970. Property Norms and Looting: Their Patterns in Community Crises. *Phylon* 31: 168–182.

Sayeed, A. 2009. Victims of Earthquake and Patriarchy: The 2005 Pakistan Earthquake. pp. 142–151 in *Women, Gender and Disaster: Global Issues and Initiatives*, edited by E. Enarson and P. Chakrabarti. Los Angeles: Sage.

Schwartz, Rob, David M. Neal and Stacy Willet. 2015. Public Health Outbreaks: The Case of Ebola. *Panel presentation at the 40th Annual Natural Hazards Workshop*, Broomfield, CO.

Sharkey, P. 2007. Survival and Death in New Orleans. *Journal of Black Studies* 37(4): 482–501.

Slovic, Paul. 1987. Perception of Risk. *Science* 236(4799): 280–285.

Stough, Laura, Amy N. Sharp, J. Aaron Resch, Curt Decker and Nachama Wilker. 2015. Barriers to the Long Term Recovery of Individuals with Disabilities following a Disaster. *Disasters*. doi:10.1111/disa.12161

Sylves, Richard. 2008. *Disaster Policy and Politics: Emergency Management and Homeland Security*. Washington, D.C.: CQ Press.

Sylves, Richard and Zoltan Buzas. 2007. Presidential Disaster Declaration Decisions, 1953–2003: What Influences Odds of Approval? *State and Local Government Review* 39(1): 3–15.

Tierney, Kathleen, Michael Lindell and Ron W. Perry. 2001. *Facing the Unexpected*. Washington, D.C.: Joseph Henry Press.

Turner, Ralph and Killian. 1987. *Collective Behavior, 3rd Edition*. Englewood, NJ: Prentice Hall.

Urby, Heriberto and David McEntire. 2015. Field, Discipline, and Profession: Understanding Three Major Labels of Emergency Management. *Journal of Emergency Management* 13(5): 389–400.

USGS. 1994. Northridge, CA Earthquake Open File Report 94-179-I. Available at https://www.usgs.gov/media/videos/northridge-ca-earthquake-open-file-report-94-179-i-0, last accessed August 30, 2016.

U. S. Fire Administration, 2004. *The Seasonal Incidents of Fire in 2000*. Topical Fire Research Series, Issue 6, Volume 3. Washington, D.C.: FEMA.

Weick, Karl E. 1976. Educational Organizations as Loosely Coupled Systems. *Administrative Science Quarterly* 21: 1–19.

Weller, Jack M. and E. L. Quarantelli. 1973. Neglected Characteristics of Collective Behavior. *American Journal of Sociology* 79(3): 665–685.

Research Methods and the Practice of Emergency Management

Objectives

Upon completing this chapter, readers should be able to:

- Outline the historical origins of disaster research and discuss the relevance of disaster research for the practice of emergency management.
- Describe the stages of the research process and understand the value of research-based knowledge.
- Provide examples of contributions made by researchers in various fields and scientific disciplines, including engineering, natural sciences, and social sciences.
- Identify the various methods used to gather data on disasters and provide examples of how they might be used.
- Describe ethical guidelines for studying human subjects and identify challenges involved in conducting disaster research.

Key Terms

- Archives
- Ethics
- GIS
- Interviews

- Multidisciplinary
- Observations
- Research process
- Surveys

4.1 Introduction

Disasters interest people for many reasons. Novelists and filmmakers craft compelling storylines celebrating selfless acts of heroism or, more commonly, images of chaos and pandemonium in the wake of catastrophe. Members of the mass media flock to the scenes of disasters, often conveying those same images of civil disorder and social breakdown to their viewers, readers, and listeners. In contrast to those who exploit disasters for sales and ratings, emergency managers, first responders, public officials, and volunteers have a professional interest in disasters and a strong desire to alleviate the suffering of those impacted.

Researchers also have a professional interest in disasters, and they share a common vision of reducing the human and financial costs of disasters. Ultimately, the goal of scholarly research is to generate insights and contribute to a safer, more sustainable future. While you may not see them on the front line throwing sandbags or delivering meals, engineers, geologists, and social scientists work hard at testing building construction practices, mapping hazardous areas, observing organizational responses to disasters, evaluating disaster-related policies and programs, and identifying vulnerable populations who are most susceptible to the devastating impacts of disasters. The results of their work may not always produce immediate benefits, but over the long term the findings of disaster research can contribute significantly to a more resilient society.

4.1.1 The Benefits of Understanding Research

As a future emergency manager, you will benefit from having a basic understanding of disaster research in several ways. First, you will develop transferrable skills. The ability to gather information, analyze data, and communicate the results of your analysis to others is a skill that is recognized and valued in virtually all professional settings. As an emergency manager, for example, you may be asked to conduct a hazard analysis, assess the degree to which your community is prepared for a disaster, or identify populations with special needs in the event of a disaster. By having some familiarity with the methods of data collection described in this chapter, you will be much better equipped to perform those kinds of tasks.

Second, having research-based knowledge of how people and organizations actually behave in disasters will enhance your effectiveness as an emergency manager. As will be discussed in Chapter 7, there are many myths about human response to disaster, all of which assume that society breaks down under extreme stress. In reality, however, rather than having to control a helpless mob of panic-stricken victims, emergency managers must instead devise strategies for coordinating the efforts of the enormous numbers of survivors and volunteers who invariably want to help.

Finally, your introduction to the tradition and practice of disaster research will benefit you by exposing you to valuable lessons learned from systematic studies of past disasters. As will be discussed later in this chapter, researchers have studied disasters in part because they have sought answers to interesting scientific questions, but they have also been driven to answer highly practical questions about how best to respond to, prepare for, or recover from large-scale disasters.

4.1.2 Sources of Knowledge for Emergency Managers

As a professional emergency manager, you will continue to learn throughout your career, and the knowledge you acquire will come from various sources, including (1) formal education, (2) field experience, and (3) disaster research. It is very likely that, as your career advances, the relative impacts of these three sources of knowledge on how you do your job will shift from time to time. For example, you may be assigned a new task about which you know very little and find yourself combing through your old class notes looking for guidance. Or, a colleague may come to you about a challenge he or she is facing in his or her community, and you will be able to share your own experiences in dealing with the same problem. Finally, you may encounter something so unique and perplexing that you decide to seek out research on the issue to see what others have learned about it.

4.1.2.1 Education-Based Knowledge

In most undergraduate degree programs, including emergency management, students are required to take classes in a wide range of disciplines including the natural sciences, social sciences, and humanities. Students often feel that their classes are disjointed and haphazard, and they do not always see the value in taking so many disparate courses. But there is a good reason for exposure to so many different topics. In addition to preparing for careers in particular fields, a college education is also aimed at equipping you with broader skills for life in general. These include critical thinking, creative problem solving, and strong communication skills. Thus, it is possible that some of your least favorite classes may pay dividends much later in life. It is also possible that certain topics covered in some of your favorite classes—such as research methods in emergency management—that may not capture your interest at the time may be vitally important to you later in your career.

4.1.2.2 Experience-Based Knowledge

Another valuable source of information about the profession will come from real-world experiences. Within your professional networks, for example, you will hear plenty of "war stories" as colleagues share their experiences from the field with you. Over time, you will also gain valuable experiences of your own that will surely serve you well. Those experiences will be critical to your development as a professional emergency manager, and they are all steps in becoming a seasoned veteran. Early in your career, it is very likely that you will feel overwhelmed, exhausted, and emotionally drained during your first encounters with large-scale disasters. Over time, however, based largely on previous experiences, you will develop much more sustainable work routines, more effective coping strategies, and more efficient solutions to the common problems you will face.

4.1.2.3 Research-Based Knowledge

It is our hope that in addition to these education- and experience-based ways of knowing, you will continue to expand your research-based knowledge throughout your career. Experience certainly matters, and the knowledge you acquire from your years of service will be invaluable. However, scientific research is also important and from it we can learn a great deal about the world around us, as described in Box 4.1.

BOX 4.1   THE VALUE OF RESEARCH FOR EMERGENCY MANAGEMENT

Dr. William A. Anderson (1937–2013)

Dr. William Anderson, a graduate of The Ohio State University and an alumnus of the Disaster Research Center, writes here about the value of research for emergency managers. Dr. Anderson, who first studied the 1964 Alaska earthquake, went on to a distinguished career at the U.S. National Science Foundation and the National Academy of Sciences. We reprise his first edition feature again in memorial. Please see the last chapter in this book for information about scholarships associated with the William Averette Anderson Fund.

Emergency managers can access and apply findings and principles from decades of disaster research when undertaking such actions as communicating risk information to the public, developing disaster preparedness plans, and undertaking crucial disaster response and recovery activities.

(Continued)

BOX 4.1 (*Continued*)   THE VALUE OF RESEARCH FOR EMERGENCY MANAGEMENT

Disaster researchers continue to produce new knowledge on such subjects. Thus, emergency managers need to periodically update their understanding of advances in the disaster research field as they pursue the goal of making their communities more disaster resilient. Staying abreast of new insights from disaster research can be rather challenging, but it should be a lifetime commitment for career emergency managers.

Many senior emergency managers have set a good example for the next generation by successfully bridging the gap between the emergency management and disaster research communities throughout their careers. Thus, the emerging generation of emergency managers can gain much in the way of their own continued growth by emulating them. There are several ways in which emergency managers have been able to access disaster research information on a career-long basis, enabling them to apply it strategically in their professional work.

Interpersonal Connections

Experience has shown that emergency managers can learn much from disaster researchers through personal contact with them. Many emergency managers have established important long-term ties with disaster researchers at their local universities or those in the immediate region for the purpose of gaining knowledge useful for their decision making. Emergency managers discover that most disaster researchers are quite eager to discuss and share their expert knowledge with them and also point them toward valuable resources such as publications, courses, workshops, and other learning opportunities. The message here is that making friends with approachable disaster scholars should be a top priority for young emergency management practitioners.

Continuing Education

Many emergency managers understand the importance of continuing education for those in their profession. Thus many obtain additional education after they have completed college and launched their careers. To help meet the needs of today's emergency management practitioners, there is quite a variety of learning experiences to choose from that are offered by disaster scholars at local universities as well as those made available online by experts at distant universities, including degree and nondegree courses, full- and short-term courses, and seminars.

Conferences and Workshops

As disasters have drawn more attention in the past several years, there has been a surge in the number of conferences and workshops that bring together disaster scholars, emergency management practitioners, and

(Continued)

BOX 4.1 *(Continued)* THE VALUE OF RESEARCH FOR EMERGENCY MANAGEMENT

disaster reduction policy makers to exchange ideas and experiences through discussions and presentations. The workshops organized by the Disasters Roundtable at the National Academy of Sciences in Washington, D.C. and the Annual Natural Hazards Workshop organized by the Natural Hazards Center at the University of Colorado in Boulder are two examples of such activities that involve the active participation of emergency managers, providing them with the opportunity to learn about discoveries in disaster research directly from researchers. Of course, disaster researchers also learn much from emergency managers during such exchanges.

Publications

The above learning strategies involve social interaction, mostly the critical face-to-face variety, between emergency managers and researchers. This is crucial because most emergency managers are seldom inclined to spend much time reading through the technical terminology and explanations of scientific research methodology found in leading scholarly research publications. However, there are publications geared to making disaster research more understandable to emergency management practitioners and these do attract a sizable number of them, including the two editions of *Emergency Management: Principles and Practice for Local Government* (Drabek and Hoetmer 1991; Waugh and Tierney 2007) published by ICMA, a leading professional association for local government managers. Newsletters like the *Natural Hazards Observer* and the online publication *Disaster Research*, both published by the Natural Hazards Center, are other sources of written information about developments in the disaster field that are reader friendly to emergency managers.

New Media

In this information technology age, emergency managers can now turn to new media sources for information on disaster research, and many are doing so. This is an area where young emergency managers may eclipse their elders in the field. Important information on disaster research can be accessed through Google searches and some disaster scholars make information available on their blogs. Also, the emergence of web-based social media, such as Facebook, Twitter and YouTube, offers unparalleled access to disaster research information of value to emergency managers.

In conclusion, acquiring relevant insights from the disaster research field throughout their careers in ways noted here, and effectively applying them, will help make the next generation of emergency managers the leaders their communities need to combat natural, technological, and human-induced disasters.

For the professional emergency manager, research findings from disaster studies can be valuable sources of knowledge for three primary reasons. First, researchers rely on *systematic observations* in which they thoroughly document what they see and hear in the field. In contrast, experience-based knowledge is often based on selective observations and anecdotal accounts of what happened in a disaster. Second, researchers gather *empirical evidence* to support their findings. Rather than relying on rampant rumors or media sensationalism and speculation, researchers report what actually happened and systematically amass evidence to substantiate their findings. Finally, disaster studies are valuable sources of knowledge to emergency managers because researchers collect *perishable information* that is critical to understanding post-disaster events fully. By deploying as rapidly as possible to the scene of a disaster, researchers can paint an accurate picture of the response effort—a task that becomes much more difficult as time passes, memories fade, response teams leave, and ad hoc ways of working are replaced by normal routines. Researchers bring a neutral stance to observing events and thus generate more objective, measurable results that can steadily improve emergency management practice.

As shown in Figure 4.1, the research process involves a systematic series of steps, beginning with the identification of a research problem, such as the factors that determine whether or not people will prepare themselves and their households for disasters. We would then conduct a review of existing literature on the topic by reading studies published in academic journals, such as the ones listed in Box 4.2. From our literature review, we would learn that income and education levels have been found to influence household preparedness levels and thus we would formulate our

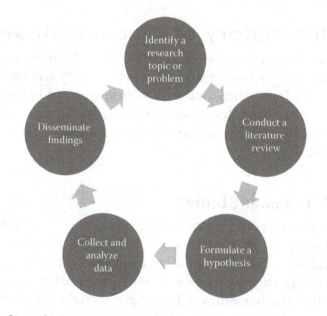

FIGURE 4.1   Steps in the research process.

BOX 4.2 ACADEMIC JOURNALS IN EMERGENCY MANAGEMENT

Australian Journal of Emergency Management
Disasters
Disaster Management and Response
Disaster Prevention and Management
Emergency Management Review
Environmental Hazards
International Journal of Emergency Management
International Journal of Mass Emergencies and Disasters
Journal of Contingencies and Crisis Management
Journal of Emergency Management
Journal of Homeland Security and Emergency Management
Natural Hazards Review
Risk, Hazards & Crisis in Public Policy

hypotheses and predict that those with higher income and education levels are more likely to prepare for disasters than those with lower levels. We would then collect data to test our hypotheses using one of the research methodologies described later in this chapter, analyze the information, and then disseminate our findings by publishing the results. The research process, as you can see, is an ongoing loop aimed at continually refining our knowledge of disasters and thereby improving the practice of emergency management.

4.2 Brief History of Disaster Research

Many students are surprised when they learn that there is an established field of research devoted to the study of disasters. They also tend to be surprised when they learn when and why the field emerged in the first place. While a few early isolated studies were pursued, systematic efforts of social scientists to examine the human dimensions of disasters began in earnest in the early 1950s.

4.2.1 Early Disaster Studies

Interestingly, the impetus for establishing a field of study devoted specifically to social aspects of disasters came from the United States military. During World War II, the U.S. military conducted extensive studies of its bombing campaigns against Germany and Japan (Fritz 1961). Those studies revealed that the bombings did not have severely debilitating effects. Both Germany and Japan demonstrated strong resilience and an impressive capacity to rebound in the wake of such massive destruction. Based on these observations, the central question for the military became, what would happen if a major U.S. city was unexpectedly attacked by an enemy? Would civil society remain intact or would social order break down into chaos?

To answer these questions, the military issued research grants to social scientists to study how people respond to disasters. Initially, studies were conducted by social scientists at the University of Chicago's National Opinion Research Center (NORC), the University of Oklahoma, and the University of Texas. Subsequent studies were conducted by researchers affiliated with the National Academy of Sciences Disaster Research Group. These early researchers studied human responses to tornadoes, airplane crashes, and chemical plant explosions (Quarantelli 1987). For their purposes, the type of event was not important as long as it happened quickly and unexpectedly. In other words, the researchers were tasked with studying events that resembled bombing attacks. As Charles Fritz (1961, p. 653), one of the pioneers of disaster research, wrote:

> The impetus for systematic studies of human behavior in disaster developed primarily from two interrelated practical needs: first, to secure more adequate protection of the nation from the destructive and disruptive consequences of potential atomic, biological, and chemical attack; and second, to produce the maximal amount of disruption to the enemy in the event of a war.

For the most part, these early studies focused on the impacts of disasters on individuals and families and reached the same conclusion as the military's investigations during World War II. They generally concluded that survivors of natural and technological disasters in the United States exhibited the same kind of resilience and recuperative capacity as residents of the cities bombed in Germany and Japan.

4.2.2 Research Centers in the United States

Beginning over 60 years ago, social scientists established research projects and centers focused on disasters. These efforts, now worldwide, have explored and pushed new areas in the field, trained the next generation of faculty for teaching and research, and generated findings that serve as the body of knowledge for undergraduate and graduate programs and degrees. Scholars from different academic areas have founded these centers, resulting in a broad scope of relevant research. In this section, we briefly highlight some of the major research centers in the United States and other centers that have formed internationally. Professional emergency managers worldwide draw upon their research findings to assist them with disaster management and policy decisions. Today, many of these centers focus on the importance of interdisciplinary research to further understand human behavior before, during, and after disaster. Below we briefly introduce the origins and perspectives of some centers.

Although not a formal "disaster" or "hazard" research center, the NORC at the University of Chicago initiated the first major series of disaster studies. Funded by the Department of Defense, they wanted to understand human behavior (specifically soldiers') during time of nuclear and chemical war. To partially replicate war scenarios, the research project focused upon human behavior in disaster. The research team established "quick response" research, traveling to the disaster site quickly to obtain an unvarnished look at what occurs. This line of research showed that such images of panic, mass hysteria, looting, and other similar behavior were generally false. Rather, disasters seemed to bring out the best in people. Charles Fritz managed this research project, and one of the graduate students on the project was E.L. Quarantelli (1987).

In the early 1960s, the focus of disaster studies shifted in an important way that would significantly shape the field's development and enhance its future relevance to the profession of emergency management. Sociologists E.L. Quarantelli, Russell Dynes and J. Eugene Haas formed the first academic center, the Disaster Research Center (DRC) at The Ohio State University in 1963. Rather than focusing on how disasters affected individuals and families, DRC researchers initially devoted their attention to a diverse array of community organizations (police and fire departments), voluntary associations (Red Cross), and other groups that responded to disasters. As described in Chapter 7, studies conducted by the DRC led to the development of a typology of organized responses to disasters that remains relevant even today, particularly for emergency managers who must coordinate the activities of various community organizations both before and after disaster strikes. Today DRC draws upon a multidisciplinary approach to study a wide range of events across all phases of disaster. In 1985, DRC moved from The Ohio State University to the University of Delaware, where it continues to reside today.

During the mid-1970s, geographer Gilbert White along with others formed the Natural Hazard Research and Applications Information Center (NHRAIC) at the University of Colorado Boulder, also commonly referred to as the Natural Hazards Center. Their initial research focused upon interdisciplinary issues related to hazard mitigation (as opposed to DRC's more sociological focus). In addition, the center established an annual, well-attended workshop, "quick response" disaster research funding, and a resource and information center for academics, professionals, policy makers, and others. The annual workshop continues to give academics, emergency management professionals, and government officials who fund research a chance to discuss new and emerging research and policy trends in the field.

In 1988, Texas A&M University established the Hazards Reduction & Recovery Center (HRRC) with Dennis Wenger serving as its first formal director. Drawing upon various disciplines (e.g., architecture, planning, sociology, policy analysis, economics, and engineering), it uses an interdisciplinary perspective for its research. Today, HRRC members devote much of their attention to land use planning and coastal issues.

Geographer Susan Cutter created the Hazards & Vulnerability Research Institute (HVRI) in the mid-1990s. Although having a strong focus on geographical issues, members also engage in interdisciplinary research from both the natural and social sciences. HVRI has developed a strong reputation especially regarding its work on vulnerability and resiliency. Other centers in the United States, such as the Center for Disaster and Risk Analysis at Colorado State University, the Center for Disaster Research and Education at Millersville University, and the Stephenson Disaster Management Institute at Louisiana State University contribute to making important research findings (see Box 4.3 for examples of research centers operating today).

BOX 4.3   RESEARCH CENTERS WORLDWIDE

Research centers have played a pivotal role in the development of disaster research in the United States and around the world. These centers typically rely on funding from various governmental agencies, nonprofit foundations, and, in some cases, corporations, and engage in cutting-edge research that has real-life applications for emergency managers. While some centers may devote more attention to a particular type of hazard (e.g., floods) or a specific disaster phase (e.g., response), most embrace the all-hazards view embodied in comprehensive and integrated emergency management.

Because most research centers are based at universities, they also serve as fertile training grounds for students at both undergraduate and graduate levels interested in the study of disasters and the practice of emergency management. In many cases, student researchers receive valuable benefits including financial stipends, tuition waivers, and course credits. By exposing students to the research process from beginning to end—from formulating a research question, to gathering data, to conducting analyses and writing the results—research centers actively groom the next generation of scholars.

In addition to training and mentoring students, research centers also provide valuable services to society at large. Researchers from these centers, for example, sometimes provide expert testimony to state and federal legislative bodies seeking to pass hazards- and disaster-related laws and policies. They also sometimes serve as consultants to governmental agencies conducting, for example, evaluation studies of new policies or programs. Researchers also regularly deliver presentations at conferences and

(Continued)

BOX 4.3 (*Continued*)   RESEARCH CENTERS WORLDWIDE

workshops attended by emergency management professionals that serve as effective strategies for breaking the barrier that often exists between the two communities. Finally, in addition to publishing the results of their studies in academic journals, including those listed in Box 4.2, some research centers maintain specialized libraries and resource collections to further facilitate knowledge transfer. The most established research centers in the United States are:

- Disaster Research Center at the University of Delaware (www.drc. udel.edu).
- Natural Hazards Center at the University of Colorado (www. colorado.edu/hazards).
- Hazard Reduction and Recovery Center at Texas A&M University (http://hrrc.arch.tamu.edu).
- Hazards & Vulnerability Research Institute at the University of South Carolina (http://artsandsciences.sc.edu/geog/hvri/front-page).

In recent years, numerous university-based research centers have been established in various countries. A few examples include the:

- Flood Research Centre at Middlesex University (http://www.mdx. ac.uk/our-research/centres/flood-hazard).
- Disaster Research Network at the Royal Melbourne Institute of Technology in Australia (http://www.rmit.edu.au/research/ find-research/research-networks/disaster-research-network).
- Risk and Crisis Research Center at Mid Sweden University (https:// www.miun.se/en/rcr).
- African Centre for Disaster Studies at North-West University (acds. co.za).
- Disaster Prevention Research Institute at Kyoto University (http:// www.dpri.kyoto-u.ac.jp/en/).

4.2.3 International Research

In recent years, the field of disaster research has grown into a global community of scholars, with researchers from all over the world studying the impacts of disasters on human societies. Although the field was born in the United States, it has a much farther reach now than ever before. The globalization of disaster research has benefitted the field in several important ways.

First, researchers outside the United States have conducted studies of the impacts of disasters on some of the least developed countries in the world. For example, they have studied cyclones in Bangladesh, flooding and landslides in Honduras, earthquakes in India and Pakistan, and the tsunami of 2004 that devastated several Asian countries. These kinds of studies are invaluable because disasters in developing countries are much more catastrophic than those experienced in the United States. Although events like the attacks on the World Trade Center and Hurricane Katrina are certainly tragic, they produce relatively low death tolls and constitute relatively low-impact events relative to the remaining financial resources, social capital, and physical infrastructure. Disasters in the least developed countries of the world, on the other hand, often produce death tolls in the tens or hundreds of thousands, completely devastate entire towns and villages, and severely disrupt community life for months or years. Fortunately, with the growth of disaster research around the world, we are beginning to learn much more about these kinds of catastrophic events.

Second, the increased involvement of scholars around the world has broadened horizons in disaster research. As explained above, the field has its origins in the U.S. military's concerns about how well American cities would survive in the event of an enemy attack. To address those concerns, researchers went into the field and studied events that resembled such attacks, that is, events that were unexpected, developed rapidly, and produced heavy but geographically concentrated impacts.

In contrast, researchers from various European countries, including Sweden, The Netherlands, and France, take a much broader view of disasters. In fact, researchers in those countries are much more likely to use the term *crisis* instead of *disaster* because it connotes a broader range of threats to society, including creeping threats. Creeping threats are crises that develop over a period of months or years, and despite their obvious potential, they often go unforeseen until it is too late. European researchers also devote considerable attention to the cascading effects of crises and disasters, particularly when the threats cross international boundaries, which is increasingly common in today's world. Cascading effects are often unpredictable and unanticipated impacts on technical systems, critical infrastructure, and social institutions, such as power failures that cross state or national lines and threaten transportation, medical care and communications. Thus, in addition to studying conventional types of disasters, European researchers, with their interests in creeping threats and cascading effects, have also studied financial crises, food contamination outbreaks, and transportation system failures.

Research centers now exist worldwide in Europe (e.g., The Netherlands, Sweden, and Great Britain), Africa, Asia (e.g., India, Japan, Thailand) and Australia. For example, recently, scholars created the African Center for Disaster Studies, located at North-West University in Potchefstroom, South Africa, and Sweden has developed a number of centers at its universities over the last 20 years (Neal 2012, see Box 4.3). Overall, research centers play an important role for the field of emergency management.

They provide the research that helps guide policy makers, train students who often become emergency managers or college professors, and generate the body of knowledge from which we teach and write our textbooks.

Finally, as the field of disaster research has grown to include scholars from many countries outside the United States, researchers have increased efforts to reach, expand, and strengthen the sense of community among those working in the field. Perhaps the strongest contribution to that effort was the creation of the International Research Committee on Disasters (IRCD) in the 1980s. Although the IRCD is a research committee within the International Sociological Association (ISA), its membership includes scholars from a range of scientific disciplines and practitioners of emergency management. Its membership also includes scholars from the Americas (North, South, and Central), Europe, Asia, Russia and Australia. In addition to convening meetings every 4 years in conjunction with the ISA World Congress of Sociology, the IRCD publishes the *International Journal of Mass Emergencies and Disasters (IJMED)*. The journal is published three times per year and serves as the flagship journal of the disaster research community. The journal contains scholarly research articles from various disciplines, book reviews, and special comments from researchers in the field. As seen in Box 4.2, in addition to *IJMED*, numerous journals now publish disaster research findings and represent valuable resources as you launch your career in emergency management.

4.3 Disaster Research as a Multidisciplinary Field

An important point to remember, which has been alluded to in the above sections, is that the field of disaster research is inherently multidisciplinary in nature. While some disciplines such as sociology and geography have older, more established, and more extensive traditions of research, numerous other disciplines have made important contributions to our understanding of disasters and how best to manage them. As described in Chapter 3, disasters are complex events that involve interactions of the natural environment, the built environment, technology, and human societies (Mileti 1999). Thus, as depicted in Figure 4.2, a comprehensive understanding of disasters requires insights and inputs from multiple scientific disciplines.

From the *natural sciences*, for example, some *geologists* specialize in the study of earthquakes, volcanoes, landslides, and other hazards, and with increased concern around the world about the problem of climate change, we are becoming more aware of the work of *climatologists* and *meteorologists*. Similarly, the threats of nuclear, chemical, and biological terrorism have enhanced the prominence and relevance of research conducted by *chemists*, *physicists*, and *biologists*. The discipline of *engineering* is also central to our understanding of

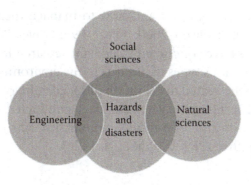

FIGURE 4.2   Interactions of scientific disciplines.

disasters and our efforts to ameliorate their effects. *Structural engineers,* for example, study different kinds of building practices and devise strategies for retrofitting or strengthening older structures that are deemed more vulnerable than newer buildings to damage or collapse in events such as earthquakes. *Civil engineers* also conduct important research on the performance of critical infrastructure systems (e.g., transportation systems and utilities) during disasters and devise strategies for improving them.

Social sciences have also played an integral role in the development of disaster research and have made profound contributions to the practices of emergency management. For social scientists:

> Disasters provide realistic laboratories for testing the integration, stamina, and recuperative powers of large-scale social systems. They are the sociological equivalents of engineering experiments that test the capacity of machines to withstand extreme physical stresses. (Fritz 1961, p. 654)

Many *sociologists,* for example, have studied how social systems—ranging from small groups to larger organizations, communities, and entire societies—prepare for, respond to, and recover from the major social disruptions caused by disasters (Kreps 1995; Quarantelli 1994).

Psychologists have also made important contributions, studying how individuals perceive and manage risks and conducting extensive research on posttraumatic stress disorder (PTSD) among children, emergency workers, and others in the contexts of natural disasters and terrorist attacks (Jenkins 1998; Norris et al. 2002a, b; North et al. 2002; Pfefferbaum, Call, and Sconzo 1999). *Anthropologists* have sought to understand how societies build cultural protections to cope with hazards in their environments and how cultural beliefs and practices change after disasters (see Hoffman and Oliver-Smith 2002; Oliver-Smith and Hoffman 1999). Scholars from *political science* and *public administration* have made significant contributions to our knowledge of disaster policies and politics and how to manage them more effectively (Birkland 1997, 2007; Olson 2000; Platt 1999; Sylves 2008; Waugh 2000, 2006). *Geographers* have conducted important research in terms of identifying and mapping various types of hazards in the environment and helping us better understand the spatial distribution of social vulnerability (Cutter 2001; Phillips et al. 2010). Finally, *economists* have conducted extensive research on the financial costs and long-term economic impacts of natural disasters (Dacy and Kunreuther 1969; Wright et al. 1979).

4.4 Types of Research

Having discussed the importance and relevance of disaster research to emergency management, its historical origins, and its multidisciplinary nature, we now turn to a more in-depth discussion of how research is actually conducted. This discussion will be beneficial to you as it provides guidance on how to conduct your own research and also give you a basis upon which to evaluate the quality and usefulness of research conducted by others. Before describing the specific methods typically used to gather data on disasters, we will discuss the different types of research.

4.4.1 Basic and Applied Research

On a general level, research can be characterized as basic or applied. Basic research is conducted to satisfy intellectual curiosity, explore previously uninvestigated topics, or address core theoretical debates in a discipline. While the results of basic research may not have immediate applicability to solving social or technical problems faced by society, it is possible that over time this kind of research will change the way scientists think about an issue, stimulate new lines of inquiry, and ultimately produce results that can be translated into practical solutions to problems. *Applied research*, on the other hand, begins with a specific problem identified by a user community and seeks to provide practical, data-based guidance for solving the problem. For example, evaluation studies are often conducted in various settings to assess the effectiveness of new policies, programs, or technologies (see Ritchie and MacDonald 2010).

Both types of research are common in the field of disaster research. As Fritz (1961) pointed out (cited earlier in this chapter), since its inception the field has sought to answer both basic and applied questions. Basic disaster research seeks to better understand how social systems respond to disruptions and refine theories about how society works. A good example of such research is Gary Kreps' work to develop a theory of organizations (Kreps 1989). Like Fritz, he views disasters as strategic sites for answering basic questions about society and sees organizations as central elements of the social structure. He has attempted to conceptually isolate the core properties of organizations and empirically document the timing and sequencing of those properties. Kreps' work may sound highly theoretical and abstract at first, but it has important implications for maximizing the efficiency and effectiveness of organizations responding to disasters.

Disaster researchers are perhaps best known for their applied research, which in some form or fashion seeks to improve some aspect of society's readiness for, response to, or recovery from disasters. For example, they have conducted extensive research on preparedness levels, warning systems, evacuation behavior, inter-governmental coordination, and many other topics. They have also performed evaluation studies of disaster-related programs such as FEMA's Project Impact, a community-based mitigation program designed to enhance disaster resilience in the United States (Wachtendorf 2001; Wachtendorf and Kompanik 2000). And they have used participatory action research (PAR) to identify strategies to improve emergency preparedness for large-scale evacuations of high-rise buildings (Gershon et al. 2008).

4.4.2 Primary and Secondary Research

Whether you are conducting a study of your own or reading research done by someone else, you will find two main sources of data: primary and secondary. *Primary research* involves the collection of original data obtained through surveys, interviews, or observations to answer a basic or applied research question. As discussed in the next section, there are various ways in which those data can be collected, but the important point is that primary research is based on new data. *Secondary research* is based on data that already exist and were gathered by someone else. As an emergency manager, you will find numerous sources of secondary data useful. For example, the U.S. Census Bureau maintains massive amounts of data that you can use to study the demographics of your community. The data cover age distribution, racial composition, income and education levels, home ownership rates, and many other characteristics. As will be seen in Chapter 5, these factors play a significant role in determining how prepared households and communities are for disasters.

4.4.3 Cross-Sectional and Longitudinal Research

Another issue to consider in conducting or reading research is the time frame over which information used in the study was or will be collected. *Cross-sectional research* is based on data gathered at one point in time and is often described as offering a snapshot of reality at a particular time. In cross-sectional research, the goal is to present a picture of how things look at the time of data collection, not predict how they might look in the future. *Longitudinal research*, on the other hand, involves prolonged data collection over time.

The goal of this kind of research is to track changes over time. As an emergency manager, you will find both approaches useful. For example, if you need a benchmark of how prepared your community currently is for a disaster, a cross-sectional study would be fine. However, if your community has recently been struck by a disaster and you want to monitor its recovery over time to see whether conditions are improving or getting worse, a longitudinal approach would be more appropriate.

4.4.4 Individual and Aggregate Research

When gathering data on disasters or any topic for that matter, you must decide the level at which you need information. Are you seeking to understand something about individuals or larger social groupings such as households or organizations? *Individual-level research* seeks to describe and explain the attitudes and behaviors of individuals. For example, if you are interested in risk perception levels of people living near a nuclear power plant, you would ask individuals how likely they think an accident is.

If you want to know whether people in your community are suffering negative psychological consequences from a recent disaster or other community emergency, you might ask them about their feelings and experiences with the event. If, on the other hand, you want to know how well the police and fire departments communicated while responding to a recent emergency in your community, you will need *aggregate-level research* to describe and explain characteristics of collectivities, including households, organizations, communities, or entire societies.

Since disasters are large-scale events that are recognizable primarily by their impacts on collectivities, much of the research you conduct or read will be based on aggregate-level data. It is important to note, however, that even if we are studying a larger social grouping, such as a fire department, we often must collect information from individuals in the department. As a result, there is an important distinction to be made between respondents and informants in our studies. *Respondents* are people from whom we gather specific information to understand their own thoughts, feelings, or behaviors. *Informants*, on the other hand, provide general information about a larger group to which they belong, whether a family or household, neighborhood association, informal search-and-rescue crew, police department, or other collectivity.

The distinction between respondents and informants is vitally important. For example, you may be involved in conducting an after-action study to assess how local governmental agencies performed while responding to an event in your community. In doing so, you would likely collect information from directors of the various departments and divisions. When it comes time to analyze the data, you will need to know whether department heads provided information on their own activities or the actions carried out by the unit as a whole.

4.4.5 Quantitative and Qualitative Research

Another important distinction you will encounter in conducting your own studies or reading works by others is between quantitative and qualitative research. At the most basic level, *quantitative research* is the application of mathematical principles and statistical analyses to the study of social life. Stated another way, quantitative studies seek to describe and explain variation in the numeric properties of some aspect of social life. For example, researchers have developed elaborate scales and indices to precisely measure and quantify levels of risk perception and disaster preparedness. They also employ sophisticated statistical techniques to identify factors that contribute to higher or lower levels of these phenomena (Bourque, Shoaf, and Nguyen 2002).

Qualitative research, on the other hand, seeks to describe and explain the processes involved in some aspect of social life. Whereas quantitative research largely assumes that social life is patterned and predictable, qualitative research assumes that reality is variable, fluid, and less predictable.

While both quantitative and qualitative studies are common in disaster research, qualitative methods are particularly useful in the early aftermath of a disaster. During that period, there is a great deal of ambiguity and a tremendous amount of activity, much of which is unplanned and improvised, as survivors, first responders, governmental agencies, and voluntary organizations converge on a scene and initiate a response. As Phillips (2002, 2014a,b) points out, because qualitative methods focus on social processes and afford the researcher flexibility, they are well suited for the post-disaster environment. Indeed, there is a long tradition of quick-response field studies in disaster research in which researchers are dispatched to the site of a disaster as quickly as possible after impact to gather valuable data that might otherwise perish (Michaels 2003; Quarantelli 2002). Researchers have also employed qualitative methods to conduct longitudinal studies of such topics as the experiences of children and extended families in Hurricane Katrina (Browne 2015; Fothergill and Peek 2015), the role of religious organizations in disaster response and recovery efforts (Phillips 2014c), and community controversies over the practice of hydraulic fracturing or "fracking" in natural gas exploration (Gullion 2015).

4.5 Methods of Data Collection

There are numerous ways in which researchers have gathered data on disasters (see Figure 4.3), and knowledge of those methods may help you as an emergency manager to measure preparedness levels in your community, monitor the performance of local agencies and departments in responding to a disaster, gauge short- and long-term recovery after a disaster, and assess community support for a proposed mitigation program or policy. In collecting information about disasters, the most important consideration is to select a methodology that will appropriately and adequately provide data on the question or questions you pose. Researchers, analysts, and other professionals certainly develop clear preferences for methods of gathering data. For example, some people are quantitatively inclined and feel best if they can see statistics on the magnitude of a problem. Others are more visually inclined and prefer to see maps and other spatial or visual representations of an issue. Still others are more qualitatively oriented and want to gain in-depth understandings of disasters from the perspective of those experiencing them. Fortunately, researchers, emergency managers, and others interested in gathering disaster data have a broad and diverse range of tools available for such purposes. Indeed, probably the best way of gathering data on any social phenomenon is through *triangulation*—the use of multiple methodologies.

4.5.1 Surveys

If you are interested in learning about a relatively large population of people, the survey is an appropriate choice. Surveys involve the administration of a standardized questionnaire to a sample of people to better understand perceptions, attitudes, opinions, preferences, and behaviors prevalent in a larger population. The most common approaches to administering surveys are by telephone, mail, face-to-face meetings, and increasingly via the Internet. Questions on surveys are usually closed-ended; respondents are forced to select one response option for each question. These kinds of questions are preferred in survey research because they are easier to quantify and subject to statistical analyses. Surveys have been used extensively in disaster

FIGURE 4.3 Methods of data collection.

research to study a wide variety of topics. For example, surveys have been administered to measure household preparedness levels, evacuation decision making, recovery outcomes, and people's willingness to pay for mitigation programs.

In designing a survey questionnaire, it is important to develop questions that are reliable and valid. *Reliability* is best described as a measure of consistency. In other words, reliable questions should elicit common responses in repeated administrations of a survey instrument. In reality, of course, a survey is administered only once to respondents, so it is important to spend a lot of time and effort crafting good questions. Pilot testing of surveys usually results in clear wording that respondents can understand and thus select responses that best fit their perceptions.

Validity is best described as a measure of accuracy. Valid questions should elicit accurate information on the phenomena they seek to address. If you are interested, for example, in understanding people's perceptions of the likelihood of a terrorist attack in their community, you do not want to ask questions that instead measure their fear of terrorism. The two concepts may be similar, but they are not the same. Indeed, to illustrate how they are actually two separate (albeit related) concepts, consider the hypothesis that those with higher levels of fear of terrorism will also perceive a greater likelihood of an attack.

Importantly, surveys typically involve *random sampling* techniques, whereby every person in the study population has an equal chance of being asked to participate. This is much better than convenience sampling in which researchers administer their surveys in a nonrandomized manner to people who are most readily available. While random sampling has many advantages, many studies still rely on convenience sampling (Norris 2006). The advantage of random sampling is that it ensures *representativeness* of a sample: the demographic, attitudinal, and behavioral characteristics of the people who complete the questionnaire should closely resemble those of others in the population who were not selected for participation. Thus, findings from properly conducted surveys are *generalizable*: statistics generated from the sample of study participants can be used to estimate and make projections about the attitudes and behaviors of others in the larger population. For example, national political polls that project how tens of millions of people will likely vote in an election are typically based on samples of approximately 1,000 respondents. That is the strength and power of applying mathematical principles and theorems to the study of social life.

4.5.2 Interviews

In some cases you may be less interested in making generalizations about a very large population and more interested in the experiences of a smaller, more select group of people or organizations. In those cases, you may find interviewing a more appropriate technique for gathering information than surveys. *Interviews* are focused conversations conducted to gain in-depth understanding of the views and experiences of respondents (Rubin and Rubin 2005). They can be conducted one-on-one or as part of a larger focus group (Peek and Fothergill 2009). Although interviews are similar to surveys in that they seek to obtain respondent answers to particular questions, they are different in several important ways.

First, while surveys ask standardized questions to all respondents, interviews are typically conducted with the assistance of an interview guide. Interview guides provide researchers with a list of topics to cover and some topical questions to ask but allow flexibility in the order in which they are covered. In contrast to the closed-ended questions common in surveys, interviews typically rely on open-ended questions designed to elicit thoughtful, detailed, and in-depth responses from interview subjects. For example, you might ask the head of a local agency or department, "What are the most important challenges your agency has faced in the days since the disaster?" In depth interviewing allows you to follow the thread of a conversation that may lead in a fruitful direction as interview subjects add depth and breadth to the topic you are studying. You may also uncover unexpected insights that yield greater understanding. These emergent pieces of data often generate productive lines of inquiry for a current study and future direction.

Second, instead of random sampling techniques, interview studies typically employ a more purposive approach. *Purposive sampling* involves selecting respondents to participate based on the relevance of their knowledge and experiences to the objectives of the study. For example, if you are interested in understanding how a recent disaster impacted those with special needs in your community, a large-scale survey may not be necessary. Instead, you might conduct interviews at nursing homes, local shelters, or other appropriate places. In addition to beginning with a purposive approach, interview studies often proceed through the use of snowball sampling. *Snowball sampling* is an approach to recruit additional participants to a study by getting recommendations from past respondents. For example, you might interview the director of public works about that department's role in responding to a recent disaster and he or she may recommend that you talk to specific people in the department to gain more detail. For disaster researchers, it may also be necessary to interview people in specific spatial zones such as the immediate impact area, outer areas, and nonaffected areas. Imagine, for example, being able to track the flow of resources into an area from the outside to the inside as a way to study donations management. Time sampling also matters with disasters: the first 20 minutes after impact certainly differ from the next 20 hours or 20 days (Killian 2002). Fatality management studies, for example, benefit from time sampling to determine how various disasters impact the ability to conduct search and rescue operations over time.

Finally, while a major objective of survey research is to generalize findings from a sample of respondents to a much larger population, interview studies and qualitative approaches to research generally follow a different approach (Lincoln and Guba 1985). Qualitative research assumes that social reality, rather than being patterned and predictable, is fluid and dynamic, and while different social settings may be similar, they will always exhibit important differences. Instead of generalizability, which assumes that patterns identified among a relatively small sample of people can be inferred to exist in a much larger population, qualitative researchers focus instead upon transferability. *Transferability* is the degree to which insights gained from studying one social setting or group of people are applicable to others. In emergency management, transferability is a very useful concept. While disasters may create unique challenges for communities impacted by them, they also produce many of the same problems. Thus, by studying how one community dealt with those problems, we can learn valuable lessons that may not be directly generalizable to another community but are certainly transferable.

4.5.3 Observations

Observational research involves the systematic identification of patterns and trends in a social setting. It is an invaluable tool for disaster researchers because it offers a holistic view of activities in a post-disaster environment. While researchers often use observations in conjunction with interviews to gain a more comprehensive understanding of disasters, in some cases they must rely heavily on observations because respondents may not be readily available for interviews or a language barrier may exist. There are several important issues to consider when conducting observational research. First, of course, you must decide what to observe. Every social setting involves a tremendous amount of activity, even when it appears that nothing meaningful is happening. After a disaster, when researchers may feel overwhelmed and bombarded with information, they must make critical decisions about focusing their observations (Spradley 1980).

Second, you must devise an effective strategy for recording observations. With so much activity over a relatively wide area, it is not realistic to think after a disaster that you will be able to carry your laptop computer everywhere and enter observations directly. More often researchers make notes of their observations throughout the day and enter them into a computer in more elaborate form later. *Visual methods* such as photographs and video recordings can supplement observations or serve as stand-alone techniques. In one unique study, researchers gave cameras to shelter residents to record their personal experiences, thus uncovering valuable lessons for shelter managers (Pike, Phillips and Reeves 2006).

Finally, researchers must make decisions about their degree of involvement in a social setting. *Participant observation* involves researchers becoming active members, at least to a degree, of the setting or group studied. PAR involves researchers and people in the setting who work together to improve some aspect of social life. For example, in a classic disaster study, Taylor, Zurcher, and Key (1970) worked alongside others in a community struck by a tornado, all the while making observations about the group's activities, and later wrote a book about the experience. *Nonparticipant observation* involves maintaining a distance from the activities observed to minimize the researcher's role in and impact on a group or setting studied. In this approach, the researcher attempts to act as a "fly on the wall" by quietly observing the group or setting. In most cases, researchers find themselves playing a role between full-fledged participant and nonparticipant observer.

As with interviewing, observational research is a useful tool for capturing dynamic social processes as they unfold. Thus, observational methods are most often used for gathering data during the *response* and *recovery* periods. During those phases, things happen very quickly. If events are not thoroughly documented "on the spot," valuable information will perish. By conducting systematic observations and recording them in notes, photographs, or videos, we can more accurately reconstruct what happened during the response phase and chart the progress of recovery.

In the immediate aftermath of a disaster, with so much happening in a relatively short and condensed time frame, the challenge for those interested in gathering systematic information is often deciding what exactly to observe. It is impossible, of course, to observe everything, so you have to determine the focus of your observations on particular topics or issues. For example, if you are seeking to improve and strengthen communications among various city departments during emergencies and disasters, you might observe and document interactions of departmental representatives at the emergency operations center when it is activated. In most cases, you will have multiple reasons for making observations, so a checklist of topics or issues upon which to focus may be helpful. In addition to the response and recovery phases, observation can also be a useful tool for gathering information about *preparedness*. Observations are often used, for example, in disaster drills and exercises to document what works and does not work and identify areas for improvement in the event of an actual disaster.

4.5.4 Archives

Archival information is another valuable source of data for those wanting to learn more about the impacts of disasters on communities (Wenger 1989).

Archives are documents that attest to or provide an account of historical happenings. As society has grown in complexity and developed new technologies for producing, recording, and storing information, the amount of archival information available has vastly expanded. Indeed, the documents of life, as Plummer (2001) refers to archives, abound and are literally all around us.

Archival sources of data include newspapers, organizational memos, after-action reports, minutes of meetings, transcripts of congressional testimony, and other useful information. The major advantages of using these kinds of data are that they are plentiful, often easily accessible, and usually inexpensive to obtain. Disadvantages are that archival collections may be scattered or disorganized, data storage and retrieval systems become outdated, documents are sometimes illegible, and, in some cases, items may have been destroyed intentionally.

Many studies in the field of disaster research are based on archival data. For example, Kreps and his colleagues conducted extensive research on archives maintained by the DRC to study organizational dynamics in the aftermaths of disasters (Kreps 1989). Similarly, Mendonça and his colleagues (2007) used archival data from the 1995 bombing of the Murrah Federal Building in Oklahoma City and the 2001 attacks on the World Trade Center to study improvisation among first responders to disasters, a topic that will be discussed in depth in Chapter 7.

Archival research may require considerable detective work as the effort may require you to move from public archives into those maintained privately by individuals and organizations. Documents present some challenges such as selective deposit by their creators (Webb et al. 1999), but they also generate useful insights, supplement other techniques, and allow a comparison of events on paper with realities, for example, the differences between a written response plan and an actual response effort.

Archives can provide useful information about the various phases of a disaster. Indeed, in launching a comprehensive study of a community and its experience with a disaster, the best place to start is often the local library. In terms of *preparedness*, published reports of special investigative commissions like those formed after September 11, 2001 and Hurricane Katrina can be valuable sources of information for understanding the degree to which various organizations were aware of potential threats and whether or not they took the threats seriously. A good example of the usefulness of these kinds of documents is a classic study by Barry Turner (1976) in which he argued that organizations often suffer from a "failure of foresight" by failing to think creatively and prepare for exigencies that in hindsight should have been foreseeable.

Although many *response* activities are unplanned, unscripted, and even undocumented, organizations nevertheless produce plenty of reports, memos, agendas, meeting minutes, and other documents that can be very useful. Archival data such as newspaper articles are well suited for studying recovery processes, particularly over the long term. Newspaper articles and other archives can also be helpful for gathering information about *mitigation*. Some researchers have examined challenges such as inter-group conflicts associated with community relocation—a strategy sometimes used in cases of severe environmental contamination (Shriver and Kennedy 2005). While these studies typically involve interviews and observations, they also tend to rely heavily on archival sources.

4.5.5 Spatial Tools

Recent advances in technology have dramatically expanded and enhanced our ability to gather massive amounts of data on all kinds of topics including disaster and emergency management. Laptop computers and other portable devices, for example, make it much easier for researchers to process information including observation notes and interview transcripts from the field. Digital voice recorders are much smaller and less obtrusive than old tape recorders and reel-to-reel machines that researchers carried into the field. Improved statistical software packages allow massive amounts of data such as those gathered from surveys to be analyzed rapidly and in increasingly sophisticated ways. All these advances have made the research enterprise much more efficient and far less daunting than it used to be.

In disaster research, perhaps the most important technological development with the greatest potential for advancing the field are those designed to enhance spatial data collection and analysis. Geographic information systems (GIS) are probably the most common and widely used spatial applications in the hazards and disaster area (Dash 2002; Thomas, Ertugay, and Kemeç 2006). These programs allow researchers to attach spatial coordinates to various sources of data, all of which can then be visually depicted on maps. With appropriate GIS software, users can overlay all kinds of information on top of their geo-coded data to show roads and bridges, waterways, and environmental hazards. In addition to GIS, researchers now have access to satellite imaging and remote sensing technologies that can be very useful after a disaster.

Spatial tools are becoming much more prevalent in the field of disaster research and as technologies continue to improve, it is likely that these tools will become even more common in the future. For researchers and emergency managers, these tools have many possible applications during the four phases of a disaster. To ensure *preparedness*, for example, maps locating hospitals, schools, nursing homes, hazardous facilities, and other sites can be produced and distributed. Additionally, survey data on levels of household preparedness could be geo-coded and mapped to provide emergency managers with snapshots of preparedness levels in their communities.

Researchers have also used GIS to identify and visually depict vulnerable populations in communities across the United States—those with high concentrations of poverty and high percentages of minority residents and those in close proximity to natural and technological hazards (Cutter 2001). GIS and remote sensing tools have also proven useful in the *response* phase, allowing researchers to rapidly, efficiently, and accurately conduct damage assessments based on visual displays of areas with high concentrations of damage. These tools can be valuable resources for emergency managers who need to prioritize response activities.

Spatial data collected during the response phase can serve as baseline data for assessing short- and long-term recovery in a community. As new maps and images are produced, they can be juxtaposed with earlier ones, allowing users to visually track recovery over time. Imagine, for example, the ability to spatially depict volunteer activities after a catastrophic event to allow better preparation for the next event (Greiner and Wikle 2008). As for *mitigation*, the maps used in the preparedness phase to identify hazardous places and vulnerable populations can and ideally would be used by city commissions, planning and zoning departments, and other public officials to make informed land use decisions that minimize future risks to their communities.

4.6 Ethics and Challenges of Disaster Research

An important consideration in all fields of research is ethics. For disaster researchers, ethical concerns are perhaps more salient than in other fields because they deal with events and circumstances that entail enormous human suffering. To some, Fritz's (1961) early characterization of disasters as "laboratories" for studying basic human social processes may seem callous and exploitative. Yet, if we want to enhance the safety of society, it is imperative that we study these tragic events to learn lessons from them that can be applied to the future. In other words, we hope that our research will produce tangible benefits to society in general and those who participate in our research in particular.

4.6.1 Research Ethics

While there are no definitive, universal standards of ethics against which to judge science and research, the U.S. government has provided helpful guidelines (Babbie 2011). The primary goal of these guidelines is to provide adequate protections to human subjects of research to minimize the risk of adverse effects—psychological, emotional, financial, or social—from their participation.

The first ethical guideline is *respect for persons*. To show appropriate respect for persons, researchers must demonstrate that subjects voluntarily consented to participate, that is, they were not tricked, misled, or coerced. Subjects must be informed of their right to withdraw their participation at any time without consequence; and researchers must take adequate measures to protect the confidentiality of information provided by subjects.

Benefits and risks constitute the second ethical guideline cited in federal policies governing research. Researchers must demonstrate that the benefits of the research to subjects, society, or the scientific community outweigh the potential risks to subjects. While the risks to subjects from social science research are far less consequential than the risks from research on new medicines or experimental treatments, we need to be mindful of and sensitive to the experiences of those who participate in our research.

The final ethical consideration is *justice*. This essentially means that both the risks and benefits of research should be distributed fairly in society. For example, it would be considered unjust if the only people who participated in test studies of new medicines were prison inmates or poor people in public hospitals. Similarly, it would be unjust if the new medicines that came from those studies were not made widely available but instead were reserved for a select group of fortunate or prominent people.

It is important to note that not all research involves the participation of human subjects. For example, as described in the previous section, archival and spatial data can be gathered without interactions with people. In many cases, however, we are required to interact with people to gather the information we need. For researchers at universities, like many of those whose work is cited throughout this book, that means getting approval for a study before going into the field. That approval comes from an institutional review board (IRB). IRBs are committees that exist at all universities that receive federal support for research. The job of an IRB is to review research proposals submitted by faculty researchers to ensure that they have provided adequate protections to their subjects based on the ethical guidelines described previously.

4.6.2 Research Challenges

In addition to providing adequate human subject protection, disaster researchers face other challenges in conducting studies. Of course, all research can be difficult, but the challenges of disaster research seem particularly pronounced. For example, disaster researchers face basic *logistical challenges* not present in other types of research. They must travel to disaster-stricken communities on very short notice, gain IRB approval for the research before they leave, find available and affordable lodging, and navigate debris-filled, barricaded communities upon arrival.

Researchers in all fields must find study participants and figure out ways to deal with those who decline participation. For disaster researchers, the problem of *respondent availability* and *accessibility* can be particularly pronounced. In studies aimed at understanding the impacts of disasters on ordinary citizens, researchers may have to travel to surrounding communities to track down survivors or visit with them in shelters or temporary "tent cities." Similarly, when researchers want to study public officials and their activities after a disaster (a common focus of research) they may find access very difficult for several reasons. First, it is possible or even likely that instead of working from their normal offices, the relevant public officials will work from an alternative temporary location such as an EOC or somewhere else in the community. Second, even when we locate such officials, it may be difficult for them to stop what they are doing and find time to talk with researchers. It is important, therefore, for researchers to be flexible and accommodating in the field.

In recent years a new phenomenon has made it more difficult for researchers to access potential respondents. Indeed, the events of September 11, 2001 led to a noticeable change in post-disaster environments. Specifically, in the era of concern about homeland security, disaster sites are increasingly treated like crime scenes. As a result, law enforcement agencies have ramped up their efforts to restrict access to disaster-stricken communities and public officials appear less willing to talk to researchers, reporters, and the public at large about their activities. This is a disturbing trend because, as stated previously, a major goal of research is to learn lessons from past disasters to prevent mistakes in the future. If officials are unwilling to talk publicly about their activities including their mistakes, the prospects for uncovering lessons learned are severely diminished.

Another prominent challenge in disaster research is dealing with *emotions* and *human suffering*. Disasters are tragic events. Although as researchers we approach them with a certain degree of scientific objectivity and emotional distance, the devastation caused by disasters cannot be totally ignored. Researchers in the field see the physical damage, social disruption, and human suffering caused by disasters. They also hear stories, both heroic and tragic, from respondents about what happened and can experience feelings of sadness, sympathy, and strong desires to help those suffering. One way of managing those feelings is to recognize the value of their own work. As stated previously, their studies may not produce immediate, tangible benefits to the community, but over time studies of disasters will contribute to a safer future.

Summary

The term *emergency management* conjures up many images, but for most people scientific research is probably not what comes to mind when thinking about the profession. Yet, as we have seen in this chapter, the profession of emergency management and the field of disaster research have much in common, including a desire to improve society's ability to prepare for, respond to, recover from, and mitigate against future disasters. As a future emergency manager, you will benefit from understanding the research methods described in this chapter and the research-based findings discussed throughout this book.

Whether you are interested in conducting a study of your own or finding out what others have already learned about a topic, this chapter provides a strong foundation to help you move forward. You are now familiar with the various methodological tools available for answering all kinds of disaster and emergency management-related questions: How prepared are households and businesses in my community for a future disaster? What kinds of problems did agencies and departments in my community confront in responding to a past disaster? What is the status of my community's recovery from a past disaster as a whole, for businesses, and for certain groups in the population? And, finally, how supportive are people in my community of a newly proposed mitigation measure?

Throughout your career, you will gain valuable knowledge through first-hand encounters with disasters. That kind of hands-on experience is essential to your professional development and will serve as a tremendous confidence builder. As we discussed in this chapter, there are many other sources of knowledge including research on which you can and should draw. Regardless of profession, whether practicing medicine or managing emergencies, experience matters, but it also important to keep up with research and stay abreast of the latest developments in the field.

Discussion Questions

1. Discuss the history of disaster research in the United States? Why did the field emerge in the middle part of the twentieth century. Who funded the early studies?

2. Which method of data collection (e.g., surveys, interviews, observations, archives, and spatial tools) is most interesting to you and which do you believe is the most useful? Provide an example of how you might use that methodology.

3. Locate and read a research article on a topic of interest to you published in one of the academic journals listed in Box 4.2. What was the primary research question? How did the researcher(s) gather data to answer the question? Do you agree with the findings? How could the research have been improved?

4. Imagine you work for a local emergency management office and your community was recently struck by a disaster, such as a tornado or a hurricane. The City Council would like to know what impact the disaster had on local businesses and how it will affect sales tax revenues, which are a primary source of revenue for local governments. How would you design a study to measure the effects of the disaster on local businesses?

5. What are some examples of ethical dilemmas that a researcher might face while studying a disaster-stricken community? What steps might she or he take to resolve those dilemmas?

Resources

- The U.S. Census Bureau regularly collects and disseminates data on communities and households throughout the country and much of the data is relevant to emergency managers. To learn more, visit the official website at www.census.gov.
- Both the Disaster Research Center at the University of Delaware (www.drc.udel.edu) and the Natural Hazards Center at the University of Colorado (www.hazards.colorado.edu) house libraries with vast amount of social science literature related to the social aspects of risks, hazards, and disasters.
- The United Nations Office of Disaster Risk Reduction maintains and shares extensive information about disasters worldwide through its International Strategy for Disaster Risk Reduction (www.unisdr.org).
- The Centre for Research on the Epidemiology of Disasters in Belgium maintains a database known as EM-DAT, the International Disaster Database, which provides information on the frequency, impacts, and consequences of disasters (www.emdat.be).

References and Recommended Readings

Babbie, Earl. 2011. *The Basics of Social Research*. Belmont, CA: Thomson Wadsworth.
Birkland, Thomas A. 1997. *After Disaster: Agenda Setting, Public Policy and Focusing Events*. Washington, D.C.: Georgetown University Press.

Birkland, Thomas A. 2007. *Lessons of Disaster: Policy Change after Catastrophic Disasters.* Washington, D.C.: Georgetown.

Bourque, Linda B., Kimberley I. Shoaf and Loc H. Nguyen. 2002. Survey Research. pp. 157–193 in *Methods of Disaster Research*, edited by Robert A. Stallings. Philadelphia, PA: Xlibris/International Research Committee on Disasters.

Browne, Katherine E. 2015. *Standing in the Need: Culture, Comfort, and Coming Home after Katrina.* Austin, TX: University of Texas Press.

Cutter, Susan L., ed. 2001. *American Hazardscapes: The Regionalization of Hazards and Disasters.* Washington, D.C.: Joseph Henry Press.

Dacy, Douglas C. and Howard Kunreuther. 1969. *The Economics of Natural Disasters.* New York: The Free Press.

Dash, Nicole. 2002. The Use of Geographic Information Systems in Disaster Research. pp. 320–333 in *Methods of Disaster Research*, edited by Robert A. Stallings. Philadelphia, PA: XLibris/International Research Committee on Disasters.

Fothergill, Alice and Lori Peek. 2015. *Children of Katrina.* Austin, TX: University of Texas Press.

Fritz, Charles E. 1961. Disaster. pp. 651–694 in *Contemporary Social Problems*, edited by Robert K. Merton and Robert A. Nisbet. New York: Harcourt, Brace and World.

Fumio Yamazaki, Masashi Matsuoka and Suha Ülgen. 2000. The Marmara Earthquake: A View from Space. pp. 151–169 in *The Marmara, Turkey Earthquake of August 17, 1999: Reconnaissance Report*, edited by Charles Scawthorn. Buffalo, NY: Multidisciplinary Center for Earthquake Engineering Research.

Gershon, R. M., Marcie S. Rubin, Kristine A. Qureshi, Allison N. Canton and Frederick J. Matzner. 2008. Participatory Action Research Methodology in Disaster Research: Results from the World Trade Center Evacuation Study. *Disaster Medicine and Public Health Preparedness* 2: 142–149.

Greiner, Alyson L. and Thomas A. Wikle. 2008. Episodic Volunteerism after Hurricane Katrina: Insights from Pass Christian, Mississippi. *International Journal of Volunteer Administration* 25(3): 14–25.

Gullion, Jessica Smartt. 2015. *Fracking the Neighborhood: Reluctant Activists and Natural Gas Drilling.* Cambridge, MA: MIT Press.

Hoffman, Susanna and Anthony Oliver-Smith, eds. 2002. *Catastrophe and Culture: TheAnthropology of Disaster.* Santa Fe: School of American Research Press.

Jenkins, Sharon. 1998. Emergency Workers' Mass Shooting Incident Stress and Psychological Reactions. *International Journal of Mass Emergencies and Disasters* 16(2): 181–195.

Kreps, Gary A., ed. 1989. *Social Structure and Disaster.* Newark, DE: University of Delaware Press.

Kreps, Gary A. 1995. Disaster as Systemic Event and Social Catalyst: A Clarification of the Subject Matter. *International Journal of Mass Emergencies and Disasters* 13(3): 255–284.

Killian, Lewis. 2002. An Introduction to Methodological Problems of Field Studies in Disasters. pp. 49–93 in *Methods of Disaster Research*, edited by Robert A. Stallings. Philadelphia, PA: Xlibris/International Research Committee on Disasters.

Lincoln, Yvonna S. and Egon G. Guba. 1985. *Naturalistic Inquiry.* Newbury Park, CA: Sage.

Mendonça, David, Carter Butts and Gary Webb. 2007. Learning from the Response to Two Extreme Events. *Contingency Today,* June 4.

Michaels, Sarah. 2003. Perishable Information, Enduring Insights? Understanding Quick Response Research. pp. 15–48 in *Beyond September 11th: An Account of Post-Disaster Research*, edited by Jacquelyn L. Monday. Boulder, CO: Natural Hazards Research and Applications Information Center.

Mileti, Dennis. 1999. *Disasters by Design: A Reassessment of Natural Hazards in the United States*. Washington, D.C.: Joseph Henry Press.

Neal, David M. 2012. The Survivability of Swedish Emergency Management Related Research Centers and Academic Programs: A Preliminary Sociology of Knowledge Analysis. *Sociologiska Forsking* 49(3): 227–242.

North, Carol. S., L. Tivis, J. C. McMillen, B. Pfefferbaum, J. Cox, E. L. Spitznagel, K. Bunch, J. Schorr and E. M. Smith. 2002. Coping, Functioning, and Adjustment of RescueWorkers after the Oklahoma City Bombing. *Journal of Traumatic Stress* 15/3: 171–175.

Norris, Fran H. 2006. Disaster Research Methods: Past Progress and Future Directions. *Journal of Traumatic Stress* 19(2): 173–184.

Norris, Fran H., M. J. Friedman and P. J. Watson. 2002a. 60,000 Disaster Victims Speak: Part II. Summary and Implications of the Disaster Mental Health Research. *Psychiatry* 65(3): 240–260.

Norris, Fran. H., M. J. Friedman, P. J. Watson, C. M. Byrne, E. Diaz and K. Kaniasty. 2002b. 60,000 Disaster Victims Speak: Part I. An Empirical Review of the Empirical Literature, 1981–2001. *Psychiatry* 65(3): 207–239.

Oliver-Smith, Anthony and Susanna Hoffman. 1999. *The Angry Earth: Disaster in Anthropological Perspective*. New York: Routledge.

Olson, Richard Stuart. 2000. Toward a Politics of Disaster: Losses, Values, Agendas, and Blame. *International Journal of Mass Emergencies and Disasters* 18: 265–287.

Peek, Lori A. and Alice Fothergill. 2009. Using Focus Groups: Lessons from Studying Daycare Centers, 9/11, and Hurricane Katrina. *Qualitative Research* 9(1): 31–59.

Pfefferbaum, B., J. A. Call and G. M. Sconzo. 1999. Mental Health Services for Children in the First Two Years after the 1995 Oklahoma City Terrorist Bombing. *Psychiatric Services* 50(7): 956–958.

Phillips, Brenda D. 2002. Qualitative Methods of Disaster Research. pp. 194–211 in *Methods of Disaster Research*, edited by Robert A. Stallings. Philadelphia, PA: Xlibris/International Research Committee on Disasters.

Phillips, Brenda D. 2014a. *Qualitative Disaster Research*. Oxford: Oxford University Press.

Phillips, Brenda D. 2014b. Qualitative Disaster Research Methods. pp. 553–556 in *The Oxford Handbook of Qualitative Research Methods*, edited by Patricia Leavy. Oxford: Oxford University Press.

Phillips, Brenda D. 2014c. *Mennonite Disaster Service: Building a Therapeutic Community after the Gulf Coast Storms*. Lanham, MD: Lexington Books.

Phillips, Brenda D., Deborah S. K. Thomas, Alice Fothergill and Lynn Pike, eds. 2010. *Social Vulnerability to Disaster*. Boca Raton, FL: CRC Press.

Pike, Lynn, Brenda D. Phillips and Patsilu Reeves. 2006. Shelter Life after Katrina: A Visual Analysis of Evacuee Perspectives. *International Journal of Mass Emergencies and Disasters* 24(3): 303–330.

Platt, Rutherford H. 1999. *Disasters and Democracy: The Politics of Extreme Natural Events*. Washington, D.C.: Island Press.

Plummer, Kenneth. 2001. *Documents of Life 2*. Thousand Oaks, CA: Sage.

Quarantelli, E. L. 1987. Disaster Studies: An Analysis of the Social and Historical Factors Affecting the Development of Research in the Area. *International Journal of Mass Emergencies and Disasters* 5: 285–310.

Quarantelli, E. L. 1994. Disaster Studies: The Consequences of the Historical Use of a Sociological Approach in the Development of Research. *International Journal of Mass Emergencies and Disasters* 12: 25–49.

Quarantelli, E. L. 2002. The Disaster Research Center (DRC) Field Studies of Organized Behavior in the Crisis Time Period of Disasters. pp. 94–126 in *Methods of Disaster Research*, edited by Robert A. Stallings. Philadelphia, PA: Xlibris/International Research Committee on Disasters.

Ritchie, Liesel Ashley and Wayne MacDonald, eds. 2010. Enhancing Disaster and Emergency Preparedness, Response and Recovery through Evaluation. *New Directions for Evaluation*, Number 126.

Rubin, Herbert J. and Irene S. Rubin. 2005. *Qualitative Interviewing: The Art of Hearing Data*. Newbury Park, CA: Sage.

Shriver, Thomas E. and Dennis Kennedy. 2005. Contested Environmental Hazards and Community Conflict over Relocation. *Rural Sociology* 70(4): 491–513.

Spradley, James P. 1980. *Participant Observation*. Fort Worth, TX: Harcourt, Brace, Jovanovich College Publishers.

Sylves, Richard. 2008. *Disaster Policy and Politics: Emergency Management and Homeland Security*. Washington, D.C.: CQ Press.

Taylor, James B., Louis A. Zurcher and William H. Key. 1970. *Tornado: A Community Responds to Disaster*. Seattle, WA: University of Washington Press.

Thomas, Deborah S. K., Kivanç Ertugay and Serkan Kemeç. 2006. The Role of Geographic Information Systems/Remote Sensing in Disaster Management. pp. 83–96 in *Handbook of Disaster Research*, edited by Havidán Rogríguez, E. L. Quarantelli and Russell R. Dynes. New York: Springer.

Turner, Barry A. 1976. The Organizational and Inter-Organizational Development of Disasters. *Administrative Science Quarterly* 21: 378–397.

Wachtendorf, Tricia. 2001. Building Community Partnerships Toward a National Mitigation Effort: Inter-Organizational Collaboration in the Project Impact Initiative. Invited paper presented at the annual workshop for the Comparative Study on Urban Earthquake Disaster Management, Kobe, Japan, January 18.

Wachtendorf, Tricia and Kristy Kompanik. 2000. An Ongoing Assessment of the Project Impact Implementation Process: Recommendations and Lessons Learned. Poster presented at the Annual Project Impact Summit, Washington, D.C., November 13.

Waugh, William. 2000. *Living with Hazards, Dealing with Disasters: Introduction to Emergency Management*. Armonk, NY: M. E. Sharpe.

Waugh, William. 2006. Shelter from the Storm: Repairing the National Emergency Management System after Katrina. *The ANNALS of the American Academy of Political and Social Science* 604: 288–332.

Webb, Eugene, Donald T. Campbell, Richard D. Schwartz and Lee Sechrest. 1999. *Unobtrusive Measures*, 2nd edition. Thousand Oaks, CA: Sage.

Wenger, Dennis E. 1989. The Role of Archives for Comparative Studies of Social Structure and Disaster. pp. 238–250 in *Social Structure and Disaster*, edited by Gary A. Kreps. Newark, DE: University of Delaware Press.

Wright, James D., Peter H. Rossi, Sonia R. Wright and Eleanor Weber-Burdin. 1979. *After the Clean-Up: Long-Range Effects of Natural Disasters*. Beverly Hills, CA: Sage.

Chapter **5**

Preparedness

Objectives

Upon completing this chapter, readers should be able to:

- Define preparedness and understand its relationship to response, recovery, and mitigation.
- Identify common types of preparedness activities and describe how prepared individuals and households, organizations, and communities are for disasters.
- Identify particular groups that remain at risk due to lack of preparedness and list suggestions for enhancing their readiness.
- Provide examples of preparedness initiatives at the state, national, and international levels.
- Identify potential places to work and volunteer in the field of preparedness.

Key Terms

- At-risk populations
- Disaster subculture
- Preparedness (household, organizational, community)
- Private sector
- Risk perception

5.1 Introduction

In this chapter, we will learn about preparedness, which serves as the most important phase prior to the onset of disasters and which can produce significant personal and social benefits (Stein et al. 2014). We will also learn that preparedness levels generally fall far short of what needs to be done. It is the work of the emergency manager and the public to ensure that they are both ready for disaster. To understand this problem, the first half of this chapter defines preparedness and outlines types of preparedness activities. The full range of preparedness activities includes educating the public for individual preparedness followed by emergency management agencies conducting training, drills, and exercises to ensure readiness. We will also learn about the startlingly low levels of preparedness for households, communities, and nations as well as the factors that influence preparedness. This chapter lays an important foundation for the chapter that follows on planning, often considered a subset of preparedness activities.

5.1.1 Defining Preparedness

Preparedness is a central concept in the fields of disaster research and emergency management, and numerous definitions have been suggested over the years (Drabek 1986; Gillespie and Streeter 1987; Kirschenbaum 2002; Mileti 1999; Tierney, Lindell, and Perry 2001). *Preparedness* commonly refers to activities undertaken prior to the onset of a disaster to enhance the response capacities of individuals and households, organizations, communities, states, and nations. But what does it really mean to "enhance response capacities?"

At the most general level, *enhanced response capacity* refers to the ability of social units to accurately assess a hazard, realistically anticipate likely problems in the event of an actual disaster, and appropriately take precautionary measures to reduce impacts and ensure an efficient and effective response. We will discuss specific types of preparedness activities in the next section, but for now the general point is that we can dramatically improve our ability to respond to disasters by taking appropriate actions before they ever strike.

By defining preparedness in a way that emphasizes improving response capacities, we make an important assumption about disasters. Despite the best efforts of societies to mitigate natural and technological hazards, we are assuming in this chapter that *disasters will occur*. That is not to say that some disasters cannot be prevented or that mitigation efforts should be abandoned. Rather, by assuming that disasters will occur, we are simply acknowledging the reality of modern living and encouraging appropriate protective actions. Households, organizations, and communities must continue to devise effective means for protecting themselves against the threat of disaster.

In discussing and thinking about preparedness, several important points should be kept in mind. First, preparedness can be viewed and

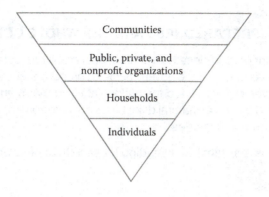

FIGURE 5.1 Levels of disaster preparedness.

measured at different *levels of analysis*. As Figure 5.1 illustrates, disaster preparedness is important at the individual, household, organizational, and community levels. Individuals and households, for example, can take protective measures such as storing first-aid kits to ensure their personal safety in the event of a disaster. Organizations can develop disaster plans and train employees on what to do in case of an emergency. And communities can stage communitywide disaster exercises and launch public education campaigns to inform people about hazards that exist in their communities. At an even higher level of analysis, nations of the world can enter into mutual aid agreements to provide disaster relief when a disaster strikes an impoverished country such as Haiti. Ultimately, preparedness is shared responsibility and successful efforts must involve the whole community (Box 5.1).

Second, we should keep in mind the varying *degrees of preparedness*. Disaster readiness is not a simple either-or proposition dictating that a household, organization, or community is *either* prepared *or* not prepared. Preparedness is a matter of degree, ranging from low to high, with some social units engaging in few or no preparedness activities and others undertaking as many precautionary measures as possible. Of course, most households, organizations, and communities fall somewhere between the two extremes and unfortunately, many lean toward the lower end of the continuum. We also know that levels of preparedness vary over time and across locations, and, as we will see later in this chapter, several important factors influence the number and type of preparedness activities undertaken by various social units.

Third, we lack a *standardized measure of disaster preparedness* at the community, state, national, and international levels of analysis. At the household and organizational levels of analysis, researchers typically use checklists to measure disaster preparedness, asking respondents to indicate which activities they have undertaken, many of which are described in the next section (Tierney et al. 2001). Using such checklists,

BOX 5.1 PREPAREDNESS AND THE WHOLE COMMUNITY

Recognizing that preparedness is a shared responsibility, it calls for the involvement of everyone—not just the government—in preparedness efforts. By working together, everyone can keep the nation safe from harm and resilient when struck by hazards, such as natural disasters, acts of terrorism, and pandemics.
Whole Community includes:

- Individuals and families, including those with access and functional needs
- Businesses
- Faith-based and community organizations
- Nonprofit groups
- Schools and academia
- Media outlets
- All levels of government, including state, local, tribal, territorial, and federal partners

The phrase "whole community" appears a lot in preparedness materials, as it is one of the guiding principles. It means two things:

1. Involving people in the development of the national preparedness documents.
2. Ensuring their roles and responsibilities are reflected in the content of the materials.

Source: www.fema.gov/whole-community-0, *(verbatim)*

we have learned a great deal about preparedness levels among households and organizations, including businesses, and identified numerous factors that influence preparedness levels. Preparedness is much more difficult to measure, however, at higher levels of analysis, including communities, states, and nations. At these higher levels of analysis, it is not simply a matter of how many items on a checklist have been performed. Rather, we must consider issues such as the strength and legitimacy of political institutions, intergovernmental relationships, locations and priorities of emergency management functions, social and financial capital, and other factors. In light of these measurement challenges, it is difficult to meaningfully compare communities, states, and nations in terms of disaster readiness (Simpson 2008).

Fourth, we must consider disaster preparedness in a *cultural context*. Culture is a central feature of every society that exerts a powerful influence over individual behavior. In talking about culture, sociologists and anthropologists typically distinguish material from nonmaterial elements. *Material culture* includes the clothes we wear, the houses we live in, the tools we use, the stories we write, the monuments we build, and other physical objects produced by societies. *Nonmaterial culture* covers shared values, our moral beliefs about right and wrong, the norms and rules governing our behavior, traditions, and the sense of collective identity that binds us together. Of course, the two elements of culture are closely interrelated. In the United States, for example, think about how values of individualism, competition, and material achievement are reflected by and embodied in the kinds of cars people drive, the houses they live in, and the places (often hazardous) where some choose to build them.

Just as culture influences decisions about buying cars and houses, it also profoundly shapes thinking about hazards and disasters (Webb 2007; Webb, Wachtendorf, and Eyre 2000). At the most general level, for individuals or social groups to attempt to mitigate or prepare for a future disaster, they must first believe that they can do something about the threat. However, this sense of self- and collective efficacy is not a cultural universal. In other words, not all societies believe they control their own destinies and can prevent disasters and other events from happening. Indeed, in many parts of the world, disasters such as earthquakes, floods, and tsunamis, are commonly viewed as "acts of God" (Ghafory-Ashtiany 2009; Schmuck 2000). As a result, local populations often develop fatalistic attitudes about disasters, attributing the widespread human suffering and loss of life to a kind of divine punishment and assuming that nothing can be done to prevent or prepare for future catastrophes.

It should be noted, however, that fatalism and apathy in the face of hazards and disasters are not limited to traditional, isolated, or impoverished regions. Even in the wealthiest and most developed countries, preparedness levels are generally low, risks may be ignored or underestimated, and dangerous decisions are made, laying the groundwork for future disasters. In the interest of promoting economic growth and development, for example, local planning commissions and city councils allow contractors to build neighborhoods in hazardous places such as flood-prone areas (Mileti 1999), and state and national governments approve high-risk ventures such as deepwater oil drilling without first considering and fully understanding the possibilities and consequences of catastrophic failures (Clarke 2005).

As these examples clearly demonstrate, culture has a major impact on disaster preparedness. In some societies, traditional religious beliefs prevent people from taking proactive precautionary measures and in others the pervasiveness of the profit motive impedes safety. It may be tempting to conclude that the key to increasing disaster preparedness is changing the way people think. Cultural beliefs, however, are firmly entrenched, slow to change, and strongly resistant to outside influence. In the context of disaster preparedness, we must respect cultural diversity and work hard to inform people about the hazards and risks they face, educate them about appropriate mitigation and preparedness measures, and motivate them to take action.

Another issue to keep in mind when thinking about preparedness is the value of the *all-hazards approach* to emergency management. As discussed throughout this book, communities face a wide range of hazards, risks, and disasters whose impacts are very similar. Thus, the typical preparedness activities discussed in the next section apply to all kinds of natural and technological disasters. Certainly some hazard-specific strategies such as installing shutters in hurricane-prone areas, purchasing an in-ground shelter in tornado-prone places, and storing a gas mask when living near a chemical weapons incinerator may be pursued. But for the most part the preparedness activities described in the next section are generic, that is, they apply to multiple hazard contexts. Rather than preparing for each threat separately—which is unrealistic—households, organizations, and communities can maximize the effectiveness of their preparedness efforts and make the most of limited resources by embracing the all-hazards approach. Basic provisions such as nonperishable food items, water, radios, flashlights, and batteries, are needed after any natural or technological disaster. The value of the all-hazards approach to planning and preparing for disasters is discussed in detail in Chapter 6.

Finally, it is important to remember that *preparedness is closely related to the other phases of emergency management*. It has already been noted, for example, that the primary goal of preparedness is to enhance response capacities, so the relationship between preparedness and response is straightforward. Although less obvious preparedness is also closely related to the mitigation and recovery phases. Drabek (1986, p. 21), for example, defines mitigation as "purposive acts designed toward the elimination of, reduction in probability of, or reduction of the effects of potential disasters," while preparedness activities "are predicated on the assumption that disasters of various forms will occur, but that their negative consequences may be…mitigated." As discussed in Chapter 6, preparedness is also relevant to the recovery phase in the sense that developing effective short- and long-term recovery plans prior to a disaster can facilitate a community's return to normalcy after an event has occurred.

5.1.2 Types and Levels of Preparedness Activities

Preparedness can involve a range of activities, whether you are an individual, a member of a household unit, or responsible in some way for a larger organization or the broader community. As Figure 5.2 depicts, some of these activities focus on securing life safety, some focus on protecting property and critical infrastructure systems, some focus on ensuring continuity of business operations, and others focus on educating the public about hazards and disasters. While each of us must accept some degree of responsibility

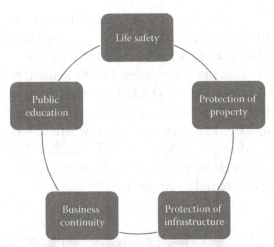

FIGURE 5.2 **Types of preparedness activities.**

for personal preparedness, as we will learn later, doing so may require support and assistance. Participating in neighborhood and community preparedness activities helps our neighbors and also allows them to help us if a disaster strikes. Furthermore, such efforts reduce the burdens of emergency responders, emergency managers, and community officials.

So, how prepared are we for disasters? The simple answer is not very. But some individuals and households are more prepared than others; some organizations have more experience with disasters and are thus better equipped to respond; and some communities devote greater resources to emergency management and disaster preparedness than others. For states and nations the picture is more complex and involves vast disparities in preparedness levels across countries and around the globe.

5.1.2.1 Individuals and Households

Individual and household preparedness activities are often measured by administering surveys that contain checklists of actions people may take prior to a disaster such as (Tierney et al. 2001, p. 34):

- Obtaining disaster-related information
- Attending meetings to learn about disaster preparedness
- Purchasing food and water
- Storing a flashlight, radio, batteries, and a first aid kit
- Learning first aid
- Developing and practicing a family emergency plan
- Bracing furniture (in earthquake-prone areas)
- Installing shutters (in hurricane-prone areas), or a safe room, or storm cellar (in tornado-prone areas)
- Purchasing hazard-specific insurance

As you can see from this list, individuals and households can take many steps to prepare for disasters. In light of all these possibilities, some people may become confused as to what exactly they should do to prepare. To simplify and clarify disaster preparation for the general public, the Federal Emergency Management Agency (FEMA) advises them to (1) get a disaster kit, (2) make a plan, and (3) be informed (www. ready.gov). FEMA recommends stocking disaster kits with three days' worth of basic provisions and other items, many of which appear on the list in Box 5.2. Photo 5.1 below depicts why it is important for households to prepare. Photo 5.2 shows how some homeowners prepared in advance.

PHOTO 5.1   Pottsboro, Texas, May 2015—Mobile homes near Lake Texoma are flooded following record rainfalls. (Courtesy of Gary Webb.)

PHOTO 5.2   Pottsboro, Texas, May 2015—Some homeowners in the community prepared for the floods by temporarily moving their mobile homes. (Courtesy of Gary Webb.)

BOX 5.2   PREPAREDNESS RECOMMENDATIONS

When preparing for a possible emergency situation, think first about the basics of survival: fresh water, food, clean air, and warmth.

Recommended Items to Include in Basic Emergency Supply Kit

- Water (1 gallon per person per day for at least three days) for drinking and sanitation
- Nonperishable food (at least three-day supply)
- Battery-powered or hand-crank radio and a NOAA Weather Radio with tone alert and extra batteries for both
- Flashlight and extra batteries
- First-aid kit
- Whistle to signal for help
- Dust mask to help filter contaminated air, plastic sheeting, and duct tape to shelter in place
- Moist towelettes, garbage bags, and plastic ties for personal sanitation
- Wrench or pliers to turn off utilities
- Can opener (if kit contains canned food)
- Local maps
- Cell phone with chargers

Source: www.ready.gov (*verbatim*)

Additional Items to Consider Adding to Emergency Supply Kit

- Prescription medications and glasses
- Infant formula and diapers
- Pet food and extra water for pet
- Important family documents such as copies of insurance policies, identification, and bank account records in a waterproof, portable container
- Cash or travelers' checks and change
- Emergency reference material such as a first-aid book or information from www.ready.gov
- Sleeping bag or warm blanket for each person; additional bedding if you live in a cold-weather climate
- Complete change of clothing including a long sleeved shirt, long pants, and sturdy shoes; additional clothing if you live in a cold-weather climate
- Household chlorine bleach and medicine dropper (When diluted 9 parts water to 1 part bleach, bleach can be used as a disinfectant; in an emergency, you can use it to treat water by adding 16 drops of household liquid bleach to a gallon of water. Do not use scented or color-safe bleaches or those containing other cleaners.)

(Continued)

BOX 5.2 (*Continued*)   PREPAREDNESS RECOMMENDATIONS

- Fire extinguisher
- Matches in waterproof container
- Feminine supplies and personal hygiene items
- Mess kits, paper cups, plates and plastic utensils, paper towels
- Paper and pencil
- Books, games, puzzles, and other activities for children

Source: www.ready.gov (*verbatim*)

Unfortunately several decades of research on individual and household preparedness reveals that overall preparedness levels are alarmingly low even in disaster-prone regions. In a comprehensive review of preparedness studies conducted after the 1970s, Tierney et al. (2001) found that most respondents in survey after survey reported that they had not undertaken a single preparedness measure, and most of those studies were conducted in areas with high seismic activity. In a more recent study Kapucu (2008) found a similar pattern of under-preparedness among households in hurricane-prone Florida with only 8% of respondents maintaining disaster supply kits stocked with enough basic provisions to shelter in place for three days (the FEMA recommendation).

While overall preparedness levels are low, there is some variation among households (Becker et al. 2014). Preparedness levels tend to be higher among those with previous disaster experience and those who are more knowledgeable about hazards and perceive the risk of a disaster as relatively high in the short term. Additionally, higher socioeconomic status and levels of education, the presence of children, and home ownership all contribute to higher levels of readiness. Conversely, the poor, racial and ethnic minorities, and those who do not own their homes tend to be far less prepared (Mileti 1999; Tierney et al. 2001). Some preparedness activities are very costly and even those that are relatively affordable to some may be cost-prohibitive to others. Thus, a major challenge for emergency managers is devising strategies to increase the preparedness levels of all the households in their communities (Becker et al. 2012). Our discussion of populations at risk later in this chapter will provide some insights into how this can be accomplished.

5.1.2.2 Organizations

For organizations including the public (government), private (business), and nonprofit sectors, typical preparedness checklists include many of the same activities that apply to households and some additional measures such as (Webb, Tierney, and Dahlhamer 2000, p. 84):

- Talking to employees about disaster preparedness
- Conducting drills and exercises
- Receiving specialized training
- Developing relocation plans
- Obtaining an emergency generator
- Purchasing business interruption insurance

As with households, organizations also vary in the degree to which they are prepared for disasters. Among public sector (i.e., governmental) organizations, for example, preparedness efforts of local emergency management agencies have improved significantly over the years (Wenger, Quarantelli, and Dynes 1986). As Mileti (1999) notes, these agencies are most effective when their activities are integrated into the day-to-day operations of local government, they coordinate their preparedness efforts with other community organizations, and engage in realistic disaster planning (Chapter 6) based on how organizations and people actually respond to disasters (Chapter 7). Police and fire departments and emergency medical services (EMS) units also devote significant effort to preparing for disasters, but researchers have identified a number of problems in the approaches these organizations take to preparedness (Mileti 1999; Quarantelli 1983; Tierney et al. 2001; Wenger, Quarantelli, and Dynes 1989). Most notably they tend to plan and prepare for disasters internally and in isolation from other community organizations, and they often fail to appreciate the significant difference between everyday emergencies and disasters. As a result, they often assume that disasters can be handled by simply expanding normal emergency procedures and fail to prepare at an appropriate scale.

Organizations in the private sector (i.e., businesses) are far less prepared than their public sector counterparts. Based on large-scale mail surveys of business owners in Tennessee, Iowa, California, and Florida, Webb et al. (2000) report that when faced with a variety of hazards, such as floods, hurricanes, and earthquakes, business owners do very little preparation. In response to a checklist of 15 possible preparedness activities, business owners on average reported engaging in only 4, the most common of which was obtaining first-aid supplies. While such safety steps are certainly important, they do little to ensure operational continuity, continued profitability, and long-term recovery and survival. As we will see in Chapters 8 (Recovery) and 10 (Public and Private Partnerships), businesses can play a vital role in a community's response to and recovery from a disaster.

5.1.2.3 Communities

Finally, at the community level of analysis, typical preparedness actions include many of the same organizational-level activities and some additional ones including (Tierney et al. 2001, p. 27):

- Testing sirens, emergency alert, and other warning systems
- Conducting educational programs and distributing disaster-related information
- Conducting multi-organizational drills and exercises
- Establishing mutual aid agreements with surrounding communities
- Maintaining an emergency operations center
- Conducting a hazard identification and risk analysis

As you can see from the lists of activities for organizations and communities, drills and exercises are fairly common. However, as with developing disaster plans (discussed in detail in Chapter 6), simply participating in a drill or exercise does not guarantee success when a disaster strikes. Disaster drills and exercises are most effective as preparedness tools when they are based on:

- Realistic scenarios, including accurate assumptions about disaster-induced demands, resource shortages, and communication difficulties.
- Accurate assumptions about how people and organizations respond to disasters, rather than myths of disaster (see Chapter 7).
- Meaningful involvement rather than ritualistic, symbolic, or mandated participation.
- Integration of multiple organizations and levels of government with citizen participants.
- Recognition that disasters do not always follow plans and often require participants to think creatively and improvise to solve unanticipated problems.

Unlike household and organizational preparedness levels, which have been measured in a relatively straightforward fashion by administering surveys containing checklists, measuring preparedness at the community level is much more difficult. As Simpson (2008) pointed out, if we wanted to compare two communities and determine which one was more prepared for a disaster, it would be very difficult if not impossible to do because we do not yet have a standardized community preparedness measure.

To fulfill that need and give communities a tool that will allow such comparisons, Simpson (2008) proposed and tested a *comprehensive community disaster preparedness index* for scoring communities based on several factors:

- Fire protection
- Emergency medical services

- Public safety and police
- Planning and zoning
- Emergency management office
- Other emergency functions (local emergency planning committees)
- Additional community measures (voluntary organizations)
- Hazard exposure
- Evacuation plans and warning systems
- Community resiliency and recovery potential (financial resources)

To test this new measure, Simpson (2008) compared two Midwest communities' overall preparedness levels: Sikeston, Missouri and Carbondale, Illinois. Which one was more prepared? According to Simpson's measure, Carbondale was 33% more prepared than Sikeston.

5.2 Factors Influencing Levels of Preparedness

In this section, we will find that preparedness is more than an issue of personal responsibility. We will uncover multiple factors that influence how much and how effectively people prepare for disasters. Before reading this section, you might refer to Box 5.2 to see how well you have prepared for a disaster. How would you grade yourself in terms of personal preparedness? Next, consider each factor explained vis-á-vis your own level of preparedness. Do any of them ring true?

5.2.1 Previous Disaster Experience

Survivors of a previous disaster are far more likely to prepare for another even if the first one affected them only indirectly. Watching the tragedy of Hurricane Katrina unfold prompted a massive evacuation when Hurricane Rita threatened Texas a few weeks later. For individuals and households, the positive effect of a recent experience with disaster on future preparedness is firmly established in the research literature (Tierney et al. 2001). Evidence also indicates that past disaster-experience stimulates preparedness at the organizational level, including in the private sector (Dahlhamer and D'Souza 1997). At the community level, repeated threats generate "local wisdom" that enhances the capacity to respond when disasters strike (Drabek 2010, p. 66).

Previous disaster experience tends to increase preparedness levels for several reasons. First, by witnessing a disaster, people and organizations develop *heightened hazard awareness and risk perception* that is positively associated with preparedness. Second, on the basis of past experience, people and organizations develop a more realistic understanding of what happens in a disaster and are thus more likely to take proactive measures to prevent or minimize potential problems from future disasters. Finally, at the community level, previous disaster experiences can contribute to the formation of what is called a *disaster subculture* of people and organizations that are extremely familiar with a threat and know what to do in a disaster (Drabek 2010). Think about "tornado alley," earthquake threats in California, and hurricane season in Florida.

While disaster subcultures often exhibit resilience in the aftermath of a disaster, they can also lead to *complacency and inaction*. As Drabek (2010, p. 67) suggests, certain "elements of the subculture … neutralize adaptive responses." He mentions hurricane parties at which people gather to "ride out" a storm despite evacuation warnings of public officials. Why do people who know better choose to stay? One reason may be that their experiences with a previous disaster were less traumatic and difficult than expected or possibly even positive. They may develop a *false sense of confidence* toward future disasters. Additionally, with the threat of a disaster always lingering in the background but usually not materializing, people tend to *normalize risk* and assume a disaster will not occur. As we will see in the next section, risk perception is an important influence on preparedness levels.

5.2.2 Risk Perception

Anyone who has watched driver education films and then ignored speed limits or traffic signs understands immediately that risk is not always respected. "It won't happen here … or to me" is a common response of people questioned about their own risks. With so many risks associated with modern living, we constantly judge what is safe and what is not. In making those judgments, we almost never calculate the statistical probabilities of illness, injury, or death. Instead, we draw on past experiences, pay vague attention to the warnings of experts, and sometimes consciously decide to take our chances. Think about the number of people who still smoke cigarettes despite their proven deleterious health effects and drivers who refuse to buckle up even when confronted with the prospects of traffic tickets, property damage, injury, or death in an accident.

Smoking and driving without a seat belt are examples of risky behaviors that present reasonably high chances of causing negative impacts. How do we act toward risks that have much lower chances of happening? Consider disasters, commonly called *low-probability/high-consequence events*. They are not nearly as common as other types of threats but have the potential to produce devastating effects. Thus, a major challenge for emergency managers is convincing a skeptical public, budget-strapped leaders, and overextended division heads and directors in local government to spend time and money to prepare for something that may not ever happen. People and organizations are much more likely to prepare when they perceive a risk as highly likely in the short-term (Tierney et al. 2001).

Fortunately, research suggests that emergency managers can influence risk perceptions and promote greater levels of preparedness in their communities via effective risk communication (Faupel, Kelley, and Petee 1992; Mileti 1999; Tierney et al. 2001). Risk communication is intended to educate people and organizations about the hazards they face, inform them about risks and likelihoods that the hazards will produce disasters, and persuade them to take appropriate measures to protect themselves and better meet the challenges resulting from disasters. Risk communication, including educational campaigns to raise hazard awareness, is most effective when it is delivered through multiple channels, consistent across the channels, details the nature of threats and their possible impacts, specific about what people and organizations can do to protect themselves, and perceived as coming from credible sources (Mileti and Fitzpatrick 1993). As we will see in Chapter 7, issuing disaster warnings is a specific risk communication used when a disaster is imminent or has already begun. In this chapter, we are referring to ongoing risk communication utilized during normal times.

5.2.3 Populations at Risk

A persistent theme throughout this text is that disasters are not equal opportunity events. Some groups bear disproportionate risk, especially when they already face exacerbating factors such as poverty. People in less developed nations bear the highest risks, as evidenced when over 300,000 died in the Indian Ocean tsunami of 2004 and about that same number perished in the Haiti earthquake of 2010. As Box 5.3 explains a community vulnerability analysis is an effective strategy that can be undertaken in the preparedness phase to identify those populations in our communities that are at greatest risk and most vulnerable to the impacts of disasters.

5.2.3.1 Race and Ethnicity

Even in developed nations, some groups are more vulnerable to risks. Hurricane Katrina caused disproportionate deaths among African Americans (Sharkey 2007). Was race the only factor? No. The answer lies in preparedness and planning at all levels. People living in urban areas lack private transportation and when plans are not in place to evacuate those at risk, they cannot leave. Urban areas such as New Orleans have higher percentages of African American residents. If those at risk and those who prepare do not coordinate efforts in advance and deploy transportation assets, these residents cannot leave. Older residents, for example, awaited social security and disability checks so that they could travel and buy gas, food, and medicines. Because Katrina hit at the end of the month, they lacked the financial resources to evacuate—and would have been hard-pressed to do so even if their checks had arrived.

BOX 5.3 COMMUNITY VULNERABILITY ANALYSIS

The first step important to any kind of preparedness, response, recovery, or mitigation initiative is a hazard identification and a subsequent analysis of the risk it poses to people and places. The next step is to map the hazards. Many existing tools such as flood-plain maps and other resources from government agencies can help you with this. As a start, visit pages of the U.S. Geological Survey (www.usgs.gov), the National Hurricane Center (http://www.nhc.noaa.gov/), and the Office of the Federal Coordinator of Meteorology (www.ofcm.gov). Hazard-specific pages may also provide information such as the Tornado Project (http://tornadoproject.com/). These resources will be enormously useful in your efforts to identify the various natural, technological, and human-induced threats facing your community.

Next, you will want to consider the overall risks to your community posed by these hazards. For example, you will need to identify the locations of utilities, infrastructure, health care facilities, and other areas critical to the community. You will want to pay particularly close attention to weakened structures that may pose increased risks, such as dams and levees.

You will also need to improve your understanding of the local population in terms of where people are most concentrated and which groups are most vulnerable. Certain populations may merit increased attention, for example, the locations of nursing homes and elementary schools. Census data (www.census.gov) will provide basic overviews of who lives in your community, the number of poor and elderly, local languages, and the ages of area housing. Census data are not always complete, however, and may mask the existence of some populations including new arrivals, immigrants, tourists, predisaster homeless, and even student populations.

In addition to locating critical infrastructure systems and understanding population dynamics, you will also need to assess the robustness of the local economy. For example, how strong is the business sector? Is it sufficiently robust economically to survive a disaster financially and physically? How strong is the tax base? It is not enough to consider only major employers. Agriculture operations, food producers, small and home-based businesses, and temporary labor must also be included.

Another element often overlooked is the environment. All communities include ecologically sensitive areas and animal life that should be considered for disaster impacts, particularly from hazardous materials. By knowing where such areas exist, a task as simple as alternative transportation routing of dangerous chemicals may safeguard both people and places.

By knowing your community, which means involving area agencies and leaders in the effort, your risk analysis will be more robust. A particularly useful (and free) tool for estimating losses from hurricanes, earthquakes, and floods is *Hazus-MH*. FEMA provides this software to assess economic, societal, and physical impacts from its website (http://www. fema.gov/hazus). The Hazus-MH software illustrates risk graphically and

(Continued)

BOX 5.3 (*Continued*)   COMMUNITY VULNERABILITY ANALYSIS

spatially to enable assessments leading to preparedness campaigns, planning initiatives, response operations, and mitigation projects.

Once you have completed a robust hazard identification and risk analysis, you are ready to develop an educational campaign to inform the public about the hazards in the community and recommend appropriate preparedness measures. Astute preparedness efforts account for both past and present disasters. Along with a risk analysis, a hazard identification takes on a new life as it demonstrates how disasters have the potential to hurt people, property, and animals. Reducing that risk is the work of the emergency management professionals and volunteers.

Sources: FEMA, Thomas et al. 2010

Historic patterns of segregation tied to lingering effects of prejudice and stereotypes increase preparedness challenges for some racial and ethnic minority groups (Heinz Center 2002). Hazardous materials sites, for example, tend to be closer to minority populations than to locations where dominant groups reside (Bullard 1990). Such sites expose minority populations to higher risk. Recent research suggests that Native Americans are also disproportionately exposed to technological hazards such as oil refineries and other petroleum-based operations (Shriver and Webb 2009).

Those involved in preparedness and planning also fail to understand the cultural processes important to minority groups. Some researchers have found that minority groups delay evacuation until they gather their family members (Lindell and Perry 2004; Perry and Mushkatel 1986). In some racial and ethnic groups, multiple generations living in multiple locations may have to be located and coordinated. Longer warnings specific to the populations likely to be affected are needed.

Lingering effects of prejudice also mean that minorities, especially older residents, are more likely to live in weak structures that fail when disasters occur (Dash 2010). Exposure, damage, and injury also lead to higher rates of psychological trauma for racial and ethnic minorities (Norris et al. 2002a, b). For racial and ethnic minorities with low incomes, the challenges to prepare for and respond to disasters increase. In short, building the capacities of those at risk by actively targeting and involving them in readiness efforts is crucial. Doing so in culturally appropriate ways is even more important.

5.2.3.2 Senior Citizens

Senior citizens represent particular concerns although research about their disaster experiences remains scattered and uneven (Bolin and Klenow 1988; Friedsam 1962; Kilijanek and Drabek 1979; Peek 2010; Poulshock and

Cohen 1975). Older residents of many nations often live at low income levels. Their resources simply do not cover the costs of preparedness items. People are told to have food, water, and medications on hand, but it may not be possible to do so. Many seniors stretch minimal budgets to cover living costs and this impedes their abilities to prepare for future events. Government plans and personal funds may not allow seniors to purchase adequate medications for future use so having them on hand for an evacuation may not be possible. Chronic medical conditions may decrease willingness to evacuate or move to a shelter and seniors often assume that the comfort of home with familiar resources is a better choice.

Other conditions exacerbate the challenges facing some senior citizens. Older residents, particularly men, may be socially isolated (Klinenberg 2002). For preparedness and warning response purposes, links to others through social networks increase the chances that people will get information and be able to respond with adequate support (Peek 2010). It is critical that community organizations, the faith-based sector, neighbors, family members, and friends reach out to widows, people who live alone, and other older residents when disaster threatens. The combination of gender-based isolation with age and/or poverty may explain why so many older African American men died during Hurricane Katrina (Sharkey 2007).

It is not enough to simply assume that seniors are at risk; it is vital to understand the combinations of factors that increase potential impacts. Consider, for example, an older woman who may be fully independent, enjoy rich networks, and have sufficient resources. The prevalence of osteoporosis is higher among women and increases with age. The medical condition of our example in combination with her gender and age increases her potential for fracture. Blizzards increase slip and fall injuries, tornadoes launch projectiles, and earthquakes topple bookcases. However, because average incomes of women typically fall below those of men, a woman is more likely to experience considerable financial challenges. She may not qualify for federal loans; available grants may not be sufficient to help her recover (Childers 2008). Frail elderly need particular attention due to the risks they may experience from a disaster event (Eldar 1992; Fernandez et al. 2002).

By targeting vulnerable populations in preparedness efforts, particularly public education tied to action initiatives, we can lessen disaster impact. In Florida and Alabama, senior centers have partnered with state agencies and local communities. They created the safe center-safe senior concept and constructed or used existing senior centers for disaster locations. With clearly visible blue roofs, the centers normally host typical senior center events and activities. But they also distribute preparedness information and convert to evacuation destinations, public shelters, and recovery centers as needed. Because the centers are familiar and people know the locations will be ready for their needs, they are more likely to use them in a disaster. The centers involve familiar and trusted social networks to prepare and respond to senior citizens facing threats and are thus far more likely to be effective.

5.2.3.3 People with Disabilities

Similar challenges exist for people with disabilities who tend to have lower incomes and until recently have not been targeted for preparedness activities. After Hurricane Katrina, the Louisiana Department of Rehabilitation had to work for nearly a year to locate the mobility devices of people with disabilities. In the massive evacuation of New Orleans after the flooding, many of those devices remained abandoned in the airport. People were hurriedly flown to safety without their wheelchairs and other critical resources. In public shelters, workers struggled to provide sign language interpretation, adequate nutrition, and assistive tools. People with disabilities remained longer in public shelters than others due to a lack of accessible temporary homes.

Conditions in the United States changed after Hurricane Katrina. The National Organization on Disability, FEMA, and the National Council on Disability led important preparedness efforts ranging from developing evacuation protocols to training first responders to move people with disabilities. A particularly important step has been involving people with disability organizations and their advocates in preparedness and planning efforts. Most recently, FEMA called on each state to include disability concerns in designing post-disaster housing (Clive et al. 2010; FEMA 2010; Government Accountability Office 2006; National Council on Disability 2009; National Organization on Disability 2005; Phillips 2009; Phillips et al. 2010).

To prepare people with disabilities and the communities and agencies that support them, the starting point is to assume such people are and can be independent, make decisions, and take care of their own needs. Preparedness efforts and planners often assume that disability equates to inability when this is simply not true. The current term in use is to prepare and plan around *functional needs* that typically include ensuring that evacuation personnel, shelters, and others are prepared to support people with varying communication (language, speaking ability, comprehension); supervisory (dementia); transportation (accessible evacuation vehicles); and medical needs (Kailes and Enders 2007). Medical needs require considerable preparedness and planning. It is essential that individuals are ready to be transported or to evacuate with their medications, assistive devices, and service animals. Those providing transportation and shelter must be adequately prepared to host and support individuals with medical needs (Klein and Nagel 2007). This is particularly important for congregate populations whose medical needs vary and who may require advanced medical support in a functional needs shelter. Providing continuity of care is critical for those undergoing dialysis, cancer treatment, and similar continuing medical needs. Health care offices and staff can assist by conducting business continuity planning and coordinating with those involved in disaster preparedness and planning to support their patients (Phillips 2009).

5.2.3.4 Children

Children constitute another group that should be covered by preparedness efforts. Schools conduct fire drills and may hold tornado or earthquake drills, but children may not know how to respond when a disaster occurs. We were vividly reminded of the importance of preparing our schools for disasters in May 2013, when a devastating tornado swept through Moore, Oklahoma, destroying numerous homes and buildings, including an elementary school (Photo 5.3). While there are many activities school administrators can undertake to prepare for disasters, children may not be at school where responsible adults can guide them when a disaster occurs. Children home alone, for example, may not know that a hazardous material has spilled nearby or where to go when a major earthquake knocks down furniture (Phillips and Hewett 2005). Research indicates that places such as day care centers and recreational facilities where children gather are not adequately prepared (Peek 2010).

Children can learn about area hazards and even become actively involved in their own preparedness. The Red Cross offers courses and online materials as do other national agencies and NGOs. Working with children to prepare them for what they may face alone or with adults will make them more resilient and more likely to survive and recover from the psychological trauma associated with disaster.

Psychological trauma is not the only issue that schools and similar facilities must manage when disaster occurs. After the September 11, 2001 attacks, FEMA assisted New York City schools with:

- Air monitoring and cleaning
- Lost instructional time

PHOTO 5.3   Plaza Tower Elementary school, Moore, Oklahoma 2013. (Courtesy of Jocelyn Augustino/FEMA.)

- Transportation costs
- Loss of perishable food
- Textbooks
- Student relocation
- Supplies and equipment
- Structural and safety inspections
- Crisis counseling

Families, child care centers, and schools bear responsibilities for preparing children to face disasters. Schools frequently conduct tornado and fire drills and require personnel to have first-aid skills. It is important to move beyond those basic steps because disaster can strike without notice. Having trained people who have prepared and drilled for a variety of scenarios on hand will result in quicker action that will save lives.

The age of a child makes a difference too. Younger children require frequent training with rewards for mastering behaviors. Older children also benefit from training and drills and can also learn from materials included in their school curricula. To prepare children, break tasks to be learned into steps. Ask first responders, emergency managers, and other disaster professionals to confirm that your training is complete and you have not forgotten an important item.

Many parents, for example, teach their children to drop and roll if clothing catches on fire. What they often miss is telling their children to "keep rolling." In training children, model the behavior you want and train them individually. Do not assume they will do what you want them to do and do not believe them when they say they know how to do it. Train and reward, and then train and reward again. Reward children positively to reinforce the behavior, and praise them for correctly following the steps.

5.2.3.5 Gender

Parents serve as critical links to children affected by disaster and some parents have a harder time preparing. This is particularly so for low-income and single parents. Female-headed families represent the largest group of single parents and according to the U.S. Census nearly a third of them live below the poverty line.

Gender, often coupled with income, matters. It influences preparedness in several ways. Historically, women have been excluded from emergency preparedness and planning efforts in what has largely been a male-dominated field (Enarson 2008; Enarson and Phillips 2008). Does representation matter? Absolutely, because presence at the preparedness and planning table surfaces concerns that others may not recognize. When Hurricane Andrew struck Florida, researchers learned how single mothers struggled to protect their homes without adequate resources. The storm severely damaged their homes, and they faced difficult battles securing recovery resources while they worked and cared for their children (Morrow and Enarson 1996). After a flood in Grand Forks, North Dakota, women who owned businesses lost their inventories and assets (Enarson 2001). Smaller businesses, many of which are owned by women, are less likely to have prepared and are thus more likely to fail.

The World Health Organization (WHO 2005, see Resources section) offers a gender-sensitive disaster assessment tool. WHO encourages us to think through how gender influences people in disaster situations. Preparedness campaign information is typically distributed via brochures and various outreach efforts. WHO asks us to consider those who have less access to that information because they lack mobility, Internet access, and literacy or may be subject to social isolation or restrictions formed by culture, religion, or patriarchy.

In short, we need to make women and girls visible in disasters so that they experience appropriate advance preparedness measures that decrease suffering and lead to quicker recovery (Fordham 1998). Preparedness thus means ensuring that those who provide relief do so in a gender-sensitive manner. Organizations involved in setting up shelters after the Indian Ocean tsunami realized too late they failed to consider health, hygiene, and privacy for girls and women, have resources on hand for pregnant and lactating mothers, and prevent personal violence (Phillips, Jenkins, and Enarson 2010). Concern also erupted over the potential for exploiting women and girls through human trafficking.

Again, the lesson is to involve the population at risk in preparedness and planning and address areas where personal resources fall short. Actively involving women's organizations such as shelters for battered women, lactation support organizations, and faith-based organizations that focus on elderly women is an important first step. WHO recommends basic principles to guide those involved in preparedness and response efforts:

- Involve women in decision making at all levels: individual, household, and community.
- Collect data on disaster impacts on women and girls; then prepare and plan accordingly.
- Identify and prepare for sex-specific needs.
- Focus on socially excluded women such as widows, heads of households, and women with disabilities.

5.2.3.6 Language

Language is another facet of culture that must be considered in preparedness and planning efforts. Language is the foundation of culture and the means by which people share information and connect. Accents, word choices, and language matter when designing brochures and outreach efforts and issuing warnings. Those at risk are more likely to listen when the person reaching out to them sounds like them and speaks their language. Using the language of a culture increases the credibility and trustworthiness of the speaker or author, especially with people who were previously excluded or harmed.

Language makes a difference in educating people about risks they face. Speaking the most common language in an area does not guarantee that all people will receive preparedness information. People who are hard of hearing (including senior citizens) or deaf will not get spoken messages. Presenting information from the view of a literate person excludes people with lower literacy levels from those who cannot read well or at all to those who do not know the language well, including tourists, recent immigrants, and family members from other countries (Morrow 2010).

Language makes a difference because people grasp content more effectively when it is presented in a familiar voice, using understood words or symbols—someone who sounds like they do (Mitchell 2007). The level at which information is presented matters too. Literacy levels for preparedness information should be pretested with a given population. A number of tools exist to test the reading levels of documents. One is the Flesch–Kincaid method. Such tools help ensure that preparedness information is readily understood. If you have ever tried to read the statistics section of a scholarly journal, perhaps you understand. Think also about grandparents or children who have different reading levels and people working on your campus who may have low literacy levels. Not everyone can read well, but they all face the same disaster threats.

5.2.3.7 Pre-Disaster Homeless

Another group that should be considered is people who are homeless before a disaster occurs (Phillips 1996). There are several categories of homeless people. First are the people we see on the street who are homeless every day. Second are people who are marginally housed and live doubled or tripled up with family or friends and join the first group as circumstances require. When Hurricane Mitch struck Honduras in 1998, an estimated 10,000 street children died. In many countries including the United States, families with children constitute the most rapidly growing group of homeless people. Recent concern focuses on homeless returning war veterans with disabilities.

Clearly, people who are homeless are not there by choice, but from circumstances often beyond their control. Organizations that reach out to and connect with the homeless via soup kitchens, mobile health care units, social workers, and faith-based activities represent the links most likely to be able to prepare these extremely vulnerable people for disasters.

5.2.3.8 Pets

Many of you probably have pets you consider important members of your family. Have you thought through how to prepare them for a disaster (Photo 5.4)? You have a personal responsibility to get them ready for a disaster because they are critically vulnerable to weather, fire, flying debris, and more. The American Society for the Prevention of Cruelty to Animals (ASPCA) recommends that you start with a few basic steps. First, put a rescue alert sticker on your home. Second, take animal training classes to increase your ability to bond with and help your pet during an emergency. Third, arrange for a safe haven for your pet that might be another family member or friend who can take in your dog, cat, bird, or other beloved pet or a pet shelter. Fourth, develop a pet preparedness kit (Federal Highway Administration). At a minimum it should contain:

- Proof of vaccination and veterinary records
- Licenses, rabies, and identification tags
- Two weeks of food, water, and medications
- Bedding and toys
- Litter box, litter, and a scoop
- Food and water bowls
- Information on medication and feeding schedules
- Newspapers, pee pads, cleaning supplies
- Collars, leashes, muzzles, harnesses
- First-aid kit
- Manual can opener and spoons
- Stakes and a break-proof rope or tie down

Who will evacuate with their pets? The best predictor is the level of attachment to their pets (Heath et al. 2001). Without us, pets remain at risk for their lives. In recent years, a number of states and emergency management agencies have partnered with other organizations to establish best practices for pet preparedness and response. Formalized planning has taken place

PHOTO 5.4 Hurricane Gustav, 2008. Pet evacuation near Beaumont, Texas. (Courtesy of Patsy Lynch/FEMA.)

and many efforts have been integrated into local, state, and national planning initiatives, usually through Emergency Support Function 11 which falls under the U. S. Department of Agriculture. The American Veterinary Medical Association (AVMA) established protocols for the care of animals and both community and professional veterinarian groups have collaborated to prepare and care for animals in pet and livestock shelters. The protocol at present, particularly in hurricane areas, is to evacuate animals with their owners. The AVMA and others have provided financial resources to some states in high-risk areas for the purchases of appropriate pet transportation vehicles.

Ideally, pets and their human caregivers enjoy co-located shelters—they are sheltered next to (but not with) each other. Livestock are harder to accommodate but increasingly county fairgrounds are used to shelter animals outside impact areas. Owners retain responsibility to care for their animals with the support of local animal care organizations and veterinarians. A veterinary medical assistance team (VMAT) may provide additional care and veterinarian schools have provided emergency care during past disasters. Pet preparedness not only saves the lives of our beloved animals, but also serves a human function. Sheltering animals with owners spurs evacuation and reduces the chances that people will return to damaged and dangerous areas to rescue their pets (Heath et al. 2000).

5.3 Preparedness Initiatives at State, National, and International Levels

Earlier in this chapter we discussed levels of preparedness at the household, organizational, and community levels, and we pointed out that preparedness levels tend to be low but with variations. We also identified various factors including risk perception, previous disaster experience, and others that influence preparedness levels. In discussing community preparedness, however, we noted that because of the lack of a standardized measure of preparedness, it is difficult, if not impossible, to make meaningful comparisons across communities. To do so at the state, national, and international levels is even more problematic. Nevertheless, in this section we discuss specific examples of preparedness initiatives at these higher levels of analysis. Our goal is not to measure how much various states, and nations are doing but instead to gain a sense of what can be and is being done to prepare for disasters at every level.

5.3.1 Examples of State-Level Preparedness Initiatives

Preparedness initiatives at the state and national levels typically involve educational campaigns, large-scale drills and exercises, and the development of disaster warning systems. A good example of a state-level educational campaign is the *Ready Oklahoma* campaign administered by the Oklahoma Office of Homeland Security (http://www.ok.gov/homeland/ Ready_Oklahoma/). This program urges individuals and households, organizations, neighborhoods, and businesses to prepare for all kinds of disasters. The activities it recommends are similar to those described in the checklists earlier in this chapter and consistent with the recommendations of FEMA's *Ready.gov* campaign mentioned earlier and described below in more detail. Importantly, specific information is provided for the elderly, those with disabilities, pet owners, and businesses. In other words, this campaign addresses the issues raised in this chapter about populations at risk.

Another example of a state-level preparedness initiative is the *Great Shake Out* earthquake drill campaign that started in California but has since widened its reach (http://www.shakeout.org/). This is an earthquake drill that aims to educate the public about earthquakes and how to prepare for them. As part of the drill, people are instructed to "drop, cover, and hold on," and practice how they would protect themselves in a real earthquake. In 2008, a shakeout drill was conducted in Southern California and the program was expanded in 2009 to include all 58 counties in California. That year, 6.9 million people participated in the drill, and in 2010, there were 7.9 million participants. The drill has been extended even further to include other countries and in 2015 more than 40 million people worldwide registered to participate.

5.3.2 Examples of National-Level Preparedness Initiatives

In many instances, national preparedness initiatives are prompted by major disasters (Mileti 1999). For example, as discussed in more detail in Chapter 7, in the months following the September 11, 2001 terrorist attacks, the U.S. Department of Homeland Security (DHS) developed the *Homeland Security Advisory System* (HSAS), a color-coded alert system to inform the public and governmental organizations about the risk of a future terrorist attack. That system drew substantial criticism, and in January 2011, DHS announced that it would be replaced by a new warning system (www.dhs.gov).

Other preparedness initiatives at the national level include FEMA's *Ready. gov* and its *National Exercise Program* (NEP). *Ready.gov* is an educational campaign for encouraging individuals, households, organizations, and communities to prepare for disasters. The campaign provides vast amounts of information on its website, including specific information for children, the elderly, the disabled, military families, pet owners, and businesses. Importantly, the campaign recognizes the need to address the special needs of populations at risk.

Since 2000, FEMA has conducted annual exercises to assess response capabilities and identify problems of inter-governmental coordination in catastrophic scenarios. In 2007, these Tier I national level exercises (NLEs), formerly known as TOPOFF due to the involvement of top officials from various federal agencies, became part of the NEP. The primary purpose of the NEP is to coordinate federal, state, and regional exercise activities. In the past, NLEs have been based on simulated large-scale terrorist attacks. The 2011 scenario was a catastrophic earthquake along the New Madrid fault in the central U.S. states involved in the exercise included Alabama, Arkansas, Kentucky, Illinois, Indiana, Mississippi, Missouri, and Tennessee. You can find more information at http://www.fema.gov/national-exercise-program.

The most recent and significant attempt to improve disaster preparedness at the national level in the United States is the establishment of the National Preparedness Goal. On March 30, 2011, President Obama issued Presidential Policy Directive/PPD-8: National Preparedness, which directed the Secretary of Homeland Security to establish a National Preparedness Goal and identify core capabilities needed to achieve that goal. The purpose of the Goal is to achieve "A secure and resilient Nation with the capabilities across the whole community to prevent, protect against, mitigate, respond to, and recover from the threats and hazards that pose the greatest risk" (U.S. Department of Homeland Security 2011, p. 1). As shown in Figure 5.3, the National Preparedness Goal consists of thirty-two core capabilities

Prevention	Protection	Mitigation	Response	Recovery
Planning				
Public information and warning				
Operational coordination				
Intelligence and information sharing		Community resilience	Infrastructure systems	
Interdiction and disruption		Long-term vulnerability reduction	Critical transportation	Economic recovery
Screening, search, and detection			Environmental response/ health and safety	Health and social services
Forensics and attribution	Access control and identity verification	Risk and disaster resilience assessment	Fatality management services	Housing
	Cybersecurity	Threats and hazards identification	Fire management and suppression	Natural and cultural resources
	Physical protective measures		Logistics and supply chain management	
	Risk Management for protection programs and activities		Mass care services	
	Supply chain integrity and security		Mass search and rescue operations	
			On-scene security, protection, and law enforcement	
			Operational communications	
			Public health, healthcare, and emergency medical services	
			Situational assessment	

FIGURE 5.3 National preparedness goal: Mission areas and core capabilities. (Data from U.S. Department of Homeland Security, 3, 2015, http://www.fema.gov/national-preparedness-goal.)

across five mission areas: Prevention, Protection, Mitigation, Response, and Recovery. In addition to directing DHS to establish a goal and identify core capabilities needed to achieve the goal, PPD-8 also requires DHS to monitor the nation's progress toward achieving the goal and to publish the results in an annual report. According to the 2015 *National Preparedness Report*, the nation continues to make progress in the area of disaster preparedness, but there are areas where improvement is needed, particularly in terms of cyber-security and dealing with complex threats such as the case of the 2014 Ebola outbreak that are not officially declared as disasters but pose significant management challenges nonetheless (U.S. Department of Homeland Security 2015).

5.3.3 Examples of International Preparedness Initiatives

Although we tend to think primarily about disasters that impact our own local communities, events, such as the earthquake in Haiti and the tsunami in Japan, have dramatically underscored the need to think about disasters on a global scale. As discussed in Chapter 7, the most impoverished and least developed nations in the world suffer the harshest impacts of disasters, including exorbitant financial costs, widespread physical damage, and massive death tolls. Given their extreme poverty under ordinary circumstances, these same nations face the greatest challenges in responding to disasters when they occur and desperately need help from the international community.

As Wachtendorf (2000) suggests, we also need to think about disasters in international terms because they sometimes defy national boundaries. For example, the 2004 tsunami impacted several countries in the region, recent floods impacted multiple countries in Western Europe, and cities in both the United States and Canada have been simultaneously inundated by floods. In these events, cooperation and coordination between governments is critical and may be facilitated through predisaster preparedness efforts. Several recent studies have also examined international preparedness levels in numerous countries, including Sweden, Turkey, New Zealand, and Japan (Guldåker et al. 2015; Karanci et al. 2005; Paton et al. 2010).

Recognizing the uneven impacts of disasters across the globe and the possibility of trans-national events, the United Nations launched the *International Strategy for Disaster Reduction* (UN ISDR) in 2000. Its primary aim is to reduce disaster losses and build resilient nations (http://unisdr. org), and it involves "numerous organizations, states, intergovernmental and nongovernmental organizations, financial institutions, technical bodies, and civil society, which work together and share information to reduce disaster risk." Its activities include coordinating international disaster relief efforts, advocating for greater investment in disaster reduction activities, conducting educational campaigns about disasters and risk reduction measures, organizing global conferences, and publishing reports on disasters across the globe.

5.4 Working and Volunteering in Preparedness

In reality, we all need to work and volunteer to achieve preparedness. It is not sufficient to be the local emergency manager who focuses on preparedness. That individual needs to be a leader who motivates others to work in the area. The emergency manager, for example, must reach out to and involve the media in crafting and disseminating preparedness messages. Other agencies also bear responsibilities for preparedness.

If a blizzard threatens an area, transportation agencies must inform the public of routes likely to close so that lives can be saved. Physicians and health care providers should ask their patients how prepared they are and distribute information to them. They can even use preparedness checklists as part of annual physical examinations. Teachers need to prepare their students for untoward events so that they respond as directed when situations warrant. Elected officials must inform themselves so that they can reach out to their constituents and encourage proper advance preparation; they bear a special responsibility for the most vulnerable among us who need protection.

Health care centers also employ preparedness experts. For example, hospitals sometimes advertise positions of emergency preparedness coordinators who will work in collaboration across the hospital and the community, design exercises and events, conduct training, and ensure continuity of operations for the hospital and its patients. These positions typically accept applications from individuals with degrees in nursing, biology, public health, environmental health, or emergency management and require some experience in emergency preparedness and planning.

Students often ask us how to get that experience. Several routes open that door. One is internship experience in an agency that works on emergency preparedness. Another route is working at an entry-level job to gain experience and earn "boots on the ground" experience with preparedness, planning, training, and exercising. A final route emerges through volunteer efforts. In the United States, the Citizen Corps offers a chance to participate in preparedness and response activities. The corps brings volunteers into several different kinds of organizations. The most common assignments since September 11, 2001 have been Community Emergency Response Teams (CERTs). Others are volunteers in police service, fire corps, Medical Reserve Corps, and Neighborhood Watch. A webinar library at www.citizencorps. gov covers topics such as collaborative planning and partnerships, youth preparedness, business continuity planning, and more.

You do not have to join a group to become more involved in preparedness. Start with your own family and neighborhood (Andrews 2001). Host a neighborhood meeting or picnic and invite the fire department and emergency management agency to visit and distribute preparedness materials. Since the most trusted information comes from social networks, use yours to prepare those around you. Canvass your community and assess what is needed. Invite professionals to create safety programs for your neighborhood. Use your school club to launch a preparedness effort directed at elderly residents with disabilities or purchase resources for local schools. Gaining experience in preparedness can be as easy as knocking on your neighbor's door with a checklist from this textbook. Preparedness starts at home.

Summary

In this chapter, we discussed both the good news and the bad news about disaster preparedness. The bad news, of course, is that disaster preparedness levels are alarmingly low for individuals and households, organizations, communities, states, and nations. Moreover, preparedness levels vary in large part because some people, households, and even nations simply do not have the resources to adequately prepare themselves. As a result, when disasters occur they impact some groups much more harshly than others, as evidenced by the earthquake in Haiti, Hurricane Katrina in the United States, and the tsunami in Asia.

The good news about preparedness is that steps can be taken to enhance readiness for disasters. Many of the activities described in this chapter are simple and relatively inexpensive. We can greatly increase the number of people taking those actions through effective educational campaigns like the ones described in this chapter, by reaching out to populations at risk, and by providing assistance when necessary. While disaster preparedness is in some sense a personal responsibility, it is also a shared, collective responsibility. By increasing readiness at all levels, from individuals and households to entire nations, we can greatly improve public safety and dramatically enhance the resilience of our communities to disasters.

Discussion Questions

1. How prepared do you believe the United States is for major disasters? What are some factors that you would consider in answering that question? Are we more prepared for natural disasters or terrorism? Why?

2. Why does the Federal Emergency Management Agency use the term whole community? What does it mean? What comprises the whole community?

3. What do you believe are the best strategies for improving disaster preparedness among at-risk populations? What are some examples of at-risk populations? What can you do as an emergency manager to assist them in preparing?

4. What is a community vulnerability analysis? What factors should be considered in conducting such an analysis? What are the most important hazards that exist in your community? Which groups are most at risk?

5. What is the National Preparedness Goal? Why was it established? What are the key mission areas and core capabilities contained in it?

Resources

- The best place to start learning more about disaster preparedness for individuals, households, and businesses in the United States is www.ready.gov.
- To learn more about disasters internationally, both in terms of their impacts and efforts to better prepare for them, visit the United Nations International Strategy for Disaster Reduction at www.unisdr.org.
- More information on the role of nonprofit, voluntary organizations in preparing for disasters can be found on the National Voluntary Associations Active in Disaster website at www.nvoad.org.
- Disaster Resilient Universities (http://emc.uoregon.edu/content/disaster-resilient-universities) is a network for college and university emergency management professionals responsible for making their campuses safer and more disaster resilient.

References and Recommended Readings

Andrews, Jill. H. 2001. Safe in the Hood: Earthquake Preparedness in Midcity Los Angeles. *Natural Hazards Review* 2(1): 2–11.

Becker, Julia, Douglas Paton, and David Johnston. 2014. Societal Influences on Earthquake Information Meaning-Making and Household Preparedness. *International Journal of Mass Emergencies and Disasters* 32(2): 317–352.

Becker, Julia, Douglas Paton, David Johnston, and K. R. Ronan. 2012. A Model of Household Preparedness for Earthquakes: How Individuals Make Meaning of Earthquake Information and How This Influences Preparedness. *Natural Hazards* 64: 107–137.

Bolin, Robert and Daniel J. Klenow. 1988. Older People in Disaster: A Comparison of Black and White Victims. *International Journal of Aging and Human Development* 26(1): 29–43.

Bullard, Robert D. 1990. *Dumping in Dixie: Race, Class, and Environmental Quality*. Boulder, CO: Westview Press.

Childers, Cheryl. 2008. Elderly Female-Headed Households in the Disaster Loan Process. pp. 182–193 in *Women and Disasters: From Theory to Practice,* edited by Brenda Phillips and Betty Morrow. Philadelphia, PA: International Research Committee on Disasters.

Clarke, Lee. 2005. *Worst Cases: Terror and Catastrophe in the Popular Imagination.* Chicago, IL: University of Chicago Press.

Clive, Alan, Elizabeth Davis, Rebecca Hansen, and Jennifer Mincin. 2010. Disability. pp. 187–216 in 256 in *Social Vulnerability to Disaster,* edited by Brenda Phillips, Deborah Thomas, Alice Fothergill and Lynn Pike. Boca Raton, FL: CRC Press.

Dahlhamer, James M. and Melvin J. D'Souza. 1997. Determinants of Business Disaster Preparedness in Two U. S. Metropolitan Areas. *International Journal of Mass Emergencies and Disasters* 15: 265–281.

Dash, Nicole. 2010. Race and Ethnicity. pp. 101–121 in *Social Vulnerability to Disasters,* edited by Brenda Phillips, Deborah Thomas, Alice Fothergill, and Lynn Blinn-Pike. Boca Raton, FL: CRC Press.

Drabek, Thomas. 1986. *Human System Responses to Disaster: An Inventory of Sociological Findings.* New York: Springer-Verlag.

Drabek, Thomas E. 2010. *The Human Side of Disaster.* Boca Raton, FL: CRC Press.

Eldar, R. 1992. The Needs of Elderly Persons in Natural Disasters. *Disasters* 16(4): 355–58.

Enarson, Elaine. 2001. What Women Do: Gendered Labor in the Red River Valley Flood. *Environmental Hazards* 3(1): 1–18.

Enarson, Elaine. 2008. Gender Mainstreaming in Emergency Management. Paper prepared for the Public Health Agency of Canada. Available at http://www.gdnonline.org/, last accessed February 7, 2011.

Enarson, Elaine and Brenda D. Phillips. 2008. Invitation to a New Feminist Disaster Sociology. pp. 41–74 in *Women in Disaster,* edited by Brenda D. Phillips and Betty Morrow. Philadelphia, PA: Xlibris/International Research Committee on Disaster.

Faupel, Charles E., Susan P. Kelley, and Thomas Petee. 1992. The Impact of Disaster Education on Household Preparedness for Hurricane Hugo. *International Journal of Mass Emergencies and Disasters* 10(1): 5–24.

Federal Emergency Management Agency. 2010. *National Disaster Housing Strategy.* Washington, D.C.: FEMA.

Fernandez, Lauren, Deana Byard, Chien-Chih Lin, Samuel Benson, and Joseph A Barbera. 2002. Frail Elderly as Disaster Victims: Emergency Management Strategies. *Prehospital and Disaster Medicine* 17(2): 67–74.

Fordham, Maureen. 1998. Making Women Visible in Disasters. *Disasters* 22(2): 126–143.

Ghafory-Ashtiany, Mohsen. 2009. View of Islam on Earthquakes, Human Vitality, and Disaster. *Disaster Prevention and Management* 18(3): 218–232.

Gillespie, David F. and Calvin L. Streeter. 1987. Conceptualizing and Measuring Disaster Preparedness. *International Journal of Mass Emergencies and Disasters* 5: 155–176.

Government Accountability Organization. 2006. *Transportation-Disadvantaged Populations: Actions Needed to Clarify Responsibilities and Increase Preparedness for Evacuations.* Washington, D.C.: GAO Report GAO-07-44.

Guldåker, Nicklas, Kerstin Eriksson, and Tuija Nieminen Kristofersson. 2015. Preventing and Preparing for Disasters—The Role of a Swedish Local Emergent Citizen Group. *International Journal of Mass Emergencies and Disasters* 33(3): 360–387.

Heath, Sebastian E., S. K. Voeks, and L. T. Glickman. 2000. A Study of Pet Rescue in Two Disasters. *International Journal of Mass Emergencies and Disasters* 18(3): 361–381.

Heath, Sebastian E., Alan Beck, Philip H. Kass, and Larry Glickman. 2001. Risk Factors for Pet Evacuation Failure after a Slow Onset Disaster. *Journal of the American Veterinary Medical Association* 218(12): 1905–1910.

Heinz Center. 2002. *Human Links to Coastal Disasters.* Washington, D.C.: The Heinz Center Foundation.

Kailes, June and Alexandra Enders. 2007. Moving Beyond Special Needs. *Journal of Disability Policy Studies* 17(4): 230–237.

Kapucu, Naim. 2008. Culture of Preparedness: Household Disaster Preparedness. *Disaster Prevention and Management* 17(4): 526–535.

Karanci, Ayse Nuray, Bahattin Askit, and Gulay Dirik. 2005. Impact of a Community Disaster Awareness Training Program in Turkey: Does It Influence Hazard-Related Cognitions and Preparedness Behaviors. *Social Behavior and Personality* 33: 243–258.

Kirschenbaum, Alan. 2002. Disaster Preparedness: A Conceptual and Empirical Reevaluation. *International Journal of Mass Emergencies and Disasters* 20(1): 5–28.

Klein, Kelly R. and Nanci E. Nagel. 2007. Mass Medical Evacuation: Hurricane Katrina and Nursing Experiences at the New Orleans Airport. *Disaster Management and Response* 5(2): 56–61.

Klinenberg, Eric. 2002. *Heat Wave: A Social Autopsy of Disaster in Chicago.* Chicago, IL: University of Chicago Press.

Lindell, Michael K. and Ronald W. Perry. 2004. *Communicating Risk in Multi-Ethnic Communities.* Thousand Oaks, CA: Sage.

Mileti, Dennis. 1999. *Disasters by Design.* Washington, D.C.: Joseph Henry Press.

Mileti, Dennis and Colleen Fitzpatrick. 1993. *The Great Earthquake Experiment: Risk Communication and Public Action.* Boulder, CO: Westview Press.

Mitchell, Louise. 2007. *Guidelines for Emergency Managers Working with Culturally and Linguistically Diverse Communities.* Emergency Management Australia. Available at www.ema.gov.au/agd/EMA/emaInternet.nsf/Page/Communities_Research_Research, last accessed March 15, 2011.

Morrow, Betty. 2010. Language and Literacy. pp. 243–256 in *Social Vulnerability to Disaster,* edited by Brenda D. Phillips, Deborah Thomas, Alice Fothergill and Lynn Pike. Boca Raton, FL: CRC Press.

Morrow, Betty and Elaine Enarson. 1996. Hurricane Andrew through Women's Eyes. *International Journal of Mass Emergencies and Disasters* 14(1): 1–22.

National Organization on Disability. 2005. *Special Needs Assessment of Katrina Evacuees.* Washington, D.C.: National Organization on Disability.

Norris, Fran. H., M. J. Friedman, and P. J. Watson. 2002a. 60,000 Disaster Victims Speak: Part II. Summary and Implications of the Disaster Mental Health Research. *Psychiatry* 65(3): 240–260.

Norris, Fran H., M. J. Friedman, P. J. Watson, C. M. Byrne, E. Diaz, and K. Kaniasty. 2002b. 60,000 Disaster Victims Speak: Part I. An Empirical Review of the Empirical Literature, 1981–2001. *Psychiatry* 65(3): 207–239.

Paton, Douglas, Robert Bajek, Norio Okada, and David McIvor. 2010. Predicting Community Earthquake Preparedness: A Cross-Cultural Comparison of Japan and New Zealand. *Natural Hazards* 54(3): 765–781.

Peek, Lori. 2010. Age. pp. 155–186 in *Social Vulnerability to Disasters,* edited by Brenda D. Phillips, Deborah Thomas, Alice Fothergill, and Lynn Pike. Boca Raton, FL: CRC Press.

Perry, Ronald W. and Alvin H. Mushkatel. 1986. *Minority Citizens in Disasters.* Athens, GA: University of Georgia Press.

Phillips, Brenda D. 2009. Special Needs Populations. pp. 113–132 in *Disaster Medicine: Comprehensive Principles and Practices.* edited by Kristi Koenig and Carl Schutz. Cambridge: Cambridge University Press.

Phillips, Brenda D. 1996. Homelessness and the Social Construction of Places: The Loma Prieta Earthquake. *Humanity and Society* 19(4): 94–101.

Phillips, Brenda D., Elizabeth Harris, Elizabeth A. Davis, Rebecca Hansen, Kelly Rouba, and Jessica Love. 2011. Delivery of Behavioral Health Services in General and Functional Needs Shelters. In *Behavioral Health Response to Disasters,* edited by Martin Teasley). Boca Raton, FL: CRC Press.

Phillips, Brenda and Paul Hewett. 2005. Home Alone: Disasters, Mass Emergencies and Children in Self-Care. *Journal of Emergency Management* 3(2): 31–35.

Poulshock, S. and E. Cohen. 1975. The Elderly in the Aftermath of Disaster. *The Gerontologist* 15(4): 357–361.

Quarantelli, E. L. 1983. *Delivery of Emergency Medical Services in Disasters: Assumptions and Realities.* New York: Irvington Publishers.

Schmuck, Hannah. 2000. An Act of Allah: Religious Explanations for Floods in Bangladesh as Survival Strategy. *International Journal of Mass Emergencies and Disasters* 18: 85–96.

Sharkey, Patrick. 2007. Survival and Death in New Orleans. *Journal of Black Studies* 37(4): 482–501.

Shriver, Thomas E. and Gary R. Webb. 2009. Rethinking the Scope of Environmental Justice: Perceptions of Health Hazards in a Rural Native American Community Exposed to Carbon Black. *Rural Sociology* 74(2): 270–292.

Simpson, David M. 2008. Disaster Preparedness Measures: A Test Case Development and Application. *Disaster Prevention and Management* 17(5): 645–661.

Stein, Robert, Birnur Buzcu-Guven, Leonardo Dueñas-Osorio, and Devika Subramanian. 2014. The Private and Social Benefits of Preparing for Natural Disasters. *International Journal of Mass Emergencies and Disasters* 32(3): 459–483.

Thomas, Deborah, Pamela K. Stephens, and Jennifer Goldsmith. 2010. Measuring and Conveying Vulnerability Analysis. pp. 323–344 in *Social Vulnerability to Disasters,* edited by Brenda D. Phillips, Deborah Thomas, Alice Fothergill, and Lynn Pike. Boca Raton, FL: CRC Press.

Tierney, Kathleen J., Michael K. Lindell, and Ronald W. Perry. 2001. *Facing the Unexpected.* Washington, D.C.: Joseph Henry Press.

U.S. Department of Homeland Security. 2011. *National Preparedness Goal,* 1st Edition. Washington, D.C.: U.S. Department of Homeland Security.

U.S. Department of Homeland Security. 2015. National Preparedness Goal, 2nd Edition. Washington, D.C.: U.S. Department of Homeland Security.

Wachtendorf, Tricia. 2000. When Disasters Defy Borders: What We Can Learn from the Red River Flood about Transnational Disasters. *Australian Journal of Emergency Management* 15(3): 36–41.

Webb, Gary R. 2007. The Popular Culture of Disaster: Exploring a New Dimension of Disaster Research. pp. 430–440 in *Handbook of Disaster Research,* edited by Havidan Rodriguez, E. L. Quarantelli, and Russell R. Dynes. New York: Springer.

Webb, Gary R., Kathleen J. Tierney, and James M. Dahlhamer. 2000. Businesses and Disasters: Empirical Patterns and Unanswered Questions. *Natural Hazards Review* 1(2): 83–90.

Webb, Gary R., Tricia Wachtendorf, and Anne Eyre. 2000. Bringing Culture Back In: Exploring the Cultural Dimensions of Disaster. *International Journal of Mass Emergencies and Disasters* 18(1): 5–19.

Wenger, Dennis E., E. L. Quarantelli, and Russell R. Dynes. 1986. *Disaster Analysis: Local Emergency Management Offices and Arrangements.* Newark, DE: University of Delaware, Disaster Research Center. Final Project Report No. 34.

Wenger, Dennis E., E. L. Quarantelli, and Russell R. Dynes. 1989. *Disaster Analysis: Police and Fire Departments.* Newark, DE: University of Delaware, Disaster Research Center. Final Project Report No. 37.

Chapter **6**

Planning

Objectives

Upon completing this chapter, students should be able to:

- Recognize that planning is a process.
- Discover that the planning process creates important social networks.
- Understand why long paper documents or boilerplate documents fail.
- Explain why evidence-based planning works.
- Describe the planning process for:
  - Households
  - Private and voluntary organizations
  - Governments.
  - Cross-national events.
- Understand the role of federal guidance in disaster planning.

Key Terms

- Business continuity planning
- Community based planning
- Comprehensive Planning Guide – 101
- Household planning
- National Incident Management System
- National Response Framework
- Planning process
- Social networks/social capital
- Whole community planning

6.1 Introduction

In Chapter 5, we discussed what preparedness means, why preparedness is important, who prepares and does not prepare, and how preparedness works. Chapter 6 covers the processes that various types of organizations in the public, private, and volunteer sectors should use to plan for disasters. Rather than considering a paper plan as an end product, this chapter shows how planning should be a participatory process among stakeholders and representatives at the local, state, and national levels. This chapter promotes the idea that planning never ceases and that many planning tools can be found through publicly available sources. It highlights the various types of planning needed for a wide range of specific issues, including socially vulnerable populations and animals. We also expose the reader to an overview of U.S. federal planning documents. This includes a special focus on the development and use of Comprehensive Planning Guide (CPG)-101, the most current federal document offering steps for any entity to use when planning. In addition to discussing key processes, the chapter also provides an overview of how plans develop through stakeholder participation, including the importance of integrating research findings. Family-level planning will be used to illustrate how planning can be done by readers in their own household. International examples of effective planning both within and across national boundaries will also be featured.

Imagine this common scenario: A disaster coordinator needs a plan *now* to meet state law requirements, initiate accreditation activities, or initiate awareness for the start of a specific disaster season (e.g., tornado, hurricane, and blizzard). In other cases, a new emergency manager may discover the 20-year-old disaster plan placed on a shelf and gathering dust. To solve the problem, the disaster coordinator asks a new hire or intern, or pays a consultant, to write a plan. Often sitting in an isolated cubicle or in a basement, the new planner will e-mail friends and colleagues, make a Facebook post, or tweet a message asking for existing disaster plans from other communities. Consultants may use their own existing boilerplate plan. The planner will then receive all kinds of plans, paste them together, do a computer generated word search to eliminate the other communities' names, and add the new community's name. While constructing the new document, the planner rarely leaves a cubicle to talk with others. Once the planner completes the document, upper management signs off, and the community or organization now has a plan and is considered "prepared." As we describe below, planners should *not* follow this planning process.

If you don't think disaster planning still occurs in this fashion, consider the disaster planning problems revealed following the April 2010, Deepwater Horizon oil spill disaster in the Gulf of Mexico (CBSNEWS 2010; National Commission on the BP Deepwater Horizon Oil Spill and Offshore

Drilling 2011). As the disaster unfolded, a BP representative stated that a plan was in place, and that the proper federal authority, the Minerals Management Service (MMS), a part of the federal government, had approved the plan (Fitzgerald 2010). In contrast, the Presidential Commission studying the aftermath of the event described the disaster planning process in the following manner (National Commission on the BP Deepwater Horizon Oil Spill and Offshore Drilling 2011, p. 133):

> If BP's response capacity was underwhelming, some aspects of its response plan were embarrassing. In the plan, BP had named Peter Lutz as a wildlife expert on whom it would rely; he had died several years before BP submitted its plan. BP listed seals and walruses as two species of concern in case of an oil spill in the Gulf; these species never see Gulf waters. And a link in the plan that purported to go to the Marine Spill Response Corporation website actually led to a Japanese entertainment site. (Congressional investigation revealed that the response plans submitted to MMS by ExxonMobil, Chevron, ConocoPhillips, and Shell were almost identical to BP's—they too suggested impressive but unrealistic response capacity and three included the embarrassing reference to walruses).

In short, planners should always engage in working with others within their own company and even across the industry to develop their plans. At its best, planning is a process that must involve a wide array of stakeholders and plan users.

As noted previously, those of us in the United States are poorly prepared for disaster. Such factors as more people defining more pressing personal or organizational priorities, managers unwilling to spend the time or money for planning, or individuals not having the time or resources to plan and prepare all affect our abilities to be ready. In the next sections, we will describe proper steps in the planning process. We base these recommendations upon a long line of research showing what works in the planning process. We focus upon households, government, the private sector, and volunteer organizations.

6.2 Planning as a Process

Researchers have discovered a lot of information on how communities and organizations can best approach disaster planning. Drawing upon extensive research, Quarantelli (1988, 1994, 1997) summarized these planning guidelines.

- *Disasters are different from day to day accidents and emergencies.* The magnitude, scope and impact of a disaster require that a fuller set of partners join in the response and recovery efforts. Accidents and emergencies use only local first responders and medical professionals that are part of planned, everyday emergency response activities. By comparison, disasters require many additional partners from both within and outside the community. Examples may include additional police, fire, paramedics and EMTs, public works employees, psychologists, faith-based community and volunteer organizations, engineering assessment teams, environmental protection specialists, animal rescue teams, shelter providers, housing reconstruction teams, and more. Representatives from state and federal government may also arrive to provide assistance and guidance. A disaster plan of any kind must consider all the people and organizations possibly needed, depending upon the hazard and its impact. Then, a community can initiate planning among all the partners likely to be part of the disaster event. In short, responding to a day-to-day emergency is much different than responding to a disaster.

- *A plan is not the final outcome of disaster planning—because planning never stops.* Plans must be living, actively revised documents. New disasters unfold over time. For example, during the last 10–15 years, new kinds of terrorism attacks, new pandemics, and cyber warfare incidents have happened that did not exist 20 years ago. Other kinds of dynamic circumstances occur as well. Employees leave their positions, new technologies emerge, and office locations change. The dynamic nature of our professional and personal lives thus compels us to revisit planning documents for currency and accuracy while also (re)connecting with existing and new representatives from other organizations to confirm or obtain new information. As one example, call down lists that are used to alert emergency response partners change frequently and require continual updating. A community's demographics may also change. Plans must reflect new groups, such as evacuees, immigrants, or even newly disabled veterans that arrive in a community. Finding and working with representatives of these groups can enhance the plan and bring new people into the process. The result? A more comprehensive and stakeholder-driven plan that serves a broader population.

- *Creating a plan means assuming an agent generic approach toward planning—not creating a plan for each specific type of hazard.* Any given community typically faces a range of threats. Planning for each type of event requires time that most agencies cannot devote to such a widespread effort. Many agencies lack the personnel and expertise to do so. Further, certain needs occur commonly across disasters such as communication, coordination, and decision-making authority. By focusing on the common areas, a planner can achieve broadly-based planning for a range of hazards. For example, creating the general components of an effective warning system is the same for a tornado or blizzard. Regardless of the event, the same organizations will be engaged with the response. In addition, the National Response Framework (NRF) in the United States, uses the all hazards approach. Within the NRF, Emergency Support Functions (ESFs) address specific areas that guide a national response. ESF #6, for example, centers on mass care (sheltering, housing, and feeding) which is a common need regardless of the type of event. For most local plans, additional annexes address concerns such as terrorism or pandemics.

- *Plans must assume that unpredictable events will occur, and that improvisation and group emergence will develop to respond to new situations.* Disasters involve problem solving. Disaster plans provide a framework or starting place for response—they do not provide all the answers. As a result, unpredictable or overwhelming events may occur. For example, how does a community quickly mobilize volunteers and sandbags to save a neighborhood? To solve these problems, emergent groups of volunteers will form. Or, various civic organizations may work together to obtain sand, bags, and a means to put sand in the bags, transport the sandbags to where they are needed, and recruit volunteers to place sandbags. New or strengthened personal or organizational relationships during the planning process often assist with the improvisation and emergent process, which in turn may provide a more rapid and effective disaster response (see Photo 6.1).

- *Plans must focus on coordination and flexibility, not on maintaining a rigid command and control bureaucracy.* Generally, rigid bureaucracies do not perform well under disaster circumstances. Disasters have a tendency to disrupt established routines and present new challenges. Keeping the day-to-day management structure for most organizations may lead to failure during a disaster. As events change,

PHOTO 6.1   Post impact planning in Nassau County, New York, to help survivors of Hurricane Sandy obtain needed benefits. (Courtesy of FEMA/Howard Greenblatt.)

so must organizational structure. Consider, for example, when an F3 tornado tore through Fort Worth, Texas in 2000. An FBI building lost its windows along with some critical case files. The same happened in New Orleans after Hurricane Katrina to police offices. Retrieving and replacing evidence presented a new challenge, one that is typically not addressed in a plan. As another example, the attack on the World Trade Center resulted in the destruction of state of the art emergency management facilities. To respond, surviving employees had to reconstruct a makeshift emergency operations center a few blocks away (Kendra and Wachtendorf 2003).

- *The planning process should create a set of general guidelines or principles for a disaster response.* Disaster planners should not adhere to a rigid set of standard operating procedures. Certainly, disaster managers and responders will draw upon some standard operating procedures such as initiating the steps for opening an emergency operations center, delineating the safety steps when responding to a hazardous materials event, or tuning on the sirens for a specific warning message. Disasters, however, generate a high degree of uncertainty. Nobody can anticipate and list out all the possible actions needed for any specific event. Even if that were possible, it would take a lifetime to generate only some of the possible standard operating procedures, and by then, everything would change. Rather, creating general guidelines and principles for planning and response are much more effective since they can be applied to a broad set of disaster threats. Consider the 2001 Super Bowl. Planners had worked diligently to protect the public from a terrorist attack at the Super Bowl. A blizzard, icy conditions, unusually low wind chills, and rolling blackouts caused unexpected disruption instead. The general set of communication guidelines established for the Super Bowl provided a foundation for managing the blizzard. More broadly, emergency coordinators can implement guidelines for communications, emergency transportation, and utility restoration regardless of the event.
- *Disaster plans must avoid integrating the myths of such events as mass hysteria, panic, looting, and other incorrect assumptions of antisocial behavior by the victims.* Rather, disasters generally bring out the best in people. If a planner anticipates that the first responders will be neighbors and friends, they can train neighborhood teams how to conduct basic search and rescue safely and render first-aid until help arrives. Consequently, dispatchers can send emergency response crews to where more immediate actions are needed. If a planner assumes that looting is actually less likely than pro-social behavior, they can deploy critical assets like National Guard troops to locations for search and rescue rather than waste their time on

unnecessary "security." When disaster threatens, knowing that people usually do not panic should prompt early warnings to inspire evacuation. Disaster planners who rely upon disaster myths may doom a community for failure during a response. Believing these myths will lead to poor decisions and a wasteful use of resources.

- *The planning process must stress people working together on the plan within and across organizations.* Planning should never be conducted within one's own "silo." Organizations that will function together in a crisis event must plan together during noncrisis times. Doing so involves a range of partners within as well as across organizations. Janitors, typically at the bottom of an organizational hierarchy, will know a great deal about building layouts and resource locations. Janitors and facilities staff are critical in an emergency. Similarly, the chief executive officer must be involved because he or she will likely make decisions that determine the fate of a business or agency. Because agencies work across their silos in a disaster they must sit at the planning table together. As an example, consider how a university might plan for a terrorist attack on a football stadium. Doing so requires involvement of university leaders as well as the temporary day labor used to route people into and out of the location. Police, paramedics, firefighters, and traffic control people are part of the operational team as are the university's communications personnel and public relations officer and high-level administrators. In short, disaster planners must network with central players when devising a disaster plan (see Box 6.1). Furthermore, planners must encourage others to work together formally and informally during the planning process. The development of pre disaster networks and building social capital during this process will enhance the disaster response.

- *The planning process and plans must be guided by the science of disaster behavior.* The use of "there I was" stories often produce biased, unrealistic assumptions about disaster behavior. Surgery requires expertise, with knowledge of what works and does not work for a given procedure. Disaster planning and operations should follow the same route. To ensure safety for any given community requires the best knowledge that science can offer. Operating on the basis of what you think would work, or what worked before, may not work this time. To illustrate, consider that the U.S. government did not offer much planning guidance on people with disabilities until well after Hurricane Katrina occurred. People could not evacuate without assistance and hundreds had to be rescued after the levees broke in New Orleans. When evacuees landed in distant cities during the evacuation, they had lost assistive devices and local shelters receiving them were hard-pressed to provide appropriate levels of support. Planners need to

BOX 6.1   BUILDING SOCIAL CAPITAL FOR EMERGENCY MANAGEMENT PLANNING

Carrie Furlong Little

Carrie Furlong Little (CEM) serves as the Director of Emergency Management for the City of Plano, Texas. She has worked for several different cities in north Texas over the last 18 years. Ms. Little has responded to many disaster events during her career including the Fort Worth tornado, Wedgwood Church shooting, hurricane evacuee sheltering, SuperBowl 45, and other regional disaster events. Ms. Little earned a Bachelor of Science in Emergency Management and a Master's in Public Administration from the University of North Texas. Ms. Little is active in several professional associations, holding committee and leadership appointments.

The local emergency manager must address a full range of threats and hazards that may affect a community. Planning must be risk-based, inclusive of the community as a whole, and serve to inform decision-making.

Citizens expect city officials to take decisive actions when hazards or other threats are imminent. The expectation is all available community resources are pressed into service to address the threat. The city then seeks support from outside agencies if necessary. Citizens, businesses, and other community groups have a responsibility to develop plans for action when disaster strikes.

Integration of representatives and stakeholders from across the community is a complex process. Inclusion of city departments, community based groups, citizens, and the business community in the planning process produces robust planning documents. The integration process begins before planning, through

(Continued)

**BOX 6.1 (*Continued*)   BUILDING SOCIAL CAPITAL
FOR EMERGENCY MANAGEMENT PLANNING**

development of an array of contacts within the community—business leaders, elected officials, volunteers, community activists, representatives from other levels of government, health care partners, city officials, school district leaders, concerned citizens, and other interested parties. Networking with individuals from across the community helps to identify the extent of risk for each identified stakeholder. Inclusion of these stakeholders in the planning process also provides an opportunity to address unique concerns related to disparate groups.

When a large tornado outbreak affected neighboring jurisdictions in North Texas, over 44 emergency management staff members from communities across the area provided support to seven jurisdictions. The responding emergency managers covered 105 shifts, totaling 1260 hours over two weeks. A comprehensive regional emergency management planning effort allowed emergency management personnel to surge into the affected jurisdictions to fill roles in the emergency operations centers, volunteer reception centers, incident command posts, and provide other support as needed. Support personnel worked on a variety of topics such as economic recovery, debris removal, disaster logistics, volunteers active in disaster, and unmet needs.

All sectors of the affected communities were impacted by the tornado outbreak. City departments responded to address immediate citizen needs for search and rescue, sheltering, debris management, short-term recovery needs, and long-term economic recovery. Business owners, faith-based groups, volunteer agencies, and community activists rallied to begin to address recovery issues. The school districts and faith-based community provided staging areas for emergency response vehicles, a collection point for donated goods, and staff to assist with unmet needs.

Prior planning conducted by the affected jurisdictions linking local emergency management plans with comprehensive regional response plans proved invaluable in the face of a regional tornado event. Moving forward, emergency management plans at the local and regional level are incorporating valuable lessons learned from the regional response to the tornado outbreak. The recovery process will be lengthy for the impacted communities. The network of community groups involved in planning before the event and now also involved with planning post-disaster will only strengthen the comprehensive emergency management efforts within the community.

consider the full range of the population including realities that may exist outside of their own frame of reference. Scientific research alerts us to those broader realities and can enhance planning.

- *Although disaster planning is part of the "preparedness" phase of disasters, planning should also integrate mitigation, response, and recovery.* As noted earlier, a range of planning exists in which a community may engage. Planners are increasingly recognizing the linkages between these kinds of plans and moving forward accordingly. For example, designing a recovery plan with mitigation initiatives improves disaster resilience for future events and reduces the burden placed on emergency management. More broadly, the planning process should never stop.

After going over these points, two principles emphasize the main elements of community or organizational disaster planning:

- *Planning is a process, not a piece of paper.*
- *Network, network, and network.*

In short, the planning process helps in the following ways. First, those involved with the planning process will learn the plan. Learning occurs not by studying it, but by becoming active participants in creating and writing the plan. People learn by doing. As a result, during a disaster they do not have to search for the plan, find the correct page number, and follow a script. Rather, they learn where and how to step into their roles through the planning process. Other activities such as training, drills, and exercises reinforce information related to the plan. In fact, when disasters strike, disaster managers become too busy to consult written plans. You need to know the plan, not look it up when conditions threaten the public.

Second, the planning process helps create and enhance connections or networks among decision makers. Today, this process of fostering social networks is known as developing social capital. Developing social capital means the mayor gets to know the fire chief better, the head of public works learns how to work with the police chief, the city manager increases trust in the emergency manager, the director of the Red Cross works more closely with the CEO of the local hospital, and a committee representing faith based groups establishes ties with similar community organizations. The social capital is the trust, the relationships, and the ability to work together that they produce through networking, training, and planning together.

Furthermore, creating plans collectively enhances opportunities for people from different jurisdictions to work together. County government representatives may have to coordinate their plans with local or municipal governments. County sheriffs may have to synchronize with local police departments. Businesses will work with various levels of government. So, not only are individuals within an organization getting to know the disaster plan through the planning process, they are getting to know even better the people they will work with during a disaster. Thus, during this planning process, people learn who they can trust, who they can count on, how they communicate, and who may just talk rather than provide supportive action. Such knowledge can be important when emergency managers must make quick decisions to save lives and properties (see Box 6.2).

BOX 6.2   DUSTING OFF THE PLAN

During one of the authors' field work training at the Disaster Research Center (DRC), the center's director Henry Quarantelli directed us to obtain a copy of the local disaster plan when possible. As part of our analysis, we would compare the written plan to the actual response. Quarantelli warned us, however, not to be surprised if the local emergency coordinator could not find the plan, or if the coordinator located the plan, he or she would pull the plan off a top shelf and brush the dust off the top of the plan. Either way, these actions showed that the disaster managers and/or others did not use the plan during the disaster. Our team seemed a bit skeptical of his observations until we would travel to a disaster site and made a request to see the plan. And yes, either the coordinator could not find the plan, or would take a second or two to wipe the dust off the top of the plan.

A few years later, one of us studied warning systems during flash floods in West Virginia for the U.S. Army Corps of Engineers. The Corps wanted to know why the warning system was so successful (i.e., no deaths). A small field team consisting of a geographer, hydrologist, and sociologist along with a consultant met at Dulles Airport and rented a car to drive to the flood stricken city. Along the way, the consultant confidently stated, "I'll bet the second they heard the flood was coming, city officials pulled out the plan and followed it exactly. ... That's why nobody was killed." The rest of us were skeptical, being well versed in the pattern of disaster plan use during response. Despite citing our experiences, the consultant felt so right, he bet us a steak. We agreed.

Upon arriving at the city offices (officials were expecting us), we started to introduce ourselves to the local emergency manager and police chief. But even before we completed our introductions (and breaking our protocol for interviewing city officials), the consultant blurted out, "I'll bet you pulled those plans right off the shelf and used them for your warning—and that's why your warning was so successful." The local emergency coordinator looked at him rather oddly, and replied, "You know, things happened so fast, we didn't even have time to use them. In fact, (she then pointed up, looking at a shelf on the wall), there they are...... the same place they were before the flood." Lesson learned—the nature of a disaster often means that local disaster managers do not pull the plans off the shelf and use them. Events unfold too fast, and good coordinators know what is in the plan. And that night, the steak tasted pretty good, too.

6.3 Types of Planning

Planning occurs across all disaster phases. The majority of planning occurs before disaster strikes, particularly in the preparedness and mitigation phases. But, it is also true that—despite recommendations from researchers and experts in the field—some mitigation and recovery planning occurs only after a disaster has struck. In this section, we review the kinds of planning typically conducted by emergency managers. Additional planning content can be found in the chapters on recovery, mitigation, and private/public sector partnerships.

6.3.1 Planning Across the Life Cycle of Emergency Management

A range of planning activities awaits those involved in managing disasters. Many think that the preparedness phase represents the time frame most important for planning. However, planners must consider the full life cycle of emergency management. Response activities influence how recovery unfolds. Recovery plans should incorporate mitigation measures to reduce future disaster impacts. Even preparedness requires planning to conduct exercises and drills, roll out public education campaigns, and offer training.

Response plans are usually referred to as Emergency Operations Plans or EOPs. They can vary in their focus, length, and format but most center on how to coordinate activities from warning the public through search and rescue and rapid restoration of services such as utilities. It is probably true that the most time spent on planning occurs around the response phase because here is where life-saving activities take place. As members of a human society, our shared value for human life compels us to concentrate on this critical planning phase.

In the United States and worldwide, response plans vary considerably, especially given available resources and expertise. In the United States, for over a decade, the NRF and its ESF (discussed in an upcoming section) drove response planning. However, with the addition of the National Incident Management System (NIMS) as a required mechanism to structure response and Community Planning Guide 101, planning has become more complex.

In some international settings, an impoverished nation lacks the resources to conduct even basic firefighting let alone more desired rescue assets such as highly skilled rescue teams, air and ground ambulances, and critical care facilities. The earthquake that struck Haiti in January 2010 required external assistance yet 300,000 lives were lost. Ten months later, a cholera outbreak claimed another 1,000 souls.

In economically privileged nations such as Israel or the United States, response planning can also vary from rural locations with minimal resources to urban areas with significant levels of planning and response capabilities (Kirschenbaum 1992). Events such as the September 11 terror attacks decimating the World Trade Center in New York heightened response planning and asset accumulation even further. The 2015 attacks in Paris and San Bernardino, California, the 2016 explosions in the Brussels airport and subway as well as the Easter Day murders in Lahore, Pakistan, demonstrated the increasingly diverse nature of preparedness and planning to involve a wide array of those likely to be involved, particularly local law enforcement.

Recovery, the phase that follows response, lacks much planning worldwide. Few jurisdictions expend time or resources to think through how they will plan out a recovery effort. Failure to do so, however, wastes valuable time in the aftermath of an event. The recovery time period, when sleep is sorely needed to drive efforts, visioning and projects, demands an organized plan. Two types of recovery planning are typical. *Pre-event recovery planning* rarely occurs but for those jurisdictions that do so, such as Los Angeles, efforts to restore normalcy can be expedited. *Post-event recovery planning* is more typical and unfortunately takes longer to conduct and implement. Sitting amidst the debris is not the time to plan, but most communities conduct recovery planning this way. Common elements of a recovery plan address housing, roads and bridges, environmental resources, historic and cultural preservation, businesses, utilities, and more. Communities with the energy, time, and funding to do so may opt to reconsider their communities and redesign to enhance traffic flow, increase green space, reinvigorate a business sector, and mitigate future risks. Increasingly, communities are seeking to rebuild in environmentally-friendly ways, as Greensburg, Kansas did after a tornado destroyed the entire town.

Emergency coordinators and planners conduct mitigation planning based upon identifying local hazards, assessing the probabilities of where and how hazards could harm people and places, and selecting feasible ways to reduce their potential impact. Mitigation planning involves stakeholders such as the business, education, utility, and health care sectors with the public in identifying and prioritizing areas for risk reduction. Mitigation measures can include structural measures, such as the construction of levees along rivers that flood or installing rebar inside homes to resist earthquake shaking. Nonstructural efforts include those that do not involve built measures. Insurance is one example, because purchasing a policy affords the means to recover. Building codes serve as another example, when cities design rules for construction. In hurricane areas, for example, the city may require that builders install hurricane clamps on roofs to help them stay on during high winds. Locations that face wildfire threats may disallow wood shingles on roofs. Both kinds of mitigation measures can be considered as a way to reduce disaster impacts.

6.3.2 Business Continuity Planning

Specialized business-related planning also occurs throughout the phases. For example, businesses must consider how they will respond given various kinds of disruptions or destruction. Certainly, private sector leaders can at least see how a major event impacting their business might negatively their bottom line. Or, they may encounter displacement where they have to relocate temporarily or even permanently. But, they must also consider the more subtle and less obvious indirect impacts. Businesses may experience downtime when they cannot receive goods and services. For example, the 2011 Fukushima Earthquake in Japan actually had a negative impact on the American Automobile industry (and also other plants worldwide). Japanese companies manufacture many essential parts, especially electronics, for vehicles made in America. In order to save money by not having a large backlog of parts, companies import parts on an as-needed basis in their supply chain. Within a month or two, automobile plants in the United States, Japan, Germany and other locations temporarily closed. Obtaining paint, electronics, and parts for engines created the larger manufacturing problems (Canis 2011).

Each day that a business is not open represents a potential threat to survival. Businesses must plan to safeguard inventory as well as buildings, employees, records, and even customers. Unfortunately, the most common form of business-related emergency planning conducted across the board results in minimal accumulation of first-aid kits and basic training (Meszaros and Fiegener 2004).

Certain factors account for the lack of planning in the business sector. Size matters. Larger firms have more resources to hire contingency planners and write plans. Companies with multiple locations can draw from those resources to recover. Smaller firms struggle more with contingency planning and consequently are more likely to fail when disaster strikes. Previous experience also influences whether and how businesses plan. Those that have faced prior threats are more likely to plan, set aside resources for that rainy day, and be ready to regroup (Webb, Tierney, and Dahlhamer 2000).

To plan for disaster requires that businesses be ready financially, physically, and emotionally. Training people really does help. The World Trade Center in New York City was attacked not once but twice. The first bombing in 1993 resulted in a slow but effective evacuation. Getting thousands people out of two massive buildings takes time. In 2001, additional training, planning and practice resulted in a more rapid evacuation that ultimately saved many lives. Businesses at the World Trade Center enhanced evacuation knowledge through training and education for those working in the building (Gershon et al. 2007). But it is also true that people in their place of employment will step up. When a supper club caught on fire near Cincinnati, Ohio, waiters and other kitchen staff led customers to safety. Though 165 died, the employees of the supper club saved lives through their knowledge of the facility and where to escape the deadly smoke (Johnson 1998). Are you ready where you work?

6.4 Planning Guidance

In this section, we review some planning guidance issued by the federal government and other sources. While a considerable body of guidance exists, it does not always follow the recommendations listed above to incorporate research, conduct planning as a process, and build networks. As we noted at the beginning of this chapter, planning should not be a cookie-cutter approach where isolated individuals cut and paste sections from other documents to create a plan.

6.4.1 Personal and Household Level Planning

Many websites and organizations tell you to be ready for disaster and to "make a plan." But what does it mean to make a plan at the individual and household level? At this point you should have some good ideas about general preparedness and understand that you bear individual responsibility for your personal safety. To the greatest extent possible, you need to develop a series of steps that you will take given a hazard that could occur in your area. Have you walked your family or roommates through steps that need to be planned out for various scenarios from fire to severe weather to an extended period of isolation from a blizzard or pandemic?

And it is not enough to be familiar with just where you live, but in your other environments including school, work, restaurant and tourist locations. Imagine, for example, going on vacation in another state and realizing that a tornado outbreak is occurring. You look at the weather map but have no idea where you are in relation to the threat. If you go outside and realize that it is hailing and need to seek immediate shelter, where do you go? Or, you are in the hotel when the fire alarm goes off. Did you read the emergency information the hotel provides in a folio or on the back of the door before that occurred? Did you count the number of doors to the closest exit so that you can crawl under the smoke to safety?

Planning at the personal level starts with familiarizing yourself with area hazards and the risks they pose to you. Many Internet sites offer content that can help you understand the disaster history of the area as does your local library. The emergency management agency probably offers information on their websites and may even have a preparedness and planning campaign with downloadable materials. At the national level, FEMA provides a Family Communication Plan tool available in Spanish, Tagalog, Vietnamese, French, and other languages (see http://www.ready.gov/publications, last accessed February 23, 2016). A National Seasonal Preparedness messaging calendar and social media toolkit for the United States also exists to alert you and other newcomers to hazards at various times of the year (http://www.ready.gov/calendar). FEMA also provides via a PDF a personal information sheet and set of cards for individuals to use in the case of disasters (https://www.ready.gov/sites/default/files/documents/files/Family_Emegency_Plan.pdf). FEMA designed these documents to be kept in the family emergency preparedness kit. Thus, when disaster strikes, family members or first responders will have helpful information on how to communicate, contact, or find and assist other family members. Why not put the book down for 15 minutes and start that process?

Several first steps should launch your plan. The first is what to do in case a disaster bears down as an immediate threat. You will need to plan out how to shelter in place or evacuate. To shelter in place requires that you know the safest place for the hazard you are facing. Should a disaster destroy your home when you are separated from family and friends, you should have a place to meet near the neighborhood. If that is possible, you will need a place within walking distance and it is good to designate a further reunification location too. Alternatively, you may be able to evacuate in advance of a threat so knowing safe nearby locations and how to get there serves as part of the planning process. Deciding how, when, and where to evacuate beyond your home requires considerably more planning effort. You will need to determine where you can go and how you will get there. Personal transportation may or may not be an option so knowing people who can assist you to travel or public transportation options is critical.

Local agencies may have a registry of people who need transportation though most communities do not. Agencies should consider such factors as income, age or even special needs. If your community has such a registry be sure to update your information when any changes occur to your location or contact information (Metz et al. 2002). However, developing such a registry for planning purposes is not a simple project. Disaster planners must identify those that may need assistance, create a list so they know where they are located, and devise a mechanism to evacuate them from a potentially dangerous area. Planners can first use a communitywide survey to determine which residents may need help. They can also begin working with organizations that deal with special needs populations (e.g., local aging agencies) to help develop a list. Many organizations may wish not to cooperate, since the Health Insurance Portability and Accountability Act of 1996 (i.e., HIPPA) has strict rules about disclosing individuals' private medical information. The use of Geographic Information Systems, coupled with demographic data and a hazard analysis, can help planners target specific areas for finding residents with accessibility needs. In addition to creating a list, planners must keep the list updated. People move, they die, or they may have been missed with previous identifying efforts. New disabilities or temporary medical conditions may arise that place some people at new or higher risk. As a result, local officials should update their list once a year, a process that can be time-consuming and expensive (Hewett 2013).

Family and household members with accessibility needs should participate actively in the planning process. Individuals who may be blind, deaf, or use mobility devices know best what works for them and can inform co-planners of their particular needs. At a minimum, planning should include ways to secure and evacuate (as needed) with medications, medical records, assistive devices and other technologies, and service animals. Caregivers must be active in the planning process so that they remain with an individual at risk during a disaster. This is particularly important during an evacuation, so plan to keep families and households together with caregivers.

Members with particular needs also include pets and livestock. Ensure that you have planned for your pet including transportable medical information, food, water, leashes, and comfort items should an evacuation warrant. As part of your plan, be sure that someone remains alert to changing weather conditions so that pets can be brought indoors to safety given heat, cold, and weather threats. Livestock can receive varying degrees of protection from the elements from farm buildings and shelters to evacuation to livestock shelters in areas outside of the immediate threat (DHS 2016a).

Finally, do not forget to develop a communication plan. Assume that you will lose your cell phone, or the charger, or that callers will overwhelm cellular capacities after a disaster. What is your next strategy to let people know where you are and what you need? Planning an alternative means to communicate is critical. Landlines, e-mail, text messaging, and social media all serve as possible alternatives (Sutton and Tierney 2007). Currently, twitter has been developed as a key means of communication by officials to the public, and even among family members and friends (e.g., Sutton et al. 2014) and serves as one of the many effective means to relay information. You should also designate certain people to serve as central communication points so that you can contact them and they can pass on information about what you may need. By planning, you can decrease the impact on your personal safety and that of your loved ones. Most planning can take place over a couple of family or household dinners, which certainly seems a worthwhile investment of time given the alternative (Sutton and Tierney 2007).

If you need a starting place to help you with taking these steps, we suggest one or two starting places (see Boxes 6.3 and 6.4) that family members can initiate and use in a planning process. Imagine household residents sitting around the kitchen table, discussing these topics. By doing so, not only will they have the form filled out, but they will have learned about hazards, communications, warnings, protective action, accessibility, older family members, and pets. An important part of household planning is also putting together a disaster kit (Red Cross n.d.b, see also Box 6.4).

BOX 6.3   MAKE A HOUSEHOLD DISASTER PREPAREDNESS PLAN

Both FEMA/DHS and the American National Red Cross provide similar suggestions for starting and maintaining a household disaster plan. Highlights of their recommendations include:

- Discuss among household members about making a plan
- Analyze the possible types of hazard that threaten you
- Review how household members might be alerted for each of these hazards and the actions household members would take when a warning is received
- Determine a location to meet if household members become separated during an event
- Ensure that each household member has contact information for other members such as:
  - Email
  - Phone
  - School or work
- Identify a contact person outside of your hazard area(s)
- Consider what important documents and medications each member may need
- Think about your pets, sheltering or evacuating with them, and their food, water, and medication needs
- Practice your plan once or twice a year.

Sources: http://www.redcross.org/prepare/location/home-family/plan; https://www.ready.gov/make-a-plan

BOX 6.4   DISASTER SUPPLY KIT: BASIC AND ADDITIONAL SUPPLIES

A basic emergency supply kit could include the following recommended items:

- Water, one gallon of water per person per day for at least three days, for drinking and sanitation
- Food, at least a three-day supply of nonperishable food
- Battery-powered or hand crank radio and a NOAA Weather Radio with tone alert and extra batteries for both
- Flashlight and extra batteries
- First-aid kit

(Continued)

BOX 6.4 (*Continued*)   DISASTER SUPPLY KIT:
BASIC AND ADDITIONAL SUPPLIES

- Whistle to signal for help
- Dust mask to help filter contaminated air and plastic sheeting and duct tape to shelter-in-place
- Moist towelettes, garbage bags and plastic ties for personal sanitation
- Wrench or pliers to turn off utilities
- Manual can opener for food
- Local maps
- Cell phone with chargers, inverter or solar charger

Additional Supplies

- Prescription medications and glasses
- Infant formula and diapers
- Pet food and extra water for your pet
- Cash or traveler's checks and change
- Important family documents such as copies of insurance policies, identification and bank account records in a waterproof, portable container. You can use the Emergency Financial First Aid Kit—EFFAK (PDF–977 Kb) developed by Operation Hope, FEMA and Citizen Corps to help you organize your information.
- Emergency reference material such as a first-aid book or free information from this web site. (See Publications)
- Sleeping bag or warm blanket for each person. Consider additional bedding if you live in a cold-weather climate.
- Complete change of clothing including a long sleeved shirt, long pants and sturdy shoes. Consider additional clothing if you live in a cold-weather climate.
- Household chlorine bleach and medicine dropper—when diluted, nine parts water to one part bleach, bleach can be used as a disinfectant. Or in an emergency, you can use it to treat water by using 16 drops of regular household liquid bleach per gallon of water. Do not use scented, color safe or bleaches with added cleaners.
- Fire extinguisher
- Matches in a waterproof container
- Feminine supplies and personal hygiene items
- Mess kits, paper cups, plates, paper towels and plastic utensils
- Paper and pencil
- Books, games, puzzles or other activities for children

Source: https://www.ready.gov/kit (*verbatim*)

We may already have some items, such as flashlights, batteries, gloves, and bottled water, around the household. But, we don't think about putting some of these items into a specific kit for a disaster. Managing to put a kit together can be expensive, so consider adding one item every month from a local dollar store.

Whereas the Red Cross provides a more generic approach to planning, The Department of Homeland Security (DHS) and FEMA provide a more specific list of recommendations for a wide range of hazards for many types of people or settings (e.g., Native Americans, the Military, Seniors, campuses, and businesses). DHS and FEMA also provide a similar set of recommendations to the Red Cross for putting together a preparedness kit. Their recommendations can be found at www.ready.gov. Any of these sites provide good initial and in-depth recommendations and information about planning.

6.4.2 Community-Based Planning

As Quarantelli (1994) has stressed, planning is a process, not a piece of paper. Whether planning involves a family in one household or a large community with thousands, people must work together to devise a plan. Within the emergency management community, we often hear the phrase, "all disasters are local." Whether local governmental offices, neighborhood associations, business organizations (e.g., Chamber of Commerce), volunteer organizations, or religious organizations, all can and should participate in disaster planning. After all, who better knows a community than those who live and work in it?

As we have noted throughout the text, disasters are not equal opportunity events. Certain groups of people, such as some of the poor, the elderly, some members of racial and ethnic minorities, and some people with accessibility needs are more likely to be exposed to disaster impacts due to historic patterns of prejudice and discrimination, coupled at times with income disparities. By involving the full community in the planning process, we can identify and anticipate those at higher risk, plan more effectively for their survival and empower a broader range of citizens to be pro-active. By leveraging the social capital that they bring to the planning table, we ultimately strengthen disaster-resilience of historically disadvantaged populations and reduce demands on emergency managers.

FEMA has drawn upon the general idea of community-based planning for close to 25 years. Today, FEMA calls this approach "Whole Community" planning. In short, FEMA encourages all stakeholders from all levels of government (including tribal nations), the public, private and volunteer sectors, and faith-based organizations to become active participants in disaster planning. FEMA (2015) best describes this rationale as follows:

Both the composition of the community and the individual needs of community members, regardless of age, economics, or accessibility requirements, must be accounted for when planning and implementing disaster strategies.

When the community is engaged in an authentic dialogue, it becomes empowered to identify its needs and the existing resources that may be used to address them. Collectively, we can determine the best ways to organize and strengthen community assets, capacities, and interests. This allows us, as a nation, to expand our reach and deliver services more efficiently and cost effectively to build, sustain, and improve our capability to prepare for, protect against, respond to, recover from, and mitigate all hazards.

This idea is embraced more widely. At the international level, The World Health Organization (WHO) serves as a center point for pandemic planning. WHO (2005, p. vii) also encourages widespread community participation in planning:

> A multisectoral approach means the involvement of many levels of government, and of people with various specialties including policy development, legislative review and drafting, animal health, public health, patient care, laboratory diagnosis, laboratory test development, communication expertise and disaster management. Community involvement means making optimal use of local knowledge, expertise, resources and networks. It is a powerful way to engage people and to build the commitment needed for policy decisions.

Drawing upon these ideas, WHO (2009) developed and now advocates a "Whole-of-Society" approach. From individuals up through government, business, and nongovernmental organizations must plan and coordinate together in order to respond to a pandemic. Pandemics impact all components of communities and nations, thus all components must be active and involved in the planning process. All of the above stakeholders maintain their involvement during the Readiness, Response, and Recovery phases of the event. In addition, WHO argues that the "Whole-of-Society" approach can also enhance disaster planning and response beyond health and pandemic events. Key societal components of this approach include (WHO 2019, p. 6):

- Health
- Defense
- Law & Order
- Finance
- Transportation
- Communications
- Energy
- Food
- Water

In addition, the U.S. federal government has provided a central document to provide guidance in local disaster planning—Comprehensive Planning Guide-101 (CPG-101). This unique document is a major step forward for assisting local stakeholders in disaster planning. This document has helped make major strides in disaster planning. First, it stresses local or community disaster planning. Second, decades of disaster research (rather than guesswork or opinions) ground many of the assumptions about disaster planning. Third, FEMA and its subcontractor relied upon the expertise of many local emergency coordinators in designing and writing the document. Fourth, although produced by the federal government, the recommendations in CPG-101 are guidelines for local disaster planners. CPG-101 developers wanted to help local disaster planners get started with the planning process—not tell local governments how they must plan for disasters. Underlying the whole approach to CPG-101 is the idea of building social capital—particularly through interacting and networking in the planning process. This assumption alone recognizes the importance of local input and participation in disaster planning (e.g., see CPG-101).

A main principle for any kind of emergency planning, then, is to involve the public to the best degree possible. Response planning requires certain levels of expertise from firefighters who know how to enter burning buildings and conduct extractions to emergency managers who coordinate behind the scenes. Public involvement, however, can be useful. For many years, communities failed to involve people with accessibility needs in response planning. More recently, however, people with disabilities have assisted first responders with how they should be moved, why their assistive devices need to be retrieved, and how to help service animals. It is also true that the first to respond to a scene are usually family, friends, and neighbors. Connecting them to the response effort ensures that they do so safely.

Recovery planning efforts need to involve community representatives as well and to inform the community about what the recovery planning team is considering. Stakeholders must come from a broad range of the public including businesses, residents, utility companies, environmental experts, and those concerned with historic and cultural preservation. Each brings a valuable perspective to the recovery planning process and can make suggestions that help restore quality of life. Community-based planning must also consider the needs of various groups when reconstruction is launched. Age matters, for example. Seniors may benefit from new codes that upgrade homes using universal design features (helpful to all of us) such as levers that open doors more easily than knobs. Children's needs might include additional park space or safe bike routes from home to school. If a community uses relocation to move structures out of floodplains, it can create parkland. The community must be consulted about their preferences that could range from establishing a nature preserve to creating soccer fields or a dog park. Community investment in any planning process means that people are more likely to return and rebuild in a way that gives meaningful social interaction for their lives.

Community involvement occurs in several ways. A typical form is to create a planning team that has representatives from various sectors. Those individuals need to stay in touch with the broader constituencies and to consult them for preferences. Communities can also hold public forums to present options and secure input. Electronic means to do so have become increasingly common, especially when residents experience displacement to other cities. Electronic surveys, websites, social media, and other sources can tap into public opinion. Radio and television shows can afford chances for the public to air their thoughts. Yet, community involvement can also be as simple as having people gather for public meetings in the bayous, city halls, or university auditoriums available locally.

Community planners can harness local energy to generate new insights and pathways for a community to take. What residents know, from the standpoint of their own lives, can positively influence all kinds of planning. By thinking through how to reach out we can further empower public input. Public outreach should reflect the community by offering information in various formats for those who cannot see or hear, with low literacy levels, and who may not speak the local language. Planning should never become an exercise in exclusion. Doing so costs lives.

6.4.3 State Planning Guidance in the United States

In the United States, the state's role generally is three-fold. First, the states take federal guidance and create training opportunities for state and local government. For example, and as we detail below, following the September 11 terrorist attacks, the federal government required that all federal, state, and local officials involved in emergency management become trained in knowing how to use the NIMS.

Second, the states model their own planning process upon the federal recommendations. This approach shows federalism at work in emergency management. Specifically, although the United States has national policies, states can take these policies and relate them to their own political and disaster climate. Considering the diverse politics and hazards throughout the United States, a federalist approach to emergency management makes sense (McEntire and Dawson 2007). CPG-101 also provides guidance for state planning. Rather than forcing each state in the union to take a specific approach to disaster planning, CPG-101 provides suggestions for different ways states can approach planning to fit their own unique needs.

6.4.4 National Planning Guidance

The notion of national planning guidance is cumbersome as the term certainly has broadly-based potential for application. On one hand, national-level planning assumes some kind of central governmental structure with responsibility for citizens under their governance. Governments, regardless of structure, may shoulder different levels of responsibility for planning. Planning may emanate from administrative components of the structure or through legislation or legal decisions. A ruling political party may lead planning or may direct that effort to a specific agency. That same ruling party may activate a plan when appropriate or may stall that decision. Those in leadership either by voter choice or through military (e.g., a dictatorship) might can thwart others from implementing plans to aid in a response. It may also be true that a centralized government could also stall response capabilities, as lower level staff remain reluctant to take action (Britton 2006). Thus, the notion of national planning needs to be understood in a widely varying set of contexts and circumstances.

National planning guidance may also emerge from within a nation or from outside, as we will see in an example of pandemic planning shortly. In the United States, a combination of choices, events and circumstances has driven national-level planning. The President, for example, can issue an Executive Order (EO) to drive forward an area of planning. Perhaps the most influential EO of the last decade occurred on October 8, 2001 when President Bush established the U.S. DHS. A portion of that EO reads (Federal Register 2001):

> The Office of Homeland Security shall coordinate national efforts to prepare for and mitigate the consequences of terrorist threats or attacks within the United States. In performing this function, the Office shall work with federal, state, and local agencies, and private entities, as appropriate, to: (i) review and assess the adequacy of the portions of all federal emergency response plans that pertain to terrorist threats or attacks within the United States.

Other Presidential Directives have also served to strengthen planning and preparedness activities for terrorist attacks and other natural and technological disasters. Homeland Security Presidential Directive-7 (HSPD-7) of 2003 focused on protecting and securing the United States' infrastructure. A number of federal agencies (i.e., Departments of Agriculture, Health and Human Services, Environmental Protection Agency, Department of Energy, Department of Treasury, Department of the Interior, Department of Defense) along with the private sector should communicate and coordinate their actions to protect the nation's infrastructure (DHS 2015). The Presidential Policy Directive-8 (PPD-8) of 2011 continued to enhance preparedness and planning activities. The ideas of improving resiliency and security drives much of this document. It also stresses a holistic approach to planning and preparedness, advocating that local communities and other stakeholders (e.g., private sector, tribal nations, and volunteer organizations) work with various levels of government (DHS 2015b).

Events also reveal the failings and limitations of plans or of not implementing plans. In the aftermath of Hurricane Katrina, both the White House and the U.S. Congress issued reports on failed systems and called for enhanced planning efforts. As a consequence, extensive review took place with reinvigorated plans and integrated planning across agencies. Certainly, lawsuits have also generated additional planning and programs. For example, *Brou v. FEMA* resulted in new efforts to increase accessible, temporary disaster housing for people with disabilities and gave momentum to a new National Disaster Housing Strategy. In summary, several means exist to influence national planning guidance.

Britton (2006, p. 365) compared national planning in Japan, New Zealand, and the Philippines. He determined that carrying out planning responsibilities tends to "reflect cultural values and assumptions, including previous disaster experiences." Japan, for example, has invested between 5% and 8% of their annual national budget to disaster reduction with the majority of that focused on mitigation initiatives. Given the significant risks they face from earthquake threats in particular, their efforts are understandable. The Great Hanshin earthquake that occurred in Kobe, Japan in 1995 killed over 6,000 citizens. A plethora of laws have since led spurred to increase Japan's capabilities and readiness. The 1998 Comprehensive National Development Act, for example, required that the government make the nation "a safe and comfortable place to live." Nonetheless, critique has centered on a lack of coordinated policies and that "public officials often consider disaster programs to be nuisances that interfere in routine administrative tasks" (Britton 2006, p. 357). In New Zealand, a task force found "unrealistically high public expectations" and that citizens assumed capabilities beyond what the government could provide. In response, the government has led initiatives to establish local civil defense and emergency management groups. Integration of scientific and empirical work has driven much of their work to situate emergency management in a local context and empower citizen involvement.

Returning to the United States, FEMA and DHS have led efforts to revise national-level planning and create a NRF. Evolution over time reflects the natural progression of planning at the national level. According to Britton (2006), the national level "is the only sector that has a commission to develop nationwide strategies with power to bind, power to commit public resources and influence private resources" (p. 366).

NIMS drives the management structure used by most response organizations in the United States. NIMS is the broad management structure for coordinating response efforts among all levels of government, the public sector, the private sector, and the volunteer sector. NIMS is based upon the Incident Management System (IMS), a management structure devised by the fire services, which we describe below.

Following the 9/11 terror attacks in the United States, expert analysis suggested that numerous management issues, including coordination and communication issues plagued the response, especially in New York City (The 9/11 Commission Report 2004). A number of experts in firefighting suggested all response organizations should use the ICS for a more effective response to disasters. As a result, this directive required all levels of government to use NIMS during all disaster events (including terror attacks). Furthermore, the federal government would assist the private sector and other nongovernmental organizations with training to they too could use NIMS (HSPD-5 2003).

Originating as a tactic to fight unpredictable wildfires in the Western United States, firefighters have used and enhanced ICS since the early 1970s. ICS is based upon five simple components: (1) the Incident Commander, (2) Logistics, (3) Planning, (4) Operations, and (5) Finance (see Figure A.2). The Incident Commander (IC) oversees and coordinates activities during an event. Individuals in charge of Finance, Logistics, Operation, and Planning report to the IC to share their information so the IC can make well-informed decisions. The Finance function pertains to keeping track of the budget and the amount of monies spent. Logistics pertains to obtaining and delivering resources to the disaster site. Finally, Planning gathers information to determine what resources (e.g., people and equipment) are needed to perform needed tasks (e.g., debris removal). In theory, ICS has a simple organizational structure that can expand or contract as driven by the situation. Firefighters can use this basic structure to fight fires, or local, state, and federal governments can use this same type of structure, but with thousands of people, to respond to a larger event (NPS 2016). For example, Figure A.2 shows how the five main components of ICS still provide the foundation for the management structure, but also how each component can have additional tasks plugged in for larger events (FEMA 2008, p. 7).

NIMS reflects the ICS structure, but also includes the idea of "unified command." In theory, each jurisdiction and major task should be operating under the ICS structure. Yet, this means that the disaster response will have multiple Incident Commanders that could lead to confusion regarding decision making and who is in charge. Thus, Incident Commanders collectively agree upon a decision and let their managers and responders know the decision (FEMA 2016). In summary, a Unified Command should have (verbatim):

- A shared understanding of priorities and restrictions
- A single set of incident objectives
- Collaborative strategies
- Improved internal and external information flow
- Less duplication of efforts
- Better resource utilization (FEMA 2016, end verbatim)

NIMS and ICS are the standard, if not required, management structure used for events ranging from day-to-day emergency response (e.g., house fires) to catastrophes (e.g., a Hurricane Katrina type of event). As disaster planners and managers implement NIMS and ICS, both disaster professionals and researchers have raised serious issues about the effectiveness of NIMS and ICS in disaster. They question such factors as flexibility, use in large scale events, plugging in volunteer and emergent groups, and training. In addition, officials made NIMS a federal policy without a set of studies demonstrating its effectiveness. In the limited studies available on ICS, variation occurred across agencies and individuals who used it, with equally varying levels of understanding how it functions (Jensen 2010; Neal and Webb 2004).

The federal government is firmly committed to NIMS. In fact, federal, state and local governments must have their employees fully trained in NIMS in order to obtain any type of federal funding or reimbursements following a disaster. In order to meet these needs, FEMA has devised a five-year plan in order to make the nation "NIMS Compliant." In short, training emergency responders and emergency managers at all levels of government is central to disaster planning in the United States (FEMA 2008).

6.4.5 Cross-National Guidance

Disasters know no political boundaries. Flooding crosses borders, blizzards and volcanic ash shut down international airports, and terrorism affects us all. Nations must work together to plan for various threats that can certainly be challenging given political differences, resource bases, and how various hazards present risks disproportionately to various populations. In this section, we look at how cross-national planning has taken place by looking at a hazard that certainly affects our readers: influenza pandemics.

No one wants to get the flu and in today's society with rapid transportation of people across national borders the potential for a major outbreak exists. We need to take the threat of influenza seriously. In 1918–1919, the

"Spanish" flu killed between 20 and 50 million people. This particular strain took its heaviest toll on young people. Later pandemics in 1957 (the Asian flu) and 1969 (the Hong Kong Flu) took a lesser toll worldwide but senior citizens and those with chronic medical conditions fared the worst (Cox, Tamblyn, and Tam 2003).

Coupled with the loss of life, pandemics also cause considerable social disruption when schools and child care centers close, hospitals and medical facilities experience massive influx and businesses lose customers. The economic impact can be significant (Cox, Tamblyn, and Tam 2003). Because we cannot eliminate influenza viruses, we must plan for their impact. The effort to do so also benefits other planning efforts, as "pandemic preparedness planning can be usefully linked to response planning for other public health emergencies, including bioterrorism threats" (Cox, Tamblyn, and Tam 2003, p. 1801).

How seriously are nations taking the pandemic threat? The World Health Organization (2005) estimates that a major influenza pandemic could result in 233 million outpatient visits, 5.2 million in-patient admissions, and 7.4 million deaths within a relatively short time period. Imagine the social and economic disruptions that would result let alone the grief that would affect so many households. To determine appropriate action steps, nations with pandemic plans rely on activation phases and levels with recommended action steps. The European Union, for example, coordinates most of their activation levels across 27 nations using WHO criteria:

- Interpandemic Period.
  - Phase 1. No new strain in humans but may be present in animals.
  - Phase 2. Virus circulating in animals.
- Pandemic Alert Period.
  - Phase 3. Human illnesses develop but not transmitted to other humans.
  - Phase 4. Illness is transmitted in small, localized clusters.
  - Phase 5. Larger clusters but still localized, pandemic possible.
- Pandemic period.
  - Phase 6. Rapid transmission across populations and locations.
- Post Pandemic Period.
  - Return to normal.

The World Health Organization (WHO 2005) recommends a series of steps for nations conducting pandemic planning. A first step sets planners on creating a task force or planning team. Planning elements for pandemics include conducting a risk assessment, focused on who would be most likely to be affected. Certainly, some populations suffer more than others as indicated by influenza history. Those living in impoverished or socially disadvantaged locations "will be among those least likely to receive effective medical counter-measures or to benefit from nonmedical public health interventions, and they will be among those most likely to die as a result of infection" (Usher-Pines et al. 2007, p. 32). Some estimates indicate that 96% of deaths would occur in developing nations but within a more advantaged nation those who are economically and socially disadvantaged would likely suffer more. In 2006, a group of experts recommended that planners (Usher-Pines et al. 2007):

- Identify historically disadvantaged populations as among those most likely to be affected by a pandemic. Depending on location, these groups may include the poor and political minorities. In recent outbreaks, poultry farmers whose livestock were destroyed suffered not only influenza but economically as well. Another group could well include people without health care insurance.
- Involve these populations in planning for a potential pandemic. They will know their life circumstances best and can identify effective means for communicating influenza information within the population, which is a main component of pandemic planning.
- List and design solutions for special needs that may exist within the population. Special needs might include disseminating information in appropriate languages, offering social services, counseling, and special housing. People who remain home-bound may need outreach, food, and medications delivered directly to them.

Initial steps also involve crafting public education information. Messaging must target those particularly at risk and should be diverse enough to reach across various populations and the information media they access. The recent outbreak of H1N1 virus illustrates the concerns of planners clearly: those most at risk were pregnant women. Delivering recommended protocol to them and their health care providers emerged as a critical action.

Public health officials must next monitor the outbreak, carefully documenting and verifying symptoms as the illness spreads. By investigating the dissemination of the illness, epidemiologists can determine who is at highest risk as well as the geographic locations of concern. You would probably not be surprised to learn that most universities and colleges have a pandemic plan in place to shut down or even quarantine your school. Some have gone a second step, to transition classes into online platforms so that students can continue to make progress toward their degrees. Some have implemented business continuity planning across their campuses to be ready (visit Ohio University for an example at https://www.ohio.edu/riskandsafety/continuity/). The traveling public may also face restrictions or health checks in passport control to reduce the spread of the disease.

Final steps address the needs of the health community as personnel respond to phases involving illness. Even they are not immune to becoming sick and staff numbers and facilities may be compromised in an outbreak. Ensuring that sufficient numbers of health care personnel can step in supports the health care system's capacity to respond. An expected patient surge in the United States is to be met by a cadre of health care professionals including the "National Disaster Medical System (NDMS), the Commissioned Corps of the U.S. Public Health Service (USPHS), the Strategic National Stockpile (SNS), and federal volunteers and temporary employees" and certainly elements of the NRF, including the Disaster Mortuary Team (Department of Health and Human Services, see Resources).

As with any good planning effort, activation of a plan during an event requires careful evaluation. Often called "hot washes" or debriefings, planners and those involved in activating the plan conduct a review. During that time it is critical that those present honestly and thoroughly critique the plan's implementation and effectiveness. This is not a time to say "job well done" but rather an opportunity to identify plan weaknesses and revise accordingly.

Recently, proper steps stopped the spread of an Ebola pandemic—but still with a major loss of life. In West Africa, the countries of Sierra Leone, Guinea, Liberia alone documented over 28,600 cases, with over 11,300 deaths. Seven other countries accounted for 36 cases and 15 deaths. A lack of public health knowledge and the contagious nature of the virus caused Ebola to spread rapidly throughout West Africa. The four cases in the United States (with one death) became a lead news story during the fall of 2014. Focused steps on prevention today have stopped the present outbreak. However, these events showed that various authorities must continue to plan to mitigate future cases (CDCa 2016).

Finally, at the time of this text going to the publisher, another possible public health threat called Zika looms. Generally, Zika can make victims feel ill and cause deformities in fetuses including microencephaly or abnormal brain development. Mosquitoes and possibly sexual contact can spread Zika. As of 2016, public health agencies are advising women not to travel to areas (e.g., South America) where scientists have detected Zika and the U.S. Congress has passed additional funding to address the health threat. With the 2016 Summer Olympics being held in Brazil, concern is spreading about the safety of participants and spectators arriving from and returning to countries around the world, and having Zika spread worldwide (CDC 2016b).

6.5 Working and Volunteering in Planning

Jobs in disaster planning may be stand-alone opportunities or embedded within a more general position. Note, for example, these listings for the Centers for Disease Control below in bullets. Components of these positions include planning elements and developing guidance materials as well as organizing training, drills and exercises to test the plans for general emergency response and for public health—which would include potential pandemics (Source: verbatim from www.cdc.gov, search Employment):

- "Emergency response specialists serve as an integral member of a team responsible for coordinating emergency preparedness and responses to natural and man-made hazards and disasters. They may provide all-hazards public health watch support; incident emergency alert, notification and escalation; and support for emergency incident drills, exercises, and actual emergencies. The specialists coordinate health consultation services; develop guidance material for response personnel; and manage and direct demonstration and training programs for state and local health personnel involved in emergency preparedness and response."
- Public Health Advisor (overseas): "perform as public health project officers of grants and cooperative agreements with emphasis on financial accountability, internal controls, strategic planning and policy. They frequently manage an extensive staff and the logistics and personnel issues that arise in a large office. They may provide guidance and assistance to host country Ministry of Health officials, other USG agencies and international organizations to plan, implement and evaluate activities for a specific public health programs. Program areas that employ public health advisors (Management and Operations) include infectious diseases, zoonotic and emerging infectious diseases, chronic diseases, environmental health and injury control." [end verbatim]

Volunteering opportunities exist also in the area of planning. This is particularly so in the areas of mitigation and post-disaster recovery planning. Because mitigation planning rolls out more slowly and in a stepwise fashion, it is easier to volunteer as part of a community-based group working to lessen area hazards. After a disaster occurs, communities also convene planning committees and usually offer the public various means to participate such as open forums, housing fairs, and planning charrettes. To become more involved in other phases, volunteer for organizations designing preparedness campaigns and help distribute and explain information to people. Encourage personal and household planning in both your own home and across your neighborhood. Form efforts with emergency management officials to support seniors and others with household planning. Response planning typically occurs within the emergency management and first responder community. Depending on the size of the community and their commitment to public involvement, you may be able to participate in the planning process as part of a formal response group dedicated to serving during emergencies. Even if you are not part of the actual planning, your participation may be useful during exercises and drills to test the plan. Remain alert for opportunities to observe these events as well as they can provide insights and instruction to you for a future career path.

Summary

The planning process should focus on creating and maintaining social networks among those who will respond to a disaster. The creation of a paper plan becomes a secondary task. Rather, disaster coordinators must engage all those involved in response with talking about and writing the plan. Those players should include, at the community level, those in local, state and even the federal government, businesses, volunteer organizations, and local residents. In addition, plans must avoid myths about disaster behavior. Research and experience by disaster responders show time and time again such incidents as looting, panic, mass hysteria, and other related negative images of human behavior are rare during disaster. Rather, disasters seem to bring the best, not the worst, out of people.

Individuals in households can help communitywide preparedness by engaging in their own planning efforts. Devising a plan, based upon local hazards, communication capabilities, and those living in a household (e.g., special needs) can help save lives. In addition, household planning can also include members acquiring proper supplies if disaster strikes.

An initial obstacle in disaster planning is where or how to start. At the local level and state level, Comprehensive Planning Guide (CPG) 101 provides helpful guidance for initiating or updating disaster plans. The NRF and the NIMS documents also provide useful information on the structure of responding to an event.

Discussion Questions

1. What are the types of activities that a local disaster manager can take to engage those in the public, private, and volunteers sector to enhance the planning process?

2. When disaster strikes, why can officials and others still manage the disaster effectively without consulting the plan?

3. Consider how disaster myths could impact a disaster response versus a reality based disaster plan?

4. Have you ever been involved in any type of household disaster planning? If so, what types of activities did you do to plan and prepare? How successful do you think these efforts were?

5. Effective disaster planning can only occur when all publics are involved. Identify different publics (e.g., those with disabilities and tribal nations) that may reside in your community. Next, how might you reach out to these stakeholders. Consider what organizations may also help you to reach out since they often represent these different groups.

6. Imagine you are a local disaster coordinator and are giving a 15 minute talk to a local club during lunch. Your talk will focus on effective disaster planning. What two or three themes would you punctuate during your short luncheon talk?

7. If you were a disaster planner, how might you explicitly draw upon CPG–101, the NRF, and NIMS to enhance your planning efforts?

Resources

- Personal planning and Preparedness: www.ready.govserves as a portal to a comprehensive set of information on planning and preparedness. As noted in part in the text, this website can assist individuals, household members, organizations, governments, tribal nations, businesses, volunteer and not-for-profit organizations. Specific links and topic may change, but it also has a useful search function so the reader can also easily find specific topics. Another website, http://www.adcouncil.org/Our-Campaigns/Safety/Emergency-Preparedness, has a lot of good information for family planning and works well in conjunction with the ready.gov web site.
- The American Red Cross http://www.redcross.org/support/emergency-preparedness gives a good overall perspective on disaster planning. Coupled with the DHS's ready.gov site, the Red Cross' site reinforces appropriate planning recommendations.
- To learn more about Comprehensive Planning Guide (CPG)-101, visit https://www.fema.gov/media-library-data/20130726-1828-25045-014/cpg_101_comprehensive_preparedness_guide_developing_and_maintaining_emergency_operations_plans_2010.pdf.
- The National Incident Management System (NIMS) can be reviewed at https://www.fema.gov/national-incident-management-system.
- The National Response Framework (NRF) can be reviewed at http://www.fema.gov/national-response-frameworkas well as http://www.fema.gov/media-library/assets/documents/32230?id=7371.
- To learn more about pandemics, visit http://emergency.cdc.gov/planning/, a web site published by the Centers for Disease Control and Prevention. This site provides informative links for planning for

specific types of agents, personal and household locations, businesses, health care facilities, government, and lists documents related to legal issues.

- European Union nation information on pandemics can be viewed at http://ecdc.europa.eu/en/healthtopics/pandemic_preparedness/ national_pandemic_preparedness_plans/Pages/influenza_ pandemic_preparedness_plans.aspx.
- Basic checklists for pandemic planning can be seen at http://apps.who. int/iris/bitstream/10665/68980/1/WHO_CDS_CSR_GIP_2005.4.pdf.
- The American Planning Association (APA) provides advice and examples on recovery, https://www.planning.org/research/ postdisaster/, https://www.planning.org/research/postdisaster/ and https://www.planning.org/divisions/hazardmitigation/.

References and Recommended Readings

Britton, Neil R. 2006. National Planning and Response: National Systems. pp. 347–367 in *Handbook of Disaster Research*, editedby H. Rodriguez, E.L. Quarantelli and R. Dynes. New York: Springer.

Canis, Bill. 2011. The Motor Vehicle Supply Chain: Effects of the Japanese Earthquake and Tsunami. Congressional Research Service. Available at https://www.fas.org/sgp/crs/ misc/R41831.pdf, last accessed February 7, 2016.

CBSNEWS. 2010. BP Didn't Plan for Major Oil Spill. Available at http://www.cbsnews. com/news/bp-didnt-plan-for-major-oil-spill/, last accessed March 5, 2016.

Center for Disease Control and Prevention (CDC). 2006. Faith Based & Community Organizations Pandemic Influeza Preparedness Checklist. Available at http://www. flu.gov/planning-preparedness/community/faithbaseedcommunitychecklist.pdf, last accessed February 9, 2016.

Center for Disease Control and Prevention (CDC). 2016a. 2014 Ebola Breakout in West Africa. Available at http://www.cdc.gov/vhf/ebola/outbreaks/2014-west-africa/case-counts.html, last accessed February 20, 2016.

Center for Disease Control and Prevention (CDC). 2016b. Zika Virus. Available at http:// www.cdc.gov/zika/index.html, last accessed February 20, 2016.

Cox, Nancy J., Susan E. Tamblyn, and Theresa Tam. 2003. Influenza Pandemic Planning. *Vaccine* 21: 1801–1803.

Department of Homeland Security (DHS). 2015a. Homeland Security Presidential Directive—7. Available at https://www.dhs.gov/homeland-security-presidential-directive-7, last accessed March 2, 2016.

Department of Homeland Security (DHS). 2015b. Presidential Policy Directive/PPD-8: National Preparedness. Available at https://www.dhs.gov/presidential-policy-directive-8-national-preparedness, last accessed March 2, 2016.

Department of Homeland Security (DHS). 2016a. Pet and Animal Emergency Planning. Available at https://www.ready.gov/animals, last accessed March 2, 2016.

Federal Emergency Management Agency (FEMA). 2008. ICS Organization. Available at https://training.fema.gov/emiweb/is/icsresource/assets/reviewmaterials.pdf, last accessed March 2, 2016.

Federal Emergency Management Agency (FEMA). 2015. Whole Community. Available at http://www.fema.gov/whole-community, last accessed February 7, 2016.

Federal Emergency Management Agency (FEMA). 2016a. Lesson 5: Unified Command. Available at https://emilms.fema.gov/IS100hcb/ICS0105summary.htm, last accessed March 2, 2016.

Federal Emergency Management Agency (FEMA). 2016b. *USAJOBS: FEMA.* Available at https://www.usajobs.gov/GetJob/ViewDetails/431383300?PostingChannelID=USA Search, last accessed March 5, 2016.

Federal Register. 2001. Establishing the Office of Homeland Security and the Homeland Security Council. Available at https://www.federalregister.gov/articles/2001/10/10/01-25677/establishing-the-office-of-homeland-security-and-the-homeland-security-council, last accessed August 30, 2016.

Fitzgerald, Alison. 2010. "BP Ready for Spill 10 Times the Gulf Disaster." Available at http://www.bloomberg.com/news/articles/2010-05-31/bp-told-u-s-it-could-handle-oil-spill-10-times-larger-than-gulf-disaster, last accessed March 5, 2016.

Hewett, Paul L., Jr. 2013. *Organizational Networks and Preparedness during Disaster Preparedness: The Case of an Emergency Preparedness Registry.* Doctoral Dissertation, Fire and Emergency Management Program (Department of Political Science). Stillwater, OK: Oklahoma State University.

HSPD-5. 2003. Homeland Security Presidential Directive-5. Available at https://www.dhs.gov/sites/default/files/publications/Homeland%20Security%20Presidential%20Directive%205.pdf, last accessed February 29, 2016.

Jensen, Jessica Anne. 2010. *Emergency Management Policy: Predicting National Incident Management System (NIMS) Implementation Behavior.* Dissertation, Department of Sociology, Anthropology and Emergency Management. Fargo, ND: North Dakota State University.

Johnson, Norris. 1988. Fire in a Crowded Theater. *International Journal of Mass Emergencies and Disasters* 6(1): 7–26.

Kendra, James M. and Tricia Wachtendorf. 2003. Creativity in Emergency Response after the World Trade Center Attack. *In Beyond September 11th: An Account of Post-Disaster Research.* Special Publication #39 Natural Hazards Research and Applications Information Center. Boulder, CO: University of Colorado.

Kirschenbaum, Avi. 1992. Warning and Evacuation During a Mass Disaster: A Multivariate Decision Making Model. *International Journal of Mass Emergencies and Disasters* 10: 91–114.

McEntire, David A. and Gregg Dawson. 2007. The Intergovernmental Context. pp. 57–70 in *Emergency Management: Principles and Practice for Local Government,* 2nd Edition, edited by William L. Waugh, Jr., and Kathleen Tierney. Washington, D.C.: ICMA Press.

Meszaros, Jacqueline and Mark Fiegener. 2004. Predicting Earthquake Preparation. Available at http://www.iitk.ac.in/nicee/wcee/article/13_571.pdf, last accessed January 31, 2011.

Metz, William, Paul Hewett, Edward Tanzman, and Julie Muzzarelli. 2002. Identifying Special-Needs Households That Need Assistance for Emergency Planning. *International Journal of Mass Emergencies and Disasters* 20(2): 255–281.

National Commission on the BP Deepwater Horizon Oil Spill and Offshore Drilling. 2011. Deep Water: the Gulf Oil Disaster and the Future of Offshore Drilling. Available at http://www.gpo.gov/fdsys/pkg/GPO-OILCOMMISSION, last accessed July 8, 2015.

National Park Service (NPS). 2016. Incident Command System. Available at http://www.nps.gov/fire/wildland-fire/learning-center/fire-in-depth/incident-command-system.cfm, last accessed March 2, 2016.

Neal, David M. and Gary R. Webb. 2006. Structural Barriers to Implementing the National Incident Management System. pp. 263–282 in *Learning from Catastrophe: Quick Response Research in the Wake of Hurricane Katrina*, edited by Christine Bvec. Boulder, CO: Natural Hazards Center, University of Colorado.

Quarantelli, E.L. 1988. Assessing Disaster Preparedness Planning. *Regional Development Dialogue* 9: 48–69.

Quarantelli, E.L. 1994. Research-based Criteria for Evaluating Disaster Planning and Managing. Available at http://www.nifv.nl/upload/179144_668_1168610952796-quarantelli-1998.pdf, last accessed March 5, 2016.

Quarantelli, E.L. 1997. Ten Criteria for Evaluating the Management of Community Disasters. *Disasters* 21: 39–56.

Red Cross. n.d.a. Make a Disaster Preparedness Plan. Available at http://www.redcross.org/prepare/location/home-family/plan, last accessed February 9, 2016.

Red Cross. n.d.b. Get a Kit. Available at http://www.redcross.org/get-help/prepare-for-emergencies/be-red-cross-ready/get-a-kit, last accessed February 5, 2016.

Red Cross. n.d.c. Prepare for Emergencies. Available at http://www.redcross.org/get-help/prepare-for-emergencies/be-red-cross-ready, last accessed February 5, 2016.

Sutton, Jeanette and Kathleen Tierney. 2006. *Disaster Preparedness: Concepts, Guidance, and Research*. Boulder, CO: Natural Hazards Center, Institute of Behavioral Sciences.

Sutton, Jeanette, Emma S. Spiro, Britta Johnson, Sean Fitzhugh, Ben Gibson, and Carter T. Butts. 2014. Warning Tweets: Serial Transmission of Messages During the Warning Phase of a Disaster Event. *Information Communication & Society* 17(6): 765–787.

The 9/11 Commission Report. 2004. *Final Report of the National Commission on Terrorist Attacks upon the United States*. New York: W. W. Norton and Company.

Usher-Pines, Lori, Patrick S. Duggan, Joshua P. Garron, Ruth A. Karron, and Ruth R. Faden. 2007. Planning for an Influence Pandemic: Social Justice and Disadvantaged Groups. *The Hastings Center Report* 37(4): 32–39.

Webb, Gary R., Kathleen J. Tierney, and James M. Dahlhamer. 2000. Business and Disasters: Empirical Patterns and Unanswered Questions. *Natural Hazards Review* 1(2): 83–90.

World Health Organization (WHO). 2005. *WHO Checklist for Influenza Pandemic Preparedness Planning*. Available at http://www.who.int/csr/resources/publications/influenza/FluCheck6web.pdf, last accessed February 20, 2016.

World Health Organization (WHO). 2009. *Whole-of-Society Pandemic Readiness: Who Guidelines for Pandemic Readiness and Response in the Non-health Sector*. Available at http://www.who.int/influenza/preparedness/pandemic/2009-0808_wos_pandemic_readiness_final.pdf?ua=1, last accessed March 4, 2015.

Chapter 7

Response

Objectives

Upon completing this chapter, readers should be able to:

- Understand the response phase in the context of comprehensive emergency management, and describe inaccuracies in the "command post" image of emergency managers.
- Define the response phase of disasters and identify some of the major activities typically undertaken during that period.
- Describe the process of issuing disaster warnings and identify the characteristics of effective disaster warnings that lead people to take appropriate protective actions.
- Discuss various myths about how individuals, organizations, and communities respond to disasters, and identify sources of those myths.
- Contrast myths with research-based findings on how individuals, organizations, and communities actually respond to disasters, and identify various sources and limitations of community resilience.
- Situate the response phase in an international context, and identify relevant issues to consider in applying research findings to developing countries.
- Identify the most common problems that arise during the response phase and discuss effective principles of emergency management to overcome those challenges.

Key Terms

- Disaster myths
- DRC typology
- EOC
- Flexibility

- NIMS
- Response-induced demands
- Warning process

7.1 Introduction

It is very likely that when you hear or think about *emergency management* you immediately think about the response phase of disaster. You might envision yourself working in an ultra-modern, high-tech emergency operations center (EOC), simultaneously monitoring network news coverage on multiple flat-panel televisions, keeping a close eye on your computer screen as response activities are logged and updated at near real-time speed into an advanced decision support software program, and handling nonstop telephone calls from colleagues out in the field and media seeking a good quote. Indeed, the image of a strong leader asserting command and control over a chaotic situation is one that many people have of the emergency manager. We will refer to this as the "command post" image of the emergency manager.

Despite the pervasiveness, and the appeal even, of this imagery, it is not entirely accurate. In fact, if your idea of an emergency manager is a person whose days are action-packed and spent in the EOC making split-second, life and death decisions, then you will likely be disappointed by the profession. There will be some of that, to be sure, but most of your time will not be spent in the trenches. You will spend much time working to make the trench time effective, efficient, and smooth (see Box 7.1).

As a point of reference, consider the law enforcement profession. When we think of the police, we tend to imagine trained professionals who spend their days chasing criminal suspects, collecting highly sensitive evidence at crime scenes, and solving cold cases. Yet, if you talk to a recently hired police officer about his or her work, you will likely sense at least some disillusionment over how much idle time they have and, even more likely, how much time they spend writing reports.

This is not to say that you will spend all of your time as an emergency manager at a desk, writing and reviewing disaster plans. Indeed, like a police officer called to the scene of a major crime, you will sometimes be sprung into action by a disaster. It is important, however, to realize that responding to actual disasters is only one, albeit a very important, component of an emergency manager's job. Our purpose here is not to shatter your hopes and dreams of saving lives during a disaster but instead to give you a more realistic view of the profession. The command post view of emergency management is inaccurate because it largely ignores the other phases of disaster and their relationship to the response

BOX 7.1   FIRST RESPONDERS AND EMERGENCY MANAGERS: KEY DIFFERENCES

Dean Findley (Courtesy of Dean Findley)

Dean Findley joined the Oklahoma City Fire Department in October 1988 and was promoted through the ranks to major. Major Findley spent the first 20 years of his career responding to emergencies including the bombing of the Alfred P. Murrah building in 1995. In 2008, he accepted a position as the fire depart-ment's liaison to the Oklahoma City Office of Emergency Management. During his time in emergency management, the city experienced multiple record breaking events, reinforcing the concept of comprehensive emergency man-agement. These experiences also highlighted the value of education and research in the area of emergency management; prompting him to pursue a doctoral degree in Fire and Emergency Management Administration through Oklahoma State University. Dean retired from the fire department in 2012 and completed his doctoral degree in 2015. Dr. Findley now teaches fire and emergency management related courses in the Industrial Safety Program at the University of Central Oklahoma.

Perhaps the best way to contrast the roles of first responders, specifically firefighters, and emergency management is through an illustration. To that end, let's examine how these two professions respond to a tornado striking their community.

Emergency management enters the response phase well in advance of a storm impact. Their work begins as the atmospheric conditions show signs of potential for tornadic activity. After reviewing weather forecasts,

(Continued)

BOX 7.1 (*Continued*)   FIRST RESPONDERS AND EMERGENCY MANAGERS: KEY DIFFERENCES

emergency management sends a threat assessment to local officials and other response partners alerting them to the potential ahead. The emergency operations center (EOC) ramps up its operations to the next level, which often signals the addition of volunteers to the mix as the approaching storm intensifies. The melding of previous experience and academic research on these type events enables the emergency manager to anticipate potential needs that must be addressed before the storm hits. Calls are made to response partners to check on their availability. Storm spotters begin staging in key areas to act as the eyes for emergency management.

Meanwhile, first responders monitor the weather and hope that the storm weakens, goes around the area, or only causes minor damage. These public servants have already confirmed that the equipment is ready, a typical activity every day on the job. They have repeatedly trained for this day, hoping these skills are never needed. They are ready but wait patiently for the lights to click on, signaling their entry into the response phase of this event.

The tornado touches down! Storm spotters and local media report structural damage with potentially trapped victims. Calls begin pouring in to 911 operators. The first responders spring into action, not knowing what awaits their arrival on the scene. Based on these damage reports, emergency management bumps the EOC operation level up one more notch. Staffing at the EOC increases to ensure the boots on the ground have what they need to overcome the storm's wrath. The knowledge gained through a recent disaster recovery course will definitely come in handy on this one.

The first responders arrive at the scene and begin pulling people from damaged homes, administering first aid, extinguishing fires, and turning off utilities to damaged structures. Often working side by side with survivors and volunteers. They work quickly and efficiently to ensure that all are accounted for and the potential for further damage is averted.

Emergency management is busy contacting various partners, both public and private, whose help is now needed. These partnerships are the results of countless hours of relationship building through meetings and planning sessions. Forging these partnerships and speaking face-to-face with these individuals and groups during the down time between disasters makes these calls for help much easier. Provisions for those displaced by the storm are coordinated through the American Red Cross, United Way, Salvation Army, and other nonprofit organizations. Most victims will turn to family for help but some have lost everything and have no one to turn to for help. Another nugget of information gleaned from a researcher's presentation at last year's tornado summit.

The first responders complete their tasks and return to the station to clean up and refuel in preparation for the next storm. Their response to the storm has ended.

(Continued)

> ## BOX 7.1 (*Continued*)   FIRST RESPONDERS AND EMERGENCY MANAGERS: KEY DIFFERENCES
>
> After the storm passes, the EOC's level of activation returns to normal. However, emergency management is still responding to the needs of the citizens. Damage assessments begin at first light. Emergency management and volunteers survey the damage and tally the numbers to submit to state and federal officials for use in a declaration request if warranted. Emergency management verifies that all displaced citizens have been take care of and thanks the assisting agencies for their help.
>
> This response phase ends. However, much work lies ahead for emergency management and the community. The emergency management office transitions into the recovery phase of this event to deal with short- and long-term issues such as infrastructure repair, housing, and long-term planning. In addition, emergency management continues to work on various projects in the preparedness and mitigation phases while continuing previous recovery projects and remaining ready for the next storm.

period, it envisions widespread chaos, and it assumes that an effective response is characterized by strong command and control over a situation.

7.1.1 Ignoring Other Phases of Disaster

As we have discussed throughout this book, the life cycle of disasters includes preparedness, response, recovery, and mitigation. Because you will spread your time across all four phases, because actual disaster events are relatively rare, and because emergency managers have numerous job responsibilities, it is simply inaccurate to assume that most of your time will be spent managing response efforts. However, it is accurate to assume that you will spend a great deal of time *thinking* about response activities. The time you spend on preparedness-related activities, for example, including educating the public about the hazards and risks in your community, talking with organizations such as schools and businesses, and conducting drills and exercises will pay tremendous dividends when it comes to responding to an actual disaster.

Similarly, if your community takes effective, proactive steps to mitigate possible threats, it is likely that disaster impacts will be less severe and will enable more manageable responses. While response is the most prevalent phase in the common view of the emergency manager's work, the concept of comprehensive emergency management assumes that the other phases are equally important.

7.1.2 Envisioning Chaos

Another reason the command post view of the emergency manager comes to mind so readily is the common notion that disasters create chaos and social disorganization. In the midst of all that confusion, it is assumed by many that we need a calm, level-headed leader to make the right decisions and keep everyone else in line. The concept that disasters create chaos and massive social breakdown, however, is a myth. Instead, as we will see, individuals, organizations, and communities typically show remarkable resilience in the face of disasters.

As Dynes (2003) points out, we continually find "order in disorder" in the immediate aftermaths of large-scale disasters like the terrorist attacks of September 11, 2001. Similarly, Drabek (2013) characterizes the post-disaster environment as "organized-disorganization." However, for reasons we will discuss in this chapter, many people, including some emergency management professionals, continue to believe that chaos prevails in disasters. As a result, the command post image of the emergency manager persists in the minds of many.

7.1.3 Assuming Need for Command and Control

Because it envisions a chaotic scene after a disaster, the command post image also assumes that the best way to effectively manage a disaster is to assert strong command and control over the situation. According to Dynes (1994), this command-and-control model of emergency management is based on numerous false assumptions and inappropriate analogies. Generally, it assumes that civil society is fragile, and the post-disaster environment is analogous to a war-time scenario. In the absence of strong and assertive leadership, the expectation is that lawlessness and anarchy will spread. From this perspective, based largely on a military model of leadership, the emergency manager is essentially a commander, establishing firm control over a situation and unilaterally issuing orders to others. As we will see in this chapter, however, emergency managers are much more effective when they emphasize coordination and communication instead of command and control.

The post-disaster environment is fluid, dynamic, and constantly changing. Decisions must be made quickly, often based on very limited information. In those circumstances, a rigid, hierarchical, and centralized approach is likely to fail. Instead, a decentralized, flexible, problem-solving approach is much better suited to the complexities of the response phase of a disaster (Dynes 1994; Neal and Phillips 1995). Therefore, in sharp contrast to the command post image, it is much more accurate to view emergency management professionals as managers and coordinators, not as commanders.

7.2 Getting Started: Definitions and Activities

Now that you understand that response is only one aspect of an emergency manager's job duties and have been cautioned against embracing a command post view of the profession, the remainder of this chapter will provide an in-depth look at the response period. In this section, we will consider various definitions of response and identify disaster-related activities typically performed during the response phase. In subsequent sections, we will discuss the process of issuing disaster warnings and identify factors that enhance their effectiveness; describe various myths about how people, organizations, and communities respond to disasters; debunk the disaster myths and describe actual responses, including typical patterns and common problems; and discuss the most effective principles of emergency management during the response phase including the all-hazards model, coordination, and flexibility. Despite decades of research on the response phase, misunderstandings about reactions to disasters are still widespread. After reading this chapter, you will have a much better sense of what really happens during disasters and obtain clear guidance on managing responses effectively.

7.2.1 Defining Response

The response phase is defined as activities "… designed to provide emergency assistance for casualties … seek to reduce the probability of secondary damage … and to speed recovery operations" (National Governors' Report 1979, p. 13). More recently, Tierney, Lindell, and Perry (2001, p. 81) define disaster response activities as "… actions taken at the time a disaster strikes that are intended to reduce threats to life safety, to care for victims, and to contain secondary hazards and community losses." They further explain that during the response phase emergency managers must address two sets of demands: those generated from the disaster and those arising from the response effort.

Disaster-induced demands are fairly obvious and arise from the needs to care for victims and deal with physical damage and social disruption caused by the event. *Response-induced demands* are far less obvious but equally important and challenging for emergency managers. They include the need to coordinate the activities of the multitude of individuals and organizations involved in the response. As we will see later in this chapter, response-induced demands are plentiful in the wake of a disaster because so many different types of actors and organizations—some without clearly delineated disaster responsibilities—become involved in response efforts.

7.2.2 Typical Response Activities

In light of the involvement of so many different individuals, groups, and agencies and the pressing needs brought on by disasters, the response period is typically packed with activity. Common components of the response effort include activating the EOC, warning the public, notifying appropriate authorities, mobilizing personnel and resources, initiating evacuation, opening shelters, providing medical services, search and rescue operations, and many others. In an effort to more accurately describe response activities,

Drabek (1986) separates them into preimpact mobilization and postimpact emergency action sub-phases. *Preimpact mobilization* involves warning the public, initiating evacuation, and establishing shelters. *Postimpact emergency actions* include searching for survivors and providing medical care to the injured. Tierney et al. (2001, p. 75) categorize response activities in even greater detail, identifying four related areas of activity:

- Emergency assessment
- Expedient hazard mitigation
- Protective response
- Incident management

Emergency assessment includes monitoring hazards (natural, technological, and human-induced) in your community and assessing damages and other impacts when a disaster occurs. One of the main tasks of an emergency manager after a disaster is to conduct an emergency assessment, which in the United States initiates the process of applying for a Presidential Disaster Declaration that releases federal disaster funding (see Box 7.2). To conduct a preliminary damage assessment (PDA), capable investigators enter the field to determine how bad things are after a tornado, flood, or earthquake has struck. The initial PDA, which will be followed by a more thorough investigation once the area is accessible, typically involves a "windshield survey" in which the emergency management team drives through the area and identifies quickly the number of houses, businesses, and infrastructure components compromised. To do so, they generally designate three levels: destroyed, major damage, and minor damage and tally a straightforward account of the apparent damage. Aerial reconnaissance and satellite imagery can also be used to assess damage, but, as with the windshield survey, the visual images just cannot reach inside a building. Therefore, the PDA is followed by more careful assessments made by qualified engineers to determine if buildings are safe to reenter or need to be torn down. The PDA thus serves to safeguard the public, determine the amount of damage to qualify for outside aid, and set up parameters by which voluntary organizations will determine the extent of their assistance. The PDA is, in short, the key step that bridges response into recovery (see more in Chapter 8).

Expedient hazard mitigation refers to activities undertaken just prior to or shortly after the onset of a disaster—sandbagging in a flood and boarding windows in a hurricane—aimed at protecting lives and containing damage. *Protective response* involves all the activities we typically think about in relation to disasters, including search and rescue, emergency medical services, sheltering, and others. *Incident management* requires establishing an EOC, inter-agency and inter-governmental coordination, media communications and public information activities, documentation, and administrative and logistic support.

BOX 7.2   PRESIDENTIAL DISASTER DECLARATIONS

The Stafford Act (§401) requires that: "All requests for a declaration by the President that a major disaster exists shall be made by the Governor of the affected State." A State also includes the District of Columbia, Puerto Rico, the Virgin Islands, Guam, American Samoa, and the Commonwealth of the Northern Mariana Islands. The Marshall Islands and the Federated States of Micronesia are also eligible to request a declaration and receive assistance.

The Governor's request is made through the regional FEMA office. State and federal officials conduct a preliminary damage assessment (PDA) to estimate the extent of the disaster and its impact on individuals and public facilities. This information is included in the Governor's request to show that the disaster is of such severity and magnitude that effective response is beyond the capabilities of the state and the local governments and that federal assistance is necessary. Normally, the PDA is completed prior to the submission of the Governor's request. However, when an obviously severe or catastrophic event occurs, the Governor's request may be submitted prior to the PDA. Nonetheless, the Governor must still make the request.

As part of the request, the Governor must take appropriate action under state law and direct execution of the state's emergency plan. The Governor shall furnish information on the nature and amount of state and local resources that have been or will be committed to alleviating the results of the disaster, provide an estimate of the amount and severity of damage and the impact on the private and public sector, and provide an estimate of the type and amount of assistance needed under the Stafford Act. In addition, the Governor will need to certify that, for the current disaster, state and local government obligations and expenditures (of which State commitments must be a significant proportion) will comply with all applicable cost-sharing requirements.

Based on the Governor's request, the President may declare that a major disaster or emergency exists, thus activating an array of federal programs to assist in the response and recovery effort. Not all programs, however, are activated for every disaster. The determination of which programs are activated is based on the needs found during damage assessment and any subsequent information that may be discovered.

Source: www.fema.gov/declaration-process (*verbatim*)

As an emergency manager, it is highly unlikely that you would ever be directly involved in all these response activities. However, it is important that you understand what happens and will happen in your community after a disaster. It is even more important that you understand how best to facilitate *coordination* of all those activities, foster *communication* among all the responding entities, and recognize the value of *flexibility* in maximizing the effectiveness of your community's response to a disaster. These core principles of effective emergency management are particularly important in the response phase, as will be evident throughout this chapter.

7.3 Disaster Warnings

Warning the public of an impending threat is a critical first step in responding to disasters. Of course, disasters vary significantly in predictability and length of forewarning. At one extreme, for example, hurricanes can be spotted and tracked well in advance, giving emergency managers and other public officials hours or possibly even days to establish an EOC, mobilize necessary resources, and urge the public to take appropriate protective actions. At the other extreme, an earthquake or chemical plant explosion offers virtually no advance warning. Between these extremes, tornadoes can be located and tracked fairly accurately, giving local officials some time, even if only minutes, to alert the public. Because of the great variability in forewarnings of disasters, it is critical in the preparedness phase for emergency managers to educate the public about the hazards in their communities, test their disaster warning systems, and provide clear guidelines for people and organizations to follow in the event of a disaster when every second counts.

In some sense, therefore, warnings be can considered both a preparedness and a response activity. In the interests of simplicity and clarity of presentation, we will focus in this chapter only on actual disaster warnings and treat them accordingly as response activities. You should recognize, however, that while disaster warnings fall under response activities, other types of risk communication cut across the phases of disaster and focus on preparedness, recovery, and mitigation. Public education campaigns that seek to inform the public about common causes of wildfires and house fires or about the value of flood insurance are intended to prevent disasters from occurring in the first place or persuading people to take preventive measures that will assist them to respond to or recover from a disaster. In weather forecasting, a distinction is made between watches and warnings. Watches indicate that conditions are favorable for the emergence of a tornado, blizzard, hurricane, or ice storm. A warning indicates that a storm has been spotted. If these efforts are effective, people will pay attention to emergency warnings and respond appropriately, lessening the burdens on emergency management agencies and first responders.

In this section, our primary objective is to gain a better understanding of the disaster warning process and the factors that enhance the effectiveness of warnings. An effective disaster warning persuades people and organizations to take appropriate protective actions. Disaster warnings have been studied extensively for more than 40 years and we have learned a great deal (Sorensen 2000; Sorensen and Sorensen 2006). Nevertheless, as we will discuss later in this section, public officials continue to develop ineffective warning systems, largely ignoring the recommendations of researchers.

7.3.1 Warning Process

In the wake of Hurricane Katrina, some observers were surprised that so many people did not evacuate New Orleans at the urging of the city's mayor. Many observers attributed much of the suffering and human tragedy that ensued to the failures of some individuals to make the right decisions and leave the area. Inherent in that view, however, are the assumptions that everyone in the impacted area received warning messages, that the messages were clear and interpreted in the same way by all who received them, and that the residents had a level playing field in terms of ability to evacuate.

In reality, people do not always receive and interpret warning messages in the same manner; messages are not always effectively worded and delivered; and social factors such as socioeconomic status, disability, and others impact the ability of people to heed warnings and take protective actions. At first glance, the warning process seems simple and straightforward: public officials issue a warning and people comply with the instructions in the warning. Research, however, suggests that warnings are far more complex. As depicted in Figure 7.1, warning is a social process that involves several steps. As shown, there is a long way to go from public officials issuing a warning to the point where people and organizations take protective action. Every step presents uncertainties and intervening factors that can negatively impact the process.

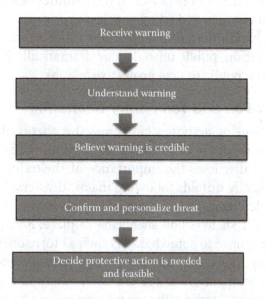

FIGURE 7.1 Warning process. (From Mileti, D. *Disasters by Design*, 1999, p. 191; National Research Council, *Public Response to Alerts and Warnings on Mobile Devices: Summary of a Workshop on Current Knowledge and Research Gaps*, 2010, p. 8; Sorensen, J.H. and Sorensen, B.V. *Community Processes*, 2006, p. 191.)

7.3.2 Taking Protective Action

By issuing disaster warnings, emergency managers and other public officials hope to enhance life safety by urging citizens and organizations within their communities to take appropriate protective actions. Of course, the nature of a hazard determines what protective actions are appropriate. In the case of a tornado, for example, people are typically urged to get below ground or go to the centers of their houses so that the walls protect against outside threats. On the other hand, in the days before a hurricane makes landfall, people may be asked to leave the area. At times, the primary purpose of a message is simply to urge people to stay tuned for more information and direct them to appropriate sources for additional information. During the winter months when inclement weather is expected, for example, public schools and universities often issue press releases and post announcements on their websites telling people to tune in to certain radio and television stations for important information about opening delays or cancellations.

For communitywide disasters, the primary protective actions are temporary sheltering and evacuation. Over the years, researchers have learned a tremendous amount about these measures and the insights they gained are extremely relevant to the practice of emergency management. If you are involved in setting up temporary shelters during a disaster, you may be surprised when very few people use them. Similarly, if you are involved in issuing an evacuation warning in your community, you may feel frustrated when many people stay put and ignore the warning. Researchers have consistently uncovered these patterns of behavior in their studies of numerous disasters, so we should not be surprised when people do not evacuate or utilize public shelters. In fact, by familiarizing themselves with research findings on sheltering and evacuation, public officials may dramatically improve their ability to persuade the public to take protective actions.

7.3.2.1 Evacuation and Temporary Sheltering

Sheltering and housing activities cut across the phases of disasters, beginning in the response phase and sometimes continuing through much of the recovery. Box 7.3 discusses the importance of sheltering and the housing process that typically unfolds following major disasters. In this section, we primarily consider temporary or emergency sheltering that falls into two broad types: public shelters and sheltering in place. *Sheltering in place* is a very common response to some hazards such as tornadoes. It involves urging people to stay where they are and giving them specific instructions on how best to protect themselves. For example, advice in a tornado is to seek shelter in a basement, storm cellar, or interior room of a house or building. A chemical or hazardous materials release may require that people remain indoors with windows closed and air conditioning systems turned off.

BOX 7.3   SHELTERING

Disasters, refugee crises, and wars cause people to move from their homes. Displaced persons typically move through four phases of sheltering and housing (Quarantelli 1982). Those four phases transition people from (1) emergency shelter they may create themselves into (2) temporary shelter established by organizations with food, water and cover from the elements. The third phase (temporary housing) and the fourth (permanent housing) will be discussed later in the chapter on recovery. However, the neat ordering of the phases does not suggest that people move efficiently through those stages. People may languish in emergency or temporary shelter that can become long term or even permanent in some locations such as refugee encampments.

Ideally, temporary shelters will be set up by experienced organizations. Internationally, the Sphere Project (2004) provides guidelines for establishing temporary shelter:

- *Strategic planning.* People should have the right to be near their homes, their economic livelihoods, and social networks. Collective settlements should be avoided. Locations providing shelter should ensure safety from future hazards. Organizations providing shelter in Haiti faced this challenge. After the 2010 earthquake, hundreds of thousands of survivors crowded into makeshift tent cities—which soon became inundated when seasonal rains moved in.
- *Physical planning.* Local practices should be used to create shelters, linking people to their families and neighbors. Safe services including water should be provided. Haiti again faced this crisis of providing access to essential, life-saving needs. Within 1 year of the earthquake, cholera broke out from contaminated water supplies. Over one thousand people died.
- *Covered living space.* People have the right to privacy and dignity within a living space. A minimum of 3.5 meters per person is recommended. Space should allow for local cultural practices, household chores, sleeping, washing, and dressing. Privacy and security proved challenging after the 2005 Pakistan earthquake killed 74,000+ people. With winter setting in, women and children reported threats to their safety and problems accessing food (Sayeed 2009).

Temporary shelter may include several types of shelter. General population shelters open to the public on an as-needed basis. Typically, emergency managers assume that about 20% of the evacuating public will go to a shelter. Most shelters in the United States are opened and operated by trained staff and volunteers from the Red Cross. Many states support that effort with other nongovernmental organizations and public agencies, like public health, on an as-needed basis. In an event as catastrophic as Hurricane Katrina in 2005, an even broader array of emergent shelters opened by nontraditional providers may occur (Phillips et al. 2012; Nigg, Barnshaw, and Torres 2006). Public shelters tend to host populations that lack resources to pay for hotels or social

(Continued)

BOX 7.3 (*Continued*)   SHELTERING

networks to provide a bed. Local animal care organizations may open pet shelters that ideally are co-located near the human population. Service animals, though, should be accommodated within general population shelters.

Another type of shelter is currently named a *functional needs shelter*, sometimes called a medical shelter that opens for people in need of services beyond what a general shelter might provide. Such shelterees might have been evacuated from a nursing home or may be in need of advanced medical care beyond what general population shelters may provide. Another example is that of a patient with dementia who may need supervisory support or security. The functional needs shelter provides a highly specialized environment with well-trained health care personnel (Phillips et al. 2011).

Most of the time, shelters open and close fairly quickly. Elongated stays can occur under some conditions such as catastrophic events or in areas where affordable, permanent housing is not available. Another factor that influences shelter stay is whether or not accessible housing becomes available, particularly for senior citizens and families with an individual who has a disability.

Developing nations typically experience different patterns of sheltering, with considerably longer stays in both emergency and temporary shelter stages. The 2005 Pakistan earthquake, for example, left nearly three million people facing long-term displacement. The geographic area affected by the earthquake spread out over 30,000 kilometers in challenging, mountainous conditions. Responding organizations and government set 144 relief camps. For the first time, the United Nations implemented its cluster approach with groups focused on health, food and water, security, communication, reconstruction and more (Brennan and Waldman 2006).

References

Brennan, Richard J. and Ronald J. Waldman. 2006. The South Asian Earthquake Six Months Later—an Ongoing Crisis. *The New England Journal of Medicine* 354: 1769–1771.

FEMA. 2010. *Guidance on Planning for Integration of Functional Needs Support Services in General Population Shelters*. Washington D.C.: FEMA.

Nigg, Joanne, Johon Barnshaw, and Manuel R. Torres. Hurricane Katrina and the Flooding of New Orleans: Emergent Issues in Sheltering and Temporary Housing. *Annals of the American Academy* 604: 113–128.

Phillips, Brenda D., Elizabeth Harris, Elizabeth A. Davis, Rebecca Hansen, Kelly Rouba, and Jessica Love. 2011. Delivery of Behavioral Health Services in General and Functional Needs Shelters. pp. 261–288 in *Behavioral Health Response to Disasters*, edited by Martin Teasley. Boca Raton, FL: CRC Press.

Phillips, Brenda, Tom Wikle, Angela Head Hakim, and Lynn Pike. 2012. Establishing and Operating Shelters after Hurricane Katrina. *International Journal of Emergency Management* 8(2): 153–167.

Quarantelli, E. L. 1982. *Sheltering and Housing after Major Community Disasters: Case Studies and General Observations*. Newark, DE: Disaster Research Center, University of Delaware.

Sayeed, Azra Talat. 2009. Victims of Earthquake and Patriarchy: The 2005 Pakistan Earthquake. pp. 142–151 in *Women, Gender and Disaster: Global Issues and Initiatives*, edited by Elaine Enarson and P. G. Chakrabarti. Los Angeles: Sage.

The Sphere Project. 2004. Minimum Standards in Shelter, Settlement and Non-Food Items. Available at http://www.sphereproject.org/content/view/100/84/lang,English/, last accessed January 28, 2011.

Public sheltering, on the other hand, involves urging people to evacuate their homes and go to designated locations for safety. These locations often include school gymnasiums, common areas in churches, and large arenas, stadiums, or convention centers. In the United States, we are starting to see communities in high-risk areas building congregate shelters to host hundreds of people at risk in a hardened facility.

In reviewing the major research findings on sheltering, we will limit discussion to public sheltering, which follows an official recommendation for people to evacuate a hazardous area. As mentioned previously, emergency managers may be puzzled when so few people actually show up at community shelters during and immediately after a disaster. Researchers have known about this pattern for a very long time. For example, in his comprehensive review of several decades of research on the topics of evacuation and sheltering, Drabek (1986) conclusively determined that most people in disaster-impacted communities do not go to public shelters.

Where do people go after a disaster, if not to public shelters? In every disaster, of course, a number of people will simply stay put. During the 1980 eruption of Mt. St. Helens in the state of Washington, a local resident named Harry Truman stubbornly refused to evacuate despite several warnings, and he is presumed to have died and been buried under several feet of ash from the volcano. According to Drabek (1986, 2010), most people who evacuate during a disaster will go to the homes of friends or relatives. While it is impossible for you to know ahead of time exactly how many people in your community will refuse to evacuate, how many will seek refuge with friends or family, and how many will use public shelters, you do not want, as many emergency managers do, to overestimate the amount of shelter use.

7.3.2.2 Factors Affecting Evacuation and Public Shelter Usage

In addition to relying largely on friends and family for safety, research has shown that several other factors affect the warning process and whether people take protective actions. These factors, described in this section, are summarized in various other publications (Drabek 1986, 2010; Mileti 1999; Tierney et al. 2001). While some of the social factors impacting people's ability and willingness to take protective actions may make perfect sense to you, others may be surprising. In both cases, you will benefit throughout your career by having a better understanding of these factors.

In their research on evacuation planning, Perry, Lindell, and Greene (1981, p. 160) identify various *community-level factors* that influence shelter usage among evacuees and suggest that "the use of public shelter increases when community preparedness is high, when the entire community must be evacuated, and when the evacuees anticipate that the necessary period of absence will be long." They go on to say that "even under these conditions, public shelters seem to attract only about one fourth of the evacuees at a given site." While Perry et al. recognize that shelter usage is typically low during disasters, they suggest that usage can be increased somewhat through enhanced community preparedness.

Researchers have also identified numerous *individual- and household-level factors* affecting warning responses and protective actions (Mileti 1999). These factors include gender, race, socioeconomic status, education level, knowledge and risk perception, and presence of children. While some of these factors positively impact the warning process, others decrease the likelihood that people will take protective action. Based on past research, it appears that protective actions are more likely to be engaged in by women, households with children, and those with higher socioeconomic status. Additionally, warning messages have more positive impacts on people with higher levels of education, greater knowledge about and heightened perception of risk, and those with more community involvement. On the other hand, racial and ethnic minorities, people of lower socioeconomic status, and those with less education are less positively impacted by official warnings and less likely to take protective actions. Social class significantly shapes exposure to hazards and the ability to escape them, as was dramatically revealed in Hurricane Katrina when many people simply did not have the necessary resources including cars to get out of the city.

Another factor stems from credibility of the person issuing the warning. A person issuing a warning should be as similar as possible to the population the warning should reach. Imagine, for example, someone with a New Jersey accent trying to convince someone in the Deep South to evacuate. A familiar voice will appear credible and thus motivate higher compliance.

Another impediment to public sheltering emerges when people believe that a shelter may not be ready for them. People with disabilities, for example, fear that shelters may not be able to accommodate their needs or perhaps a previous experience was unpleasant (van Willigen et al. 2002). We may also erroneously assume that everyone is warned. National Weather Service meteorologists noted a "hole" in the weather warning system: many systems bypass people with hearing disabilities (Wood and Weisman 2003). Senior citizens may prefer to remain in the comfort of their homes where they have medications, assistive devices, neighbors or family to help them, and pets to comfort them. Both groups experience lower incomes than the general public and have difficulties affording travel to, at, and from a shelter. Hurricane Katrina, for example, occurred at month end when many people waited for government entitlement checks to buy food, gasoline, and medicines.

Other factors you may not have considered are far less intuitive. After Hurricane Katrina and other events, we learned that one major impediment to people seeking safety in public shelters was care of pets and service animals (Heath et al. 2001). Public shelters typically do not allow pets even though owners, particularly the elderly, consider pets essential members of their families and are reluctant to leave them behind. Moreover, service animals provide necessary assistance to the vision impaired. Although public shelters are mandated to accept service animals (U.S. Department of Justice n.d.), not every shelter provider understands this (National Organization on Disability 2005).

Another less obvious impediment to evacuating and seeking refuge in public shelters is the fear of looting (Drabek 2010). As we will see later in this chapter, the idea that looting and stealing are rampant after a disaster is a major myth to which many people subscribe. Although these crimes are rare, people nevertheless make decisions about what protective actions they take on the basis of the looting myth. They fear that looters will target their property and steal their belongings if they leave their homes.

As all of this suggests, several impediments prevent people from taking protective action, in particular going to a public shelter after a warning is issued. Nevertheless, public officials and emergency managers often over-estimate how much shelter space will be needed. Envisioning shelters overrun by thousands of frightened evacuees, they sometimes prepare for a massive onslaught that never occurs. As Fischer (2008) notes, it is important for emergency managers to recognize these factors and the actual behavioral patterns during disasters and open shelters accordingly. He suggests opening shelters "as needed," opening new shelters only after existing ones begin to fill.

Finally, we would be remiss if we did not also consider disaster warnings themselves as potential impediments to protective actions. Public officials sometimes wait too long to issue a warning; issue a warning that is too vague about who will be impacted by the impending threat and what actions should be taken; or convey contradictory messages to the public as events unfold. Because it is important for you to understand how to craft warning messages that are timely and accurate and effectively persuade as many people as possible to get out of harm's way, the next section discusses the research-based characteristics of effective warning systems.

7.3.3 Characteristics of Effective Disaster Warnings

Effective warning messages persuade those who receive them to take appropriate protective actions. Several established warning systems have been in operation for many years and new technologies promise to expand the reach and enhance the effectiveness of disaster warnings. Established warning systems include outdoor sirens used to warn of tornadoes and other weather events, the Emergency Alert System that scrolls messages across television screens, weather radio, and others. Newer technologies include cell phones, short message service (SMS) and text alerts, and social media websites including Facebook and Twitter (NRC 2010; Sutton et al. 2015). In the wake of the tragic shootings at Virginia Tech University in 2007, for example, many universities across the United States implemented text alert systems for informing students, faculty, and staff about emergencies on campus and providing brief instructions on what to do.

While researchers and emergency management professionals are hopeful that the new technologies can fill crucial gaps left by the older warning systems, we actually know very little about how and the extent to which people use new technologies during disasters. One thing we do know about various advanced technologies is that they often improve the lives and safety of some but not all, that is, there is often a technological divide between those who have access to the technology and those who do not. Thus, in the realm of emergency management and disaster warnings, we would be wise to acknowledge that reality and recognize the limits of technology for keeping the public safe. Past research suggests that several factors can enhance the effectiveness of disaster warnings (Aguirre 1988; Mileti 1999; NRC 2010; National Science and Technology Council 2000). All of these studies suggest that disaster warnings are most effective when they are

- Frequently broadcast across multiple media
- Consistent in content and tone over time and across media outlets
- Crafted to reach diverse audiences
- Specific and accurate about where the hazard is and to whom the message applies
- Clear (no technical jargon), containing specific instructions on what actions to take, when, and why
- Truthful and authoritative and delivered by an identifiable and credible source

Drabek (2010, p. 105) offers additional advice for improving the effectiveness of disaster warnings. He suggests that community evacuation can be enhanced when emergency managers and other public officials:

- Encourage family planning for evacuation
- Promote media consistency
- Utilize forceful but not mandatory evacuation policies
- Allay public fears of looting
- Facilitate transportation
- Establish family message centers

Although research is fairly clear on what constitutes an effective disaster warning, warning systems that largely ignore the guidelines continue to be devised. For example, consider DHS's Homeland Security Advisory System

(HSAS) put into place by Homeland Security Presidential Directive #3 and unveiled by the newly created DHS in the months following the attacks of September 11, 2001. Its purpose was to educate the public about the threat of terrorism, inform them about changes in risk levels, and encourage them to take precautionary measures.

To achieve those objectives, a color-coded scheme was implemented in which green indicated a low risk of terrorist attacks, blue indicated a general risk, yellow indicated a significant risk, orange indicated a high risk, and red indicated a severe risk. However, based on the characteristics of effective disaster warnings described in this section, the HSAS had major shortcomings. As Aguirre (2004) aptly demonstrated, the terrorism alert system offered only a vague description of the hazard, was nonspecific in terms of to whom or even what region it applied, and failed to provide explicit instructions as to what people should do to protect themselves.

Additionally, the HSAS potentially suffered from what has been termed "warning fatigue" whereby the impact of a warning system on behavior is diminished when the public is continually warned about a hazard that does not materialize into a disaster (Sorensen and Sorensen 2006). Because of these and other potential problems, former Secretary of Homeland Security Janet Napolitano ordered a review of the system. In September 2009, the Homeland Security Advisory Council submitted its written report, *Homeland Security Advisory System: Task Force Report and Recommendations,* concluding, "The system's ability to communicate useful information in a credible manner to the public is poor. Significant rethinking of how to communicate to this audience is warranted" (p. 1). As a result, in January 2011, Secretary Napolitano announced that the HSAS would be replaced by a new warning system, which is now called the National Terrorism Advisory System.

To better understand what constitutes an effective disaster warning system, consider news network coverage of severe weather in "tornado alley." If you live in or visit Texas, Oklahoma, or Kansas in the spring, you will undoubtedly experience severe weather and television coverage of it. During a typical broadcast, after a tornado has been spotted, meteorologists and weather forecasters inform viewers of its precise path including its future trajectory and time estimates. Importantly, they tell viewers exactly what to do when the storm reaches their area. For example, viewers are typically told to go to a basement, storm cellar, or the center of the house away from windows. If you find yourself responsible for writing a disaster warning message in the future, think about the contrast between a detailed, highly specific tornado warning and the vague, ambiguous terrorism warning. To maximize the effectiveness of your warning message, model it more after the tornado warning than the terrorism alert.

7.4 Disaster Response: Myths and Realities

Despite what we have learned over the years about effective disaster warnings, some emergency managers and other public officials are still sometimes hesitant or reluctant to issue warnings to the public. Like the individual who refuses to go to a shelter out of fear of his or her home being looted, some officials fear that a premature warning will spark widespread panic in their communities. Indeed, fears about looting and panic in the aftermaths of disasters are fairly widespread among the public, and alarmingly, even among emergency managers. Looting and other anti-social behaviors are exceedingly rare in disasters and commonly called myths by researchers (Fischer 2008). In this section, we will explore these and other response myths in much greater detail, identify some of the sources of these myths, and contrast them with a more realistic, research-based view of the response phase.

At the most basic level, myth-based and research-based views differ in terms of what they assume about social order in disasters. The *myth-based view* assumes that society is fragile, and disasters cause a breakdown in social order, which leads to lawlessness, conflict, and chaos. On the other hand, the *research-based view* recognizes that society is resilient, and disasters typically result in increased helping behavior, consensus, and enhanced social solidarity during the response phase. In fact, since the early 1950s, researchers have continually attempted to debunk the myths of disaster and instead document the recuperative and resilient capacities of societies (Fischer 2008; Fritz 1961; Quarantelli 1960; Quarantelli and Dynes 1977).

In this section, the myth-based and research-based views are contrasted in terms of how they characterize disaster response at the individual, organizational, and community levels. The myth-based view assumes that individuals will suffer from reduced coping capacity, organizations will lack personnel, and communities will be torn apart. Conversely, the research-based view recognizes that individuals will actively contribute to the response effort, organizations will adapt and change to meet heightened demands, and communities will exhibit significant resilience. The primary purpose of our discussion is to introduce you to the research-based view and demonstrate its relevance to the effective practice of emergency management.

7.4.1 Myth-Based View of Disaster Response

When most people think of disasters, the myth-based view often comes immediately to mind. They envision massive piles of rubble, burning fires, blaring sirens, and traumatized victims milling around a devastated town.

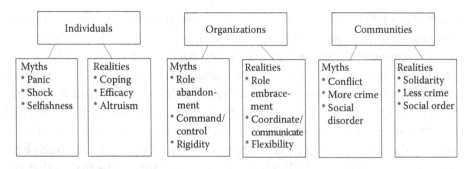

FIGURE 7.2 Myths and realities of disaster response.

Under those tragic circumstances, it is difficult for many people to imagine anything but chaos and disorder. Associated with this imagery is the notion that the best way of dealing with the aftermath of a disaster is for authorities to swoop in and establish strong command and control over the highly disorganized scene. As illustrated in Figure 7.2, there are numerous myths about how individuals, organizations, and communities respond to disasters.

At the *individual level,* the myth-based view assumes that panic and psychological breakdown will impede the ability of people to respond in an orderly, rational, and productive manner. In the simplest sense of the term, *panic* refers to highly individualistic or selfish, nonrational, flight behavior accompanied by a complete disregard for social rules and attachments (Quarantelli 1954). Thus, the epitome of a panic-stricken person would be a mother who abandons her own child to escape an impending threat or a man who pushes, shoves, and tramples others to escape a burning building. The myth-based view assumes that because panic is a common response to disaster, emergency officials should postpone warning the public of a hazard until absolutely necessary. It also assumes that a major part of the official response will involve controlling and containing all the panicked people in the community.

Another core assumption of the myth-based view about individuals is that disasters will cause severe psychological *shock and dependency.* Because of their psychological impairments, it is assumed that individuals will become immobilized and dependent on response agencies for basic needs. As with the panic myth, the assumption here is that individuals will not be available to participate actively in or contribute to the response. Rather, it is assumed that much of the official response effort must be devoted to addressing the pervasive and widespread psychological trauma brought on by the disaster. As Quarantelli (1960, p. 72) states, "the picture is one of docile and impotent individuals, waiting childlike for someone to take care of them."

At the *organizational level,* the myth-based view assumes that organizations will suffer personnel shortages and be largely ineffective. This assumption has two major components. First, it is often assumed that the only organizations that will respond will be those with clearly delineated disaster responsibilities such as police and fire departments and hospitals. Second, in light of the centrality of these organizations to the response effort, there is concern about the problem of role abandonment. *Role abandonment* is the failure of emergency workers to report to work and instead tend to their own personal or family needs. Because the myth-based view assumes that emergency-relevant organizations will not receive much help from other agencies and individuals in the community, the fear is that the effects of a disaster will be exacerbated if emergency workers do not report to work. Disaster myths also assume that organizations must assert strong command and control to counter the panicked and selfish responses of individuals, and that it is best to conform to rigid bureaucratic policies and procedures.

Finally, at the *community level,* the myth-based view assumes there will be intense community conflict, increased crime, and widespread social disorder. If you have watched any network news coverage of a recent disaster, the first thing you will notice is a focus on looting. Indeed, after Hurricane Katrina, the media devoted considerable attention to looting, playing a continuous loop of video footage of people removing merchandise from department stores and conveying reports of organized gangs terrorizing people in public shelters at the Superdome and New Orleans Convention Center. In addition to looting, the myth-based view emphasizes the breakdown of social order more broadly, for example, price gouging by greedy vendors who capitalize on the suffering of others and the emergence and spread of conflict and strife throughout a community.

If panic, looting, and social breakdown are myths, why do so many people including the public, government officials, and even some emergency managers believe them? As discussed in the next section, these myths persist despite several decades of debunking research. We can identify at least three primary reasons for the persistence of disaster myths. First, the *mass media* certainly plays a role in perpetuating disaster myths (Fischer 2008). In an effort to capture the attention of readers, listeners, and viewers (and thus satisfy advertisers), media outlets typically sensationalize disasters, focusing primarily on rare and isolated cases of anti-social behavior and presenting them as the norms rather than the exceptions. Second, as Tierney (2003) points out, various *institutional interests* benefit from depicting disasters as chaotic and lawless, including private security firms, advanced technology companies, and those seeking to establish an increased role for the military in civilian disaster response operations. Finally, Quarantelli (2002) suggests that the myth of panic and social breakdown may serve a useful function for *society at large.* Drawing insights from a classical sociologist named Emile Durkheim who argued that images of crime and criminals are functional for society because they reaffirm the importance of social rules, Quarantelli similarly suggests that perhaps images of panic, chaos, and social breakdown remind us all of the need to conform to cultural norms, maintain social relationships, and preserve social order, even during disasters.

7.4.2 Research-Based View of Disaster Response

The research-based view of disaster response contrasts sharply with the myth-based view. Its central premise is that individuals, organizations, and communities exhibit resilience in the face of disaster. In this context, *resilience* refers to the ability of individuals and social units to absorb and rebound from the impacts of a disaster. As will be discussed in more detail later in this section, certain vulnerable populations are at greater risk and some individuals, organizations, and communities rebound more easily and quickly than others, but the overall pattern of resilience is well established in the research literature (Dynes 2003).

At the *individual level,* the research-based view recognizes that disaster survivors participate actively in the response effort. Indeed, individuals possess important coping skills, and in times of disaster they typically exhibit remarkable self-efficacy and respond in an altruistic and caring manner. In virtually every disaster, survivors are typically the first responders on a scene, initiating search and rescue activities and providing preliminary care to the injured. Rather than having to control panic-stricken people as they flee en masse, emergency managers instead find themselves struggling to manage and coordinate all the people and donations that quickly arrive at disaster scenes.

This mass influx of people and supplies at the scene of a disaster is known as *convergence behavior.* In the first systematic study of the issue, Fritz and Mathewson (1957) identified several types of people who converge on a disaster site: returning survivors, curious spectators, volunteers, and those who seek to exploit the situation for economic gain. In addition to this kind of *personal convergence,* these researchers also discussed *informational convergence,* which in today's world would certainly include the mass media and its round-the-clock coverage of disasters, and *material convergence—* heavy equipment, other relief supplies, and donated items. In a much later study of convergence behavior, Neal (1994, 1995) documented the problems emergency managers faced in South Florida following Hurricane Andrew in 1992 when they were bombarded with unrequested donations including winter coats and mismatched shoes. A similar pattern of excessive donations followed the explosion of a fertilizer plant in West, Texas in 2013 and a tragic mass shooting at an elementary school in Newtown, Connecticut in 2012. As Box 7.4 describes, donations management is a critical emergency management function and must be taken seriously.

BOX 7.4   DONATE WHAT IS TRULY NEEDED: MONEY

You might be surprised that, most of the time, most things that people want to donate after a disaster are not needed. In disaster after disaster, people empty their closets and cupboards and send their used clothing and canned goods, often to places and people who do not need or cannot use what has been sent. Such unsolicited donations can cause significant problems when they require staff or volunteer time to sort and manage (Neal 1994). Though it is through a spirit of generosity that such donations arrive, the impact can be massive and cause problems.

Even more importantly, people who have lost everything need the right things at the right time in the right place, and your help in serving them *effectively* is needed. People who wear uniforms to work will need them replaced. If you do not have such uniforms in your closet (firefighter, police, medical, maid, delivery worker) then the most effective thing you can donate is money to purchase replacement uniforms—ones that are clean and in the right size. People may also need specialized, assistive devices like hearing aids, wheelchairs, scooters, walkers, canes, eyeglasses—and ones that work specifically for their specific needs. By donating money, an aid organization can move your money quickly through electronic means to that person with a specific need. Or, imagine the teenager who just desperately wants to fit in again—by wearing clothes that fit, that are current, and that help them to express their own sense of individuality. Clothing symbolizes who we are and when we donate money, aid organizations can issue vouchers so that teenagers can make their own selections. Re-gaining control in this manner also produces psychological benefits. Using the money locally stimulates the economy as well, and since most items can be purchased fairly close to a disaster area most of the time, your money can help re-start local businesses.

Instead of holding a clothing or food drive, think about how to raise money for a reputable aid organization. Hold a garage sale, pass a bucket, or donate online. Sell used clothing at a yard sale. Set up a bake sale. Ask for donations from area businesses and hold a silent auction. Talk to companies in your area about donating a percentage of sales. Host a pancake breakfast. Put on a car wash. Donate your labor to mow yards in exchange for a donation. The money will be the most useful thing that you will send because it is the most flexible (see Photo 7.1).

What happens when unsolicited donations do arrive? In big disasters, outside organizations help inventory, organize, and distribute goods or funds donated. In most disasters, the Seventh Day Adventists (a faith-based organization) set up a warehouse. They may get help from Americorps, the military, and other volunteers. From an online inventory, voluntary organizations can then log in to see what is available, then distribute items to people in need. Leftover items may be stored or offered to distribution sites set up by Goodwill or the Salvation Army stores. Used clothing is often sold to businesses that convert them into rags or other recyclable items and the

(Continued)

BOX 7.4 (*Continued*)   DONATE WHAT IS TRULY NEEDED: MONEY

voluntary organization then receives funds from the sale. The time that this can take might go on for months.

Do not be part of the problem. Be part of the solution and do the right thing.

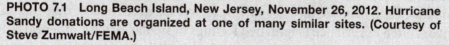

PHOTO 7.1   Long Beach Island, New Jersey, November 26, 2012. Hurricane Sandy donations are organized at one of many similar sites. (Courtesy of Steve Zumwalt/FEMA.)

As far as the panic myth is concerned, extensive research suggests that it is rare or nonexistent (Clarke and Chess 2008; Johnson 1987, 1988; Quarantelli 1954, 1957). Norris Johnson (1987), a leading authority, studied victim behavior in a major nightclub fire in which 160 people perished and a crowd surge at a rock concert where 11 people died. On the basis of extensive research, he concluded that in both instances social norms and attachments continued to regulate behavior. For example, in the crowd surge he found that people upheld norms of civility as evidenced by the fact that helping behavior became widespread. Moreover, helping behavior appeared to have been guided by prevailing gender role expectations. Specifically, he found that most women reported receiving help while men were twice as likely to report giving than receiving help. In terms of social attachments, he found in the nightclub fire that the overwhelming tendency was for patrons to attempt to evacuate in the same social groupings—friends and family members—with whom they arrived, a very common phenomenon in building fires.

Many observers point to the attacks on the World Trade Center and remember the images of people leaping to their demise from the upper floors of the burning towers. Even in those desperate circumstances, we heard numerous reports of people first attempting to place phone calls and connect with loved ones before they perished. Indeed, the persistence of social norms and relationships in even the most extreme environments has led scholars in emergency management to question whether the concept of panic serves any useful purpose (Quarantelli 2002). Perhaps Johnson (1987, pp. 181–182) has addressed the matter most succinctly: "throughout the analysis I was struck not by the breakdown of social order but by its strength and persistence; not by the irrational, individual behavior of popular myth, but by the socially structured, socially responsible, and adaptive actions of those affected." He goes on to conclude that "ruthless competition did not occur, and it did not occur because a functioning social order prevented it."

The issue of psychological stress and impairment has also been the subject of extensive research (for an excellent summary see Edwards 1998). The basic conclusion is that disasters are capable of producing *both* negative and positive mental health effects. While the myth-based view focuses only on the negative effects and the debilitating impacts on individuals, the research-based view also calls attention to the possible positive effects. As Fritz (1961, p. 657) states, "The traditional emphasis on pathological 'problems' has focused only on the destructive and disintegrative effects of disaster; it has wholly neglected the observable reconstructive and regenerative human responses." Thus, although we should certainly be sensitive to the mental health needs of disaster survivors, we also need to recognize that survivors often experience heightened feelings of solidarity with others around them and a sense of empowerment as they contribute actively to a response effort. This is not to say that there is no need for psychological services after disasters, but just as they do with public sheltering decisions, emergency managers and other public officials sometimes dramatically overestimate demands for mental health services.

At the *organizational level,* the research-based view suggests that organizations are adaptive and resilient in the face of disasters. Rather than having to deal with personnel shortages from role abandonment, as assumed by the myth-based view, research suggests that organizations, especially those with disaster-related responsibilities will instead be confronted with a massive onslaught of workers and volunteers. Consider the search-and-rescue and clean-up efforts at Ground Zero following the attacks on the World Trade Center. Firefighters, police officers, construction workers, and volunteers from all parts of the country toiled in the rubble for months, working exceedingly long hours and stopping only periodically to recuperate or attend funerals. Far from abandoning their roles, these workers overextended themselves, even placing their own health and safety at risk. Many of the first responders later suffered serious health problems as a result of the toxic exposures they faced at the site of the disaster, and, as a result, the U.S. government passed legislation to address their medical needs.

The research-based view recognizes that numerous and diverse organizations are typically involved in responding to disasters. While police and fire departments and hospitals may be the operations that come to mind first, many other organizations step up after disasters. Thus, rather than focusing on command control within a single organization, the greatest need after a disaster is for improved communication between and coordination of multiple organizations. In an effort to more accurately describe the range of organizations involved in responding to disasters, the Disaster Research Center (DRC) developed what is now commonly known as the *DRC typology* (Dynes 1970).

As you can see in Figure 7.3, organizations are classified in terms of their structures and the tasks they perform. Type I, or *established organizations,* such as police and fire departments, perform their regular tasks in a disaster and in so doing rely on existing structures. Type II, or *expanding organizations,* such as the Red Cross or Salvation Army, also perform regular tasks, but they rely on new structures—that is, they grow or expand from a small cadre of full-time professionals to large-scale operations of tens or hundreds of volunteers. Type III, or *extending organizations* have established structures, but take on new tasks in the aftermath of a disaster—for example, a construction crew working on a project in town may lend its personnel and equipment to the clean-up effort. Finally, Type IV, or *emergent organizations,* such as informal search-and-rescue groups, do not exist prior to a disaster, form only after impact, and thus rely on new structures and perform nonregular tasks. The involvement of so many different organizations, as we will see later in this chapter, can create problems in terms of coordination and communication, and that is why rather than adhering to rigid bureaucracy, organizations must be flexible after disasters strike.

At the *community level,* the research-based view emphasizes resilience and social order, rather than lawlessness and social breakdown. Instead of stealing from and fighting with each other, disaster survivors are much more likely to assist family members, friends, and neighbors. This increase in helping behavior after disasters led early researchers in the field to characterize the post-disaster environment as therapeutic in some respects for

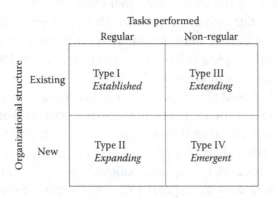

FIGURE 7.3 Types of organized responses to disasters. (Adapted from Dynes, Russell R., *Organized Behavior in Disaster,* 1970, p. 138.)

disaster-stricken communities. For example, Fritz (1961, p. 694) argued, "Contrary to the traditional pictures of man and society in the process of disintegration, disaster studies show that human societies have enormous resilience and recuperative power."

7.4.2.1 Sources and Limitations of Community Resilience

Researchers have identified various sources of community resilience in the face of disasters. First, although they are certainly tragic when they occur and disruptive to those they impact, many disasters are relatively low-impact events in relation to remaining community and societal resources, which allows societies to largely absorb the effects (Wright et al. 1979). Second, disasters are collectively shared experiences that often produce a unifying effect whereby people feel heightened attachment to and responsibility for others, and social distinctions and inequalities are temporarily suspended (Fritz 1961). Third, during a disaster, an emergency consensus typically arises, whereby community priorities that are ordinarily are subject to competition and debate are simplified and oriented toward life safety activities (Dynes 1970). Finally, social capital including cultural values, social norms and obligations, social relationships, and cultural traditions, ensures community survival and provides guidance and resources for responding to disasters (Dynes 2003).

Researchers also recognize, however, that disasters can and do produce negative effects and that societies can do much more to prevent them (Tierney 2014). Indeed, Tierney (2007) cautions researchers against overstating or exaggerating what she refers to as the "good news" paradigm in disaster research. Researchers have begun to identify various limitations of community resilience. First, for example, catastrophic events may severely limit the ability of a community or society to effectively rebound. The scope and magnitude of impact of a catastrophe, such as Hurricane Sandy that caused widespread damage along the Eastern seaboard of the United States in 2012, are so wide and devastating that even the capacity of surrounding communities to offer assistance is diminished. It is important to note, however, that even in catastrophes people remain capable of and typically do exhibit pro-social, helping behavior, as demonstrated in Hurricane Katrina (Rodriguez, Trainor, and Quarantelli 2006).

Second, as discussed throughout the text, vulnerable populations including the elderly, racial and ethnic minorities, the poor, and others often suffer much greater impacts from disasters and steeper challenges responding to and recovering from them. Third, problematic predisaster conditions such as high crime rates and widespread political corruption may also limit the ability of a community to respond in a productive, pro-social manner, as these same dynamics will likely play out during the disaster (Fischer 2008).

Fourth, a growing body of research in the field of environmental sociology suggests that technological disasters such as oil spills, rather than producing the therapeutic effects commonly observed in natural disasters, may instead create corrosive communities characterized by heightened psychological stress, intensified conflict over whom is to blame, and, in some cases prolonged litigation (Picou, Marshall, and Gill 2004).

Finally, some types of disasters, such as riots, can involve intense conflict between first responders and community members, and in some cases, the response effort is actually thwarted by crowd members throwing rocks, bottles, and other objects at responders and otherwise attempting to undermine the response effort. These kinds of confrontations were observed in the summer of 2014 and spring of 2015 when riots erupted in Ferguson, Missouri and Baltimore, Maryland, respectively. In light of the conflict that accompanies these kinds of events, researchers have historically made a distinction between natural disasters, which typically evoke consensus and solidarity and conflict-type events, such as riots, which involve intentional acts of property damage and disruption (Peek and Sutton 2003).

7.5 Disaster Response in an International Context

The myths and realities of human response to disaster discussed in this chapter are based largely on research conducted on events in the United States. In light of that fact, it is reasonable to question whether the same kinds of response patterns would be present in another country. Do people in other countries respond to natural disasters in the same pro-social manner described above? Do they rely as heavily on informal social networks including family and friends? Does the outpouring of support occur in response to international disasters? The simplest answer to these questions is that there are some basic similarities in disaster responses across countries but there are also important differences.

As described in Chapter 4, some research focuses on disasters outside the United States, and a sizable international network of scholars from many countries conducts it. At the most basic level, international research suggests that societies across the globe exhibit varying degrees of resilience in responding to disasters. In the wealthiest, most developed countries of the world such as the United States, Canada, Australia, Japan, European Union nations, and others, disaster impacts are typically absorbed relatively effectively, and the general response pattern resembles the research-based view of response described in this chapter. While the financial impacts of disasters in those nations can be very high, loss of human life is typically relatively low. Indeed, on virtually any indicator including financial loss, damage to the built environment, and death toll, the ratio of disaster impacts to remaining societal resources is usually relatively low in the most developed nations.

However, disaster impacts on all of these dimensions are typically very high in developing nations and in the least developed countries of the world. But the initial social response to disaster in those countries is often very similar to the pattern observed in developed nations, including survivors actively engaging in search and rescue and other activities; friends, family members, and neighbors helping each other; and volunteers, supplies, and resources converging on the scene. In other words, *social capital*, such as interpersonal relationships, community ties, cultural traditions, and other factors, serves as a source of survival and resilience in all societies, from the most impoverished and least powerful to the wealthiest and most powerful (Ritchie 2012).

Disasters in the developing world, however, typically produce much greater devastation and much more complex and difficult response challenges than those in developed nations. Developing nations include Brazil, Guatemala, Honduras, Mexico, Haiti, Honduras, the Dominican Republic, India, Indonesia, Pakistan, Turkey, Thailand, Sri Lanka, and many others. There are many reasons for the *heightened disaster vulnerability* of these countries.

First, substantial portions of their populations live in *extreme poverty*. As a result, in daily life and certainly when disaster strikes, people have far fewer resources to draw upon than those living in wealthier nations. Second, these societies typically have *vulnerable physical infrastructures*. Because of that vulnerability, the physical impacts of disasters on their built environments are often far more extensive than what we see in the United States and other developed countries. Third, stemming from the vulnerable built environment, disasters in developing countries often produce *sizable death tolls*. The January 2010 earthquake in Haiti and the 2004 Asian tsunami, for example, each resulted in approximately 300,000 deaths, and a devastating earthquake in Nepal in 2015 killed thousands more. With such widespread loss of human life, disasters in the developing world cause much greater losses in social capital—a primary source of resilience—than they typically do in developed countries.

Fourth, developing countries often have *weak or ineffective political institutions*. Countries like Turkey, for example are known to have reasonable building codes governing development but lack enforcement mechanisms, leading to questionable building practices and massive damage and loss of life when earthquakes occur. In 1999, for example, approximately 20,000 people died in an earthquake in Turkey, largely from building collapses. Fifth, in many cases developing countries are more vulnerable to disasters due to a *lack of effective warning systems*. The death toll in the Asian tsunami in 2004, for example, was so high in large part because the Indian Ocean, unlike the Pacific, was not protected by an advanced tsunami warning system. Finally, developing nations face increased technological hazards. As the wealthiest and most developed countries shift their manufacturing operations to the developing world in search of cheaper labor power and weaker environmental regulations, they are exposing people in those nations to new technological risks. In 1984, for example, thousands of residents of Bhopal, India died from a toxic release at a chemical plant owned by Union Carbide, a U.S. company.

7.6 Disaster Response and Principles of Effective Emergency Management

Based on the topics covered in this chapter, it should be clear that disasters, even in an international context, generally do not produce the kind of chaos and social breakdown envisioned by the myth-based view. Problems arise, to be sure, particularly in developing nations, but they typically do not center on the need to control hordes of unruly people. Instead, the greatest challenge in effectively responding to disasters is organizing and focusing the activities of the numerous individuals, informal groups, voluntary organizations, and public agencies that invariably arrive at the scene of a disaster.

Indeed, probably the two most common problems identified in after-action reports about disasters are the lack of coordination among responding organizations and breakdowns in communication. Throughout your career you can do your part in overcoming those challenges by remembering the principles of effective emergency management introduced in this book. In particular, the most effective strategies to embrace during the response phase are comprehensive emergency management, integrated emergency management, and flexibility.

7.6.1 Comprehensive Emergency Management

As discussed throughout this book, many hazards and disasters confront modern society. These threats vary, of course, in terms of the length of forewarning they afford and the scope, magnitude, and duration of their potential impacts. Each disaster agent is unique. Responding to a chemical, biological, or nuclear attack, for example, would certainly require the involvement of highly trained specialists and the use of specialized equipment not typically needed for natural disasters. *Comprehensive emergency management*, however, recognizes that various types of hazards share a great deal in common. For example, they are all capable of producing extensive physical damage, causing major injuries and deaths, and, importantly, creating major social disruption. Indeed, an event is only recognized as a disaster when it impacts human societies.

As social events, then, disasters of all types create some common social responses that have been described in this chapter, and produce common management problems. Convergence behavior, or rushing to the scene of a disaster, is very likely to occur, regardless of the hazardous agent. Additionally, as predicted by the DRC typology, numerous organizations, both formal and informal and official and unofficial, will invariably become involved in responding to disasters of all types. As a result, regardless of the type of disaster involved, emergency managers will always have to organize and focus the activities of multiple response organizations. By embracing the *all-hazards view*, emergency managers maximize their ability to respond effectively to the broadest range of threats.

7.6.2 Integrated Emergency Management

Integrated emergency management recognizes that all kinds of organizations are involved in responding to disasters. From this perspective, a major challenge for the emergency manager is coordinating, organizing, and focusing the activities of so many different response agencies. Coordination is a vital and far-reaching task. Emergency managers must facilitate coordination of multiple levels of government, coordination of government and NGOs, coordination within single organizations and across multiple organizations, and interactions among official and unofficial response groups and organizations. They must also manage the flow of information throughout the community and through the media and direct the movement of equipment, supplies, and donations.

Based on such a tall order and complex and important tasks, it may be helpful to consider some strategies for improving coordination. Keep in mind that none of these strategies is guaranteed and each has limitations. First, for example, emergency managers can improve coordination through enhanced EOC design, setting a center up in a way that maximizes communication among responding organizations (Neal 2003, 2005). An EOC is best viewed as a communication hub, not as a command post, where emergency management professionals and representatives from all of the responding organizations can come together to identify and address emergency response needs. Whether the EOC is set up as a stand-alone facility in a city-owned building or as a mobile operation in a motor home or trailer, its purpose is to monitor, manage, and share information so that officials can make proper decisions. To facilitate communication and assist in the decision-making process, EOCs today are equipped with numerous advanced technologies, including web-based software programs, such as Web EOC, that allow stakeholders to communicate and share information remotely.

Unfortunately, many modern EOCs are so oriented toward advanced technology that they actually impede communication because representatives from agencies sit staring at computer screens rather than interacting with others. Thus, EOCs should always be set up and designed in a manner that maximizes communication and facilitates collaboration and coordination among the multitude of responding organizations.

Second, *incident management frameworks,* such as the National Incident Management System (NIMS), predicated largely on the Incident Command System (ICS) developed by the fire services, can be useful for improving coordination. These systems are aimed at providing common terminology and organizing response activities into standard, recognizable areas (finance, logistics, operations, and planning). Box 7.5 presents the key components of NIMS and discusses the benefits of using the system to respond to wide range of disaster events. It is expected that all levels of government will use NIMS in a consistent manner, but as with all federal policies, actual implementation varies significantly. In their study of the use of NIMS in responding to Hurricane Katrina, Neal and Webb (2006) visited the EOC in New Orleans and the Joint Field Office in Baton Rouge and found wide variation in organizational training in and use of NIMS.

Finally, numerous *advanced technologies* can assist emergency managers in coordinating response activities. Geographic information systems (GISs) and global positioning systems (GPSs) can be used to locate and track response teams or map areas of heavy damage. Remote sensing technologies can produce aerial images for damage assessment, and decision support software can be used to log, track, and prioritize response activities. Advanced technologies, however, should be approached with some caution. One reason for caution is that not all jurisdictions have access to the most advanced technologies, creating somewhat of a technological divide in community readiness for disasters. Further, satellites cannot see inside a building to assess damage and may require ground truthing (Eguchi et al. 2003). Another reason is that technological glitches invariably arise, including data compatibility problems and lack of system interoperability. Finally, technology should be viewed with caution to the extent that it may foster overdependence and constrain the flexibility and creativity of users.

7.6.3 Flexibility in Emergency Management

In addition to embracing comprehensive and integrated emergency management, emergency managers can enhance their ability to overcome response challenges by recognizing the value of flexibility. As discussed in Chapters 5 and 6, preparedness and planning are critical aspects of emergency management. If done successfully, these activities can greatly reduce the amount of damage and disruption caused by a disaster, lessen

BOX 7.5   NATIONAL INCIDENT MANAGEMENT SYSTEM

What Is the National Incident Management System?

- Comprehensive, nationwide systematic approach to incident management
- Core set of doctrine, concepts, principles, terminology and organizational processes for all hazards
- Essential principles for a common operating picture and interoperability of communications and information management
- Standardized resource management procedures for coordination among different jurisdictions and organizations
- Scalable and applicable for all incidents

Key Benefits of NIMS

- Enhances organizational and technological interoperability and cooperation
- Provides a scalable and flexible framework with universal applicability
- Promotes all-hazards preparedness
- Enables a wide variety of organizations to participate effectively in emergency management/incident response
- Institutionalizes professional emergency management/incident response practices

NIMS Audience:

NIMS is applicable to all incidents and all levels of stakeholders, including levels of government, private sector organizations, critical infrastructure owners and operators, nongovernmental organizations and all other organizations who assume a role in emergency management. Elected and appointed officials and policy makers, who are responsible for jurisdictional policy decisions, must also have a clear understanding of NIMS to better serve their constituency.

NIMS Components:

Built on existing structures, such as the Incident Command System (ICS), NIMS creates a proactive system to assist those responding to incidents or planned events. To unite the practice of emergency management and incident response throughout the country, NIMS focuses on five key areas, or components. These components link together and work in unison to form a larger and comprehensive incident management system.

(Continued)

BOX 7.5 (*Continued*)   NATIONAL INCIDENT MANAGEMENT SYSTEM

NIMS Components Include:

- Preparedness
- Communications and Information Management
- Resource Management
- Command and Management
- Ongoing Management and Maintenance

What NIMS Is NOT

- A response plan
- Only used during large-scale incidents
- Only applicable to certain emergency management/incident response personnel
- Only the Incident Command System (ICS) or an organizational chart

Source: www.fema.gov/nims (*verbatim*)

the number of physical injuries and deaths, and dramatically improve a community's ability to respond. During the response phase, however, emergency managers and other public officials will invariably encounter new problems and unforeseen challenges for which they may not have been trained or to which they may not have given much consideration. When that happens, responders need to think creatively and be flexible about possible solutions.

There are two broad categories of flexibility in responding to disasters. *Individual-level* flexibility refers to improvisations enacted by individual responders and can take various forms (Mendonca et al. 2014). For example, a responder may have to perform a task without his or her usual equipment and rely instead on makeshift provisions. In the aftermath of the bombing of the Murrah Federal Building in Oklahoma City in 1995, for example, first responders used blown-out doors in the fallen debris as stretchers for carrying victims of the blast. As one contributor to the final report on the bombing observed, "Probably the greatest tool of all was the rescue workers' ingenuity. In the early stages of the incident, I saw many circumstances in which rescue workers adapted standard tools to complete tasks for which the tools were not originally designed." The report concludes, "This expedited the rescues of dozens of people in the early stages of the incident" (The City of Oklahoma City 1996, p. 154).

Organizational-level flexibility involves adaptations on the part of organizations. Similar to individual improvising, organizational adaptations can take several forms and usually result from resource shortages, unforeseen contingencies, or unmet needs and demands. For example, in the aftermath of the September 11, 2001 attacks, New York City's EOC had to be relocated when the building housing it was destroyed (Kendra and Wachtendorf 2003). Also in that event, thousands of people were evacuated from lower Manhattan in an unplanned water rescue operation (Kendra and Wachtendorf 2016; Kendra, Wachtendorf, and Quarantelli 2003). At both the individual and organizational levels, flexibility is often necessary to fill gaps left by the planning process and meet heightened demands of a disaster.

Certainly there will be times in your career when you will need to think creatively and exhibit this kind of flexibility. In fact, in all professions, not just emergency management, a premium should be placed on creativity and flexibility because it typically produces positive results. Of course, improvisations occasionally fail or backfire and create undesirable outcomes. In other words, at times doing things "by the book" is the best way to go and at other times it is necessary to "think outside the box." Like the football quarterback who must decide in a split second whether to run a play as called by the coaches or make a quick change at the line of scrimmage, the most effective leaders in any context decide, based on past experience or intuition, which path to follow. As you gain experience in the field of emergency management, your skills in this area will sharpen over time.

Some organizations, however, develop *important limitations on flexibility*. As Webb and Chevreau (2006) suggest, several *internal organizational characteristics* limit flexibility. For example, many organizations actually stifle flexibility and creativity due to their strict adherence to written rules and procedures, extensive specialization of tasks with accompanying diffusion of responsibility, and over-reliance on technology to solve basic problems. Rather than producing innovators and problem solvers, these organizations instead create conformists and ritualists who define their jobs in very narrow terms and rely exclusively on protocol and standard operating procedures to perform tasks. There are also important *external constraints* on organizational and individual flexibility. Drabek (2010) calls attention to the climate of litigation so prevalent in modern society and the possibility that individuals and organizations may be legally liable for damages possibly resulting from failures to follow proper protocol. Additionally, we could consider the broader bureaucratic context under which emergency management falls as a possible external constraint on flexibility. With the creation of DHS, for example, many observers feared that FEMA would lose its autonomy and flexibility to respond to natural disasters when it was placed under the umbrella of homeland security. Those concerns were validated by the federal government's initially slow and ineffective response to Hurricane Katrina (Waugh 2005).

7.7 Working and Volunteering in Response

As described in Box 7.1, considerable differences exist between first responders and emergency managers. Working in the response phase is only one of the activities of the emergency manager and is a role that involves coordination, communication, and collaboration across multiple agencies. In a small town, the emergency manager will likely play the role of EOC facilitator. In larger areas, emergency management professionals play more specific roles during the response period such as specializing in mass care (food and shelter), coordinating debris removal, handling massive unsolicited donations, assessing infrastructure damage and repair needs, re-establishing communications, and working with the media.

To be effective, an emergency manager must pursue education, training, and experience. Anyone who works in an EOC during a response period must be a highly trained professional capable of managing significant amounts of stress, working across agencies, and moving the community through crisis stage by stage. Although you are at the first stages in moving toward working in the response period, you can start by acquiring some knowledge beyond this chapter through the FEMA independent study courses. These free, online courses offer insights into incident command, the National Incident Management System, voluntary organizations and more.

Volunteering during the response period also requires training. You can start with basic first-aid and cardio-pulmonary resuscitation (CPR) courses. Many disaster organizations like the Red Cross also offer shelter manager training and integrate volunteers well in advance into disaster action teams. After September 11, 2001, the United States also established the Citizen Corps (www.ready.gov/citizen-corps). Within your state, community, or possibly your university, you may be able to train for a community emergency response team (CERT) and be activated for crisis events or help with crowd management at a major sporting event.

Perhaps you have other kinds of interests. The Medical Reserve Corps integrates medical professionals into volunteer service. When coastal hurricanes threaten nursing home populations, for example, many residents are evacuated inland or to other host states. The Medical Reserve Corps receives, assesses, and cares for arriving evacuees. A fairly new program, called Map Your Neighborhood, in the states of Washington and Oklahoma involves neighbors in identifying people who may need assistance and where neighborhood resources can be located for rescue purposes. If you volunteer for response, do not just show up and hope to help. Known as spontaneous unaffiliated volunteers (SUVs), such convergences of people create more problems than help. Enter a damaged area through an established organization for your own safety as well as that of those you seek to help.

Summary

This chapter has addressed several important aspects of the response phase of disaster. Having read this chapter, you should now have a much better understanding of what actually happens during the response phase and how to maximize the effectiveness of response efforts. For example, we identified the major characteristics of effective disaster warnings: consistency, specificity, and credibility. Additionally, we discussed the myth-based view of disaster that envisions chaos and pervades the popular imagination and contrasted it with the research-based view emphasizing resilience and adaptability.

While the public response to disasters is often productive, adaptive, and pro-social, we have also identified the most common response problems including communication and coordination. We also discussed strategies for overcoming these challenges including enhanced EOC design, appropriate incident management frameworks, and reasonable use of advanced technologies. For international disasters, we identified specific vulnerabilities of developing countries such as extreme poverty, vulnerable infrastructure, weak and ineffective political institutions, and other factors. Finally, we suggested that the key to effectively managing the response phase of disasters is to embrace core principles discussed throughout this book including comprehensive emergency management, integrated emergency management, and flexibility.

Discussion Questions

1. Which word do you believe best describes an emergency manager: a commander or a coordinator? Why?

   Managers and Coordinators NOT commanders!

2. Based on what you have learned about the response phase in this chapter, how can we improve community disaster preparedness efforts to improve our ability to respond more effectively to future disasters?

3. If you were an emergency manager, how would you make use of social media (e.g., Facebook and Twitter) to issue disaster warnings?

4. Think about a disaster-themed movie or television show you have seen recently. How did it portray people's response to the event? Was it realistic or based on disaster myths? Why is it important for emergency managers to understand the myths of disaster?

5. International disasters, such as the 2010 Haiti earthquake and the 2015 Nepal earthquake, often cause massive damage and devastating death tolls. Why are disasters so destructive when they strike impoverished nations? What can be done to lessen their impacts, particularly on human lives?

Resources

- To learn more about training and educational opportunities available to first responders and emergency managers, visit the FEMA Emergency Management Institute (EMI) at training.fema.gov/emi.aspx.
- To learn about Citizen Corps and various educational and volunteer opportunities that may be available to you visit www.ready.gov/citizen-corps.
- To gain some critical insights into Hurricane Katrina and how the response to it was shaped by post-9/11 changes to the U.S. emergency management system, visit the Social Science Research Council understandingkatrina.ssrc.org.
- To learn more about the National Terrorism Advisory System, which replaced the color-coded Homeland Security Advisory System, visit www.dhs.gov/national-terrorism-advisory-system.

References and Recommended Readings

Aguirre, Benigno E. 1988. The Lack of Warnings Before the Saragosa Tornado. *The International Journal of Mass Emergencies and Disasters* 6(1): 65–74.

Aguirre, Benigno E. 2004. Homeland Security Warnings: Lessons Learned and Unlearned. *International Journal of Mass Emergencies and Disasters* 22(2): 103–115.

The City of Oklahoma City. 1996. *Final Report: Alfred P. Murrah Federal Building Bombing, April 19, 1995*. Stillwater, OK: Fire Protection Publications.

Clarke, Lee and Caron Chess. 2008. Elites and Panic: More to Fear than Fear Itself. *Social Forces* 87(2): 993–1014.

Drabek, Thomas E. 1986. *Human System Responses to Disaster: An Inventory of Sociological Findings*. New York: Springer-Verlag.

Drabek, Thomas E. 2010. *The Human Side of Disaster*. Boca Raton, FL: CRC Press.

Drabek, Thomas E. 2013. *The Human Side of Disaster*, 2nd edition. Boca Raton, FL: CRC Press.

Dynes, Russell R. 1970. *Organized Behavior in Disaster*. Lexington, MA: Health Lexington Books.

Dynes, Russell R. 1994. Community Emergency Planning: False Assumptions and Inappropriate Analogies. *International Journal of Mass Emergencies and Disasters* 12(2): 141–158.

Dynes, Russell R. 2003. Finding Order in Disorder: Continuities in the 9–11 Response. *International Journal of Mass Emergencies and Disasters* 21(3): 9–23.

Edwards, Margie L. Kiter. 1998. An Interdisciplinary Perspective on Disasters and Stress: The Promise of an Ecological Framework. *Sociological Forum* 13(1): 115–132.

Eguchi, R., C. Huyck, B. Adams, B. Mansouri, B. Houshmand, and M. Shinozuka. 2003. *Resilient Disaster Response: Using Remote Sensing Technologies for Post-Earthquake Damage Detection*. Buffalo, New York: Multidisciplinary Earthquake Engineering Research Center.

Fischer, Henry W. 2008. *Response to Disaster*, 3rd edition. Lanham, MD: University Presses of America.

Fritz, Charles E. 1961. Disasters. pp. 651–694 in *Contemporary Social Problems,* edited by Robert K. Merton and Robert A. Nisbet. Riverside, CA: University of California Press.

Fritz, Charles E. and J. H. Mathewson. 1957. *Convergence Behavior in Disasters: A Problem in Social Control.* Washington, D.C.: National Academy of Sciences, National Research Council.

Heath, Sebastian, Philip Kass, Alan Beck, and Larry Glickman. 2001. Human and Pet-related Risk Factors for Household Evacuation Failure During a Natural Disaster. *American Journal of Epidemiology* 153(7): 659–665.

Homeland Security Advisory Council. 2009. *Homeland Security Advisory System, Task Force Report and Recommendations.* Washington, D.C.: Department of Homeland Security. Available at http://www.dhs.gov/xlibrary/assets/hsac_final_report_09_15_09.pdf, last accessed May 26, 2011.

Johnson, Norris. 1987. Panic and the Breakdown of Social Order: Popular Myth, Social Theory, and Empirical Evidence. *Sociological Focus* 20(3): 171–183.

Johnson, Norris. 1988. Fire in a Crowded Theater: A Descriptive Investigation of the Emergence of Panic. *International Journal of Mass Emergencies and Disasters* 6(1): 7–26.

Kendra, James M. and Tricia Wachtendorf. 2016. *American Dunkirk: The Waterborne Evacuation of Manhattan on 9/11.* Philadelphia, PA: Temple University Press.

Kendra, James M. and Tricia Wachtendorf. 2003. Creativity in Emergency Response after the World Trade Center Attack. pp. 121–146 *In Beyond September 11th: An Account of Post-Disaster Research,* edited by Jacquelyn L. Monday. Boulder, CO: Special Publication #39 Natural Hazards Research and Applications Information Center, University of Colorado.

Kendra, James M., Tricia Wachtendorf, and E. L. Quarantelli. 2003. The Evacuation of Lower Manhattan by Water Transport on September 11: An Unplanned Success. *Joint Commission Journal on Quality and Safety* 29(6): 316–318.

Mendonca, David M., Gary R. Webb, Carter T. Butts, and James Brooks. 2014. Cognitive Correlates of Improvised Behaviour in Disaster Response: The Cases of the Murrah Building and the World Trade Center. *Journal of Contingencies and Crisis Management* 22(4): 185–195.

Mileti, Dennis. 1999. *Disasters by Design.* Washington, D.C.: Joseph Henry Press.

National Governors Association. 1979. *Comprehensive Emergency Management.* Washington, D.C.: National Governors Association.

National Organization on Disability. 2005. *Special Needs Assessment of Katrina Evacuees.* Washington, D.C.: National Organization on Disability.

National Research Council, Committee on Public Responses to Alerts and Warnings on Mobile Devices: Current Knowledge and Research Gaps. 2010. *Public Response to Alerts and Warnings on Mobile Devices: Summary of a Workshop on Current Knowledge and Research Gaps.* Washington, D.C.: The National Academies Press.

National Science and Technology Council, Committee on Environment and Natural Resources. 2000. *Effective Disaster Warnings: Report by the Working Group on Natural Disaster Information Systems, Subcommittee on Natural Disaster Reduction.* Washington, D.C.: National Science and Technology Council.

Neal, David M. 1994. Consequences of Excessive Donations in Disaster: The Case of Hurricane Andrew. *Disaster Management* 6(1): 23–28.

Neal, David M. 1995. Crowds, Convergence, and Disasters. *Crowd Management* 2(1): 13–16.

Neal, David M. 2003. Design Characteristics of Emergency Operating Centers. *Journal of Emergency Management* 1(2): 35–38.

Neal, David M. 2005. Case Studies of Four Emergency Operating Centers. *Journal of Emergency Management* 3(1): 29–32.

Neal, David M. and Brenda D. Phillips. 1995. Effective Emergency Management: reconsidering the bureaucratic approach. *Disasters* 19: 327–337.

Neal, David M. and Gary R. Webb. 2006. Structural Barriers to Implementing the National Incident Management System. pp. 263–282 in *Learning from Catastrophe: Quick Response Research in the Wake of Hurricane Katrina*, edited by Christine Bvec. Boulder, CO: Natural Hazards Center–University of Colorado.

Peek, Lori A. and Jeannette N. Sutton. 2003. An Exploratory Comparison of Disasters, Riots, and Terrorist Acts. *Disasters* 27(4): 319–335.

Perry, Ronald W., Michael K. Lindell, and Marjorie R. Greene. 1981. *Evacuation Planning in Emergency Management*. Lexington, MA: Lexington Books.

Picou, J. S., B. K. Marshall, and Duane Gill. 2004. Disaster, Litigation, and the Corrosive Community. *Social Forces* 82: 1497–1526.

Quarantelli, E. L. 1954. The Nature and Conditions of Panic. *American Journal of Sociology* 60: 267–275.

Quarantelli, E. L. 1957. The Behavior of Panic Participants. *Sociology and Social Research* 41: 187–194.

Quarantelli, E. L. 1960. Images of Withdrawal Behavior in Disasters: Some Basic Misconceptions. *Social Problems* 8: 68–79.

Quarantelli, E. L. 2002. The Sociology of Panic. pp. 11020–23 in *International Encyclopedia of the Social and Behavioral Sciences,* edited by Paul B. Baltes and Neil Smelser. New York: Elsevier.

Quarantelli, E. L. and Russell R. Dynes. 1977. Response to Social Crisis and Disaster. *Annual Review of Sociology* 3: 23–49.

Ritchie, Liesel A. 2012. Individual Stress, Collective Trauma, and Social Capital in the Wake of the Exxon Valdez Oil Spill. *Sociological Inquiry* 82: 187–211.

Rodriguez, Havidán, Joseph Trainor, and E. L. Quarantelli. 2006. Rising to the Challenges of a Catastrophe: The Emergent and Prosocial Behavior following Hurricane Katrina. *The ANNALS of the American Academy of Political and Social Science* 604: 82–101.

Sorensen, John. 2000. Hazard Warning Systems: A Review of 20 Years of Progress. *Natural Hazards Review* 1: 119–125.

Sorensen, John H. and Barbara Vogt-Sorensen. 2006. Community Processes: Warning and Evacuation. pp. 183–199 in *Handbook of Disaster Research*, edited by Havidan Rodriguez, Enrico L. Quarantelli, and Russell R. Dynes. New York: Springer.

Sutton, Jeannette, C. B. Gibson, E. S. Spiro, C. League, S. M. Fitzhugh, C. T. Butts. 2015. What It Takes to Get Passed On: Message Content, Style, and Structure as Predictors of Retransmission in the Boston Marathon Bombing Response. *PLoS One* 10(8): e0134452. doi:10.1371/journal.pone.0134452.

Tierney, Kathleen J. 2003. Disaster Beliefs and Institutional Interests: Recycling Disaster Myths in the Aftermath of 9-11. pp. 33–51 in *Terrorism and Disaster,* edited by Lee Clarke. New York: Elsevier.

Tierney, Kathleen J. 2007. From the Margins to the Mainstream? Disaster Research at the Crossroads. *Annual Review of Sociology* 33: 503–525.

Tierney, Kathleen J. 2014. *The Social Roots of Risk: Producing Disasters, Promoting Resilience*. Stanford, CA: Stanford University Press.

Tierney, Kathleen J., Michael K. Lindell, and Ronald W. Perry. 2001. *Facing the Unexpected*. Washington, D.C.: Joseph Henry Press.

United States Department of Justice. n.d. *The ADA and Emergency Shelters*. Available at http://www. ada.gov/pcatoolkit/chap7shelterprog. pdf, last accessed January 25, 2011.

van Willigen, Marieke, Bob Edwards, Terri Edwards, and Shaun Hessee. 2002. Riding Out the Storm: The Experiences of the Physically Disabled during Hurricanes Bonnie, Dennis, and Floyd. *Natural Hazards Review* 3(3): 98–106.

Waugh, William. 2005. The Disaster That Was Katrina. *Natural Hazards Observer*. Available at http://www.colorado.edu/hazards/o/archives/2005/nov05/nov05d1. html, last accessed January 25, 2011.

Webb, Gary R. and Francois-Regis Chevreau. 2006. Planning to Improvise: The Importance of Creativity and Flexibility in Crisis Response. *International Journal of Emergency Management* 3: 66–72.

Wood, V. T. and Weisman, R. A. 2003. A Hole in the Weather Warning System. *Bulletin of the American Meteorological Society* 84(2): 187–194.

Wright, James, Peter Rossi, S. R. Wright, and E. Weber-Burdin. 1979. *After the Clean-Up: Long-Range Effects of Natural Disasters*. Beverly Hills, CA: Sage.

Chapter **8**

Recovery

Objectives

Upon completing this chapter, readers should be able to:

- Identify and define various ways to understand recovery.
- List and illustrate common recovery challenges.
- Discuss the need for pre-disaster planning.
- Outline steps in the process of recovery planning (pre or post).
- Understand best practices for volunteering in a recovery context.
- Be familiar with the types of social capital available for recovery and how to leverage such human resources.
- Describe the community, civic, and voluntary organizations active in disasters.
- Link recovery to a more resilient future response to disasters.

Key Terms

- Civic organization
- Community based-organization
- Pre-disaster recovery planning
- Post-disaster recovery planning
- Reconstruction
- Recovery
- Rehabilitation
- Resilience
- Restitution

- Social capital
  - Bonding
  - Bridging
  - Cognitive
  - Linking
  - Structural
- Sustainability
- Voluntary organization
- Voluntary organization active in disaster (VOAD)
- Volunteer

8.1 Introduction

After a disaster, we have to think about a wide array of concerns that face families, communities, organizations, leaders, and managers. Recovery, while daunting, provides an opportunity for these kinds of people and the places that they love. Even though a disaster occurred, an opportunity has also presented itself. Now, we can re-think how we build homes so that they are more resistant to future disasters. We can also design new outdoor, green spaces to provide for both recreation and environmental preservation. The business community can work with city government to transform transportation arteries in order to attract more customers and clients. The infrastructure, which may have led to some of the disasters (such as a levee failure) can be strengthened. In short, recovery presents the chance to offer enhancements and improve local quality of life. To start our discussion, we begin by considering the concept of "recovery."

8.2 Defining Recovery

Recovery can mean different things to different people and it is wise to keep that in mind when using the term (Quarantelli 1998). It is not unusual for a local official to go on television and proclaim that the community will rebuild. *Reconstruction*, though, is not the only term that describes recovery. The rebuilding process needs to be thought through carefully as the post-disaster time frame allows for re-thinking *how* we rebuild. Reconstruction might be thought of, for example, as a chance to bring in greener materials to allow for more energy-efficient homes and businesses. The reconstruction period might also allow for a chance to promote green space, improve storm water systems, and relocate utilities underground before the next disaster. Reconstruction could also reduce the impacts of future disasters by incorporating storm-resistant hurricane shutters and roof clamps, safe rooms, elevations and similar features. Reconstruction should not just be thought of as building back, but as building back better toward a more resilient future.

Restoration serves as another term that people use during the recovery period. Restoration, or returning to the way things were before, may be appropriate in some cases such as with the historical and cultural elements of a community. The meaningful parts of an historic structure, for example, can be rebuilt with elements saved during debris removal. We can also integrate mitigation features to restored buildings. By elevating a structure above anticipated flood levels, an historic building can be kept in its historic context but made safe from future risks. By doing so, we safeguard our ancestry and the places that mean so much to each of us.

Rehabilitation is yet another term used during recovery. To rehabilitate means to make things better, typically in a way that improves some element of a structure or a community. Rehabilitation, though, may result in low-income areas being demolished or changed so much that original residents cannot return. Some communities may disallow trailer parks after a tornado, but not reintroduce affordable housing. After Hurricane Katrina, public outcry arose when the U.S. Housing and Urban Development in conjunction with the Housing Authority of New Orleans tore down public housing and introduced mixed income housing. The decision, according to protestors, resulted in fewer homes for those at lower income levels. Rehabilitation, though, may also provide a chance to improve deteriorated facilities and incorporate desirable aspects such as accessibility.

The term *restitution* carries with it the suggestion that some kind of legal action or compensation is expected. This is usually the case where an entity or agent is deemed to be at fault, such as with hazardous materials releases, the failure of a levee system, or a terrorist attack. Assigning blame and securing compensation can take considerable time as was experienced after the attacks of September 11th and with the levee failures in New Orleans after Hurricane Katrina.

Experts suggest that *recovery* is best thought of as a process involving a series of stages or steps. The *short-term recovery* stage would include restoring key utilities and infrastructure and placing people into temporary housing. *Long-term recovery* involves the community in tackling how, when, and where to rebuild, lays out a timeline to do so, and organizes people, resources, and organizations in moving toward a consensus-based vision of normalcy.

Typically, emergency managers are most involved in short-term recovery. Long-term recovery is more likely to be managed by elected officials, special task forces, and relief organizations. This is unfortunate because the expertise of emergency managers may not be tapped. Emergency managers should remain well-integrated into the various tasks of recovery in order to leverage their expertise and insights. Recovery is sufficiently daunting without involving those most knowledgeable about what to do and why.

8.3 Recovery Challenges

Where to start? When facing the destruction caused by a massive hurricane, unexpected earthquake, or a terrorist attack, recovery may seem like an insurmountable task. However, emergency managers who anticipate recovery will face a more manageable set of challenges. To do so, emergency managers should have:

- Conducted mitigation planning with the community to identify hazards, assess risks, and prioritize solutions with stakeholders involvement.
- Worked with local stakeholders to improve their resilience or ability to bounce back from a disaster.
- Engaged in pre-disaster recovery planning.
- Developed a set of tools to expedite the recovery process.
- Become familiar with the potential challenges ahead and established effective partnerships and procedures to launch an immediate recovery.
- Created a holistic, comprehensive way in which to launch a recovery process (NHRAIC 2005).

Although mitigation planning will be addressed more fully in a coming chapter, the process involves area stakeholders in identifying hazards and assessing risk. They then look into ways to reduce risks, such as building safe rooms or buying insurance. Mitigation planning teams then prioritize such solutions and seek funding to implement the mitigation measure, through perhaps establishing a state-wide safe room initiative. If the mitigation planning team has been successful, the effects of disasters should reduce the burden of recovery. In essence, mitigation planning should have built a culture of prevention in which resilience—or the ability to bounce back more quickly—becomes a reality after a disaster (see Box 8.1).

Other measures that can be taken to reduce recovery difficulties include pre- and post-disaster recovery planning with an eye on specific areas such as housing, jobs, or the environment.

8.3.1 Pre-Disaster Recovery Planning

Two kinds of recovery planning may occur: the kind that occurs before an event and the kind that takes place afterwards. *Pre*-disaster planning is ideal as it allows communities to anticipate recovery challenges, build partnerships to tackle recovery tasks, and determine the best ways to move forward. Conversely, *post*-disaster recovery planning often occurs in the context of confusion, sadness, and long work days. Though this text urges readers to conduct prerecovery planning, the reality is that most will do so after an event. The purpose of this section is to walk through the various challenges that will be faced in either a pre- or post-disaster planning context.

BOX 8.1   RESILIENCE

What is resilience? Most people describe resilience as the ability to bounce back from a disaster or an ability to learn, adapt, and self-organize when a disturbance (like a hurricane) occurs (Folke 2006; Peacock 2010). Disasters require such an ability in order to avoid loss of life, property damage and losses, or significant external assistance (Mileti et al. 1995; Mileti 1999). Resilience is also viewed as a means to flip vulnerability (Galderisi et al. 2010).

But how does resilience happen? In 2012, the U.S. National Academies released a report titled *Disaster Resilience: A National Imperative*. As a foundational element of increasing national resilience, the report said that "bottom-up interventions—the engagement of communities in increasing their resilience—are essential" (National Academies 2012, p. 4). Toward this goal of whole community engagement, the report recommends (verbatim):

- Engaging the whole community in disaster policymaking and planning;
- Linking public and private infrastructure performance and interests to resilience goals;
- Improving public and private infrastructure and essential services (such as health and education);
- Communicating risks, connecting community networks, and promoting a culture of resilience;
- Organizing communities, neighborhoods, and families to prepare for disasters;
- Adopting sound land-use planning practices; and
- Adopting and enforcing building codes and standards appropriate to existing hazards [end verbatim]

Who is responsible for becoming more resilient? The National Academies report gives this responsibility to all including all levels of government. Or, as the Committee on Increasing National Resilience to Hazards and Disasters stated (National Academies, 2012, p. vii), "Disaster resilience is everyone's business and is a shared responsibility among citizens, the private sector, and government."

Source: For a free pdf of the National Academies report, visit http://www.nap.edu/catalog/13457/disaster-resilience-a-national-imperative, last accessed February 3, 2016.

To start, recovery planning must be done by locals and must involve the whole community (FEMA 2005; Norman 2004; Quarantelli 1997; Schwab et al. 1998). Local people know their people and places best including how they want to live in a post-disaster context. The New Zealand Ministry of Civil Defence and Emergency Management empowers local Civil Defence Emergency Management groups (CDEMs) to work collectively. Their CDEM groups involve citizens, officials, utility companies, educators, and others who know their community well and can serve as active participants in a planning process. Such a configuration is considered ideal for recovery planning as a broad array of expertise and insights come into the planning process.

Ideally, such efforts will view recovery planning as an opportunity to identify risks and form strategies to reduce those risks. For example, a pre-disaster recovery plan might identify historic and cultural resources in museums, neighborhoods, and outdoor sites. They could specify that such places, which help to form a community's sense of identity, should be protected. Planners could build teams of residents living in historic neighborhoods, architects, and historic preservation officers to design ways to salvage and reuse historic elements. Their efforts would help to recapture the community look and feel that people deem to be meaningful.

Recovery plans should address:

- *Housing*: How should housing be rebuilt after a disaster? Recovery can provide an opportunity to alter the built environment and make it safer. Doing so, however, should not be at the expense of people who cannot afford to rebuild (Kroll-Smith, Baxter, and Jenkins 2015). By preidentifying locations of high risk vis-à-vis area hazards, it may be possible to design affordable post-disaster alternatives that also provide increased safety. Other new ideas can also be brought in including more sustainable, energy efficient housing, or an increase in green space to enhance quality of life and decrease energy expenses.
- *Businesses*: People need to work to be able to afford post-disaster expenses, feed their families, and pay rent or mortgages. From small businesses to large corporations, issues such as displacement, downtime, loss of inventory, effects on human resources, damage to records, and more must be considered. How, where, and under what circumstances can you reopen businesses to help business owners, employees, and the local economy rebound?
- *Environmental resources*: While one might argue that natural disasters are an inevitable part of the physical environment, the human impact may worsen the impact. Floods, which may occur on a regular basis, may also move hazardous materials out of homes and businesses. Subsequent contamination can leave soil, water, vegetation, and wildlife at risk as well as the humans who will live in or near the inundated area. Wildfires also worsen when humans build homes in the wildland–urban interface, fueling massive conflagrations. Pre-disaster planning can identify ways to protect endangered areas or species and provide a means to restore the tree canopy, increase native plants to resist area weather, and restore damaged eco-systems.
- *Historic and cultural resources*: Places are important to people and their shared love for them will bring them to the planning table. Debris removal teams can salvage historic bricks and facade elements

so that the "old look" can return. To imagine Paris without the Eiffel Tower, Moscow without St. Basil's Cathedral, or Spain without its plazas is to understand how important places are economically, historically, and in terms of people's pride in their identities. Outdoor sites should be considered as well including sacred Native American sites or historic battlefields (Barthel 1996). Even disaster sites, such as Oklahoma City, New York City's World Trade Center, the Pentagon, and a field in Pennsylvania have become places to preserve (Sather-Wagstaff 2011).

- *Infrastructure*: Transportation systems, utilities, cell systems, Internet access and more comprise the built infrastructure. Earthquakes can move roadways. Hurricanes can take out cell towers and disrupt Internet service. Terrorist attacks can shut down airports. In addition, the infrastructure in many areas is already in deteriorating condition. The American Society of Civil Engineers (ASCE 2013) gave the United States a D+ for its infrastructure. After a disaster, planners should be well-poised to implement changes that alter and improve waterways, transit systems, wastewater, drinking water, dams, and more.
- *Psychological recovery*: Helping people deal with the trauma they may experience in a disaster should be a planning action item. Though most people face and manage disasters fairly well (Norris et al. 2002a, b), we should be concerned about the effects of major disasters. Terrorist attacks, particularly those that attack soft targets like a mall or café, are intended to cause psychological distress. Being ready for such events and fostering internal and collective resilience can make a difference (see Box 8.2, Photo 8.1).

Ultimately, we recover, rebuild, rehabilitate, and restore communities because people live and work in places that mean something to them. Recovery planning must involve these stakeholders as they move toward a newly envisioned post-disaster home, workplace, and community.

8.3.2 Leveraging Human Resources for Recovery

How, where and when homes, businesses, and infrastructures are rebuilt impacts each of us. By participating, we bring ideas, insights, and resources to the planning table. When we bring people in to participate in events that impact our futures, like recovery planning, we bring something else as well: *social capital*. Think of social capital as akin to money: it is an intangible resource that develops when people socially interact (Nakagawa and Shaw 2004; Uphoff 2000; Woolcock 2000).

BOX 8.2 THE HOPE TRUNK FROM OKLAHOMA CITY

PHOTO 8.1 The Hope Trunk. (Courtesy of Brenda Phillips, with permission.)

In 1995, 168 people died in a bombing at the Murrah Federal building in Oklahoma City as the result of a domestic terrorist attack. The building housed a number of federal functions including social security, drug enforcement, housing, firearms, and military recruiting offices. The site also included a day care center, where nineteen children died. Over 700 people sustained injuries as well when the side of the nine-story building collapsed. While many people focus on the building, it is important to know that adjacent sites were affected as well including area businesses, state offices, and places of worship. The bomb could be felt within a six-mile radius of the site, including at least six schools. The attack, occurring well before the massive attacks of September 11th, shook the heartland of the United States.

How do you recover from such a traumatic event? How do you find the will to go on and to heal? In the aftermath, Oklahoma launched efforts to provide mental health support to survivors and to first responders. Children became a particular focus of the efforts, with the Oklahoma Department of Mental Health developing outreach programs for teachers and students. Their efforts took place right after the attack, as well as during the ensuing criminal trials.

The Murrah building became the site of a national memorial and museum (https://oklahomacitynationalmemorial.org/). It includes the Gates of Time, where visitors walk through gates marked by the moment of the attack.

(Continued)

BOX 8.2 (*Continued*)   THE HOPE TRUNK FROM OKLAHOMA CITY

"Places of Remembrance" also include sites where people can learn, remember, mourn, and come to terms with lingering grief. On the lawn, a reflective pool allows contemplation of the 168 chairs symbolizing the lives taken. A Survivor Wall includes the names of those who survived, carved on granite from the building. Called the Survivor Tree, an American elm has survived not only the attack but also severe weather. Arborists have taken graftings from the tree, which are given to those who enter the annual Memorial Marathon. And those who run leave their entry bibs on a remnant of fence still in place today.

So many items have been left on the chairs or the fence, or sent to the museum, that they became part of an archive and a traveling exhibit. The Hope Trunk (see Photo 8.1) centers on teaching people, particularly school children, about the event. When the Hope Trunk arrives at a school, specially marked bags contain items from the fence and the building. Educational materials also come with the Hope Trunk, designed to help students develop an understanding of violence including bullying. Exercises can be used from the Trunk as well—and a stuffed teddy bear will remain with the new "Hope School" when it completes its exercises.

To view videos and hear audios of the event, visit https://oklahomacity-nationalmemorial.org/about/the-memorial-museum/. To learn more about the Hope Trunk and how to bring it to your school, visit https://oklahomacitynational-memorial.org/learn/education/hope-trunk/, last accessed February 3, 2016.

Several kinds of social capital can be present after a disaster. *Bonding* social capital occurs when people connect across similarities. After Superstorm Sandy and Hurricane Katrina, for example, planning events provided opportunities for people to express their opinions (see Photo 8.2). Similarities might result from neighborhood or family ties, jobs, or personal interests (e.g., outdoor pursuits and sports). People who share similar

PHOTO 8.2 Long-term recovery planning, with community input. (Courtesy of Marvin Nauman/FEMA. New Orleans, LA.)

interests may be more likely to support or work on post-disaster initiatives like reinvigorating green space for a neighborhood park, restoring an historic character to the area, or designing day care centers for workplaces.

People also hold *linking* social capital that occurs when new partners come to the recovery planning table, such as city officials, nongovernmental organizations and the faith community (Woolcock 2000). Without the links from government financing to faith-based volunteers, many people will struggle to rebuild, especially those at low incomes or with challenging medical conditions. Linking social capital thus generates crucial recovery resources useful to many (see Box 8.3).

BOX 8.3   THE VOLUNTARY COMMUNITY AND RECOVERY

Jessica Bettinger

Jessica Bettinger currently serves at the Salvation Army as their National Community Relations Department Emergency Disaster Services/Government Relations specialist. Previously, she worked as the Member Services Manager at National Voluntary Organizations Active in Disaster, where she was responsible for the organization's communications and member engagement for over 60 national organization members and 56 state/territory VOADs. In this role, Jessica served as the lead on grant distribution and supported coordinating efforts for a multitude of domestic disasters. Jessica is recognized for her ability to effectively lead programs that address member services, development, external relations, and community resiliency. Raised in Oklahoma, Jessica has completed a Master of Science degree in Sociology from Oklahoma State University with particular emphasis on nonprofits involved in disaster relief.

(Continued)

BOX 8.3 (*Continued*)   THE VOLUNTARY COMMUNITY
AND RECOVERY

National Voluntary Organizations Active in Disaster (National VOAD) was founded over 40 years ago in response to the challenges many disaster organizations experienced following Hurricane Camille, a category 5 hurricane that hit the Gulf Coast in 1969. The storm was one of the worst of the twentieth century, killing 256 people and causing over 1 billion dollars of property damage. A national organization dedicated to facilitating a more coordinated, cooperative response by multiple agencies was a revolutionary concept. At that time, agencies- both government, private and nonprofit, worked independently of each other. The result was a mixture of gaps and duplicative services to the affected communities. Ultimately, it was the disaster survivor and their communities that suffered.

In 1970, seven voluntary organizations came together to solve the problem. They identified four key factors necessary for a more efficient and successful approach to disaster response, recovery and preparedness. These four factors are the foundation of National VOAD and are referred to as the 4Cs: Communication, Coordination, Cooperation and Collaboration. National VOAD members and partners recognize the 4Cs as guiding principles for how they operate and are based on building and maintaining trusting, mutually capable relationships.

By the end of the 1970s, interagency coordination and collaboration during national-level disasters was the expectation. In the 1980s, the concept of the 4C's began to filter from the national level to the state level and finally, the local level. The 1990s showed the true strength of the voluntary sector as the concept of the 4C's and VOAD shifted into a national movement. Over the past 44 years, the VOAD movement has grown to include more than 115 members and partners.

Functions

National VOAD is a nonprofit, nonpartisan, membership-based organization that builds resiliency in communities nationwide. It serves as the forum where organizations share knowledge and resources throughout the disaster cycle—preparation, response, recovery and mitigation—to help disaster survivors and their communities. To fulfill this mission, National VOAD fosters more effective service to people affected by disaster through convening mechanisms, outreach, advocacy, and as a champion and facilitator for the application of its values and core principles. Since its founding in 1970, National VOAD Member organizations have worked tirelessly to assist communities affected by disasters.

National VOAD focuses a great deal on preparedness and recovery efforts. As an entity, National VOAD does not provide direct service, rather it provide the convening mechanisms for its national organization members and state/territory VOADs. Its role in the disaster space is to bring together

(Continued)

BOX 8.3 (*Continued*)   THE VOLUNTARY COMMUNITY AND RECOVERY

organizations with disaster programs and give them opportunities to organizations with disaster programs and give them opportunities to share best practices, lessons learned, challenges and successes. Its two primary convening functions are as follows:

1. Committees. National VOAD currently has 12 committees, each of which focuses on a major role within disasters. For example, it has Advocacy, Donations Management, Long-Term Recovery, and Volunteer Management. Each committee is made up of representation from National VOAD members with expertise in that particular subject area, state/territory VOAD representatives, partners and subject matter experts (SMEs). One of their primary functions is to create guidance documents that share best practices and lessons learned. These documents are vetted by its membership, ratified by its Board of Directors and then made public. The Long-Term Recovery Committee has created two guidance documents: The Long-Term Recovery Guide and the Long-Term Recovery Quick Reference Guide. Each guidance document highlights how to organize a Long-Term Recovery Group (LTRG), the role of disaster case management, communications, spiritual care and much more.

2. National VOAD Conference (NVC). The NVC is an annual event hosted by National VOAD and is open to all members, partners, and those affiliated with the VOAD Movement or wanting to become involved. This is the largest gathering of voluntary organizations with a focus on disaster relief and recovery efforts. Each year, over 600 participants come together facilitating discussions around pertinent issues, sharing lessons learned, and raising awareness. This conference gives all those involved with disaster sector an opportunity to meet one another in-person and to develop and maintain relationships.

Goals

Guided by the core principles of the 4Cs—cooperation, communication, coordination, and collaboration—National VOAD is led by member organization volunteers and staff who are champions in the disaster services community. Many volunteer their time to serve on Committees and Task Forces, as members of the Board of Directors, or as participants at the annual National VOAD Conference. It is committed to caring for all people affected by disaster and it is their ultimate goal to facilitate a more coordinated, inclusive approach to disaster recovery by provide a nurturing environment in which disaster agencies will flourish. Providing hope and offering opportunities for true collaboration are the heart and soul of the organization.

Structural social capital refers to the places we hold in our communities. An architect brings knowledge of how to build structures, often with disaster-resistant designs that reflect local historical and cultural character. Bankers and corporate executives know from where donations and grants can be obtained. But not only should the higher-paid occupations be considered. The person who picks up trash every day views the impact of debris on the environment and where storm water drains may be clogged. Mothers offer insights into what teenagers, who may be at risk for domestic violence, need and how to support schools. In short, no one should be excluded from participating because of his or her position in society.

Finally, *cognitive* social capital is defined as the attitudes that people bring to the planning table (Woolcock 2000). Those attitudes may stem from cultural backgrounds, faith traditions, and ways of thinking. Attitudes can spur or impede community planning. As one example, viewing recovery as an opportunity opens the door to possibilities: mitigation, serving low income families, harnessing solar and wind power, increasing accessibility, and more. By amassing the energies that people produce through social interactions we can leverage their energy, visions, and collective resources to face the recovery period.

8.4 Facing the Challenges of Recovery

How do we get people back home? When can businesses reopen to provide services and restore paychecks? Will the environment recover from disaster debris and contamination? What kinds of psychological impacts may people experience as they move through the recovery process? In the United States, the National Recovery Framework serves as a way to think about and move through returning people and places (see Box 8.4). At the local level, the recovery may play out as a collective, new vision.

Why a *new* vision? Because the disaster impacts should have—and possibly could have—been avoided. Recovery presents an opportunity to not only return to a normal routine but also a transition into a safer, more sustainable and resilient place to live, work, and enjoy.

8.4.1 Getting People Back Home

Where do you live? You may live in a mobile home or perhaps rent an apartment. Maybe you own a house or live with your parents. If you are older, you might reside with your children or in an assisted living facility. Perhaps you have a disability and receive government-funded public housing. Depending on where you were born, you may live in a refugee camp, a small village of mud huts, or a densely packed urban area. Or, you may have been homeless

BOX 8.4   FEMA NATIONAL RECOVERY FRAMEWORK

In 2011, FEMA published the National Recovery Framework for the United States with support from the Department of Homeland Security and the Department of Housing and Urban Development. The plan considers:

- *Individual and family empowerment.* Families, in all their diversity, must be considered in order to promote a full and robust recovery.
- *Leadership and local primacy.* Local leadership must be involved in any recovery effort as a basic, underlying principle including local, state, and tribal governments.
- *Pre-disaster Recovery Planning.* Preplanning is essential and must involve an array of stakeholders including public and private sectors.
- *Partnerships and Inclusiveness.* Stakeholder include all who might be affected particularly those historically excluded because of accessibility barriers, racism, or lack of sensitivity to matters of age.
- *Public information.* It is important to ensure that the entire public receives and understands recovery messages particularly those who historically have lacked access to information because of language or accessibility.
- *Unity of effort.* Consensus and transparency in the planning process must be consistently provided including respecting all who participate toward a common goal of recovery.
- *Timeliness and flexibility.* People should not fall through the cracks of available assistance and should receive aid in a manner that avoids delays or lost opportunities.
- *Resilience and sustainability.* Risks to future disasters must be reduced so that communities can rebound from future shocks.
- *Psychological and emotional recovery.* Communities and individual will benefit from addressing the shocks associated with a disaster from the initial impacts through long-term recovery needs.

Source: FEMA, visit http://www.fema.gov/media-library-data/20130726-1820-25045-5325/508_ndrf.pdf, last accessed February 3, 2016.

before a disaster occurred. In the aftermath, securing safe shelter and new housing may be challenging.

Displaced persons typically move through four phases of sheltering and housing although not at the same pace (Quarantelli 1982). Those four phases transition people from *emergency* shelter they may create themselves into *temporary* shelter usually established by organizations to provide food, water, and cover. With sufficient resources (money, insurance, family, friends, the help of agencies, government funding, and even luck), they may move into temporary housing where they can establish a household routine. Ideally, they will then move into permanent housing.

People do sometimes skip these steps, moving right from displacement into permanent housing. For example, renters may be able to rent a new place if available units exist. Or, displaced residents may be able to go into temporary housing quickly if their insurance allows for such relocation. However, if communities, families, and individuals cannot secure sufficient resources (remember Socio Political Ecology theory from Chapter 2), then they may experience longer times before they return home. Hurricane Katrina, which happened in 2005, ended up becoming such a case. Many homeowners could not afford to rebuild and remained displaced. The population of New Orleans changed, with some neighborhoods never recovering 10 years later (Kroll-Smith, Baxter, and Jenkins 2015).

The first step in post-disaster recovery efforts involves finding safe and secure housing for people, which is usually temporary. Doing so can be harder than expected. In many developed nations, people assume they will find temporary housing locations like a rental unit or another house while their home is repaired. Some countries, such as the United States, may provide eligible applicants with funding to rent units or in some instances, a travel trailer or mobile home. The latter strategy is used when there is massive damage to housing or in areas that lack rental units and/or affordable housing.

In countries where large numbers of people experience dislocation, the effort to provide housing can be overwhelmingly difficult and minimal. Years after the 2010 Haiti earthquake, hundreds of thousands of people remained in temporary settlements. An international engineering assessment determined that of 289,491 postearthquake existing structures, only 52% were habitable with another 26% in need of repairs to make them safe while 21% remained unsafe (USAID 2010). The Nepal earthquake of 2015 proved equally challenging when it destroyed 490,000 homes, damaged another 265,000, and affected nearly 10 million people.

One model to help with post-disaster housing is called *capital-infusion* where outside aid arrives through nongovernmental agencies. The Nepal earthquake represents such an example. In these cases, the majority of the relief must come from the outside due to a lack of sufficient resources within the nation. The Government of Nepal conducted a post-disaster needs assessment that revealed the extent of the recovery challenges. Heavily hit, the event was estimated to push an additional 3.5% of Nepalis (about 700,000 people) into poverty by 2016 (World Bank 2015). One year after the event, the World Bank (2015) worked to build 55,000 multi-hazard homes that would prove resilient to future disasters—as people lingered in temporary shelters. Other international nongovernmental organizations also set up efforts as well in this external capital-infusion approach.

An alternative *redevelopment model* involves national-level or governmental agencies in designing a recovery. Agencies will work together to create a systematic master plan. This type of plan is most likely to occur under a highly centralized government and in a context of extensive damage. In many countries where homeowners carry insurance, such a model is unlikely to occur. The model also assumes government support of the population and sufficient resources to do so. This was the case in Tangshan, China, after the 1976 earthquake when the Chinese government organized the rebuilding of an entire city (Mitchell 2004).

A third model for permanent housing recovery is more typical in developed nations and is called the *limited-intervention model*. Here, insurance is used to help people recover from their losses with governmental resources, grants, expertise, loans or personnel. The critique is that the approach does not always cover all needs. Low-income and historically marginalized communities often fail to hold or secure sufficient resources to recover (Peacock and Girard 2000).

The last model is termed as the *market model*. In this scenario, people must survive on their own with limited support from others. Clearly, this model results in "winners and losers" that are sorted out on the basis of personal funds (Comerio 1998, p. 127).

What should be noted about all of these models is that they involve external agencies, with limited influence from those directly affected. Conversely, evidence suggests that stakeholders must be involved in making decisions about their homes and futures if the effort is to be successful. Nongovernmental agencies have been criticized, for example, for coming into an area with predesigned ideas and approaches. Lacking an understanding of local practices, their well-intentioned efforts can undermine not only housing preferences but also environmental conditions, religious beliefs, and local construction practices. This happened in Sri Lanka and India after the 2004 tsunami. In Sri Lanka, kitchens were created for a type of fuel not normally used. The new Sri Lankan homes did not accommodate critical resources like fishing gear, which people used to feed their families and earn a living (Karunasena and Rameezdeen 2014). Indians in a tsunami-affected area returned to concrete structures created by contractors—that proved to be hot and humid as they failed to take into account local environmental conditions and prevailing winds (Barenstein 2006).

8.4.2 Businesses

Preparedness is crucial to surviving disaster within the business community, yet most business owners do little to prepare (Webb, Tierney, and Dahlhamer 2000). Take a minute and think about the place where you or a family member work. What would happen should that business have to close due to a disaster? How long would the business have to be closed? Would you receive a paycheck?

Downtime is defined as the length of time when a business cannot provide its goods and services to the public. Without being open for business, wages may be lost, the tax base for the area economy can be undermined, and the business may fail. Reopening businesses so that people can work and things can return to normal is an important first step during recovery.

But businesses may not be able to reopen if they lose their location. FEMA (2001) estimates that one foot of flood water displaces a business for 134 days. With two feet of water, a business must relocate for 230 days and with three feet or more of water the business must operate from a new location for at least a year. This is called *displacement* and means that the business has to find a new site, restore its customer or client base, restock its inventory and other critical assets (desks, phones, computers), and enable its employees to return to work. The business may not only need a site, but utilities, routes to the business that are open and accessible, and a visible presence that they have reopened (see Photo 8.3).

All kinds and sizes of businesses will need to reopen, from gas stations so that employees can travel to organizations that provide health care to major corporations whose absence could affect the broader economy. Small businesses, including micro- and home-based businesses, face the highest risk of disaster impact because they tend to have less cash flow and fewer resources. Smaller businesses are also more likely to be operated by women and minorities. Small businesses that are home-based are particularly at risk including home repairs, carpentry and cabinetmaking, consulting, child care, and sewing (Enarson 2001). Larger businesses have more employees to help with the recovery and may have alternative locations to provide an infusion of goods, services, and funds (Webb, Tierney, and Dahlhamer 2000). They are also more likely to have employed business continuity or disaster managers who helped the firm to prepare.

The Leidenheimer Baking Company in New Orleans, owned by four generations, faced catastrophic losses from Hurricane Katrina in 2005 (FEMA, n.d.). They responded first by enacting their family evacuation plan. The company president then organized upper management to put their disaster

PHOTO 8.3 Businesses reopen in 2012 along the Ocean City boardwalk in New Jersey. (Courtesy of Steve Zumwalt/FEMA.)

plan into place. They shut down the bakery and told employees to evacuate with their families. Meanwhile, the company president evacuated with his emergency kit including contact information, back-up files, computer hard drives, and customer and employee lists. During the evacuation, he contacted insurance and legal support for the company and then set up a satellite office in Baton Rouge. The plant was indeed flooded and had sustained severe damage—which the company addressed with a transportation plan to bring employees in to work while the city recovered (FEMA, n.d.).

How do businesses recover financially? In the United States, the Small Business Administration offers loans for both physical and economic damages which must be repaid. Businesses may also need to use insurance and savings to recover. Insurance must include coverage for specific hazards and for critical resources—from ovens and yeast replacement in the bakery to computer hardware and software in a bank. Still, financial resources may not be enough. Customer traffic needs to return, which can be challenging if people are not aware the business has reopened. The businesses most likely to survive are those with appropriate advance preparedness and contingency planning. Those most likely to need support include small businesses, particularly those in developing nations and those operated by historically disadvantaged populations.

8.4.3 Infrastructure and Lifelines

One study in Memphis, Tennessee in the United States found that businesses needed electricity the most followed by phone services, water, wastewater treatment, and natural gas (Tierney, Nigg, and Dahlamer 1996). The study revealed that the businesses most likely to close first from disaster-related utility disruptions were business and professional services, followed by manufacturing and construction, wholesale and retail firms, and then banks, insurance, and realtors. It is worthwhile bearing in mind that these were *indirect effects* caused solely by utility disruption. A *direct impact* could cause even more significant impacts. The 1994 Northridge, California (U.S.) earthquake, for example, resulted in an average loss of $156,273 to affected businesses (Tierney 1996). Superstorm Sandy had significant impacts on New Jersey tourism, primarily in two counties. In 2013, the U.S. Department of Commerce estimated a loss of $950 million in tourism revenue that would cost the jobs of 11,000 workers. In contrast, the estimated $29.5 billion required to rebuild was expected to bring in 281,000 new construction jobs.

There are also social impacts, namely the disruption to our personal lives from managing personal hygiene to getting to and from work and school. A 1998 ice storm that affected Canada put four inches of ice on the ground. One in five Canadians lost power for up to three weeks. Senior citizens were a particular concern as they are more affected by heat, cold, and social isola-tion than younger residents. Canada sent out large numbers of military to find and support those affected, the largest peacetime deployment in the nation's history (Scanlon 1999).

We also need a functioning infrastructure including roads, ports, and bridges to travel to school, work, and home. We need utilities to shower, make food, and take care of the sick. Cell phones are commonplace in most countries as are social media that connect people to each other and allow for the exchange of information in times of crisis.

Disaster recovery can also provide an opportunity to upgrade dated infra-structure systems. To do so, recovery must incorporate best practices to miti-gate future risks such as adding flood reduction features. Another consideration when rebuilding is to examine interconnected infrastructure elements, such as a power blackout that results in traffic signal outages, street congestion, or communication disruptions (Zimmerman 2003). Recovery must thus promote increasingly resilient and alternative routes, such as wireless connectivity in addition to dedicated lines. Opportunities to increase public transit options can also reduce traffic congestion. Ports can also be hardened to resist storm surge, terrorist attacks, or wind projectiles. Bridges can be rebuilt to be more flexible for earthquakes. Communications systems and electrical grids can build in redundancies and flexibility for rerouting. Such mitigation can be done if the political will, public support, and financial means to do so are in place.

8.4.4 Psychological Impacts

Many misconceptions exist about the impact of disasters on the human spirit. Media messages often lead us to assume that everyone impacted is immediately subject to Post Traumatic Stress Disorder (PTSD). However, diagnosing such a condition takes, at a minimum, six months. Perhaps sur-prisingly, most people respond fairly well to disasters and PTSD does not occur as readily as we might think. What does make a difference is the degree of exposure to fatalities and trauma, the availability of support networks, and personal resilience (Norris et al. 2002; Norris, Friedman, and Watson 2002). Some individuals may be at higher risk than others, suggesting that we pro-vide a range of post-disaster care and support for affected populations.

Age may make a difference as can how we assist people at various ages. Smaller children can usually be comforted with hugs and words of encouragement. With children, pre-disaster conditions can influence the trajectory of their recovery. Those impacted by poverty, for example, may find limited resources to flee a disaster and thus encounter higher degrees of exposure (Fothergill and Peek 2015). Older children can benefit from interactions with school counsel-ors or grief counselors by working through their own stories via crafts or play.

Teenagers and adolescents can become more involved, serving as supervised volunteers in disaster sites or raising funds to donate. However, most children never receive specialized counseling. One study after September 11th discovered that about 18% of children exposed to the trauma experienced a stress reaction but only 27% received counseling. Those who did go to counseling (social workers, therapists or clergy) did so at parental request (Fairbrother et al. 2004). People like parents, who range from young to middle-age, typically receive more social support from friends and family but also serve as caregivers and employees and sometimes for multiple generations. These overlapping roles can increase stress of those in middle ages (Norris, Friedman, and Watson 2002; Norris et al. 2002). Older survivors may actually react better than we expect, in part because they have a lifetime of coping skills to draw upon from similar experiences (Prince-Embury and Rooney 1988).

Gender may also influence psychological recovery, although studies suggest that other factors may be influential. While women report higher levels of stress or anxiety, they are also more likely to have experienced pre-disaster trauma such as interpersonal violence. When disaster strikes, we need to have resources in place as well as have processed such previous experiences. Doing so increases our knowledge of and experience with coping strategies (Norris et al. 2002a, b). Gender may also influence post-disaster outcomes including an increased risk of interpersonal violence including human trafficking—such was the case after the 2004 tsunami in Sri Lanka and the 2015 earthquake in Nepal. Recovery managers would be well advised to develop relationships with gender-based pre-disaster organizations who address such social problems in an effort to stem their reappearance after a disaster.

We should also be alert to racial and ethnic minorities who may experience higher rates of trauma. Researchers believe this may occur because of their proximity to disaster sites, such as historic patterns of segregation that marginalize them in floodplains or in lower-income homes less resistant to disasters (Cutter 2006). Because of their proximity to disaster, traumatic exposure may be more likely. Race and ethnicity may also be influenced by patterns of prejudice and discrimination that reduce wages, which means fewer resources for a disaster. Complicated by age or disability, people may bear higher risk for death or injury when facing disaster as was the case after Hurricane Katrina (Kelman and Stough 2015; Sharkey 2007). Imagine the circumstances of Syrian refugees in 2015–2016 as they fled internal war. It is believed that thousands perished through drowning or starvation. Those who arrived in refugee camps and then moved on into countries of refuge will likely bear the burden of significant traumas (see the chapter on humanitarian response for recommended best practices).

Occupation may also put some people at risk, though the pre-disaster training that they receive will increase their chances of recovering well.

As with other conditions, exposure is the key element to consider. The closer someone is to trauma and violence, the more difficulty they may experience, even first responders and emergency managers. By participating in pre-disaster training and post-disaster debriefing, potentially lingering traumas can be addressed pro-actively. Others may be at risk as well, including social workers (Pulido 2007), therapists, or clergy. What they may experience is called "secondary traumatic stress" as they absorb and deal with the traumas of their clients or parishioners (Bride 2007; Pulido 2007).

What can we do to help ourselves before disaster? By strengthening social relationships before disaster, we can improve our chance to respond in a more resilient manner. After the 1995 Oklahoma City (U.S.) bombing, for example, firefighters turned to their family and relatives as their most common strategy for addressing stress (North et al. 2002). Vulnerability theory (see Chapter 3), though, suggests that not everyone enjoys equal access to resources including strong social relationships or extensive sets of resources. Finding ways to bring people together to support each other, such as through reuniting families, developing support groups, forming neighborhood work teams, and convening community-based recovery committees, can be helpful. As survivors described in one study, it is the arrival of volunteers who restore hope by bringing back not only labor to rebuild but people who come to listen (Phillips 2014b). Known as the therapeutic community, the arrival of volunteers who listen sympathetically and allow people to tell their story can produce an alternate set of social relationships that promote healing (Phillips 2014a).

Programs for post-disaster psychological recovery tend to be funded in an ad hoc manner and often through donations made to faith-based or voluntary organizations. The American Red Cross does offer trained and credentialed mental health support. Church World Services outlines a code of conduct for disaster spiritual care and Lutheran Disaster Response trains and certifies chaplains and offers Camp Noah for children.

Community memorials are common after disaster, often at the one month and one year anniversaries, and bring people together to mourn and provide comfort (Eyre 2006). In the aftermath of the 2015 Paris and San Bernardino terrorist attacks, people brought flowers, stuffed animals, messages, and candles to impromptu memorials. School programs can also be offered to children, an especially important step when their school or community is directly impacted. Involving mental health professionals in working with children is essential as is restoring normal elements of children's worlds (see Box 8.2 again, the Hope Trunk). Encouraging people to take time off, pursue personal fitness, eat nutritionally, and minimize the use of alcohol and drugs is usually advised by professionals. These techniques are things we can work anytime to enhance our own personal resilience should a disaster occur.

8.4.5 Environmental Concerns

There are many areas of concern with the environment after a disaster: hazardous materials that have traveled during floods, animals injured or displaced by wildfire, and the best means in which to rebuild. In recent years, attention has turned to the options available to rebuild in a "green" manner that promotes the use of renewable resources, energy efficiency, and environmental-friendly designs. The process begins when we start to pick up the pieces after a disaster.

Consider post-disaster debris for example—what do we do with it and where should it go? It might surprise you to discover that you can re-use mud, sand, and dirt from floods and landslides. Properly managed, it can be used as topsoil or as landfill cover. Shingles torn off by hurricanes can be re-used to resurface asphalt roads. Metals torn from vehicles, billboards, and homes can be sorted and sold for scrap, producing a profit for the affected community. Flooded buildings can be stripped and salvaged and windows, cupboards, and doors can be resold or reused. Communities can also mulch tree limbs and green matter and then use it in parks, schools, and other public locations. To minimize further the amount of debris, we also incinerate clean, woody debris. Creative thinking can reduce the amount of debris sent to landfills and even generate recovery funds (Brickner 1994; EPA 1995; FEMA 2007).

Some events represent environmental disasters by themselves. In 2010, BP Petroleum had an accident with its Deepwater Horizon Well. The explosion and resulting damage leaked extensive amounts of oil into the U.S. Gulf. As a result, commercial and recreational fishing shut down. Happening right at the start of shrimping season, as well as the onset of summer tourism (hotels, restaurants, beaches), the economic damage became significant. Agencies and organizations worked diligently to save wildlife, endangered wetlands, and fragile estuaries (see Photo 8.4). Continued monitoring will need to occur. Effects of the 1989 oil spill into Prince William Sound in Alaska found

PHOTO 8.4 State and federal partners work together to rescue a pelican affected by the Deepwater Horizon oil spill. (Courtesy of John Miller/U.S. Coast Guard. Jefferson Parish, LA.)

that environmental damages continued for some time, affecting not only aquatic life and beaches but tribal economics and family relationships—a concern raised again after the 2010 BP oil spill for communities along the Gulf Coast (Gill, Picou, and Ritchie 2011; Picou and Gill 2004; Picou, Gill, Dyer, and Curry 1992; Ritchie, Gill, and Picou 2011; Short et al. 2004).

8.4.6 Historic and Cultural Resources

Historic properties are defined as "any prehistoric or historic district, site, building, structure, or object included in, or eligible for inclusion in, the National Register of Historic Places" (FEMA 2005). Cultural resources include the built environment, monuments, the art and sculpture found inside museums and around our communities, and the ways of life that represent a shared cultural heritage.

Besides the historical and cultural value, places also offer economic importance. We travel to coastal areas to enjoy the beaches and ocean, to capital cities to tour museums, or into areas that preserve and celebrate the culture and history of First Nations/Native American people. Related travel and tourism generates significant amounts of dollars and taxes that support local economies. Restoration of those locations means people retain their livelihoods along with the meaning of places in their hearts and minds.

The National Historic Preservation Act (NHPA) requires FEMA and other federal agencies to consider how demolition, relocation, or rebuilding (prime tasks during recovery) would affect the historic value of the property including tribal areas. A Heritage Emergency National Task Force of 41 federal agencies and historic preservation organizations provide support (Quarantelli 2003). Each state or tribal area in the United States also has a State/Tribal Historic Preservation Officer to serve as a resource for identifying and protecting historical and cultural resources. Many communities have local historical associations that work to preserve locally meaningful places. Together, they can serve as important resources for a community recovery planning effort.

The downtown area of Chillicothe, Ohio—the first capital of Ohio—has suffered several devastating blows. The 1913 flood that affected multiple states inundated the downtown, closing businesses and disrupting households (Williams 2013). Today, a massive levee and U.S. Army Corps of Engineer efforts protect residents and businesses from Scioto River flooding. However, in 2003, a fire destroyed the interior of the historic Romanesque-style Carlisle Building in downtown Chillicothe. The roof collapsed and a portion of the back caved in. Sitting open and exposed to the elements for some time, the local hospital decided to purchase and restore the building for medical residents. An historic preservation architecture firm took on the job, maintaining the unique exterior and character of the Carlisle while rebuilding the structure to current building codes. The building reopened in 2015 (see Photo 8.5 and Photo 8.6).

PHOTO 8.5   The damaged Carlisle building in Chillicothe Ohio. (Courtesy of Adena Health System.)

PHOTO 8.6   The rebuilt Carlisle Building, Chillicothe Ohio. (Courtesy of Adena Health System.)

What made the difference in the Carlisle? Community and civic leaders came together in a united vision to maintain the First Capital District as a signature piece to a downtown reinvigoration project.

8.5 Working and Volunteering in the Field of Recovery

When we think of recovery, the first people who come to mind may be volunteers—they are certainly those most likely to be featured by the media, which is well-deserved. But a lot more goes on behind-the-scenes during recovery. Should a recovery earn a Presidential Disaster Declaration in the United States, for example, many resources will become available from technical expertise to funding specific programs. Thus, a full set of governmental and nongovernmental options develop to work in the area of recovery.

Governmental organizations, for example, may include those who come to assess needs, explain programs, set up recovery centers, support voluntary organizations, and explain mitigation opportunities. They will include debris removal experts and contractors, utility companies and crews, environmental and animal rescue teams, and historic preservation officers. Outsiders will work with state and local government to clear the roads, restore power, and enable the recovery to begin. Experts in energy-efficient designs or structural mitigation projects may arrive to improve the area post-disaster.

Local recovery efforts will necessarily involve elected officials who make decisions and authorize funding as well as emergency managers and designated recovery leaders. Consultants may come to provide expertise and guide local stakeholders through a post-disaster recovery planning process. Long-term recovery teams will be formed with locally appointed leadership. Case managers may be hired to help people though the confusing recovery process (Stough et al. 2011). Faith-based organizations will manage donations, set up distribution centers, and identify future work sites. Soon, volunteer teams (preferably those affiliated with experienced disaster organizations) will arrive for initial repairs and then set up for long-term reconstruction efforts.

Business leaders will, ideally, launch their pre-disaster recovery plans so that people can work again. They may need construction crews to help rebuild or other franchises to provide temporary employees and replace lost inventory. Home- and micro-level businesses may need loans or grants to replace damaged or lost tools for sewing, child care, construction, or other work done out of one's home or vehicle. With adequate support, they can return to being productive members of the local economy.

Depending on the magnitude and scope of the disaster, extensive opportunities to work or volunteer usually develop during recovery. This time period may also provide temporary work for new graduates or for student internships. Securing such experience can add significantly to a resume and could lead into full-time employment. Volunteering with an experienced disaster organization (see nvoad.org for a list) can help you understand the therapeutic community. You may also acquire new understandings of people living in different cultures and places. The connections that you make with disaster survivors could be meaningful not only to them, but also to you as you work alongside people of similar beliefs in a shared experience (Phillips 2014a).

Summary

Recovery is defined in a number of ways but generally describes the process of getting people back into permanent housing and work. Recovery, for many, means re-establishing normal routines like going to school again. But recovery can also be seen as an opportunity, particularly to become more resilient. The idea of resilience means to bounce back from future shocks. A number of strategies can be tried to increase resilience including the ways in which communities rebuild or restore damaged areas, a topic we will turn to in the next chapter.

Recovery planning is considered essential to returning, restoring, and becoming more resilient. Ideally, pre-disaster recovery planning will take place although the majority of the time, it is post-disaster recovery planning that actually occurs. Doing so during the pressures and stresses of post-disaster times can be difficult. Recovery planning teams must face these challenges with an eye on a comprehensive and holistic recovery encompassing many elements. People will want to return to their household routines after a disaster, but may not be able to do so for some time. This means offering temporary housing while re-envisioning and planning for reconstruction. The permanent housing phase may require different strategies from rentals to repairs to complete reconstruction. Many people may face personal challenges due to limited resources, which will require governmental and nongovernmental assistance.

Other elements of a holistic recovery include restoring the business sector, which means that people can earn a living and the economy can rebound. This may require attention to infrastructure and lifelines that could have sustained serious damage, disrupting transportation arteries or power, gas, water, and communications. Employers and community recovery teams may also need to recognize that people have been traumatized by the event and provide appropriate levels of support. Their broader environment may also have been damaged, from waterways where people earn a living to the green spaces and wildlife that people find therapeutic. Restoring such locations, including historic locales and cultural artifacts, can help to bring back local identify and a quality of life deemed valuable by residents. A number of opportunities exist to help across these components of recovery from volunteering on rebuilding sites to leading recovery planning teams.

Discussion Questions

1. Why does the way in which we define recovery matter? How do the various terms influence how people think about and approach recovery? Do some kinds of recovery emerge as more influential than others?

2. Who should be on a recovery planning team before a disaster? Who should be on a post-disaster planning team? Why does the composition of the team matter?

3. What kinds of barriers exist to prevent people from returning home after a disaster? How do various organizations and agencies try to help?

4. Are most businesses ready for a disaster? What can they do to improve their ability to recover?

5. What kinds of psychological impacts should you expect after a disaster happens? How can a community and its leaders leverage resources to provide psychological support?

6. Investigate the BP and Exxon oil spills in the United States. What kinds of impacts happened to people, wildlife, fisheries, and livelihoods? If this kind of an event happened in your community (on land or sea), what might you expect where you live?

7. If a disaster happened, what kinds of infrastructure changes would you want where you live and work?

8. Look around your community and identify historic and cultural resources. What kinds of disaster threats exist and what might be done to protect them in a disaster? Consider also the architectural character of your community and identify the features that you would want to restore.

Resources

- The U.S. National Recovery Framework, http://www.fema.gov/national-disaster-recovery-framework, last accessed February 3, 2016.
- The Flight 93 National Memorial can be found at http://www.honorflight93.org/presskit/passengers.html, last accessed February 4, 2016.
- The 9/11 Memorial website is here http://www.911memorial.org/, last accessed February 4, 2016.
- Voluntary organizations can be viewed on a long list, with links to their websites, at www.nvoad.org, last accessed February 1, 2016.

References and Recommended Readings

American Society of Civil Engineers. 2013. *America's Infrastructure G.P.A.* Available at http://www.infrastructurereportcard.org/a/#p/grade-sheet/gpa, last accessed February 4, 2016.

Barenstein, Jennifer. 2006. Challenges and Risks in Post-tsunami Housing Reconstruction in Tamil Nadu. *Humanitarian Exchange* 33: 39–40.

Barthel, Diane. 1996. *Historic Preservation: Collective Memory and Historical Identity.* New Brunswick, NJ: Rutgers University Press.

Brickner, Robert. 1994. How to Manage Disaster Debris. *C & D Debris Recycling*, pp. 8–13.

Bride, Brian E. 2007. Prevalence of Secondary Traumatic Stress among Social Workers. *Social Work* 52(1): 63–70.

Comerio, M. 1998. *Disaster Hits Home: New Policy for Urban Housing Recovery.* Berkeley, CA: University of California Press.

Cutter, Susan. 2005. *The Geography of Social Vulnerability.* Available at http://understandingkatrina.ssrc.org, last accessed February 10, 1996.

Enarson, Elaine. 2001. What Women Do: Gendered Labor in the Red River Valley Flood. *Environmental Hazards* 3: 1–18.

Environmental Protection Agency (EPA). 1995. *Planning for Disaster Debris.* Washington, D.C.: U.S. Environmental Protection Agency.

Eyre, Anne. 2006. Remembering: Community Commemoration after Disaster. pp. 441–455 in *Handbook of Disaster Research*, edited by Havidán Rodríguez, Enrico L. Quarantelli, and Russell R. Dynes. New York: Springer.

Fairbrother, G., J. Stuber, S. Galea, B. Pfefferbaum, and A. R. Fleischman. 2004. Unmet Need for Counseling Services by Children in New York City After the September 11th Attacks on the World Trade Center: Implications for Pediatricians. *Pediatrics* 113(5): 1367–1374.

FEMA. 2001. *Understanding Your Risks: Identifying Hazards and Estimating Losses, #386-2.* Washington D.C.: FEMA Publication.

FEMA. 2005. *Integrating Historic Property and Cultural Resource Considerations into Hazard Mitigation Planning, #386-6.* Washington D.C.: FEMA Publication.

FEMA. 2007. *FEMA 325.* Available at http://www.fema.gov/government/grant/pa/demagde.shtm, last accessed July 28, 2008.

FEMA. n.d. *Sandy Whann Case Study.* Washington D.C.: FEMA.

Folke, C. 2006. Resilience: The Emergence of a Perspective for Social–Ecological Systems Analyses. *Global Environmental Change* 16: 253–267.

Fothergill, Alice and Lori Peek. 2015. *Children of Katrina.* Austin, TX: University of Texas Press.

Gill, Duane A., J. Steven Picou, and Liesel A. Ritchie. 2011. The Exxon Valdez and BP Oil Spills: A Comparison of Initial Social and Psychological Impacts. *American Behavioral Scientist* 56(1): 1–21.

Karunasena, Gayani and Raufdeen Rameezdeen. 2014. Post-disaster Housing Reconstruction: Comparative Study of Donor vs. owner-driven Approaches. *International Journal of Disaster Resilience in the Built Environment* 1(2): 173–191.

Kelman, Ilan and Laura Stough, editors. 2015. *Disability and Disaster: Explorations and Exchanges.* New York: Palgrave MacMillan.

Kroll-Smith, Steve, Vern Baxter, and Pam Jenkins. 2015. *Left to Chance: Hurricane Katrina and the Story of Two New Orleans Neighborhoods.* Austin, TX: University of Texas Press.

Mileti, Dennis. 1999. *Disasters by Design.* Washington D.C.: Joseph Henry Press.

Mileti, Dennis S., JoAnne Darlington, Eve Passerini, Betsy Forrest, and Mary Fran Myers. 1995. Toward an Integration of Natural Hazards and Sustainability. *The Environmental Professional* 17(2): 117–126.

Mitchell, Ken. 2004. Reconceiving Recovery. pp. 47–68 In *New Zealand Recovery Symposium Proceedings*, edited by S. Norman. Wellington, NZ: Ministry of Civil Defence and Emergency Management.

Nakagawa, Y. and R. Shaw. 2004. Social Capital: A Missing Link to Disaster Recovery. *International Journal of Mass Emergencies and Disasters* 22(1): 5–34.

National Council on Disability. 2009. *Effective Emergency Management*. Washington D.C.: National Council on Disability.

Natural Hazards Research and Applications Information Center (NHRAIC). 2005. *Holistic Disaster Recovery, revised*. Boulder, CO: NHRAIC/Public Entity Risk Institute.

Norman, Sarah. 2004. Focus on Recovery: A Holistic Framework for Recovery. pp. 31–46 in New *Zealand Recovery Symposium*, edited by S. Norman. New Zealand: Ministry of Civil Defence & Emergency Management.

Norris, F. H., M. J. Friedman, and P. J. Watson. 2002. 60,000 Disaster Victims Speak: Part II. Summary and Implications of the Disaster Mental Health Research. *Psychiatry* 65(3): 240–260.

Norris, F. H., M. J. Friedman, P. J. Watson, C. M. Byrne, E. Diaz, and K. Kaniasty. 2002. 60,000 Disaster Victims Speak: Part I. An Empirical Review of the Empirical Literature, 1981–2001. *Psychiatry* 65(3): 207–239.

North, C. S., L. Tivis, J. C. McMillen, B. Pfefferbaum, J. Cox, E. L. Spitznagel, K. Bunch, J. Schorr, and E. M. Smith. 2002. Coping, Functioning, and Adjustment of Rescue Workers after the Oklahoma City Bombing. *Journal of Traumatic Stress* 15(3): 171–175.

Peacock, Walter Gillis. 2010. *Advancing the Resilience of Coastal Localities: Developing, Implementing and Sustaining the Use of Coastal Resilience Indicators: A Final Report*. Prepared for the Coastal Services Center and The National Oceanic and Atmospheric Administration. Under Cooperative Agreement Award No. NA07NOS4730147.

Peacock, Walter Gillis and Chris Girard. 2000. Ethnic and Racial Inequalities in Hurricane Damage and Insurance Settlements. pp. 171–190 in *Hurricane Andrew*, edited by W. Peacock, B. Morrow and H. Gladwin. Miami, FL: International Hurricane Center.

Picou, J. Steven, Duane A. Gill, and Christopher L. Dyer. 1991. Disruption and Stress in an Alaskan Fishing Community. *Organization and Environment* 6(3): 235–257.

Picou, J. Steven, Brent K. Marshall, and Duane Gill. 2004. Disaster, Litigation, and the Corrosive Community. *Social Forces* 82(4): 1493–1522.

Phillips, Brenda. 2014a. *Mennonite Disaster Service: Building a Therapeutic Community after the Gulf Coast Storms*. Lanham, MD: Lexington Books.

Phillips, Brenda. 2014b. Therapeutic Communities in the Context of Disaster. pp. 353–371 in *Hazards, Risks, and Disasters in Society*, edited by Andrew Collins. Amsterdam, the Netherlands: Elsevier.

Prince-Embury, S. and J. F. Rooney. 1988. Psychological Symptoms of Residents in the Aftermath of the Three Mile Island Accident and Restart. *Journal of Social Psychology* 128(6): 779–790.

Pulido, Mary. L. 2007. In Their Words: Secondary Traumatic Stress in Social Workers Responding to the 9/11 Terrorist Attacks in New York City. *Social Work* 52(3): 279–281.

Ritchie, Liesel Ashley, Duane A. Gill, and J. Steven Picou. 2011. The BP Disaster as an "Exxon Valdez" Rerun. *Contexts* 10(3): 30–35.

Quarantelli, E. L. 1982. *Sheltering and Housing after Major Community Disasters: Case Studies and General Observations*. Newark, DE: Disaster Research Center, University of Delaware.

Quarantelli, E. L. 1997. Ten Criteria for Evaluating the Management of Community Disasters. *Disasters* 21(1): 39–56.

Quarantelli, E. L. 1998. The Disaster Recovery Process: What We Do and Do Not Know from Research. Available at http://dspace.udel.edu:8080/dspace/handle/19716/309?mode=simple, last accessed January 28, 2011.

Quarantelli, E. L. 2003. The Protection of Cultural Properties: The Neglected Social Science Perspective and Other Questions and Issues That Ought to be Considered. University of Delaware, Disaster Research Center, Preliminary Paper #325.

Sather-Wagstaff, Joy. 2011. *Heritage That Hurts: Tourists in the Memory Scapes of September 11*. Walnut Creek, CA: Left Coast Press, Inc.

Scanlon, Joseph. 1999. Emergent Groups in Established Frameworks: Ottawa Carleton's Response to the 1998 Ice Disaster. *Journal of Contingencies and Crisis Management* 7(1): 30–37.

Schwab, James, Ken. C. Topping, Charles. C. Eadie, R. E. Deyle, and R. A. Smith. 1998. *Planning for Post-Disaster Recovery and Reconstruction*. Washington, D.C.: FEMA/ American Planning Association.

Sharkey, Patrick. 2007. Survival and Death in New Orleans. *Journal of Black Studies* 37(4): 482–501.

Short, Jeffrey W., Mandy R. Lindeberg, Patricia M. Harris, Jacek M. Maselko, Jerome J. Pella, and Stanley D. Rice. 2004. Estimate of Oil Persisting on the Beaches of Prince William Sound 12 Years after the Exxon Valdez Oil Spill. *Environmental Science & Technology* 38(1): 19–25.

Stough, Laura M., Amy Sharp, Curt Decker, and Nachama Wilker. Disaster Case Management and Individuals with Disabilities. *Rehabilitation Psychology* 55(3): 211–220.

Tierney, K. 1996. *Business Impacts of the Northridge Earthquake*. Newark, DE: University of Delaware Disaster Research Center.

Tierney, K., J. Nigg, and J. Dahlhamer. 1996. The Impact of the 1993 Midwest Floods: Business Vulnerability and Disruption in Des Moines. pp. 214–233 in *Cities and Disaster: North American Studies in Emergency Management*, edited by Richard T. Sylves and William L. Waugh. Springfield, MA: Charles C. Thomas.

U.S. Agency for International Development. 2010. Haiti Earthquake, Fact Sheet #3, Fiscal Year 2011. Available at http://www.usaid.gov/our_work/humanitarian_assistance/ disaster_assistance/countries/haiti/template/fs_sr/fy2011/haiti_eq_fs03_10-15-2010.pdf, last accessed October 25, 2010.

U.S. Department of Commerce 2013. Economic Impact of Hurricane Sandy. Available at http://www.esa.doc.gov/sites/default/files/sandyfinal101713.pdf, last accessed February 9, 2016.

Uphoff, N. 2000. Understanding Social Capital: Learning from the Analysis and Experience of Participation. pp. 215–250 in *Social Capital: A Multifaceted Perspective*, edited by P. D. a. I. Serageldon. Washington, D.C.: The World Bank.

Webb, G., K. Tierney, and J. Dahlhamer. 2000. Businesses and Disasters: Empirical Patterns and Unanswered Questions. *Natural Hazards Review* 1(3): 83–90.

Williams, Geoff. 2013. *Washed Away: How the Great Flood of 1913, America's Most Widespread Natural Disaster, Terrorized a Nation and Changed it Forever*. New York: Pegasus Books.

Woolcock, M. 2002. *Social Capital in Theory and Practice* 2000. Available from http:// poverty.worldbank.org/library/view/12045/, last accessed 2002.

World Bank. 2015. International Development Association Project Appraisal Document on a Proposed Credit from the IDA Crisis Response Window/Earthquake Housing Reconstruction Project. Available at http://documents.worldbank.org/curated/ en/2015/07/24702721/nepal-earthquake-housing-reconstruction-project, last accessed February 4, 2016.

Zimmerman, Rae. 2003. Public Infrastructure Service Flexibility for Response and Recovery in the Attacks at the World Trade Center, September 11, 2001. pp. 241–267 in *Beyond September 11th*. edited by J. Monday. Boulder, CO: Natural Hazards Center.

Chapter **9**

Mitigation

Objectives

Upon completing this chapter, readers should be able to:

- Distinguish between and give examples of structural and nonstructural mitigation.
- Discuss the advantages and disadvantages of various kinds of mitigation measures.
- Link mitigation to a more resilient community that rebounds from disasters.
- Understand why some mitigation measures are more likely to occur than others due to economic, social, and political influences.
- Walk through a series of steps in basic mitigation planning.
- Identify work and volunteer opportunities in the mitigation phase of disaster management.

Key Terms

- Building codes
- Code enforcement
- Elevation
- Insurance
- Land use planning
- Mitigation
- Mitigation planning
- Nonstructural mitigation
- Relocation
- Resilience
- Retrofit
- Structural mitigation

9.1 Introduction

Resilient communities embrace mitigation, defined as a set of strategies to reduce future risks. Two kinds of mitigation are typically pursued. Structural mitigation efforts include the built environment such as safe rooms, levees, dams, floodwalls and seawalls, blast resistant structures, barricades, and seismic bracing. Structural mitigation work may rely on nonstructural (or nonbuilt) measures, such as when building codes (intangible rules) require hurricane clamps or fire-resistant shingles on roofs. Other kinds of nonstructural mitigation may include insurance, public education, first aid training, or evacuation practice. The goal of mitigation is to increase public safety from individual homes to entire communities. This chapter describes and explains examples of both kinds of mitigation measures with an eye on making communities more resilient in the face of area hazards.

9.2 Structural Mitigation

Structural mitigation centers on the built environment. This section gives several examples to prevent a hazard from becoming a disaster. Examples include dams that hold back water, levees alongside waterways, blast-resistant windows for tornadoes, or concrete barriers that deter curbside attacks. Before disaster, it can be very challenging to get the public excited about disaster mitigation work. Those who do are often considered champions for an uncelebrated cause (see Box 9.1; Meo, Ziebro, and Patton 2004).

BOX 9.1   CHAMPIONS OF MITIGATION

Mitigation requires both solid, scientific knowledge of what works (like how to build a levee) as well as how practitioners can design and implement the best ways to become more resilient. Coming from both the scholarly and practitioner communities, two leaders in the United States have emerged as tireless champions for mitigation. To conduct their work, they have relied on both science and application to make a difference.

Gilbert White

Gilbert F. White, known worldwide as the "father of floodplain management" joined the University of Colorado-Boulder (CU) faculty in 1970 as a professor of geography and director of the Institute of Behavioral Science where he remained active in academic work till 1990s. He founded CU's Natural Hazards Research and Applications Information Center, the nation's leading repository of knowledge on human behavior in disasters, in 1974. White's work in natural hazards changed the way people deal with nature and made the world safer for people to inhabit. "Floods are 'acts of God,' but flood losses are largely acts of man" he wrote in 1942 in his doctoral dissertation, which has since been called the most influential ever written by an American geographer.

(Continued)

BOX 9.1 (*Continued*)   CHAMPIONS OF MITIGATION

Gilbert White (Courtesy of University Communications, University of Colorado, Boulder, CO.)

White earned his degrees from the University of Chicago, then worked for the federal government in the late 1930s where he studied the Mississippi River Basin. White served as the Gustavson Distinguished Professor Emeritus of Geography at CU-Boulder where he founded and led the Natural Hazards Center. He was a member of the National Academy of Sciences, the American Academy of Arts and Sciences and the Russian Academy of Sciences. His numerous awards include the nation's highest scientific honor, the National Medal of Science, presented in 2000. Among White's numerous other honors are the National Geographic Society's highest award, the Hubbard Medal; the United Nation's Sasakawa International Environmental Prize; and the Association of American Geographer's Lifetime Achievement Award. He received an honorary doctorate from CU-Boulder in May, 2006.

FEMA Director David Paulison recalls him as: "a pioneer in a field that protects people and their homes."

"At a time when the mainstream thought was to build bigger and stronger flood control devices, Mr. White was investigating creative—and effective— methods that promoted safety, but not at the cost of damaging rivers and waterways. His legacy is a program that keeps people safe, protects the environment and makes smart investments in mitigation activities at all levels of government"

(FEMA 2006, Release Number: HQ-06-145; see also Mabey 1986).

(Continued)

BOX 9.1 (*Continued*) CHAMPIONS OF MITIGATION

James Lee Witt

James Lee Witt served as the director of the Federal Emergency Management Agency under President Bill Clinton (Photo 9.1). His career began in Arkansas, where he owned a construction company, served as a county judge, and then became head of the Arkansas Office of Emergency Services. While Witt was serving in FEMA, President Clinton made the FEMA directorship a cabinet-level position. As the first politically-appointed director with a background in emergency management, Witt made significant transformations in the agency (Goss 2015).

In his book, *Stronger in the Broken Places*, he said "Mitigation—which means to moderate in force or intensity—should be the goal of every crisis manager. Why prepare to clean up more efficiently after a disaster when you can prepare to lessen its effect in the first place" (Witt and Morgan 2002, p. 6). One of FEMA's signature projects during his tenure was Project Impact. The effort partnered government with private and non-profit communities to design mitigation efforts such as tornado safe rooms or flood reduction works (Holdeman and Patton 2008). Project Impact began as a grass-root program, which encouraged local stakeholders to determine what worked best for them—and to work together to design and implement solutions. Although Project Impact ended in 2001, the partnerships it inspired continued in a number of communities. Tulsa, Oklahoma's Project Impact efforts, for example, dramatically reduced flooding following widespread disasters in the 1980s (Meo, Ziebro, and Patton 2004; Wachtendorf et al. 2002). As James Lee Witt said, "mitigation is the ultimate application of common sense to the challenges the world throws our way" (Witt and Morgan 2002, p. 7).

PHOTO 9.1 Deerfield Beach, FL, 1998: FEMA Director James Lee Witt and Vice President Al Gore retrofit hurricane shutters. (Courtesy of FEMA.)

(*Continued*)

BOX 9.1 (*Continued*)   CHAMPIONS OF MITIGATION

After leaving FEMA, Witt formed his own consulting business and went on to manage reconstruction projects for the state of Louisiana after Hurricane Katrina and remains active in the field (Goss 2015).

Source: Information on Gilbert White provided courtesy of University Communications, University of Colorado-Boulder. With permission.

9.2.1 Living with Hazards and the Built Environment

Nature has always had a plan for when and where to let the rains come and flow. From a systems theory perspective, though, people do not always respect what Mother Nature intended and build homes and businesses on beautiful coastlines, along recreational lakes and rivers, and in or near floodplains. When we build a structure on the ground, water flows differently around it. The ground has less potential to absorb runoff. Ideally, communities will respect such areas of high rainfall with a propensity for flooding including stormwater drainage. Given that flooding represents the top hazard in many nations, including the United States, we need to think through where we allow building. Costs to recover from flooding (and other) disasters can be significant for people, workplaces, and responding organizations.

One example of a planned environment that strives to reduce risks comes from physical structures such as dams or levees. In the United States, the U.S. Army Corps of Engineers typically takes responsibility for the creation of major projects to increase safety from flooding. Across the nation, thousands of such structures—large, small, and even makeshift—exist. Often, local and state governments shoulder responsibility for dam and levee maintenance while citizens have responsibility for dams on private land.

U.S. dams are in trouble, though. The American Society of Civil Engineers (ASCE 2013) awarded the grade of "D" to our dams nationwide, a grade that has not changed in some time. Thousands of high hazard dams (with an increased likelihood of failure) exist across the United States according to the ASCE, with the bulk of responsibility for maintenance and repair existing at the state government level. The ASCE estimates that billions of dollars annually would be needed for repairs, a sum that would have to be shouldered mostly through taxpayer dollars.

Many times, hard choices have to be made to put such structural mitigation measures into place. The 2005 levee failure in New Orleans after Hurricane Katrina represents a measure that failed to protect—in large part because political and economic choices had to be made about how much could be spent on the levee protection system, where to place structures including homes and businesses, and how much to spend to maintain them. The pre-Katrina system provided protection from a Category 3 storm. Hurricane Katrina pushed a Category 5 surge into the levee system.

9.2.2 Elevations

Such flooding risks continue. In 2013, the U.S. Department of Commerce estimated that most businesses affected by Superstorm Sandy sustained short-term damage though again the losses were in the billions of dollars. However, the tourism industry suffered extensively with an estimated loss of $950 million in New Jersey alone affecting employment of over 11,000 workers.

One way to deal with flood risks is to raise a home or business above expected flooding levels, which is called elevation. Unfortunately, elevation levels are often determined (or recalculated) after an event when people have already sustained damage. Nonetheless, with new post-disaster awareness, people may be willing to accept new codes that require elevations (see Photo 9.2). The cost of elevation, though, may be difficult to afford. In such cases, it may be economically harder or even impossible for some households to return or businesses to re-open with new elevation requirements.

A number of successful elevations took place after Hurricane Katrina in both Louisiana and Mississippi including many that took on the challenge

PHOTO 9.2 A post-Superstorm Sandy elevation in Seabright, NJ. (Courtesy of Rosanna Arias/FEMA.)

of affordability for low-income homeowners. The community of Pass Christian, Mississippi created a long-term recovery committee and recommended clients to disaster voluntary organizations, such as Mennonite Disaster Service. Donations to the Mennonites included extensive funding from the Naperville, Illinois Rotary Club which subsidized about 20 homes including expensive elevations. In Louisiana, the Southern Mutual Help Association provided grant money to voluntary organizations. One community, Grand Bayou, had ten homes rebuilt on elevations by Mennonite Disaster Service. The combination of funds and supervised volunteer labor were essential to enabling people to return home, including those owned by single parents, elderly residents, African Americans, and Native Americans (Phillips 2014).

9.2.3 Retrofit

Another structural mitigation option is to bring an older building up to the current codes. An excellent example of predisaster earthquake retrofit occurred at the University of California-Berkeley in the United States. UC-Berkeley conducted a hazard assessment and loss estimation given the very real probability of earthquake damage from the Hayward Fault (Comerio 2000). The assessment included examining soil maps, the potential for ground shaking and the position of various campus buildings. The team looked at how faculty and students used those buildings and when the peak number of occupants would be inside. Then they considered occasional, rare, and very rare earthquake events. A rare event of a 7.0 magnitude (using the Richter scale at the time) would cause the university to disrupt normal schedules for 2 years. A very rare event of 7.5 magnitude would close the campus for a year, affecting 800 university and community jobs with an associated loss of $680 million in personal income and $861 million in related sales.

Where would you start to mitigate such impacts? Berkeley determined that seventeen buildings hosted about 75% of the university's externally generated research funds. Because research funds keep universities economically sound and represent the university's mission, administrators determined that a 20 year timeline to retrofit buildings would be needed and set aside $1 billion for projects (Comerio 2000).

The University of California-Berkeley is not alone in facing threats. Hurricane Katrina prompted the Department of Homeland Security to provide $2 million for rebuilding the Southern University in New Orleans. FEMA allotted $26 million to the University of Southern Mississippi's Gulf Park campus. The choice is really quite clear: pay now or pay later. By paying predisaster mitigation costs, future and repetitive losses can be reduced.

Oklahoma State University shouldered such mitigation efforts as part of its comprehensive emergency planning process (see http://ehs.okstate.edu/ mit_activities.pdf). Their mitigation master list identified seventeen potential disasters from natural events to hazardous materials, pandemics, and terrorism and listed a range of all-hazard mitigation measures. Particular risks, such as attacks, were addressed through hazard-specific mitigation measures like security barriers on game days or training staff on what to look for when admitting patrons (for more on university disaster resistance, see FEMA 2003). What has your university done?

9.2.4 Safe Rooms

About 1,200 tornadoes occur annually in the United States although they have also been reported in South America, Europe, Africa, Asia, Australia and New Zealand (National Weather Service n.d.). Although tornadoes range from the more likely EF #1 to the less likely EF #5 (see appendix), any tornado has the potential to damage homes and businesses and cause harm to the people within them. One of the worst tornadoes to hit the United States occurred in Joplin, Missouri in 2011. An EF #5 level tornado, the twister stretched as far as a mile wide. It devastated Joplin, including homes, businesses, schools, and the local hospital. The human toll was enormous, with 158 lives lost and well over 1,000 people becoming injured. Seventeen people died in a single assisted living facility including residents and staff.

One way to mitigate risk to people in a tornado threat is through the use of a safe room. The main cause of injuries in a tornado comes from projectiles picked up and thrown at tremendous velocity. Safe rooms, built to specific standards, can protect people from very strong storms including tornadoes and hurricanes (see Photo 9.3). FEMA documents

PHOTO 9.3 Community Safe Room, Poplarville, Mississippi. (Courtesy of Christopher Mardorf/FEMA.)

#P-320 (homes and businesses) and #P-361 (community and residential) offer guidance on safe rooms, which can be built either underground or above ground. In the aftermath of Joplin, Kansans determined that larger safe rooms needed to be provided in their community. Three such facilities were built in Baxter Springs schools to protect 730 students and staff (see resources section of this chapter).

State emergency management agencies may also provide safe room programs to residents using a combination of federal, state, and homeowner funds. After a series of tornadoes tore destructive paths across Oklahoma in one year and killed 44 people, the federal and state governments launched initiatives to install interior or underground safe rooms. With grants available up to $2,000 (and most safe rooms cost $2,500 to $3,000), homeowners moved quickly to build the safety features. Newly built homes with safe rooms sold rapidly. Funded through the Federal Hazard Mitigation Grant Program, the program emerged as one of the most successful intergovernmental mitigation partnerships in history.

9.2.5 Dams and Levees

A *dam* is an engineered structure designed to hold back water, such as water that flows along a river or moves from a lake into a downstream area. Worldwide, problems exist. By the time you read this, it may be possible that The Mosul Dam in Iraq has collapsed. Estimates suggest that one million people could be left homeless without action to protect the downstream population (Leslie 2016). In Zambia, the Kariba Dam is in similar straits. In addition to affecting people downstream, a collapse would undermine the dam's power production. Approximately half of Zambia relies on Kariba Dam for energy (Leslie 2016).

The American Society of Civil Engineers (2013) gives a grade of D or "poor" to dams in the United States. Why should we be concerned? There are approximately 84,000 dams in the United States with an average age of 52 (ASCE 2013). This includes about two thousand "deficient high-hazard dams" out of a total of 14,000 high-hazard dams. In addition to the risk to people, the ASCE notes that the United States relies on dams for "drinking water, irrigation, hydropower, flood control, and recreation" (ASCE 2013, website, see http://www.infrastructurereportcard.org/a/#e/hh-dams-state to view high hazard dams by state). Such losses could be significant. In 2010, the Iowa Lake Delhi dam failed with $120 million of economic losses (see Photo 9.4). To consider the potential risk and losses, note that California has 807 high hazard dams, Texas has 915, and Missouri has 1,588 (ASCE 2013). In contrast, the percent of state *regulated* dams includes California (45%; $11,142,000 state dam budget available for repairs), Texas (65%; $2,104,634), and Missouri (43%; $585,470).

PHOTO 9.4 Iowa Lake Delhi Dam failure. (Courtesy of Josh deBerge/FEMA.)

Levees are situated alongside rivers and are designed to prevent overtopping when floods occur in riparian areas. As many of you know from this textbook already, a number of levee failures occurred in the City of New Orleans from Hurricane Katrina's storm surge. Levees were overtopped by water, collapsed or split from the pressure of the storm surge, or failed when water pushed out the base from under the levee structure. In short, a number of failures characterized the levee system in New Orleans, resulting in most of the city experiencing 2–8 feet of water in homes, businesses, schools, hospitals, and other structures, causing massive economic losses, sustained displacement of people and businesses, and more than a decade of recovery work. The city will never be the same and many people will never return home.

Levees in the United States include 100,000 miles of flood-mitigation works that, in the ASCE estimation, earn a grade of D. Although the National Committee on Levee Safety estimates $100 billion would be needed to improve existing levees, such structures were noted as *preventing* $141 billion in losses for 2011 (ASCE 2013). How many people do they protect? FEMA estimates that about 43% of the U.S. population benefits from levee protection, which includes about "14 million people who live or work behind the structures" (ASCE 2013). The 1993 flooding along the Mississippi River revealed significant challenges, when dozens of cities flooded causing massive losses. How can losses be mitigated? The ASCE recommends creating a National Levee Safety Program, a levee mapping and classification systems to assess the risks, insurance, and emergency plans as part of an essential effort (ASCE 2013).

9.2.6 Building Resilience

Buildings must be able to withstand significant impacts. Even in concrete buildings, high winds can push projectiles through windows and doors and injure the people inside. Tornadoes caused major damage when airborne objects penetrated hospitals in Joplin, Missouri (2011), and Moore, Oklahoma (1999 and 2013). And, as the 1995 domestic terrorism attack on the Murrah Federal Building in Oklahoma City indicated, buildings need to be able to withstand an improvised explosive device—which caused the deaths of 168 people including 19 children. All manners of potential impacts need to be thought through, as we found on September 11th when international terrorists used airplanes to take down the World Trade Center towers and destroy part of the Pentagon. Terrorists are not the only potential threat, as concern also exists for armed intruders in "soft target" areas like malls, schools, or airports.

Blast performance is one element of making a building more structurally resilient in the face of a natural disaster or terrorist attack. Efforts might include placing barriers around buildings to reduce the possibility that explosive-laden vehicles could penetrate the perimeter. Fencing, guards, and security procedures can also reduce the possibility that someone intent on harm can carry out their plans. Windows, doors, and storefronts can be strengthened by installing blast resistant products. Sometimes called "hardening," the process of assessing and incorporating materials and procedures—when coupled with emergency planning and public education—can save lives, reduce injuries, and minimize economic losses (see Box 9.2).

BOX 9.2   ASSESSING BUILDING VULNERABILITY TO TERRORISM

Are you safe where you work or go to school? How about places you visit such as a hospital or public mall? FEMA has published guidance on ways to assess vulnerability and mitigate terrorist attacks, and many of the items mentioned below also fit with other hazards (such as a flood entering a building and disrupting utilities). Their materials include assessments of many things you should start looking at when visiting public buildings (this is a selective list, for more, see the full document at the source given below):

- *The site.* Where is the facility and what kinds of other facilities are around it? Could they become targets and your building be affected? Can a vehicle (with an explosive) be parked close to your building? Are access procedures in place to prevent entry, such as key cards or barriers?
- *The architecture.* Does the building design allow for being able to see visitors and others coming into the location? Do the windows have blast resistance? Would the way the building was put together allow for places to hide from an intruder? Do places exist where explosive devices could be hidden? Are there ways to safely exit the building?

(Continued)

BOX 9.2 (*Continued*) ASSESSING BUILDING VULNERABILITY TO TERRORISM

- *Structural systems.* Will the building withstand the impact of an explosion? Is it wood, steel, or concrete? What kinds of impacts would happen under certain circumstances? What can be done to strengthen or reinforce the building? Will parts of the building fail or pancake in an attack? Where are the weaknesses?
- *The building envelope.* Can the exterior withstand an assault or explosion? The building itself, as well as the windows and doors?
- *Utility systems.* Where do water, gas, and electricity come from? What kinds of dependencies exist? Are any of these sources vulnerable to penetration or disruption? What about transformers in the area? Backup units? Generators? Is there a reliable source of utilities that can be depended on externally in a major attack?
- *Mechanical systems.* Are any parts of heating or air conditioning open to penetration or assault? What about air intake and air filtration? What would happen in a biological or chemical attack? Are there fire walls and fire doors?
- *Fire alarm systems.* Are the fire extinguishers, smoke detectors, and alarms working? Are there sprinklers? Are fire drills conducted? Are fire alarm panels protected from unauthorized people?
- *Communications and information technology (IT) systems.* How are telephones organized and operated? Is there a backup system? Is the emergency alert system secured and how many people have access to it? Is the wiring secured? Will the Internet be accessible in an emergency? Are records secured? What is the backup?
- *Security systems.* Is there a television system that monitors and records what happens? How long are these materials saved? Who can access them and what procedures are in place when such information is needed in an emergency? Are they exterior, interior, or both?

Source: For an even more extensive set of ideas and suggestions, see: FEMA. 2005. *FEMA 452, A How-To Guide to Mitigate Potential Terrorist Attacks against Buildings.* Washington D.C.: FEMA. Available at http://www.fema.gov/media-library/assets/documents/4608, last accessed March 3, 2016.

9.2.7 Advantages of Structural Mitigation

The benefits of implementing structural mitigation measures should be obvious. In short, lives are saved. The costs of rebuilding homes, infrastructure, and buildings lessen. People can return home faster, earn livelihoods, and commute to work. Insurance companies do not have to raise premiums to offset payments. The psychological impacts of being injured or grief stricken, living in tents or temporary housing, or trying to return to work diminish because exposure lessens. Mitigation promotes resilience of the built environment, made possible through human choices, in a way that means things can return to normal quickly for people and places.

Given that all areas where people live have hazards and associated risks, making hazard adjustments through mitigation is just a smart thing to do. Consider also, that structural mitigation measures have side benefits. Have you enjoyed boating, fishing, or skiing on a lake created by a dam? Recreational opportunities abound in such locations and generate tourist income for the local economy too. Large-scale hydro-electric dams can provide enormous amounts of energy for communities and smaller facilities can power specific industries. Such dams do not come without controversy, however, as some have been charged with causing damage to the ecosystem, particularly riparian habitats with native flora and fauna. The advantages of structural mitigation must always be offset with the disadvantages—and hard choices will have to be made by those affected and those who serve the public.

9.2.8 Disadvantages of Structural Mitigation

Along with the clear benefits of mitigation, disadvantages also exist. The most common critique concerns the high costs of structural mitigation. The costs to rebuild the New Orleans area levee system reached the $14 billion mark 7 years after the storm (2005–2012). However, the newly strengthened levees may will not afford 100% protection from the same kind of storm given that they were rebuilt to similar levels of protection. Choices to rebuild structural mitigation measures and at what level and cost come with the harsh reality that there is no perfect system of protection, even in an area historic, culturally rich, and as economically important as the major port city of New Orleans. Conversely, there may always be events exceeding the design of the structural mitigation measure. Putting a levee into place for a 100 year flood event sounds good—until the 500 year event comes along. Making choices about mitigation means considering the risks faced and determining what is feasible.

Other consequences may result as well. People may place their faith in structural mitigation measures that could fail. People also stay in areas subject to flooding because levees or seawalls exist. Experienced homeowners as well as those unfamiliar with the area sometimes stay, including tourists who simply do not know any better. Rather than evacuating before a massive tornado outbreak, homeowners huddle in hallways believing the walls and roof will hold or that the twister will miss them. We also tend to put off mitigation measures because disasters are simply not forefront in our daily lives and we assume we can get around to it later.

9.3 Nonstructural Mitigation

Nonstructural mitigation includes disaster reduction efforts that are not tangible or built. They include intangibles like decisions over land use or written building codes. When we create such rules for construction, we also need to make sure they are followed, which includes code enforcement. Other kinds of nonstructural mitigation can consist of land use planning, insurance, and relocations as just a few examples.

9.3.1 Land Use Planning

Land use planning is considered a best practice to determine what should happen in concert with the local environment and area hazards. Land use planning relies heavily on making informed choices about both location and design by involving stakeholders in those decisions (Burby 1993; Burby et al. 2000; Godschalk, Kaiser, and Berke 1998).

Planning for area growth or site use requires a process in which those involved identify areas of potential growth and determine what they deem best for the area. Planners, elected officials, community members, builders, and developers may all be involved in the process. They will consider various scenarios and options including zoning regulations, subdivision rules, building codes, land acquisition, and the environment. Part of their work will necessarily involve hazards identification and risk assessment—are new locations being considered where hazards might generate losses and impacts? Or perhaps cause runoff that impacts other areas? To mitigate those risks, land use planning and community involvement is essential to make informed choices that reduce future risks (Burby et al. 2000).

Experts suggest that land use planners create sustainable communities "where people and property are kept out of the way of natural hazards, where the inherently mitigating qualities of natural environmental systems are maintained, and where development is designed to be resilient in the face of natural forces" (Godschalk et al. 1998, p. 86). Such an approach embraces living in concert with nature rather than in opposition. Sustainable communities would accept that rivers go where Mother Nature intended and that humans imperil themselves when they situate homes and businesses in the wrong place.

Still, while land use planning makes sense in terms of disaster risks, it has not always been supported by public officials or developers. A city council member may find themselves in a bind trying to determine how to support a range of stakeholders: city planners, developers wanting to invest in the community, and constituents who may want to live in a desirable but hazardous location. Should you develop an area to help the community's economic well-being? Or, should the area be preserved or have limited growth to preserve environmental resources (Burby et al. 2000)? These kinds of decisions represent potential ways to build a more resilient community, but one that may be challenging to work through with differing opinions.

9.3.2 Building Codes and Enforcement

Many communities put building codes into place and require developers, builders, and homeowners to secure permits, go through inspections, and comply with the code. Such rules exist to increase public safety though some builders and developers avoid them as an added cost. However, for a few hundred dollars, hurricane clamps can decrease roof damage or loss. When a roof leaves its structure, it can cause further damage or harm to others. By installing relatively inexpensive clamps, we can increase not only our own safety but that of others. Another option is to require companies to install utility lines underground, except for flood-prone areas, to reduce damage from storms and ice.

Cost really does make a difference. Consider the outcomes of the 2010 earthquakes in Haiti (Richter 7.0) and Chile (Richter 8.8). Approximately 800 people died in Chile (the higher magnitude quake) while about 300,000 souls perished in Haiti. Considerable differences existed between the two nations, with the primary difference being the ability to afford and enforce mitigation. Population density in areas close to the quake also made a difference with the Haiti earthquake striking a highly populated capital city. Chile, with a stronger economic base, has dedicated considerable resources and expertise to increasing infrastructure and building safety through careful design and strict building codes. Despite enduring one of the most powerful earthquakes ever recorded, they came out far better than Haiti. Questions remain, though, over how developing nations such as Haiti will ever be able to enhance mitigation for their population. Without external assistance it is likely that considerable risk will remain, as was evidenced in the 2015 Nepal earthquake.

Code enforcement is usually the work of city planning offices and code inspectors. The degree to which code enforcement is kept has been questionable in some areas. After Hurricane Andrew tore off roofs across southern Florida in 1992, it was clear that codes did not match wind speeds (Ayscue 1996). To their chagrin, public officials watched as television crews filmed inside homes where nails had clearly failed to attach the roof to the rafters—something that inspectors should have caught during construction. Allegations of bribery and corruption erupted. Stronger building codes (structural mitigation) coupled with code enforcement (nonstructural mitigation) through inspections during construction could have made a difference. Haiti's earthquake serves as another example.

The building code for the nation was a scant four or so pages. Code enforcement was nearly nonexistent. Buildings pancaked, entombing many of the victims.

After a disaster, people take greater interest in new codes as planners, engineers, and architects look for ways to mitigate future damage. Most communities take advantage of the moment to write new codes and commit to stronger enforcement. Additional challenges emerge, though, as people want to rebuild and return home and may not be able to do so quickly as the new codes are worked out. New codes may also displace people, as with the example of elevations given earlier. To illustrate further, some communities have chosen to disallow mobile home parks after a tornado. Although the effort to ensure safer housing is laudable, affordable housing may not be in sufficient supply to provide for people who are displaced. Most students would understand this conundrum—you want to live in a safe place but the rent may be too high. When decisions to build safer housing are made, it is also necessary to ensure that people do not lose homes overall.

9.3.3 Relocations

When people and places face repetitive losses from disasters, it may be worthwhile to consider moving out of harm's way. Called a "relocation," the process involves selecting a new location outside of storm surge, the floodplain, an area contaminated with hazardous materials, or a location dealing with noxious fumes. Relocation is often fraught with difficulty because people do not want to leave homes, neighborhoods, and familiar locales that mean something to them. Conversely, staying in place may increase exposure, risk their lives, and damage their properties.

Why do people end up in harm's way? They may have moved to or live in a beautiful location, such as a Caribbean island, which faces continual threats from hurricanes. Or, race-based segregation could have kept generations of their family in a place of risk, literally on the floodplain side of a river. Perhaps they need to live close to their work, like the ocean that can push a tsunami on to shore. Maybe they feel a spiritual or cultural tie to the land, as when Native Americans feel called to protect the environment and its resources. Relocation in such instances might be embraced as a way to push away continued risk, which is itself the result of racism. But relocation might also be viewed as a threat to a way of life, a commitment to the land, and a social network that enables survival and provides rich, meaningful relationships.

Relocation, sometimes called a "buyout" can occur voluntarily or it can happen through dedicated funds. In the United States, relocations have occurred in places of significant risk due to chemical contamination like

Love Canal, New York where a breached chemical containment area led to serious health issues, miscarriages, and birth defects. Ultimately, the federal government assisted families through the Superfund Act and relocated over 800 families (Gibbs 2010). But people do not always want to move (Handmer 1985; Handmer and Nalau 2013). In Princeville, North Carolina, repetitive floods threatened a community of about 1,000 residents. Mostly female and older, the community boasted a heritage of being the first town in the United States incorporated by African Americans. Flooded again in 1999, the community refused a buyout in a close vote. They did so out of allegiance to previous generations who survived race-based attacks, economic deprivation, and segregation as well as close kinship among trusted social networks (Phillips, Jenkins, and Stukes 2012).

Similar responses have happened in other places. After the 2004 tsunami, efforts to move fisher families away from the Sri Lankan shoreline failed. People needed to stay closer to their livelihoods and moved back into the buffer zone (Karunasena and Rameezdeen 2014). A volcano that threatened families near Colima, Mexico resulted in some relocation amid great suspicion that the effort was actually a land grab. Many stayed in place with the government creating an evacuation plan instead (Cuevas Muñiz and Luján 2005; Gavilanes-Ruiz et al. 2009). In short, relocation efforts must be discussed carefully with those involved in order to identify and address their concerns. Otherwise, relocations may very well fail as a mitigation measure.

9.3.4 Insurance

Carrying personal insurance, even if you are a renter, gives you the chance to replace a computer, clothing, or furniture. Renter's insurance can be surprisingly inexpensive and although you may not want to pay even a small amount on a limited budget, contrasting your potential losses with the monthly amount (called a premium) you pay may put things into perspective. Still, people may not have the financial means to purchase insurance, especially when specific coverage (wind, floods, earthquakes) increases the premium. Even then, people do not always purchase sufficient coverage when they can, thinking that the probability of an event is low (Kunreuther 2006).

Take the time now to inventory items in your home or where you work. Given that flooding is the most common hazard worldwide, think about what is below the one or two foot line of a flood—and remember that floods move and break up furniture and appliances, enter walls where electrical lines are located, and wick water upwards into sheetrock and insulation. These kinds of hidden losses may be more than you had envisioned.

Next, take time to visit with an insurance provider to determine the extent of your coverage including any limitation. Many insurance policies do not cover flooding and sometimes wind damage. To make up for this, the U.S. government offers the National Flood Insurance Program. Private insurance companies sell and service the policies that insure homes and contents up to certain amounts (see link in resources). A number of conditions must be in place for the program. For example, communities that offer the insurance must adopt and enforce ordinances that prohibit building in floodplains. You will also have to pay a deductible (a set amount you agree on when you sign a policy) before your insurance will cover any losses. Should these and other conditions be in place, people who face the possibility of flooding can stay in homes closer to where they earn a livelihood. Moving out of harm's way is not always economically possible, so insurance can mitigate potential economic losses (for more information, visit www.floodsmart.gov).

9.3.5 Advantages of Nonstructural Mitigation

Because structural elements can be so costly to install and maintain, nonstructural measures may represent an affordable option for many individuals and communities. In the case of pandemic planning, for example, educating the public to engage in healthy behaviors as simple as the low cost of washing your hands can stem a potential outbreak. Targeting public education to those most likely to become ill from particular outbreaks, such as seniors or expectant mothers, can save lives. That was the focus of the 2016 Zika virus efforts, to focus on those at risk—particularly pregnant mothers and their fetuses—who might be harmed by exposure or transmission.

Though some degree of financial investment in a nonstructural mitigation measure is usually needed, such as with insurance, the payoffs can be enormous. With sufficient coverage, you will be able to build back and replace furniture, clothing, and computers. Or, land-use planning can serve the public good and enhance quality of life by setting aside green space and reducing flood risks. Building codes protect people inside, from employers to employees and the customers, clients, and patients who visit their facilities. Code enforcement ensures that roofs stay on, safe rooms stop projectiles, and people emerge safely from the tornado that passed over.

9.3.6 Disadvantages of Nonstructural Mitigation

Not everyone engages in nonstructural mitigation although some of it is free—like sneezing into your elbow rather than your hands to avoid spreading germs. Another problem with nonstructural mitigation is the cost, such as insurance coverage. For low income families, the costs can be prohibitive. It is not unusual to discover that the cheapest insurance fails to cover particular hazards like wind or water. Or, insurance may not cover portions of the reconstruction process such as removing debris or a concrete foundation slab.

Another disadvantage is that we all pay when people fail to adopt mitigation measures—when homes and businesses are destroyed, our tax dollars and donations will be needed as well as our volunteer time. When someone sneezes into their hand and touches a doorknob—that we then touch—the potential for being ill increases. Those exposed may pay a price with their health, including their lives, for those at highest risk. We may also lose income from missing work—not to mention the impacts on grades from missed classes, exams, or assignments. See Box 9.3 for suggestions on how to mitigate such a risk.

BOX 9.3   TAKING PERSONAL RESPONSIBILITY

The Centers for Disease Control tell us that washing our hands can prevent the spread of illness and influenza. Wash your hands frequently (verbatim):

- Before, during, and after preparing food
- Before eating food
- Before and after caring for someone who is sick
- Before and after treating a cut or wound
- After using the toilet
- After changing diapers or cleaning up a child who has used the toilet
- After blowing your nose, coughing, or sneezing
- After touching an animal, animal feed, or animal waste
- After handling pet food or pet treats
- After touching garbage

Wash your hands like this (verbatim):

- Wet your hands with clean, running water (warm or cold), turn off the tap, and apply soap.
- Lather your hands by rubbing them together with the soap. Be sure to lather the backs of your hands, between your fingers, and under your nails.
- Scrub your hands for at least 20 seconds. Need a timer? Hum the "Happy Birthday" song from beginning to end twice.
- Rinse your hands well under clean, running water.
- Dry your hands using a clean towel or air dry them.

9.4 Mitigation Planning

Mitigation efforts can make a difference. One study suggests that the benefit can be significant, with FEMA mitigation grants returning a monetary investment average of 4:1 (Rose et al. 2007). Ideally, communities and workplaces will develop and implement a mitigation plan to reduce the effects of a disaster. In reality, though, mitigation planning often takes a backseat to other activities. Those who do engage in mitigation planning in the United States, as part of local, state, and federal initiatives, will likely experience fewer impacts, a shortened recovery, and a faster return to normalcy. But it is also true that mitigation probably has the biggest level of attention after a disaster when people want to avoid a repeat event. Communities and workplaces that have not conducted mitigation planning may now find great interest in prioritizing and funding mitigation measures. In this section, we walk readers through common steps taken during a mitigation planning effort and encourage such activities to take place well in advance of a disaster.

9.4.1 Launching Mitigation Planning

The public may not hold the collective memory to recall the potential for or consequences of a 100-year flood event if it has not occurred in recent decades. Politicians may have other priorities besides mitigation work as well, and feel they need to address more immediate concerns like homelessness, crime, drugs, violence, economic downturns, or deteriorating facilities. The first step then is to inspire the public to understand and support mitigation planning efforts as part of public safety needs.

Planning must involve an array of partners that represent all sectors: education from preschool through university levels, businesses of all sizes, utilities, recreational and tourist facilities, government (including tribal), and residential sectors including homes, apartments, and congregate care facilities. Within neighborhoods, planners must consider and involve those who may be the most vulnerable: single parents, racial and ethnic minorities, seniors living alone or in assisted living facilities, people with disabilities, pets, and livestock.

Mitigation planners should invite a wide array of people from within these sectors. High school teachers and university administrators should be there. People who are blind or use assistive devices should participate. Children should have input. Veterinarians can contribute as can medical providers. Business settings need to be represented too, from home-based through massive factories. People who live in doorways, trailer parks, expensive downtown apartments, public housing, and single family homes should be able to weigh in. No one should be excluded and efforts must be made to make meetings accessible and to offer appropriate languages and literacy levels (National Council on Disability 2009; Peguero 2006; Santos-Hernández and Morrow 2013).

Planning should also reflect a community's culture. Perhaps your community has a history of appointing formal committees to accomplish public tasks—or maybe you live in an area that relies on talking circles, which are more common to Native American locales (Krajeski and Peterson 2013; Picou 2000). Honoring the local way of meeting and connecting leverages the community's existing social networks and knowledge bases and makes people feel more welcome at the planning table. Going to where people live and work to invite their insights also helps, as not everyone can come to a formal meeting. They may be able to join in workplace-based focus groups, respond to a survey, or offer comments on social media. By respecting how people prefer or are able to interact, we generate more interest in their participation for mitigation along with their personal, economic, and political support.

In California, three separate jurisdictions including the Berkeley Unified School District, the City of Berkeley, and the University of California-Berkeley worked together to reduce risks from earthquakes, wildfires, and other events (Chakos, Schulz, and Tobin 2002). Berkeley benefited from a community culture that believed truly in "participatory democracy" where people join in actively over collective matters. With such broad stakeholder involvement, Berkeley residents voted to fund $30 million in mitigation projects. The community also addressed risk in small businesses and residences by "developing appropriate seismic standards, finding affordable solutions and providing new incentives for retrofit." Why was Berkeley so successful in tackling mitigation? "The impetus for change came from a handful of champions who tirelessly kept the issues in front of political leaders and the public, and who unashamedly lobbied at the local, state and national level for information and resources" (Chakos, Schultz, and Tobin 2002, p. 64).

9.4.2 The Hazard Mitigation Planning Process

FEMA recommends that the planning process involve several basic steps: (1) organize resources, (2) assess risks, (3) develop a mitigation plan and (4) implement the plan. It sounds straightforward, but it can take time—even years to complete and longer to secure financial resources for implementation. *Step one* involves a mitigation leader in assessing community support (see resources for FEMA Mitigation Planning materials). To do so first requires you to identify the planning area, such as the jurisdictional boundaries of your city or perhaps an area as focused as a given neighborhood. Next, you need to determine if the community is ready to begin and then address roadblocks to their participation and support like child care or work shifts (Krajeski and Peterson 2013). It is likely that you will spend considerable time explaining the process and value of mitigation planning to the public and to community officials. A public education effort might take the form of a series of media stories that take people back in time to area disasters, describe their impacts, and map out risk areas. Efforts to convince public officials could center on the long-term cost effectiveness of mitigation, with the idea that investment now pays dividends later (FEMA, see resources section).

The *second step* actively involves the mitigation planning team in assessing local hazards. Where can you find hazards information? You can interview people who survived or remember disaster events and their impact. Leverage that information to inform others and motivate supporters. People will remember an ice storm that cut off their power for three weeks and be more likely to fund underground utilities as a mitigation measure. Newspapers and historical records also serve as documents that provide past information. Libraries, historical centers, museums, and archives all contain materials on past disasters. Internet websites list severe weather and other disasters from previous times. Take good notes, then map the physical locations, types of impacts, the present built environment, and the locations of vulnerable populations and places. By visually presenting the information that has and will affect a community, you can build a strong case for mitigation projects.

Another way to get people's attention is to conduct loss estimation. First, estimate losses to each location such as a school, business, hospital, or home. For each, consider the loss of the structure and its contents. What kinds of economic impacts would result? Would you have to rent another home or business location, and at what cost? Would the tax base of the community be undermined, thus potentially affecting local government's ability to provide police, fire, public works, or other essential services? Who might be injured or killed in the scenario? Are some populations more at risk than others, such as trailer parks located in or near floodplains? Have historically diverse communities been sited near a hazardous materials location? Are some facilities subject to potential attack or assault (see Box 9.3)?

Once the data are accumulated and analyzed, present the information to the public to raise concern and support—and be creative. Attend worship services, speak at service organizations, hand out flyers, involve scout troops in walking door to door, distribute information at parent teacher meetings, go to senior centers, and invite civic and neighborhood associations to hear your concerns (FEMA, see resources). Get people concerned and excited, noting the considerable payoffs that could result.

Step three leads the community, in all its residential and workplace diversity, through mitigation planning (Burby 2001; Fordham 1998; Krajeski and

Peterson 2013). Present the information to the community or, better yet, have the community present the information to each other, allowing them to speak in their own words and to their own concerns. List out the hazards and let them discuss what they have learned about the risks that each presents. Ask them to become involved in determining which hazards post the greatest threats to the community. Then, who among the people in the community face the most significant impacts? Which locations, homes, businesses, schools, hospitals, or other facilities could be damaged? What would that mean to the community and its ability to survive?

The discussion process then moves toward identifying a set of mitigation measures and prioritizing what comes first—for implementation and for funding. Doing so may be daunting as the planning team decides which locations and populations require the most immediate action (FEMA, see resources). Mindful consideration of vulnerability, both physical and human, must be weighed into determining the top priorities for action. This is the time when powerful voices may lobby for their own interests and strong leadership will be required to stay on task to reduce risk for as many as possible, particularly those least able to represent themselves. Finding the way forward between collective efforts to safeguard the community and individual interests will be challenging.

In *step four*, the planning team develops an implementation strategy and timeline to mitigate future risks. Continual efforts will need to be made to secure funding as once the planning is complete, the process may fall from public view and interest. By continuing to present mitigation efforts and successes to the public, emergency managers can keep the issue alive. When disaster happens, either in your community or one nearby, it can be used as a visible reminder of the need to mitigate. Though your work in mitigation may seem unending and the payoff far in the future, it will come someday. The lives you save may be your grandchildren, your neighbors, those with whom you worship, or people you don't even know. Mitigation is a payment toward the future and a more resilient community.

9.5 Working or Volunteering in Mitigation

Many emergency managers work in the field of mitigation on a regular basis. In quite a few locations, they may be the only person in their city or county, thus the work of all four phases falls on their shoulders. To accomplish mitigation work, they would likely collaborate with planners, public officials, community members, business leaders, school personnel, health care providers and others. They will also work with state, regional, tribal, or national level governments to align their plans with those outside of their jurisdiction, because disasters do not recognize jurisdictional boundaries. They may interact with insurance companies, engineers, construction firms, and others to design and implement mitigation measures. Emergency managers will also connect with many people and places to educate them about risk reduction measures and to motivate them to join in.

Emergency managers may also work exclusively in mitigation activities (see Box 9.4). In larger cities or in state, regional, tribal, or national

---

BOX 9.4 MITIGATION EMPLOYMENT

FEMA offered this position in March, 2016 as a Senior Emergency Management Specialist in the FEMA Regional Office of Denton, Texas for a salary ranging from $75,167.00 to $97,717.00. Duties are described verbatim:

In this position, you will serve as a Senior Emergency Management Specialist providing advice to senior level staff in FEMA Regional Offices, as well as emergency management partners engaged in supporting hazard mitigation. Typical assignments include:

- Implementing programs to engage all stakeholders in reducing the frequency, severity, and cost of disasters, injuries, fatalities, and impact on critical infrastructure and the environment.
- Promoting The National Flood Insurance Program (NFIP) that has a goal to reduce the impact of flooding on private and public structures by providing affordable insurance for property owners. Encouraging communities to adopt and enforce floodplain management regulations, which will mitigate the effects of flooding on new and improved structures. Helping communities reduce the socioeconomic impact of disasters by promoting the purchase and retention of insurance through the NFIP.
- Enrolling communities in the NFIP and monitoring all compliance activities. Engaging in outreach activities in promoting floodplain management and flood mitigation measures. Monitoring local administration of the NFIP to include review of ordinances to assure compliance with federal regulations.
- Performing technical writing functions, requiring substantial knowledge of the various areas of emergency management and of the specialized terminology required. Writing and/or editing technical materials, including reports of research findings, regulations in technical areas, technical manuals, and specifications.
- Performing as a spokesperson at regional conferences, meetings, committees, and working groups on the implementation of the floodplain management regulations.

Source: FEMA, https://www.usajobs.gov/GetJob/ViewDetails/43138 3300?PostingChannelID=RESTAPI, last accessed March 4, 2016.

government, they may be the sole person tasked with developing a mitigation planning process and implementing the prioritized results. Grant writing will likely serve as one of their chief activities, as they work to secure funds for various projects. Perhaps they will focus exclusively on a mitigation project, like dam construction or a state-wide safe room initiative. They could also work within an industry, conducting loss estimations and recommending strategies to remain economically strong. Perhaps insurance could serve as a place of employment, with the goal of risk reduction and overall savings to people, organizations, communities, and governments.

But mitigation work can and should involve the rest of us too. Everyone should be involved in being personally responsible to mitigate what risks they can for themselves as well as their families, friends, and co-workers. We can also volunteer to serve on a mitigation planning process. As citizens in a community at risk, we can help with fundraising and educational efforts to reduce dangers. We can volunteer on projects to increase public safety, from hosting insurance fairs to setting up public displays of safe rooms. Mitigation is everyone's responsibility.

Summary

Mitigation is an intentional effort designed to reduce losses from hazards. Two main kinds of mitigation can be pursued, structural or nonstructural. The first focuses on the built environment and involves creating or altering structures to be more resilient. An example might be an elevation, which raises a home or business out of an area of repetitive flooding. Earthquakes can also threaten structures, so building them to be more seismically resistant is another example of structural mitigation. Hurricane-centered structural mitigation might include metal shutters, hurricane clamps on roofs, or siting buildings away from areas of risk.

Nonstructural mitigation includes a range of nonbuilt measures. For example, communities will decide about how land should be used away from potential hazards. Public officials will also design and implement building codes, often based on nationally and internationally accepted standards, about how structures should be constructed. They will also enforce those codes through permits and inspections. Insurance can also serve as a nonstructural mitigation effort designed to reduce losses experienced by homes and businesses. Mitigation planning represents a means to involve a wide range of stakeholders in identifying hazards, assessing risks, determining vulnerabilities, and prioritizing mitigation measures.

Discussion Questions

1. Distinguish between structural and nonstructural mitigation and give examples of each.

2. Identify three hazards that have occurred in the area where you live or work (or hope to live or work) and determine a structural and a nonstructural way to reduce your own risks.

3. What are the standards for hand-washing and why are they important? Can you find similar recommendations for cyber-security or personal safety?

4. How safe is the building in which you live or work? Using the relevant boxed feature, conduct an initial overview of what risks might exist, then consider some ways to reduce those risks.

5. What is the cost of insurance to cover your potential losses given the hazards in your area?

6. What are the advantages and disadvantages of both structural and nonstructural mitigation?

7. Who should be involved in mitigation planning in your community and why these people?

8. What are the essential steps in mitigation planning?

Resources

- For a worksheet to help you determine your insurance needs, visit http://www.ready.gov/sites/default/files/documents/files/insurance-form%5B1%5D.pdf, last accessed February 23, 2016.

- For information on residential and community safe rooms, visit https://www.fema.gov/safe-rooms. For the case study on Baxter Springs, Kansas school safe rooms, visit http://www.fema.gov/media-library-data/1427461301284-fd429255aad8dfbff0d2622d08642e9b/School_Community_Safe_Room_Southeast-Kansas.pdf.

- National Flood Insurance Program information can be found at https://www.floodsmart.gov/floodsmart/pages/about/nfip_overview.jsp which has a tool to estimate your risk and premium.

- FEMA Mitigation Planning Series. The FEMA Local Mitigation Planning handbook is available at https://www.fema.gov/media-library/assets/documents/31598. Additional materials and books on terrorism, building design, and more can be found at https://www.fema.gov/what-mitigation.

References and Recommended Readings

American Society of Civil Engineers. 2013. *Report Card for America's Infrastructure 2013.* Washington D.C.: American Society of Civil Engineers. Available at http://www. infrastructurereportcard.org/grades/, last accessed February 23, 2016.

Ayscue, Jon. 1996. Hurricane Damage to Residential Structures: Risk and Mitigation. Working Paper #4. Available at http://www.colorado.edu/hazards/publications/wp/ wp4/wp4.html, last accessed January 31, 2011.

Birkland, Thomas, Raymond J. Burby, David Conrad, Hanna Cortner, and William K. Michener. 2003. River Ecology and Flood Hazard Mitigation. *Natural Hazards Review* 4(1): 46–54.

Burby, Raymond J. 1998. Natural Hazards and Land Use: An Introduction. pp. 1–28 in *Cooperating with Nature*, edited by Raymond J. Burby. Washington D.C.: Joseph Henry Press.

Burby, Raymond J., Robert E. Deyle, David R. Godschalk, and Robert B. Olshansky. 2000. Creating Hazard Resilient Communities Through Land-Use Planning. *Natural Hazards Review* 1(2): 99–106.

Chakos, Arrietta, Paula Schulz, and L. Thomas Tobin. 2002. Making it Work in Berkeley: Investing in Community Sustainability. *Natural Hazards Review* 3(2): 55–67.

Comerio, Mary. C. 2000. *The Economic Benefits of a Disaster-Resistant University.* Berkeley, CA: University of California Berkeley.

Cuevas Muñiz, Alicia and José Luis SeefooLuján. 2005. Reubicación y Desarticulación de La Yerbabuena: Entre el riesgovolcánico y la vulnerabilidadpolítica. *Desacatos* 19: 41–70.

FEMA. 2003. *Building a Disaster-Resistant University.* Washington, D.C.: FEMA Publication 443.

Fordham, Maureen. 1998. Participatory Planning for Flood Mitigation: Models and Approaches. *Australian Journal of Emergency Management* 13(4): 27–34.

Gavilanes-Ruiz, Juan et al. 2009. Exploring the Factors That Influence the Perception of Risk: The case of Volcán de Colima, Mexico. *Journal of Volcanology and Geothermal Research* 186: 238–252.

Gibbs, Lois. 2010. *Love Canal and the Birth of the Environmental Health Movement.* Washington D.C.: Island Press.

Godschalk, David, Timothy Beatley, Philip Berke, and Davis Brower. 1998. *Natural Hazard Mitigation: Recasting Disaster Policy and Planning.* Washington D.C.: Island Press.

Godschalk, David, Edward J. Kaiser, and Philip R. Berke. 1998. Integrating Hazard Mitigation and Local Land Use Planning. pp. 85–118 in *Cooperating with Nature*, edited by Raymond J. Burby. Washington D.C.: Joseph Henry Press.

Godschalk, David R., Samuel R. Brody, and Raymond Burby. 2003. Public Participation in Natural Hazard Mitigation Policy Formation: Challenges for Comprehensive Planning. *Journal of Environmental Planning Management* 46(5): 733–754.

Goss, Kay C. 2015. James Lee Witt. *The Encyclopedia of Arkansas History and Culture.* Available at http://www.encyclopediaofarkansas.net/encyclopedia/entry-detail. aspx?entryID=3709, last accessed March 3, 2016.

Handmer, John. 1985. Local Reaction to Acquisition: an Australian study. Working Paper #53, Centre for Resource and Environmental Studies, Australian National University.

Handmer, John and Johanna Nalau. 2013. Is relocation transformation? Available at http://research-hub.griffith.edu.au/display/nb44819abc2abb41486d9f5b324cc5921, last accessed January 5, 2016.

Holdeman, Eric and Ann Patton. 2008. Project Impact Initiative to Create Disaster-Resistant Communities Demonstrates Worth in Kansas Years Later. *Emergency Management Magazine*, December 12, 2008. Available at http://www.emergencymgmt.com/disaster/Project-Impact-Initiative-to.html, last accessed March 4, 2016.

Karunasena, Gayani and Raufdeen Rameezdeen. 2014. Post-disaster Housing Reconstruction: Comparative Study of Donor vs. Owner-Driven Approaches. *International Journal of Disaster Resilience in the Built Environment* 1(2): 173–191.

Krajeski, Richard and Kristina Peterson. 2013. Involving the Community in Mitigation and Outreach. pp. 151–194 in *Natural Hazard Mitigation*, edited by Alessandra Jerolleman and John J. Kiefer. Boca Raton, FL: CRC Press.

Kunreuther, Howard. 2006. Disaster Mitigation and Insurance: Learning from Katrina. *ANNALS of AAPS* 604: 208–227.

Leslie, Jacques. 2016. One of Africa's Biggest Dams Is Falling Apart. *The New Yorker*, February 2, 2016.

Mabey, Richard. 1986. *Gilbert White: A Biography of the Author of The Natural History of Selbourne*. Charlottesville, VA: University of Virginia Press.

Meo, Mark, Becky Ziebro, and Ann Patton. 2004. Tulsa Turnaround: From Disaster to Sustainability. *Natural Hazards Review* 5(1): 1–9.

Meszaros, Jacqueline and Mark Fiegener. 2004. Predicting Earthquake Preparation. Available at http://www.iitk.ac.in/nicee/wcee/article/13_571.pdf, last accessed January 31, 2011.

Mileti, Dennis, JoAnne DeRouen Darlington, Eve Passerini, Betsy C. Forrest, and Mary Fran Myers. 1995. Toward an Integration of Natural Disasters and Sustainability. *The Environmental Professional* 17: 117–126.

National Council on Disability. 2009. *Effective Emergency Management: Making Improvements for Communities and People with Disabilities*. Washington D.C.: National Council on Disability.

National Weather Service. No date. Severe Weather 101: Tornado Basics. Available at http://www.nssl.noaa.gov/education/svrwx101/tornadoes/, last accessed March 1, 2016.

Nauteghi-A., F. 2000. Disaster Mitigation Strategies in Tehran, Iran. *Disaster Prevention and Management* 9(3): 205–211.

Peguero, Anthony. 2006. Latin Disaster Vulnerability: the Dissemination of Hurricane Mitigation Information among Florida's Homeowners. *Hispanic Journal of Behavioral Sciences* 28(1): 5–22.

Phillips, Brenda. 2014. *Mennonite Disaster Service: Building a Therapeutic Community along the Gulf Coast*. Lanham, MD: Lexington Books.

Phillips, Brenda, Patricia Stukes, and Pam Jenkins. 2012. Freedom Hill Is Not for Sale and Neither Is the Lower Ninth Ward. *Journal of Black Studies* 43(4): 405–426.

Picou, J. S. 2000. Talking Circles as Sociological Practice: Cultural Transformation of Chronic Disaster Impacts. *Sociological Practice* 2(2): 77–97.

Prater, Carla S. and Michael K. Lindell. 2000. Politics of Hazard Mitigation. *Natural Hazards Review* 1(2): 73–82.

Rose, Adam, et al. 2007. Benefit-Cost Analysis of FEMA Hazard Mitigation Grants. *Natural Hazards Review* 8(4): 97–111.

Santos-Hernández, Jennifer and Betty Morrow. 2013. Language and Literacy. pp. 265–280 in *Social Vulnerability to Disasters*, edited by D. Thomas et al. Boca Raton, FL: CRC Press.

U.S. Department of Commerce. 2013. *Economic Impact of Hurricane Sandy: Potential Economic Activity Lost and Gained in New Jersey and New York*. Washington D.C.: U.S. Department of Commerce.

Wachtendorf, Tricia, Rory Connell, Kathleen Tierney, and Kristy Kompanik. 2002. Final Project Report #4 Disaster Resistant Communities Initiative: Assessment of the Pilot Phase-Year-3. University of Delaware, Disaster Research Center.

Witt, James Lee and James Morgan. 2002. *Stronger in the Broken Places*. New York: Times Books.

Chapter **10**

Public and Private Sectors

Objectives

Upon completing this chapter, readers should be able to:

- Describe the role of local, state, and federal government in disaster.
- Understand the Presidential Disaster Declaration process.
- Illustrate the importance of the private sector's capability to deal with disaster before, during and after an event.
- Demonstrate that the private and public sectors must work together before, during, and after disasters.
- Show how relationships can be built between the public and private sector regarding disasters.

Key Terms

- Business continuity
- Disaster recovery
- Presidential Disaster Declaration
- Private sector

- Public/private sector relations
- Public sector
- Resilience
- Retrofitting
- Stovepipes

10.1 Introduction

Preparing for, responding to, recovering from, and mitigating for disasters involves many stakeholders. Two central stakeholders include both the public and private sectors. In the past, members of both sectors would not talk to each other about disaster issues. During James Lee Witt's directorship of FEMA, he encouraged government and business to work together to enhance disaster management. Such an approach made better use of resources, highlighted that disasters were a community issue (not just the local emergency management office), and enhanced disaster activities across all four phases. In this chapter, we first describe the role of the public sector in disaster. Next, we outline how the private sector should approach disasters. Finally, we discuss how to develop public–private partnerships, and how they can improve disaster management.

10.2 The Public Sector

As many have stated, all disasters are local. With this assumption, we will begin our discussion of the public sector by looking at the roles of local public officials. In addition to emergency managers, we include city managers, mayors, city council members, and elected county officials. A discussion of the public section should also include other parts of local government such as public works, parks and recreation, planning departments, and emergency services (e.g., police, fire, and medical). Next, we look at the role of state government, including the governor, the state office(s) of emergency management and/or homeland security, and other related state agencies. Finally, we review the role of the federal government, focusing primarily on the duties and responsibilities of the Executive Branch (including FEMA) and Congress. We also outline the process of a Presidential disaster declarations, which involves all levels of government. Overall, we stress that the public sector's approach to disaster is "multi-organizational." By that, we mean that government representatives from local, state, and federal sectors much work together, perhaps in different or new ways from every day operations, in order to succeed before, during, or after disaster (Drabek 2013).

10.2.1 Local Government

In this section, we will identify various local governmental actors and agencies and describe their roles and activities in emergency management. As you read this section, you will notice that in addition to departments that have clearly delineated disaster-related responsibilities, such as police and fire departments, many others contribute to emergency management activities.

10.2.1.1 *Elected Officials and the Emergency Management Offices*

In general, by law the highest elected local official carries the main decision-making responsibilities for emergency management. For county government in many states this could be the county judge or the head county commissioner. For city governments, depending upon the exact type of local government structure, it could be the mayor or the president of the city council. These elected officials have many different tasks to manage on a day-to-day basis, so they do not have time to oversee an emergency management department on a full-time, daily basis. As a result, elected officials delegate these crucial emergency management tasks to the designated local emergency manager.

Furthermore, local governments may locate the office of emergency management differently. Generally, we see the office of emergency management embedded within fire or police departments. Such a pattern has developed historically because officials did not see emergency management as a separate profession. Instead, local officials saw the office as part of "emergency services" with a focus on response. Thus, local officials would fill the position with a person having experience in a "command and control" or emergency response background. Thus, when a police officer or firefighter was given the title and duties of the local emergency manager, he or she had a fire or police chief to report to, the chief reported to the city or county manager, who in turn reported to the elected official. As a result, the position of emergency manager often got buried under local government bureaucracy. Being buried under bureaucracy and many bosses, their job became more difficult before, during, and after disaster (Waugh and Streib 2006).

Today, we see some increasing evidence that an office of emergency management reports directly to the top official in local government. In many ways, this location is ideal to promote outreach, networking, and interacting across government, private, and volunteer sectors. But the problem is not unique to local government, as this same problem of organizational location plagues state government and FEMA. This problem can also be observed in the private sector, where business continuity planners are either part of the IT/computer offices, or fall under safety and security. Overall, emergency managers and business continuity planners may pass through many layers of a bureaucracy to get to the main decision maker. Rare is the case where the emergency manager has direct access – even during a disaster—to key decision makers (Edwards and Goodrich 2007; McEntire 2006). Since the creation of the Department of Homeland Security (DHS), the problem of access has further developed with an implicit "top down" or command-and-control approach to emergency management (Waugh and Streib 2006). More recently,

DHS has been moving to a command and "manage" approach with an emphasis on collaboration and communication among DHS partner agencies.

10.2.1.2 Local Departments

Before disaster strikes, local government departments do their normal day-to-day tasks. When disaster strikes, some of these operations may continue, or will focus on bringing capabilities back to normal. Sanitation departments work on debris removal and disposal. The utilities ensure that power and gas lines are safe to use. Water and sewage departments test the water and sewage systems for safety and that they work properly. As Dynes (1974) and Drabek (2013) stress, during and after disaster, many parts of local government (and others from government, business and volunteer organizations) may change their tasks or integrate themselves into a broader local response. For example, workers from parks and recreation may be moved to other departments to help, or their facilities may be used as staging sites for material resources or coordinating outside volunteers. Budget and finance offices will keep track of monies spent so that the federal government can reimburse local government for disaster expenses. In broader situations, mutual aid agreements come into effect where police or fire departments may cross jurisdictions to help another community. In extreme cases, such as the City of Salt Lake during extreme flooding in 1983, a city may totally alter its organizational structure and tasks to focus strictly on preventing the whole city from flooding (Neal 1985).

Following disaster, local government must find ways to work with state and federal government, and with local residents to enhance the recovery process (Phillips 2015; Smith and Wenger 2007). In short, local departments become central players before, during, and after a disaster, and must be willing to work together for the response and recovery to be effective. Pre-existing relationships and effective communication built before the disaster can assist with effective event management.

10.2.2 State Government

State governments also play an important role in emergency management. Governors, for example, declare states of emergency after disasters strike, which is a crucial step in initiating subsequent response activities on the part of the federal government. Some state agencies refer to themselves as offices of emergency management while others are known as offices of homeland security. In other locales, they may have both a Department of Homeland Security and Office of Emergency Management. Regardless of their names and bureaucratic locations, these agencies play vital roles in promoting preparedness at the local level, assisting in response activities, and facilitating recovery. For example, state offices play central roles in obtaining monies for local training, preparedness, and mitigation activities. They also assist in gathering information for the governor to obtain additional funding for presidentially declared disasters. Interorganizational coordination between local governments and state agencies during normal times must exist so that response and recovery will go more smoothly when disaster strikes.

10.2.2.1 Role of the Governor

Similar to the model of local government, the highest elected official of any state, the governor, is the state's lead emergency manager. The state director of emergency management (see below) typically serves at the will of the governor and promotes his or her policies. Although a state director of emergency management and/or homeland security can make recommendations, the ultimate decisions related to emergency management rest with the governor (Sylves 2015, pp. 114–115).

A state's governor has a number of important roles during a disaster response. First, only the governor has the power to activate the state's National Guard to assist with response-related activities. Second, only through the governor can a State make the formal request to the FEMA regional office to secure funding through a Presidentially declared disaster. Third, the governor can lobby both the President and Congress for additional funding or changes in policy in order to assist states with disaster issues. Governors' interactions with the FEMA regional offices before, during, and after disasters can also assist in obtaining a wide range of federal resources. Overall, the office of the governor becomes a central conduit between local and federal governments to work together to meet their goals (Sylves 2015, pp. 114–115). Overall, governors must set a leadership example by being willing to work with local government, and the federal government, including the FEMA regional office, Congress and even the President. Importantly, the governor sets the tone for developing intergovernmental relationships and partnerships.

10.2.2.2 Emergency Management and Homeland Security Offices

In general, the state office of emergency management and/or homeland security takes care of day-to-day operations of emergency management. Similar to FEMA, these organizations are much more than a response agency such as providing training opportunities for local governments. It also helps to fund some initiatives for local emergency management offices. These state emergency management agencies also serve as an important conduit for federal information and monies to local government. The state office also assists local governments in gathering data for disaster declaration applications, and provides the information to the regional FEMA office. In general, state offices help to promote effective and responsive emergency management.

The development of the DHS as a cabinet level post following the September 11, 2001 terror attacks further complicated matters for state officials. The creation of DHS placed FEMA within the DHS structure, and the Director of FEMA reported to the DHS director (DHS 2015). Many states created their own Homeland Security office, adding further bureaucracy to their disaster management capabilities. Similar to the situation with local emergency management offices, one could find the state emergency management or homeland security office in many possible organizational locations. Possible options among states include (FEMA 2016a):

- Governor
- Adjutant General/Military
- Homeland Security
- Public Safety
- State Police
- Other

Thus, except for those organizations reporting directly to the governor, emergency management or homeland security directors may have bureaucratic roadblocks reaching the governor. For example, the State of Minnesota has the Division of Homeland Security and Emergency Management as one office. However, the division is located within the State Department of Public Safety, thus having no direct organizational access to the governor (Minnesota Department of Public Safety 2016).

Following the 9/11 terrorist attacks, California created its own DHS in addition to keeping its Governor's Office of Emergency Services. However, within a few years, the governor and state legislature merged the two offices and changed the name to the California Emergency Management Agency. In 2013, further organizational changes occurred and the name changed back to its historical roots—Office of Emergency Services. Although the office today covers a wide range of hazards and potential terror attacks, much of its budget and grants it receives focuses upon homeland security (AllGov 2015; California Office of Emergency Services 2016).

Oklahoma takes another approach. The Oklahoma Department of Emergency Management reports directly to the governor, and the governor appoints the state director. Tasks of this office include assisting with emergency and disaster declarations, helping victims and communities to obtain financial assistance following a disaster, and providing training opportunities for a wide range of hazards across all four phases of disaster (Oklahoma Department of Emergency Management 2016). On the other hand, the Office of Homeland Security is located within the Oklahoma Department of Public Safety (Oklahoma Department of Public Safety 2016). Although appointed by the governor, the Director of Homeland Security reports to the Director of Public Safety. Homeland Security's main purpose is to protect the state from various types and forms of terrorist attacks. In addition, this office also manages most of the grants the state receives related to homeland security and emergency management (Oklahoma Office of Homeland Security 2016). In sum, no one model exists where emergency management and security are located within state organizational charts.

10.2.3 Accrediting State and Local Governments

The Emergency Management Accreditation Program (EMAP) focuses upon improving state and local government (i.e., organizational) capabilities. During the National Emergency Management Agency (NEMA) annual meetings in 1997, the organization decided to create a set of emergency management standard for state and local governments. If state and local governments met these standards, they would become an "accredited" organization. Since NEMA's efforts are directed by the state directors of emergency management in the United States, this effort carried a lot of weight. The criteria that governmental organizations must follow are known as the Emergency Management Standard. These standards, developed by state and local emergency managers and emergency management organizations (e.g., NEMA, IAEMS, DHS), consist of (EMAP 2016b):

- Self assessment and documentation
- On-site assessment by a team of trained, independent assessors
- A committee review and recommendation
- Accreditation decision by an independent commission
- Maintaining accreditation

In all, EMAP uses 16 general standards that a state or local government must meet to become accredited. Although too many to list here, examples of some of the general criteria include (EMAP 2016c, *verbatim*):

- Program Management
- Administration and Finance
- Laws and Authorities
- Hazard Identification, Risk Assessment and Consequence Analysis
- Hazard Mitigation
- Prevention
- Operational Planning
- Incident Management
- Resource Management and Logistics
- Mutual Aid
- Communications and Warning
- Operations and Procedures
- Facilities
- Training

- Exercises, Evaluations and Corrective Action
- Crisis Communications, Public Education and Information (end *verbatim*)

At this time, 31 states have EMAP accreditation as does the District of Columbia. A number of major United States cities, disaster-related federal agencies, and even three universities have achieved EMAP accreditation (2016a).

10.2.4 Federal Government

The federal government helps set disaster policy and guidance for state and local governments and other organizations. It also provides money for activities related to preparedness, response, recovery, mitigation, and prevention. Whereas all disasters may still be local, the federal government drives and helps finance much of these activities. Here, we review the main activities by the Executive Branch (including the Presidential Disaster Declaration process) and Congress.

10.2.4.1 The Executive Branch

Generally, the President obtains emergency powers through the Constitution. Article 2 Section 3 of the U.S. Constitution says that the President must ensure that laws of the nation are executed properly. Article 2 of the Constitution makes the President the Commander in Chief of the Military, giving the President the power to use military resources. In addition, the Constitution also allows the President under times of crisis to use the authority given to the two other branches of government: legislative and judicial. Only twice have Presidents used this power. Abraham Lincoln used it during the Civil War and Franklin Roosevelt used it during World War II. Although rarely used, the President could draw upon this authority in time of a catastrophic event (Sylves 2015, pp. 91–92).

The President also has various cabinet level posts that generally make up a large percentage of what we refer to as the "Federal Bureaucracy." Over the last 50 years, cabinet level posts have stayed generally the same. In 2016, the current 15 cabinet level posts include (The White House 2016):

- Department of Agriculture
- Department of Commerce
- Department of Defense
- Department of Education
- Department of Energy
- Department of Health and Human Services
- Department of Homeland Security
- Department of Housing and Urban Development
- Department of the Interior

- Department of Justice
- Department of Labor
- Department of State
- Department of Transportation
- Department of the Treasury
- Department of Veteran Affairs

FEMA currently resides under the Department of Homeland Security. Beginning with President Clinton's administration in 1993, FEMA had become a designated Cabinet-level post. As a result, the FEMA director had direct access to the President and matters dealing with disasters often moved much more quickly and efficiently. However, with the formation of the Department of Homeland Security (DHS) in 2003, FEMA moved under DHS. Many in emergency management expressed concern about the organizational location of FEMA, its perceived diminished importance due to the change, and potential problems with direct communication with the President. These fears became reality during and following Hurricane Katrina in 2005 (Waugh 2005, 2006). The added layer of bureaucracy proved to be a major hindrance to the response effort.

DHS, with FEMA now under its jurisdiction, serves as the central cabinet post for disaster and homeland security issues. Yet, resources and expertise within all layers of the cabinet enhance the federal government's response capabilities during a disaster. As laid out in the National Response Framework and its Emergency Support Functions (ESFs), a representative from one Cabinet level post may coordinate the efforts to mobilize resources from other cabinet organizations. For example, to coordinate the activities related to public health during any disaster (ESF #8), Health and Human Services would serve as the primary agency and ESF coordinator. Thirteen federal agencies from different cabinet posts would support or assist with ESF #8. To illustrate, some of these thirteen agencies would include the Department of Justice, Department of Labor, Department of State, and the Environmental Protection Agency (FEMA 2008).

Coordinated activities by DHS and FEMA (i.e., executive branch) also lay the foundation for assisting state and local governments. For example, the CPG-101 disaster planning guide promotes communication and coordination among federal, state, local agencies, and other entities. CPG-101 stresses that disaster planning should be local and it must include stakeholders from the whole community. Thus, partnerships among public, private, and volunteer organizations are crucial if planning and response are to be effective. The whole document stresses engaging all parts of a community (FEMA 2010a).

The President makes the final decision on Presidential Disaster Declarations (PDD). Through these declarations, the executive branch passes monies through State governments that directly or indirectly reimburse or assist locally affected entities. For many, including politicians and victims, the Presidential declaration process may seem confusing, and it has changed through the years. To initiate the process, local government officials provide detailed damage assessments to the State's governor. The governor then sends these reports to the FEMA Regional office. Both of their assessments then go to FEMA National Headquarters. Top officials at FEMA make their assessment, and the Director of FEMA passes along a recommendation to the President. The President makes the final decision (FEMA 2016b). The President does not accept all requests. In fact, from 1989 to 2013 Presidents rejected almost 20% of all disaster declaration requests (Sylves 2015, p. 119).

Some declarations may be controversial despite the President and others following guidelines. For example, a localized event (EF 4 tornado) with extensive damage and deaths may not meet a threshold for a disaster declaration, but a wide spread event lasting days (e.g., a slow rising flood) with no deaths and few injuries may quickly be declared a disaster. As a result, disaster declarations may appear to be political decisions rather than one based on need. Related research (Reeves 2009; also see Sylves and Buras 2007) suggests that at times small, subtle political factors may influence the declaration process. States with large populations that appear friendly to the President may have a slight advantage in obtaining a Presidential declaration over other states with large populations that may not always support the President. The annual percentages of requests accepted by a President since May 1953 generally vary from 75% to 80%. In sum, politics may enter the equation, but probably only slightly.

10.2.4.2 Congress

Congress has a much less hands-on role than the Executive Branch. Certainly, Congress passes the budgets that allow the Executive Branch to operate, and it provides funding (e.g., grants and matching funds) to state and local governments for specific disaster projects and initiatives. Congress also provides funding for the President's Disaster Relief Fund. Although the President authorizes monies for disaster relief, Congress must approve the funding—and, to date, Congress has always approved the majority of needed funding. Congress may also provide emergency supplements in bills related to disaster needs (Sylves 2015, pp. 111–114).

Finally, a constant tension often exists regarding how much the federal government can explicitly dictate specific local disaster policy to local governments. This issue of federalism runs constant through United States history, and is part of emergency management policy. On the one hand, federal mandates can provide consistent standard approaches to disasters nationwide. On the other hand, each community and state has different cultures and ways of seeing the world, meaning how one state approaches a disaster issue may be different from another. Federalism can both improve and impede disaster management issues across the four phases of emergency

**PHOTO 10.1 European Commission assisting with the Ethiopian Drought.
Extensive and long term drought has caused significant loss of animal life. The
European Commission has provided money to create water boreholes. (Courtesy
of European Union/ECHO/Anouk Delafortrie; http://ec.europa.eu/echo/field-blogs/
photos/ethiopia-thirsty-rain_en [last accessed August 26, 2016].)**

management. Some claim that federalism in part created the poor response
to Hurricane Katrina (Burby 2006; Menzel 2006).

Throughout this chapter, we have discussed the roles and responsibilities
in the United States of the local, state, and federal government. We also need
to consider transnational government. The European Union (EU), for example, consists of more than two dozen countries throughout Europe. While
each country has local, regional, and national governments, they also participate in the EU. Because of major flooding and heat waves in EU countries
in recent years, and because of large-scale disasters in other nations outside
of Europe, the EU changed its emergency management infrastructure. In
2001, the EU created the Community Civil Protection Mechanism (CCPM)
(Wendling 2010). Now known as the Emergency Response Coordination
Centre (ERCC), this unit today monitors events and disasters within the
EU and worldwide. When necessary, the ERCC coordinates resources and
activities among EU nations to assist in providing aid within the EU or
other nations. In addition to response capabilities, the ERCC also assists
with preparedness activities, disaster exercises, and hazard awareness (EU
2016). For example, Photo 10.1 shows a recent EU ERCC project to provide
water for animals during a severe drought in Ethiopia.

10.3 The Private Sector

When we think about disasters and emergency management, we think of
police and fire departments, local emergency management agencies, FEMA,
and other public agencies rather than businesses and the private sector. For
their part, researchers have also largely ignored the private sector. As we
have seen throughout this book, much of what we know about disasters and
emergency management is based on studies of households, broader communities, and organizations, primarily those in the public sector.

10.3.1 The Importance of the Private Sector

In recent years, however, the situation has begun to change with people paying more attention to the private sector. There are three primary reasons why it is important to consider the private sector in the context of disasters and emergency management. First, a major impetus for increased concern about the private sector is the growing awareness of the staggering *financial costs of disasters*. For example, Mileti (1999) reports that disasters in the United States between 1975 and 1994 cost the nation an estimated $500 billion dollars in financial losses. Benson and Clay (2004) estimate that disasters worldwide during the 1990s produced average losses of $66 billion per year (in U.S. dollars). More recently, between 2000 and 2015, United States insurance companies paid out an annual average of $175 billion for losses due to disaster (Veysey 2016). Disasters do put many businesses at great risk for closure. The federal government's Small Business Administration reports that possibly 25% of all business close after a disaster (SBA 2016). Internationally, such losses increase annually. A recent report to the United Nations documents that natural hazards generated $10 billion in losses in 1975 and $400 billion in losses in 2011. Since 2000, losses have mounted over $2.5 trillion. United Nations Secretary General Ban Ki-moon characterized the situation as "out of control" (Brinded 2013).

These eye-opening losses over long periods of time and worldwide are startling. Yet, large scale or catastrophic events, such as the 2001 September 11 attacks, the 2012 Hurricane Sandy, or the 2015 Nepal Earthquake produce economic impacts reaching into the tens of billions of dollars. Unfortunately, most projections are that these costs will continue to rise exponentially in the coming years as we continue to face more and worse disasters.

Second, the private sector now plays a larger role *responding to disasters*. During the authors' fieldwork, for example, we have seen companies provide transportation, computers, food, and other supplies to assist with the response. In the United States and other countries, private companies own and operate much of the critical infrastructure including electricity, telecommunications, and transportation. When those systems sustain damage or fail during a disaster, the effectiveness of the overall response effort largely hinges on the ability of company workers to restore services in a timely fashion. As we emphasize throughout this chapter, with so much involvement by the private sector, the challenge of coordinating response activities is even more pronounced for emergency managers. Thus, in order to aid communication and coordination during the response period, all levels of government must reach out to businesses and include them in broader community preparedness initiatives before a disaster strikes.

Finally, we need to pay more attention to the private sector because of its integral role in *stimulating overall community recovery from disaster*.

Local governments rely heavily on sales tax revenues to support their basic operations, provide essential services, and launch new community initiatives. When disasters strike, those funds can be dramatically impacted if numerous businesses are damaged and forced to close. Not only do individual businesses suffer from disaster-induced interruptions and sales losses, but the broader community also suffers as a result of reduced sales tax income. The sooner local businesses are able to resume normal operations, the sooner the community as a whole can get on the long path to recovery (e.g., Hackerott 2016). Recovery is a process involving numerous stakeholders, including individuals and households, community groups, and governmental agencies. And, we must also add businesses to that list.

Clearly, the private sector is highly relevant to the study of disasters and the practice of emergency management. In the next section, we will describe the typical kinds of impacts that disasters have on the private sector, including physical damage to businesses, loss of electricity and other lifeline services, and many others. Then, we will discuss the private sector in relation to the life cycle of disasters and emergency management, highlighting the types of preparedness activities that best equip businesses to cope with disaster impacts, the typical kinds of things private sector companies do during the response phase, factors that affect business recovery outcomes, and the role of the private sector in mitigation. Given the centrality of the private sector to all four phases, we conclude the chapter by discussing and emphasizing the need for greater cooperation and coordination between the public and private sectors in preparing for, responding to, recovering from, and mitigating future disasters.

10.3.2 The Impacts of Disasters on the Private Sector

Disasters can produce enormous financial impacts. In measuring those impacts, we often think about losses over an extended period of time or at broad levels such as state, regional, or national economies (Webb, Tierney, and Dahlhamer 2000). These measures give us useful information about the economic consequences of disasters, but they can overshadow and distort what happens to individual businesses. To understand what happens, in this section we look at the direct, indirect, and remote impacts on businesses.

10.3.2.1 Direct Impacts

In addition to their broader financial impacts, disasters can directly affect individual businesses in a number of ways. Indeed, when we think about businesses and disasters, the direct impacts are the ones that come immediately to mind (see Photo 10.2). Direct disaster impacts on businesses include:

PHOTO 10.2   St. Mary, Missouri floods after the Mississippi River inundates the downtown businesses and area homes, 2016. (Courtesy of Steve Zumwalt/FEMA.)

- *Physical damage* to the building in which a business is housed.
- *Forced closure* of a business as a direct result of damage.
- *Loss of utility lifelines* at the site, including electricity, water, sewage, and telecommunications.

In their study of disaster impacts on businesses and long-term recovery of businesses from disasters, Webb, Tierney, and Dahlhamer (2002) found that these kinds of impacts are widespread. In South Florida, for example, fewer than 10% of business owners reported experiencing no physical damage to their facility as a result of Hurricane Andrew in 1992. Among owners whose businesses were damaged, more than 75% indicated that the damage was disruptive or very disruptive to their operations. The vast majority of businesses were forced to close for at least some period of time, with 35% of those businesses closing for more than 22 days. Beyond physical damage to the property, loss of utility lifelines, such as electricity, water and sewer, and telephone services, can also force businesses to close after a disaster.

Research suggests that the immediate disaster impacts felt by businesses can have significant long-term consequences. In particular, what happens in the immediate aftermath of a disaster can profoundly shape recovery outcomes for individual businesses and the community as a whole. For individual businesses, those forced to close over longer periods of time are less likely to experience positive long-term recovery outcomes than those not forced to close or closed for shorter periods of time (Webb, Tierney, and Dahlhamer 2002). When businesses suffer losses, sales tax revenues also decline, which negatively impact broader community recovery efforts.

10.3.2.2 Indirect Impacts

In addition to physical damage, lifeline outages, and forced closure, businesses can also experience a range of indirect disaster impacts. These are things that occur off-site but that nevertheless negatively affect the ability of a business to operate. Typical indirect effects include such things as (Webb, Tierney, and Dahlhamer 2000):

- Employees unable to get to work
- Suppliers unable to deliver necessary items
- Customers declining

In each of these instances, the effects on business operations can be significant, yet individual business owners can do little to prevent this from happening. For example, workers may be unavailable because they must deal with their own disaster-induced problems at home. Similarly, supply chain disruptions may be the result of direct physical damage to a supplier's facility, blocked transportation routes that impede deliveries, or even employees getting to work. Customers may need to manage damage to their own homes, navigate damaged routes to businesses districts, shift spending priorities in the aftermath of a disaster, leading to gains for some businesses and losses for others.

As with physical damage, utility outages, and forced closure, indirect impacts experienced immediately after a disaster can also have longer-term consequences. For example, the more operational problems a business faces, like the ones described here, the less likely they are to have positive recovery outcomes over the long-term (Webb, Tierney, and Dahlhamer 2002). Therefore, owners should develop realistic business continuity plans to help them deal with the full range of direct and indirect disaster impacts they may face. As we will see in our discussion of private sector preparedness, in developing those plans, business owners must consider employees, suppliers, nearby businesses, local government agencies, and others to maximize their effectiveness.

10.3.2.3 Remote Impacts

Disasters can produce remote impacts on businesses, which are similar to but larger in scope and more difficult to predict and control than the indirect impacts described in the previous section. We have already illustrated that disasters are becoming increasingly complex in modern society. A driving force behind the growing complexity of crises and disasters is the increased interdependence of nations and the emergence and growth of a global economy. When a disaster strikes in one part of the world, its impacts are often felt in many different places at once. In other words, disasters are now capable of producing remote effects, many of which directly impact businesses in the private sector. As Quarantelli, Lagadec, and Boin (2006) point out, the effects of modern disasters multiply rapidly and are increasingly felt across geographical boundaries.

To illustrate the remote effects of disasters on the private sector, consider some recent examples in which an event in one place produced cascading effects across an entire region or even the entire world. In 2010, for example, a volcanic eruption in Iceland affected air travel worldwide. To start, a massive cloud of volcanic ash stranded passengers going to or from major airports throughout Europe. For days flights airlines cancelled, delayed, or re-routed flights all around the world. The airline industry suffered major disruptions and enormous financial losses. Similarly, in January 2011, several severe winter storms and blizzards crippled airports in Chicago, Dallas, Atlanta, New York, Washington, D.C., and other major cities. As another example, consider the Deepwater Horizon spill in the Gulf of Mexico in 2010. It certainly dealt a major blow to the local communities along the Gulf Coast, but it also adversely impacted the supply and prices of seafood and other commodities for the entire nation. We already noted earlier in this text how the combined impacts in Japan of the 2011 earthquake, tsunami, and nuclear power plant meltdown ceased production of automobile parts in Japan. American and other automobile manufactures relied upon these parts. They had to stop car production until the Japanese manufactures got back on line.

All of these examples show how economic impacts transcend the local level and reverberate across large geographic regions. As a result, business owners and emergency managers promoting higher levels of preparedness must consider a wide range of hazards. Direct impacts, including physical damage, utility outages, and forced closure are the most obvious ones. But, planners must not neglect considering indirect impacts, and remote effects when preparing for disasters and developing effective business continuity plans.

10.3.3 The Private Sector and the Life Cycle of Emergency Management

Before looking at the life cycle, we need to point out that some of the private sector disaster language is different from the public sector. The public sector, for example, will use such interchangeable terms as "emergency coordinator" or "disaster manager" to designate the person(s) dealing with the hazard or event. Within the private sector, we often hear "disaster recovery" or "business continuity" related to the position and tasks in the private sector. These terms have two different meanings.

Business continuity planning refers to the basic process of preparing and planning for a disaster. The main steps of business continuity include (DHS 2016a):

- Conducting a business impact analysis
- Identifying, documenting, and implementing ways to recovery business functions and processes and functions
- Organizing a team to write the business continuity plan
- Undertaking training for the business continuity group
- Testing and exercising the plan

Figure 10.1, the Business Continuity Plan, provides more detail of the business continuity planning process (DHS 2016b).

Within the business sector, disaster recovery has little to do with getting operations back to normal. Rather, disaster recovery means focusing upon materials and actions related to Information Technology (IT). Simply, the matter of disaster recovery refers to cell phones, e-mail, various types of computers, computer networks, cyber security, electronic data interchange, servers, remote access, and data backup. Imagine any business today not able to communicate electronically, including using debit or credit cards for business transactions. Such a conditions would destroy a business (DHS 2016c).

As we have seen, the private sector is a crucial part of emergency management. McEntire, Robinson, and Weber (2003, p. 453) explain:

> It is apparent that the private sector plays both vital and varied roles in emergency management. In fact, it is not an exaggeration to state that the contributions of businesses in mitigation, preparedness, response, and recovery activities have been woefully underestimated ......The private sector interacts frequently with the public sector to fulfill necessary community disaster functions. Therefore, the lines between the public and private sectors appear to be blurring, disappearing, or perhaps even artificial.

Now let's turn to the four phases of emergency management for the private sector.

10.3.3.1 Preparedness

Disasters are not a priority for most businesses and many do little to prepare. For example, on surveys containing checklists of 15 to 20 possible preparedness actions, such as storing a first aid kit, purchasing hazard-specific insurance, developing business continuity plans, or having their building assessed by a structural engineer, business owners on average report undertaking only about four of the items on the lists (Webb, Tierney, and Dalhamer 2000). However similar to trying to persuade individuals in households, businesses generally are not prepared for what they see as low probability events. Business owners, particularly those who own small, local establishments, have more pressing concerns. With bills to pay, payrolls to meet, and profits to protect, paying for engineering assessments, continuity plans, or higher insurance premiums becomes a low priority.

When they do prepare, businesses tend to prefer certain types of activities, namely, those that are *simple, inexpensive, site-specific,* and geared toward *life safety* (Webb, Tierney, and Dahlhamer 2000). By site-specific preparedness measures, we are referring to activities that businesses can do independently, without having to coordinate with other businesses or governmental agencies. Thus, the most common types of preparedness measures undertaken by businesses include obtaining first aid supplies, storing water, and talking

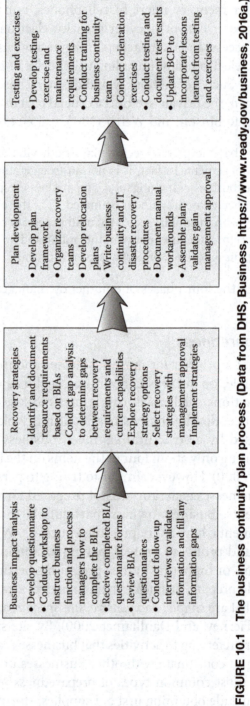

Business impact analysis
- Develop questionnaire
- Conduct workshop to instruct business function and process managers how to complete the BIA
- Receive completed BIA questionnaire forms
- Review BIA questionnaires
- Conduct follow-up interviews to validate information and fill any information gaps

Recovery strategies
- Identify and document resource requirements based on BIAs
- Conduct gap analysis to determine gaps between recovery requirements and current capabilities
- Explore recovery strategy options
- Select recovery strategies with management approval
- Implement strategies

Plan development
- Develop plan framework
- Organize recovery teams
- Develop relocation plans
- Write business continuity and IT disaster recovery procedures
- Document manual workarounds
- Assemble plan; validate; gain management approval

Testing and exercises
- Develop testing, exercise and maintenance requirements
- Conduct training for business continuity team
- Conduct orientation exercises
- Conduct testing and document test results
- Update BCP to incorporate lessons learned from testing and exercises

FIGURE 10.1 The business continuity plan process. (Data from DHS, Business, https://www.ready.gov/business, 2016a.)

to employees about disasters. While important to ensure the life safety of business owners and employees, these kinds of activities do little to prepare businesses for the kinds of impacts described in the previous section, particularly those originating off-site, such as supply chain interruptions.

To prepare for the diverse impacts of disasters, initial steps reflect what other types of organizations and even household members must engage in. These activities include hazard identification and risk assessment of threats and hazards. Next, owners must focus on how these different threats or hazards could affect their business. As a result, businesses must develop comprehensive business continuity plans, possible relocation plans, and longer-term recovery plans (DHS 2016b).

Unfortunately, however, few businesses engage in that kind of proactive planning (Webb, Tierney, and Dahlhamer 2000). As Clarke (1999) points out, planning in the private sector often amounts to little more than the production of *fantasy documents*. These are symbolic plans businesses produce to give the public, governmental regulators, and themselves the sometimes false impression that they are ready for a disaster. Clarke focused his research on the oil industry and its lack of readiness for the *Exxon Valdez* oil spill in 1999, but the concept of fantasy documents applies much more broadly to all kinds of businesses.

While overall business preparedness is alarmingly low, some factors do influence readiness levels. These include *size, sector, property ownership*, and *previous disaster experience* (Webb, Tierney, and Dahlhamer 2000). For the most part, larger businesses with more employees tend to be more prepared than their smaller counterparts. This pattern actually can threaten the well-being of most communities since a high number of small businesses are central to the overall economy. Businesses in finance, insurance and real estate tend to be more prepared than others, particularly those in the retail and service sectors. When a business owns rather than leases a property, the owners will more likely engage in disaster preparedness. Finally, disaster experience can help in some cases with higher levels of preparedness.

Based upon the direct, indirect, and remote impacts of disasters, the following *preparedness principles* might assist in enhancing private sector readiness. First, business owners need to think beyond simple life safety measures. Although important, they are not enough to deal with the complex problems brought on by disasters. Second, business owners need to expand their activities beyond their own specific location. Business can suffer disaster-induced interruptions even if their own property sustained no damage. For example, an event can damage or destroy transportation routes. Thus, manufacturers cannot ship products, workers cannot get to work, or customers cannot travel to the business. Thus, business owners must also consider and prepare for a variety of off-site contingencies. Finally, businesses must coordinate their own preparedness activities with other businesses and with local governmental agencies. Fostering cooperation among businesses can be difficult because they are accustomed instead to competing with each other for customers. Yet, existing institutions, such as a local Chamber of Commerce, emphasize the shared interests of businesses and promote their collective well-being that can be used to promote increased preparedness.

10.3.3.2 Response

The private sector has a diverse and varied role during response (McEntire, Robinson, and Weber 2003). To illustrate, restaurant franchises, large-scale retailers, home improvement chains, heavy equipment rental stores, and many others often donate badly needed provisions, supplies, and services in the aftermath of major disasters. Telecommunications and computer hardware and software companies may provide necessary equipment and technical expertise. Other important response activities, such as debris removal, typically rely heavily on the services of paid subcontractors.

Examples exist of major disasters in which the private sector played pivotal roles during the response phase. For example, after the 1995 bombing of the Murrah Federal Building in Oklahoma City, much of the media coverage of the event focused on the heroic efforts of firefighters and emergency medical teams, but working alongside them at the scene were numerous representatives from the private sector. Workers from natural gas and electric companies in the state were there to shut down those services and ensure the safety of the site, telecommunications companies set up mobile equipment to facilitate the use of cellular telephones, and contractors from major construction firms operated heavy equipment to lift and clear debris for rescue workers (Fire Protection Publications 1996). Similarly, the response to the September 11th attacks at the World Trade Center relied heavily on private utility and telecommunications companies, construction workers, and others to perform numerous critical tasks. These actions included debris removal, technical software support, mass fatality management, sanitation services, perimeter security and fencing, donations management, infrastructure repair, and others (McEntire, Robinson, and Weber 2003). During the response to hurricane Katrina, Wal-Mart provided trucks and supplies to the devastated area, often times beating federal and state aid efforts (ABC News 2005). The private sector played a central role with debris removal. Because of its wide scope of impact, the hurricane produced enormous amounts of wreckage and debris (Mendonça and Hu 2006), and numerous private entities, including waste management companies, landfill operators, and other contractors were involved (U.S. Government Accountability Office 2008). FEMA (2015) recently reported on the central role the private sector played during and just following Hurricane Sandy's impact on New Jersey and New York. Utility companies provided free information to victims in their utility bills on how to deal with a wide range of response and recovery items. A fast food chain anonymously donated over 7,000 sandwiches in 32 New Jersey locations. About 2,000 realtors donated resources to assist victims with finding housing. Companies provided free space for community meetings and activities during and after the hurricane.

Our examples punctuate the private sector's active role in disaster response. Such widespread involvement magnifies the importance of coordination and communication during the preparedness and planning phase. While the private sector often provides necessary equipment, skills, and expertise that local governments may not have, we must also point out the potential for abuses with so much private sector involvement. For example, some companies may win contracts that others may see as unfair or biased. In other cases, some companies may exploit the situation and overcharge for services provided. Thus, appointed officials, including emergency managers, must recognize the importance of the private sector to the overall response effort but also keep a close eye on potential abuses, always striving for integrity, fairness, transparency, and maximum effectiveness.

10.3.3.3 Recovery

The private sector also plays an important role in the community recovery process. When businesses quickly resume operations and return to profitability, the entire community benefits from sales tax revenues used to fund various services, including public safety, parks and recreation, public works, and many others. In this section, we will discuss what we know about business during the recovery period, including factors that promote or impede business survival.

There are two common ways to think about the economic impacts of disasters (Webb, Tierney, and Dahlhamer 2000). On the one hand, disasters have devastating impacts, driving many firms out of business altogether. On the other hand, regional, state and national economies absorb local disaster impacts (Wright et al. 1979). Disasters appear not to have negative long-term economic impacts. In reality, the answer lies somewhere between these two extremes.

Perhaps the best way to think about the issue is to recognize that disasters produce *winners and losers*. At a broad level, most businesses do recover from disasters—that is, they at least return to their predisaster level of functionality and profitability. However, some businesses have an easier time getting there and may even come out ahead. Factors associated with positive recovery outcomes over the long term include size, sector, financial condition, and market scope. Large businesses and those in good financial shape prior to a disaster typically fare better during the recovery phase than their smaller and financially struggling counterparts. Also, businesses in certain sectors, including the construction industry, often experience dramatic increases in profits as the rebuilding process begins. Conversely, small retail stores often suffer severe declines, primarily because that sector tends to be crowded and highly competitive under normal conditions, so even modest short-term declines in sales can have devastating effects. Finally, businesses whose primary markets extend beyond the local area, such as those with high internet sales, tend to rebound more quickly because they are less dependent on local customers (Scanlon 1988; Webb, Tierney, and Dahlhamer 2000, 2002).

Two factors that we would expect to facilitate recovery among businesses—namely, preparedness and the use of post-disaster financial aid—do not always produce the desired results. In other words, businesses with higher levels of preparedness and those who receive some form of financial aid are no more likely to report positive recovery outcomes than those who prepare less and do not make use of post-disaster aid. To explain the apparent ineffectiveness of business disaster preparedness, researchers have suggested that the efforts of business owners are misguided. As noted above, business owners are primarily interested in protecting themselves and their employees. Yet, they fail to prepare themselves for the indirect and remote impacts we discussed earlier. Many owners instead turn to personal savings and help from friends and family to get through a disaster (Haynes, Danes, and Stafford 2011; Webb, Tierney, and Dahlhamer 2000).

In short, we need to pay more attention to businesses during the recovery process. Their survival and continued profitability is central to the recovery of the broader community. However, we should point out that close relationship between business recovery and community recovery can potentially be a source of conflict. Following a major disaster, as recovery money begins flowing into the community from various sources, community stakeholders may disagree on how best to use those funds. Some, for example, may promote the idea of economic development and want to use the money to help businesses. Others may be more interested in providing support to families and households. Therefore, local officials, including emergency managers, must be aware of these conflicts, and implement a recovery process that considers multiple perspectives and develops sensible, fair, and effective solutions.

10.3.3.4 Mitigation

As with the preparedness, response, and recovery, the private sector is also very important to the mitigation phase. Because of its innovation, entrepreneurship, and willingness to take chances, the private sector has enhanced the quality of life in our local communities and for society. Businesses create jobs, perform critical services, and provide us with limitless opportunities for leisure and recreation. However, business activity can also be risky, not just for the entrepreneur with money at stake, but for society as a whole when things go wrong.

Think, for example, about the 2010 Deepwater Horizon oil spill in the Gulf of Mexico. British Petroleum (BP) obviously saw the potential for huge profits by drilling for oil offshore in extraordinarily deep waters and decided that it was an acceptable risk. The company had to convince governmental regulators and a skeptical public that these activities were safe. As a result, catastrophic damage was done to the environment and local communities, many of which depended heavily on tourism and fishing. Related impacts included mental health issues, standard of living, and joblessness (Gill et al. 2014).

Businesses make choices about activities, risk, and (short- and long-term) profit. To find an effective middle ground, businesses and communities must work together to create a business friendly environment that also keeps hazard mitigation and safety in mind. Therefore, local officials, emergency managers, the public, and the business community must in concert devise and implement strategies that satisfy the demand for growth and development while at the same time maximizing safety.

In his influential book, *Disasters by Design*, Mileti (1999) proposes a model of *sustainable hazards mitigation*. This approach simultaneously allows for continued economic success for businesses, maintains and protects safety and quality of life for residents, and preserves the surrounding natural environment. Some of the tools for achieving sustainable mitigation include:

- Land-use planning and management
- Building codes and standards
- Insurance
- Prediction, forecast, and warning
- Engineering

While all of these elements currently exist, this approach provides substantial room for improvement. Some local city councils and planning commissions, for example, continue to allow builders to develop flood-prone and other hazardous areas. In addition, as building codes evolve, newly constructed buildings continue to get safer, but many older buildings badly need retrofitting. In places like Florida and California, people find it extremely difficult if not impossible to afford hazard insurance, so there is clearly a need for some kind of innovation or reform in the insurance industry.

Ultimately, the solutions to the problems we face in preparing for, responding to, recovering from, and mitigating disasters will require increased coordination and cooperation between the public and private sectors. In this section, we have discussed the relevance and importance of the private sector to all four phases of disasters and emergency management. The remainder of this chapter discusses strategies for enhancing the relationship between the public and private sectors.

Emerging in part from the ideas of mitigation and resilience, we now have the notion of resilience. For businesses, resilience has become an important term for survival, and can be defined as "the capacity of the people and systems that facilitate organizational performance, to maintain functional relationships, in the presence of significant disturbances as a result of a capacity to draw upon their resources and competencies to manage the challenges, demands and changes encountered (Paton and Hill 2006, p. 249). Simply, we can think of private sector resiliency as how a business or businesses can absorb a disaster impact while continuing its business activities, or rebound as quickly as possible to continue its business. One way to manage such issues is to make business continuity and disaster resilience part of a business's organizational culture. In short, decisions should incorporate understanding how various types of disruptions (including disasters) can impact a business' profits, and take those types of disruption into consideration for any type of business decision (Alesi 2008).

In summary, probably one of the least studied areas is the private sector. Furthermore, private sector actions should occur in collaboration with the public sector. The Risk and Crisis Research Center (RCR) at Mid Sweden University is initiating studies related to these (and other) issues. We highlight the activities of the RCR in Box 10.1.

BOX 10.1   MID SWEDEN UNIVERSITY'S RISK AND CRISIS RESEARCH CENTER

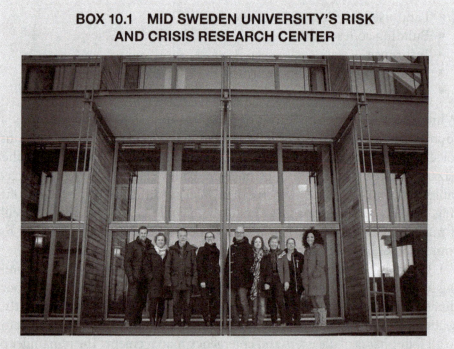

*A few of the 35 RCR members. From left to right: **Olof Oscarsson**, PhD candidate in Sociology; **Anna Olofsson**, Professor of Sociology and Director of RCR; **Roine Johansson**, Professor of Sociology; **Minna Lundgren**, PhD candidate in Sociology; **Jörgen Sparf**, Assistant Professor in Sociology; **Sara Ekholm**, PhD candidate in Sociology; **Erna Danielsson**, Associate Professor in Sociology; **Elin Montelius**, PhD candidate in Sociology; **Evangelia Petridou**, PhD candidate in Political Science.* **(Courtesy of RCR.)**

(Continued)

BOX 10.1 (*Continued*)   MID SWEDEN UNIVERSITY'S RISK AND CRISIS RESEARCH CENTER

The Risk and Crisis Research Centre (RCR) at Mid Sweden University at Östersund is one of Sweden's leading research centres within risk, crisis and security. Through RCR, public and private organizations have a unique opportunity access research results at how risk is perceived and assessed and how crises are managed.

RCR researchers represent scientific expertise from nine different disciplines with a certain preponderance of social science perspectives. The research is conducted in two partially converging areas of research—risk research and crisis research. They are both multidisciplinary and consist of a number of subareas. The common ground is societal aspects of risks and crises.

In the risk research area, RCR study how risks are calculated, understood, communicated and agreed upon. The research is conducted in computer and systems sciences, industrial management, criminology, economics, and sociology. A few of the recent projects focus no household vulnerability in situations where infrastructures break down, and home-owners perceptions of climate changes and behaviors regarding home insurance related to this. The researchers are also developing an intersection risk theory called "doing risk."

In the crisis research area, RCR study how different actors and organizations manage crises. Research is conducted in computer and systems science, informatics, quality engineering, law, sociology, and political science. The research includes crisis management collaboration between national rescue services and police departments in border region, improved community policing in the European Union, and voluntary organizations in disaster management, to mention a few examples.

Within the area of crisis research, RCR is at the early stages of developing a crisis lab. The lab will be a flexible environment where physical as well as virtual emergency exercises can be performed. This is primarily a research lab, but it will also be used for education, method development, and emergency exercises for public and private organizations.

RCR's outreach activities include open seminars and workshops, and the conference Åre Risk Event, where researchers and professionals from the risk and crisis management field meet and exchange knowledge.

RCR is directly connected to the Risk and Crisis Management program (Bachelor's degree) and has links to the Master of Science in Business Administration program. Students from these programs regularly write their essays within RCR projects. Former students work as project assistants or continue their academic journey as PhD students.

10.4 Public and Private Sector Relationships

In the past, government organizations or businesses worked in a stovepiped setting. By that, each organization worked alone, failing to communicate within its own organizational structure, or with other organizations. Today, we know that successful organizations must work across all sectors before, during and after disaster. Since the private and public sectors play such a central role in most parts of a community, they can promote partnerships to enhance a community's ability to manage disasters and hazards. In fact, current FEMA Director Craig Fugate has made public and private partnerships a central part of his administration. Director Fugate says, "There's no way government can solve the challenges of a disaster with a government-centric approach. It takes the whole team" (FEMA n.d., p. 1). Because of this reality, Director Fugate has provided the needed personnel and resources to promote public and private partnerships at the local, state and federal level. At this time, FEMA also has specific grants available to help start public/private disaster planning initiatives. Drawing upon in part Director Fugate's original comments, dimensions of developing the partnerships include (FEMA 2015b, *verbatim*):

- Enhance situational awareness
- Improve decision making
- Access more resources
- Expand reach and access for communication efforts
- Improve coordination with other efforts by segments of the private sector
- Increase the effectiveness of emergency management efforts
- Maintain strong relationships, built on mutual understanding
- Create more resilient communities (end *verbatim*)

Below, we suggest how such relationships can develop and grow to make a community more resilient to disasters.

10.4.1 Developing Public and Private Sector Relationships

As we have shown in this chapter, members of both the public and private sectors experience a number of barriers to effective communication. While individuals from different governmental organizations may speak the same technical language, in many cases they must interface with business owners and consultants who are far less fluent in the acronyms commonly used by government officials. Over the last decade or so, various organizations have recognized the importance of breaking down these communication problems and have devised means to get these organizations and sectors working together. In addition, along these lines, the use of NIMS and ICS, which promotes a common and simple terminology among all organizations, should help communication during crises (FEMA 2006). Clearly, without cooperation, coordination, and communication, any activity among the four phases will not succeed.

Rather than explicitly locking organizations into one type of planning format, FEMA encourages state and local governments to work together to find what works best in their jurisdiction. This idea also includes the private sector in the disaster planning process. For example, as the planning document CPG-101 states, "The private sector plays a critical role in any disaster, and it is important to ensure that they are active participants in the process, including involvement in jurisdictional training and exercise programs. An effective outreach program is critical in developing these partnerships" (FEMA 2010b, p. 53).

For example, following the September 11th terrorist attacks, the State of Illinois started working with the private sector on issues related to infrastructure. They called this initiative the Illinois Private Sector Alliance Project. Information sharing and the building of partnerships between the public and private sector drove this alliance with infrastructure protection being one of their central goals. Without a functioning infrastructure, both business and government suffer, and as their report points out, the private sector owns 85% of the infrastructure in the United States. Another goal of the public–private partnership in Illinois was enhancing mutual aid and resources. As a result, the private sector would have representation in the state's Emergency Operating Center during a disaster. All groups would participate and share information through a terrorism information center. The private sector would be included in disaster exercises in the state. In addition, workshops, training, and websites would be part of the effort to enhance public/private relationships (FEMA 2010c). As an example, managing material convergence following a disaster involves the effective coordination of private and public sector. Box 10.2 details the importance of communication and coordination between these two sectors (and the volunteer) to manage donations and providing resources to victims.

The International Association of Emergency Managers (IAEM) also strongly promotes the development of public–private relationships. An IAEMs report highlights some basic steps in developing relationships coming from the perspective of a local emergency manager. These recommendations focus on creating partnerships with local and regional businesses that can help provide supplies to assist with a disaster response and recovery. Stovall (2007, p. 4) recommends the following types of businesses to initiate relationships (*verbatim*):

- Utilities
- Transportation companies
- Engineers/Engineering companies
- Building inspectors
- Communications
- Debris monitoring and management

BOX 10.2   MATERIAL CONVERGENCE AND THE FOUR RIGHTS: THE RIGHT RESOURCES TO THE RIGHT PEOPLE IN THE RIGHT LOCATION AT THE RIGHT TIME

John Ricketts (Courtesy of John Ricketts.)

John Ricketts is the Director of Domestic Programming and Disaster Services for Feed the Children. As the organization's representative to National Voluntary Organizations Active in Disasters (VOAD), he serves on the Board of Directors and multiple committees: Mass Care, International, and is past Chair of Donations Management (2013–2015). He serves as Chair of the Oklahoma VOAD. He is a member of the International Association of Emergency Managers and the Humanitarian Logistics Association. He resides in Edmond, Oklahoma with his wife and three daughters.

Thousands of black trash bags, hundreds of bins and containers filled with miscellaneous product, intended for families in need. This describes Feed the Children's Distribution Center in June 2013, after one of the largest tornados in State history ripped through Moore and four other Oklahoma communities. Generosity from the public was overwhelming. Material donations came from all across the country. Feed the Children alone received nearly $12 million worth of in-kind goods to support relief and recovery efforts. During that time, there were over 90 points of distribution (PODs) in the central Oklahoma region. It is not realistic to think disaster survivors would go to each POD for all of their material needs to be met. Large-scale events with strong media coverage can generate large amounts of donations that overwhelm the local community's ability to get the right resources to the right people at the right time in the right locations. This is just one example of well-intended donations from the public maximizing the local community's abilities to sort, glean, process and distribute to those in need after a disaster. However, with proper planning, donations management can meet needs of those impacted by disaster and it can be done effectively.

(Continued)

BOX 10.2 (*Continued*)   MATERIAL CONVERGENCE AND THE FOUR RIGHTS: THE RIGHT RESOURCES TO THE RIGHT PEOPLE IN THE RIGHT LOCATION AT THE RIGHT TIME

Donations Management planning begins at the local level. It is important for local communities to prepare for the influx of material donations after disasters. Ideally, Emergency Managers should work to establish relationships with organizations which can specialize in donations management. Local nonprofits can absorb a good deal of this work but in some cases, the response can overwhelm the local ability to handle the public's generosity. It is in these situations a Donations Management Annex in the Local Emergency Operations Plan and practicing the plan can be valuable. In my experience, being a part of several Donation Task Forces help to preidentify potential warehouse space, future POD locations and organizations with specialty emphasis in handling in-kind donations can become extremely valuable in the time of crisis. These task forces can build relationships with Public Information Officers and local media contacts to prescript messaging for the public concerning donations.

Establishing public–private relationships before a disaster event can also be valuable. For example, with recent lead contamination in Flint, MI. thousands of residents are in need of clean water. Feed the Children's established partnership with Niagara helped minimize the effects of this man-made disaster. Initially Niagara partnered to bring 28.5 truckloads of bottled water to Flint, with a future commitment of 13 additional truckloads when this resource is needed. Before this generous donation from Niagara could be accepted, Feed the Children worked to first verify the need on the ground for such a donation. The organization worked alongside the Michigan State Police Department's Logistics Division, the Federal Emergency Management Administration Voluntary Agency Liaisons and local community based nonprofits to ensure donated water was in fact a need, it could be stored, processed and distributed effectively. Collaborating with Niagara and the State's warehouse allowed for adequate staffing and equipment requirements to process the donation in a timely manner. The contrast of this type of operation is collecting bottled water from the general public, which is not palletized, must be sorted and gleaned. Relationships like that between Niagara Bottling and Feed the Children do help those in times of need.

Once the need was established, Feed the Children worked to fund the transportation of each truckload from Columbus, Ohio to Flint. Calling on individual, corporate and church donors, shipments of water were transported at zero cost to the operating budget of Feed the Children. The key to this specific response for Feed the Children was having established relationships to identify the need, formulate the logistics plan and then execute and restock the supply as the community had need.

In Flint, Michigan, planning has helped ensure the right resources reach the right people in the right location at the right time. For Feed the Children, lessons are learned from each disaster. Material donations can quickly overwhelm the local community but with proper planning occurring beforehand, the negative effects of material convergence can be minimized if not all together mitigated.

- Temporary housing manufacturers
- Construction companies
- Food, water, ice retailers
- Hardware retailers
- Health care facilities
- Temporary staff services
- Corporations
- Private security companies
- Private ambulance services
- General rental or supply outlets
- Restoration companies
- Warehouse space/temporary storage facilities (end *verbatim*)

Furthermore, emergency managers must provide outreach to companies to assist them with their own disaster planning. Although large corporations do have disaster planners, smaller companies either do not have the resources or desire to spend money on disaster preparedness.

The U.S. Chamber of Commerce is also heeding the message that businesses need to work with government to prepare for disasters. For example, the Chamber stated, "Improving our emergency response strategies would prevent the loss of billions of dollars in future damages and business interruptions, which is typical of major disasters ... Now is the time to advance 'disaster 2.0' principles—focusing on readiness and resiliency, rebuilding communities to be more sustainable, and educating the different sectors on how to work together effectively (U.S. Chamber of Commerce 2009)." Following up on this message, another emerging thrust has focused on cyber security. Business and government representatives worked together on making a series of recommendations to enhance cybersecurity within both sectors (U.S. Chamber of Commerce 2011). More recently, both sectors together advocating and creating more resilience buildings in the case of disaster or terror attacks (U.S. Chamber of Commerce 2014).

Public–private partnerships do work. Box 10.3 details the efforts of the G8 Economic Summit in Fredrick, Maryland. World leaders from major countries arrived to discuss economic policies, and were met by protesters. Cooperation among public and private sectors made the management of this event a success. As the case in Box 10.3 illustrates, emergency managers from government and business must be proactive in making sure partnerships develop and work. Even today, top executives of companies may not see the full value of disaster planning (except for having data back-ups), may be concerned about the public sectors' encroachment upon private sector businesses, and could be focused upon a company's short-term rather than long-term existence. Developing partnerships among all sectors and educating top executives on the importance of overall disaster management must be a top priority now and in the future (Box 10.4).

BOX 10.3   PUBLIC PRIVATE PARTNERSHIPS: THE 2012 G8 SUMMIT IN FREDRICK, MARYLAND

Mark Landahl (Courtesy of Mark Landahl.)

Sergeant Mark Landahl, PhD, CEM, is a 14-year member of the Frederick County (MD) Sheriff's Office and currently serves as Supervisor of the School Resource Officer Unit. He received his PhD in Fire and Emergency Management Administration from Oklahoma State University in 2015 and earned his masters in Security Studies at the U.S. Naval Postgraduate program in 2006. He has published research articles in the Journal of Homeland Security and Emergency Management *and* Homeland Security Affairs.

In May 2012, the Presidential Retreat at Camp David in Frederick County, Maryland was the site of the Group of 8 (G8) Summit. The G8 Summit is an annual meeting of the leaders of the eight highly industrialized nations— Canada, France, Germany, Great Britain, Italy, Japan, Russia, and the United States. Fourteen world leaders attended the meetings that took place on May 18–19, 2012. Previous G8 and G20 (Group of Twenty industrialized nations) events, resulted in clashes between police and protesters. The results of these included disruptions to communities, property damage, mass arrest, and in one example death (Genoa, Italy, 2001). Recent examples of these events with large-scale disruptions include G8 summits in Genoa, Italy (2001); Gleneagles, Scotland (2005); Rockstock, Germany (2007), and G20 Summits in Pittsburgh, US (2009); and Toronto, Canada (2010).

The 2012 G8 summit was unique. Only a few weeks before the event, officials split the G8 Summit from the immediately following NATO Summit and moved the event from Chicago, IL to Frederick County, MD. This change compressed the usual months of planning for an international event into just weeks. It also resulted in a change in the designation of the event. When paired with the NATO Summit in Chicago, the G8 Summit was a National Security Special Event (NSSE). When split and moved, the G8 Summit itself did not receive designation as an NSSE.

(Continued)

BOX 10.3 *(Continued)* PUBLIC PRIVATE PARTNERSHIPS: THE 2012 G8 SUMMIT IN FREDRICK, MARYLAND

Local officials designated the Frederick County Sheriff's Office (FCSO) as the lead local agency for planning, preparedness and response to the event with support from the County Division of Emergency Management (FCDEM). The United States Secret Service (USSS) served as the lead federal agency. The Maryland State Police (MSP) served as the lead state agency. Dozens of other local, state and federal agencies participated in the event planning process and response.

Due to the remote location of Camp David and the potential for demonstrations in the City of Frederick (16 miles south of the event site), the event was coordinated using the Frederick County emergency operations center (EOC) as a Unified Area Command (UAC). Two distinct incident command posts managed event operations, one in the Northern part of Frederick County near Camp David and one in the Central part of the County in the City of Frederick. The UAC Area decided overall event strategy and priorities and determined the distribution of resources across the two commands.

The EOC/UAC consisted of local representatives from Frederick County Government including the FCSO, FCDEM, Department of Public Works, Emergency Communications Center, and Division of Fire & Rescue Services. Municipal representatives included the Frederick City Police. State of Maryland agencies included MSP, State Highway Administration, and Maryland Emergency Management Agency. Federal representatives included USSS, Federal Bureau of Investigation, Bureau of Alcohol Tobacco & Firearms, and the Department of Homeland Security. A Joint Information Center established at the FCSO headquarters managed event information.

An example of the function of the EOC/UAC came on Saturday May 19, 2012 when a large peaceful demonstration developed in the small town of Thurmont, MD. At the same time, the Frederick Command had no on-going demonstrations. The EOC/UAC shifted staged crowd control resources from the Frederick Command to the Northern Command.

Overall, the G8 Summit resulted in only a few minor peaceful demonstrations in the City of Frederick and Town of Thurmont (near Camp David). These demonstrations resulted in no property destruction and no arrests.

BOX 10.4 BUSINESS CONTINUITY JOB ADVERTISEMENT

Business Continuity Analyst

Aptask Inc.—Rutherford, NJ
$60–$77 an hour—Contract
Industry: Banking/Financial/Information and Technology
Job title: Business continuity analyst

(Continued)

BOX 10.4 (*Continued*)   BUSINESS CONTINUITY JOB ADVERTISEMENT

Job location: 700 Edwin L. Ward, Sr. Memori, Rutherford, NJ-07070
Duration: 1 year contract with possibility of extension
Pay rate: $60–77/h

Job Description

CoB operations process reengineering analyst (resolution planning)

Project Description

Banking's CoB Program Operations organization within Global Operations & Technology Risk and Control (OTRC) is seeking an experienced analyst to provide Continuity of Business (CoB) operations support. The candidate will join a core team which is part of the organization leading client's global business continuity program responsible for the CoB Program at client. The candidate will be involved in various aspects of CoB operations under the direction of the CoB Operations Process Re-Engineering Team Leader, including: providing in-depth and sophisticated analysis of current processes and metrics to suggest areas for improvements inclusive of resolution planning. Monitor changes to business recovery plans that may impact resolution planning, develop metrics, and work with shared services resolution planning team to highlight the potential issues including, tracking these issues to resolution once dispositioned. Facilitating the process to ensure that business continuity plans are viable, executable, implemented, and tested. Working closely with the CoB tools team on enhancements to align the CoB tool with the reengineered processes. Working closely with the CoB metrics and reporting team to enhance and define new operating performance and risk metrics. Assisting in the development of CoB policy and standards. Promoting business continuity awareness and education. Participating on special projects as assigned.

Required Qualifications

- 5+ years of data analytics or reporting development experience.
- 5+ years business continuity/disaster recovery/business resiliency experience, preferably within a business and technology risk management environment.
- 5+ years in process analysis and process improvement, business analysis, project management, and/or related business experience.
- Strong analytical skills and ability to see the big picture and take ideas from the concept to execution.
- Exceptional technical skills regarding pulling and interpreting data and tying the findings with business judgment to drive actionable outcome.

(Continued)

BOX 10.4 (*Continued*)   BUSINESS CONTINUITY JOB ADVERTISEMENT

- Demonstrated strong written and verbal communication skills with the ability to develop and articulate actionable, fact-based, insights and recommendations and deliver these by telling a simple, compelling story to varying types of audiences to guide decision-making.
- Strong interpersonal skills, including the ability to partner with others and deal effectively with multiple projects and changing priorities.
- Excellent influencing and negotiation skills and ability to work effectively with all levels of the organization as well as geographically disbursed teams.
- Strong problem solving and critical thinking skills.
- Strong meeting organization and facilitation skills.
- Ability to work independently in a fast-paced multitasking environment.
- Team player with strong conflict resolution and influencing skills.
- Experience with advanced analytical technologies (e.g., R, Python, SQL, etc.) and reporting and data mining tools (e.g., SAS, Teradata SQL, Tableau, Business Objects, Crystal Reports, IBM Cognos etc.) is a plus.

Job Type

Contract

Required Experience

- Business Continuity: 2 years

Source: http://www.indeed.com/cmp/ApTask-Inc./jobs/Business-Continuity-Analyst-8e2034239366f0a1?q=Business+Continuity

10.5 Working and Volunteering in the Private Sector

As we noted earlier in this text about the public sector, the private sector also has numerous opportunities to volunteer or work in. So, when you think about volunteering, seeking out an internship, or applying for jobs, you should look beyond the most obvious places and consider the private sector. For example, business continuity and/or disaster recovery specialists are needed for banks, chemical companies, hospitals, manufacturing firms, accounting firms, social services, and more. Looking for internships and jobs in the private sector may also suggest slightly different thinking about other majors or minors. Those looking for internships and jobs in the private sector must show a wide range of skills and capabilities. For example, some business offices for business continuity include health and safety or security. Those with additional background, training, or experience in occupational safety, fire, or law enforcement can enhance their internship and job opportunities. In many industries, such as chemical companies and manufacturing plants, they need safety compliance officers, risk managers, and emergency response personnel. Computer skills, especially with networks and communications backgrounds or training, can also complement those interested in disaster recovery. In some cases, if you have basic computer skills, the company will provide additional training while on the job.

Box 10.5 provides a detailed example of a paid internship. Unlike many internships in the public or volunteer sector, this one is paid. Although certainly not reflective of all internships in the private sector, this should

---

BOX 10.5   INTERNSHIP AND JOB REQUIREMENT EXAMPLES

[*verbatim*]

Internship

The National Rural Electric Cooperative Association (NRECA) … is the trade association for over 900 consumer-owned electric cooperatives serving more than 42 million people.

The purpose of an internship in the OGC/Compliance department is to introduce a college student to areas of risk management, content management, business continuity, benefit plan compliance, and securities compliance.

Learning Objectives
- Gain hands-on risk monitoring and internal controls experience.
- Work with pension and welfare plans information and testing requirements.
- Become familiar with regulatory laws such as ERISA, HIPAA, and SEC.
- Work in areas of enterprise risk management and content management.
- Exposure to multiple project areas and multi-tasking workload.
- Develop both oral and written communications skills and interacting in a team environment.

Requirements and Qualifications
- Preferred Degree: Business, Risk Management or Accounting
- Proficient in Microsoft Outlook, Excel, Word, Access, PowerPoint, SharePoint
- Knowledge of Internet functions and capabilities

(*Continued*)

**BOX 10.5 (*Continued*)   INTERNSHIP AND
JOB REQUIREMENT EXAMPLES**

- Knowledge or interest in health plan related laws (ERISA, HIPAA, COBRA)
- Knowledge or interest in SEC laws
- Analytical skills
- Attention to detail and accurate proof-reading skills
- Strong organizational skills

This is an intern position

- 3.0 or above GPA required and Must be a rising junior or senior
- Dates: May 16th through August 5th
- Wages: $18.50 per hour

Source: https://nreca.jibeapply.com/jobs/IRC26036/
Arlington-VA-Intern-Compliance-department?lang=en-US

Business Continuity Analyst

Aptask Inc.—Rutherford, NJ
$60–$77 an hour—Contract
Industry: Banking/ Financial/ Information & Technology
Job Title: Business Continuity Analyst
Duration: 1 Year Contract with possibility of extension
Pay Rate: $60–$77/h

Required Qualifications:

- 5+ years of data analytics or reporting development experience.
- 5+ years Business Continuity/Disaster Recovery/Business Resiliency experience, preferably within a Business and Technology Risk Management environment.
- 5+ years in process analysis and process improvement, business analysis, project management and/or related business experience.
- Strong analytical skills and ability to see the big picture and take ideas from concept to execution.
- Exceptional technical skills regarding pulling and interpreting data and tying the findings with business judgment to drive actionable outcome.
- Demonstrated strong written and verbal communication skills with the ability to develop and articulate actionable, fact-based, insights and recommendations and deliver these by telling a simple, compelling story to varying types of audiences to guide decision-making.
- Strong interpersonal skills, including the ability to partner with others and deal effectively with multiple projects and changing priorities.

(Continued)

BOX 10.5 (*Continued*)   INTERNSHIP AND
JOB REQUIREMENT EXAMPLES

- Excellent influencing and negotiation skills and ability to work effectively with all levels of the organization as well as geographically disbursed teams.
- Strong problem solving and critical thinking skills.
- Strong meeting organization and facilitation skills.
- Ability to work independently in a fast-paced multitasking environment.
- Team player with strong conflict resolution and influencing skills.
- Experience with advanced analytical technologies (e.g., R, Python, SQL, etc.) and reporting and data mining tools (e.g., SAS, Teradata SQL, Tableau, Business Objects, Crystal Reports, IBM Cognos etc.) is a plus.

Required experience:

- Business Continuity: 2 years

Source: http://www.indeed.com/cmp/ApTask-Inc./jobs/
Business-Continuity-Analyst-8e2034239366f0a1?q=Business+Continuity

help you understand think about how to prepare yourself through experience, training, and academics to obtain a similar position.

As you may recall, the International Association of Emergency Managers awards the Certified Emergency Manager (CEM), which is generally oriented toward the public sector. For those seeking careers in the private sector, one can also obtain various levels of certification oriented toward the business community. With the growing interest and opportunities, we have identified at least three different organizations providing certification opportunities for those in the private sector. For example, the Disaster Recovery Institute International (DRII) offers seven different types of accreditation based upon different foci and areas of expertise. These include (DRII 2016b):

- Certified Functional Continuity Professional (CFCP)
- Certified Business Continuity Auditor (CBCA & CBCLA)
- Certified Business Continuity Professional (CBCP)
- Master Business Continuity Professional (MBCP)
- Certified Public Sector Continuity Professional (CPSCP)
- Certified Healthcare Provider Continuity Professional (CHPCP)

Obtaining and maintaining these various certifications include attending pre exam seminars (not required but helpful), taking exams, attending continuing education related training, and paying an annual membership fee (DRII 2016a, b).

The Business Continuity Management Institute (BCMI) also offers a wide range of certification options. They include (BCMI 2015, verbatim):

- BC Certified Planner (BCCP)
- BC Certified Specialist (BCCS)
- BC Certified Expert (BCCE)
- DR Certified Specialist (DRCS)
- DR Certified Expert (DRCE)
- BC Certified Auditor (BCCA)
- BC Certified Lead Auditor (BCCLA)
- Crisis Management Certified Planner (CMCP)
- Crisis Management Certified Specialist (CMCS)
- Crisis Management Certified Expert (CMCE, end verbatim)

Obtaining each of these certificates requires obtaining specific levels of education/training and experience (BCMI 2015).

The Business Resilience International Consortium (BRCI 2016) provides certificates in business continuity, IT, and business continuity/disaster resilience auditing. Training classes provide much of the foundation for obtaining these certificates.

These are just some of the examples of certification opportunities that could enhance one's job entrée and advancement in the private sector. We do not endorse any of these programs. Rather, this information may serve as a starting point for exploring options. We recommend that you talk with experienced employees in the private sector to see which type of certification may be best for you. You may also obtain an understanding which certification is recognized by your profession in your geographical area.

Although we commonly think of emergency management as a responsibility of the public sector, the private sector has an equally valuable role. This role also increases opportunities for internships, volunteer work, and jobs. As disasters continue to threaten our communities and their financial impacts continue to climb, we believe that positions in business continuity and disaster recovery will continue to expand.

Summary

Both the public and private sectors play vital roles before, during, and after disasters. Government, especially at the local level, is the starting place for effective emergency management across all disaster phases. Local government must work with its state and federal government to enhance its disaster capabilities. An important component for local government after a disaster strikes is understanding and using properly the process to obtain a Presidential Disaster Declaration. Otherwise, local government (and its residents) may not get proper funding and reimbursement, and in a timely manner, to provide assistant for response and recovery.

The private sector has a number of priorities, and managing disasters is not one of them. Yet, many businesses suffer greatly and may even go out of business from a disaster. Business managers and executives must recognize that surviving disturbances and disasters are a central component to having, in the long run, a successful and profitable business. Making disaster awareness and resiliency as part of the organizational culture creates an important step for a successful business to survive a disaster.

Discussion Questions

1. Research your own state's organizational structure of emergency management. Are the offices of Homeland Security and Emergency Management two distinct offices or are they combined? Do these offices report directly to the governor, or another office (e.g., Adjunct General) who then reports to the governor? What implications might these arrangements have for dealing with disasters or terrorism before, during, or after any event?

2. Identify any major events in your home county (e.g., tornado, flood and hurricane) and if they were Presidentially declared disasters or not. If not, see if any controversy followed.

3. What are some examples of having businesses making disaster resilience as part of their organizational culture? As a starting point, you might want to consider from whom they buy products, the types of transportation routes (e.g., roads, rail, ports, and airports), location of their offices and/or manufacturing areas) used, where they locate their offices and other facilities, and how those facilities are constructed.

4. Thinking of your own hometown, consider some of the following questions. What might be some important business representatives (e.g., both businesses and organizations that represent businesses) that could team with local government to develop public–private relationships? What type of organizations representing the private sector could help initiate or maintain the idea of developing public–private relationships? What do you think might be some good forums or opportunities that would provide officials from the public and private sector to meet? In what settings may they already gather

that could be used to initiate a discussion? What related activities could also enhance these relationships?

5. Why must the public and private sectors must work together before, during, and after disasters? Consider the types of resources, regulations, and personnel each sector has that the other does not. Think on how these capabilities before, during and after a disaster may complement each other rather than duplicate each others' tasks.

Resources

- If you are interested in the number or type of disaster declarations in your county (or any county), the following link can provide this information: https://www.fema.gov/disasters/.
- To enhance business continuity planning, DHS has developed a software package. DHS designed it so small or large businesses can use it to create, adapt, or enhance new or existing business continuity plans. It can be found at https://www.ready.gov/business-continuity-planning-suite.
- FEMA has an extensive web page with links to a wide range of documents to assist with business continuity planning. Topics include case studies, risk assessment tables, worksheets, insurance guidance among other related topics. This site can be found at https://www.fema.gov/media-library/collections/357.
- Small, often family-owned business, have their own preparedness needs to consider. The Small Business Administration provides information and related documents to help those with small businesses prepare, respond, clean-up, and recover during disaster. This site can be found at https://www.sba.gov/managing-business/running-business/emergency-preparedness/emergency-preparedness.
- In conjunction with the American National Red Cross, the Occupational Safety and Health Administration developed a two page checklist to assist small businesses with disaster planning. This document can be found at https://www.osha.gov/dte/grant_materials/fy07/sh-16618-07/sm_business_emergency_checklist.pdf.
- FEMA has a number of resources available to assist communities and others initiating or maintaining public–private relationships for disaster planning. A few good starting places include https://www.fema.gov/public-private-partnerships, https://www.fema.gov/tools-resources-0.

- Although not having a specific link to public–private partnerships, the International Association of Emergency Managers link http://www.iaem.com, has an excellent search function that can help you find a number of helpful documents on the topic.
- To have an overview of disaster recovery and business continuity trends, the professional magazine, *Disaster Recovery Journal*, is a good place to start. You can find the information at http://www.drj.com/.

References

ABC News. 2005. What Can Wal-Mart Teach FEMA about Disaster Response? Available at http://abcnews.go.com/WNT/HurricaneRita/story?id=1171087, last accessed March 27, 2016.

Alesi, Patrick. 2008. Building Enterprise-Wide Resilience by Integrating Business Continuity Capability into Day-to-Day Business Culture and Technology. *Journal of Business Continuity and Business Planning* 3: 214–220.

AllGov. 2015. California Office of Emergency Services. Available at http://www.allgov.com/usa/ca/departments/office-of-the-governor/california_emergency_management_agency?agencyid=217, last accessed March 26, 2016.

BCMI. 2015. Certification. Available at http://www.bcm-institute.org/certification, last accessed April 5, 2016.

Benson, C. and E. J. Clay. 2004. *Understanding the Economic and Financial Impacts of Natural Disasters*. Washington, D.C.: The World Bank.

BRCI. 2016. Certification Program. Available at http://www.brcci.org/index.php/certification/business-continuity-certification-overview, last accessed April 5, 2016.

Brinded, Lianna. 2013. Businesses Face Billions in Natural Disaster Economic Losses. *International Business Times*. Available at http://www.ibtimes.co.uk/catastrophe-risks-costs-pwc-imf-hurricane-storms-468976, last accessed March 27, 2016.

Burby, R. J. 2006. Hurricane Katrina and the Paradoxes of Government Disaster Policy: Bringing about Wise Governmental Decisions for Hazardous Areas. *The Annals of the American Academy of Political and Social Science* 604: 171–191.

California Office of Emergency Services. 2016. About Cal EOS. Available at http://www.caloes.ca.gov/Cal-OES-Divisions/About-Cal-OES, last accessed March 26, 2016.

Clarke, L. *Mission Improbable: Using Fantasy Documents to Tame Disaster*. Chicago, IL: University of Chicago Press, 1999.

Drabek, Thomas E. 2013. *The Human Side of Disaster, 2nd Edition*. Boca Raton, FL: CRC Press.

DHS. 2015. Creation of the Department of Homeland Security. Available at https://www.dhs.gov/creation-department-homeland-security, last accessed March 25, 2016.

DHS. 2016a. Business. Available at https://www.ready.gov/business, last accessed March 27, 2016.

DHS. 2016b. Business Continuity Plan. Available at https://www.ready.gov/business/implementation/continuity, last accessed April 4, 2016.

DHS. 2016c. IT Disaster Recovery. Available at https://www.ready.gov/business/implementation/IT, last accessed April 4, 2016.

DRII. 2016a. Certification. Available at https://www.drii.org/certification/maintaincert.php, last accessed April 5, 2016.

DRII. 2016b. Certification—Maintaining Certification Overview. Available at https://www.drii.org/certification/maintaincert.php, last assessed April 5, 2016.

Dynes, Russell R. 1974. *Organized Behavior in Disaster*. Columbus, OH: Disaster Research Center.

Edwards, Frances L. and Daniel C. Goodrich. 2007. Organizing for Emergency Management. pp. 39–56 in *Emergency Management: Principles and Practice for Local Government*, 2nd edition, edited by William L. Waugh and Kathleen J. Tierney. Washington, D.C.: ICMA Press.

EU. 2016. Emergency Response Coordination Centre. Available at http://ec.europa.eu/echo/what/civil-protection/emergency-response-coordination-centre-ercc_en, last accessed April 8, 2016.

Emergency Management Accreditation Program (EMAP). 2016a. EMAP Accredited Programs. Available at https://www.emap.org/index.php/what-is-emap/who-is-accredited, last accessed March 31, 2016.

Emergency Management Accreditation Program (EMAP). 2016b. EMAP History. Available at https://www.emap.org/index.php/program-resources/steps-to-accreditation, last accessed March 26, 2016.

Emergency Management Accreditation Program (EMAP). 2016c. "Emergency Management Standard". Available at https://www.emap.org/index.php/what-is-emap/the-emergency-management-standard, last accessed March 26, 2016.

FEMA. 2006. NIMS and Use of Plain Language. NIMS Alert. Available at http://www.fema.gov/pdf/emergency/nims/plain_lang.pdf, last accessed March 31, 2016.

FEMA. 2008. Emergency Support Function Annexes: Introduction. Available at http://www.fema.gov/media-library-data/20130726-1825-25045-0604/emergency_support_function_annexes_introduction_2008_.pdf, last accessed March 26, 2016.

FEMA. 2010a. *Comprehensive Planning Guide 101*. Available at http://www.fema.gov/pdf/about/divisions/npd/CPG_101_V2.pdf, last accessed April 5, 2016.

FEMA. 2010b. *Comprehensive Planning Guide 101*. Available at http://www.fema.gov/PDF/about/divisions/npd/CPG_101_V2.pdf, last accessed October 21, 2016.

FEMA. 2010c. State Partnership—Illinois' Private Sector Alliance Project. Available at http://www.fema.gov/pdf/privatesector/illinois_partnership.pdf, last accessed April 5, 2016.

FEMA. 2015a. Three Year after Sandy: New Jersey's Private Sector Continues the Work of Recovery. Available at http://www.fema.gov/news-release/2015/10/21/three-years-after-sandy-new-jerseys-private-sector-continues-work-recovery, last accessed March 27, 2016.

FEMA. 2015b. Public-Private Partnerships. Available at http://www.fema.gov/public-private-partnerships, last accessed April 5, 2016.

FEMA. 2016a. Emergency Management Agencies. Available at https://www.fema.gov/emergency-management-agencies, last accessed March 25, 2016.

FEMA. 2016b. The Declaration Process. Available at http://www.fema.gov/declaration-process, last accessed March 30, 2016.

FEMA. n. d. Building Better Resiliency—Together. Available at http://www.fema.gov/media-library-data/1383654912681-508c2ec178c9741b3eb78ddddf106428/Public_Private_Partnerships.pdf, last accessed April 5, 2016.

Fire Protection Publications. 1996. *Final Report: Alfred P. Murrah Federal Building Bombing, April 19, 1995*. Stillwater, OK: Fire Protection Publications.

Gill, Duane A., Liesel A. Ritchie, J. Steven Picou, Jennifer Langhinrichen-Rohling, Micha Long, and Jessica W. Shenesey. 2014. The Exxon and BP Oil Spills: A Comparison of Psychosocial Impacts. *Natural Hazards* 74: 1911–1932.

Hackerott, Caroline. 2016. *A Jolt to the System: Measuring Disaster-Induced Social Disruption through Water Consumption, Sales Tax Revenue and Crime Data.* PhD Dissertation. Stillwater, OK: Fire and Emergency Management Program, Oklahoma State University.

Haynes, George W., Sharon M. Danes, and Kathryn Stafford. 2011. Influence of Federal Disaster Assistance no Family Business Survival and Success. *Journal of Contingencies and Crisis Management* 19(2): 86–98.

Indeed. 2016. Business Continuity Analyst. Available at http://www.indeed.com/cmp/ ApTask-Inc./jobs/Business-Continuity-Analyst-8e2034239366f0a1?q=Business+ Continuity, last accessed April 5, 2016.

McEntire, David A. 2006. Local Emergency Management Organizations. pp. 168–182 in *Handbook of Disaster Research*, edited by Havidán Rogríguez, Enrico L. Quarantelli, and Russell R. Dynes. New York: Springer.

McEntire, David A., Robie J. Robinson, and Richard T. Weber. 2003. Business Responses to the World Trade Center Disaster: A Study of Corporate Roles, Functions, and Interaction with the Public Sector. pp. 431–457 in *Beyond September 11th: An Account of Post-Disaster Research.* Special Publication #39. Boulder, CO: University of Colorado, Natural Hazards Research and Applications Information Center.

Mendonça, David and Yao Hu. 2006. Hurricane Katrina Debris Removal Operations: The Role of Communication and Computing Technologies. pp. 283–304 in *Learning from Catastrophe: Quick Response Research in the Wake of Hurricane Katrina*, edited by Christine Bvec. Boulder, CO: Natural Hazards Center – University of Colorado.

Menzel, D. C. 2006. The Katrina Aftermath: A Failure of Federalism or Leadership? *Public Administration Review* 666: 808–812.

Mileti, Dennis. 1999. *Disasters by Design.* Washington, D.C.: Joseph Henry Press.

Minnesota Department of Public Safety. 2016. Homeland Security and Emergency Management. Available at https://dps.mn.gov/divisions/hsem/about/Pages/default. aspx, last accessed March 26, 2016.

Neal, David M. 1985. *A Comparative analysis of Emergent Group Behavior in Disaster: A Look at the United States and Sweden.* PhD Dissertation. Columbus, OH: Department of Sociology, The Ohio State University.

NRECA. 2016. NRECA Careers. Available at https://nreca.jibeapply.com/jobs/IRC26036/ Arlington-VA-Intern-Compliance-department?lang=en-US, last accessed April 5, 2016.

Oklahoma Department of Emergency Management. 2016. About Us. Available at https:// www.ok.gov/OEM/About_OEM/index.html, last accessed March 26, 2016.

Oklahoma Department of Public Safety. 2016. Home. Available at http://www.dps.state. ok.us/, last accessed March 26, 2016.

Oklahoma Office of Homeland Security. 2016. About OKOHS. Available at https://www. ok.gov/homeland/About_OKOHS/index.html, last accessed March 26, 2016.

Paton, Doug and Rosemary Hill. 2006. Managing Company Risk and Resilience through Business Continuity Management. pp. 249–266 in *Disaster Resilience: An Integrated Approach*, edited by Doug Paton and David Moore Johnston. Springfield, IL: Charles C. Thomas.

Phillips, Brenda D. 2015. *Disaster Recovery, 2nd Edition.* Boca Raton, FL: CRC Press.

Quarantelli, Enrico L., Patrick Lagadec, and Arjen Boin. 2006. A Heuristic Approach to Future Disasters and Crises: New, Old, and In-Between Types. pp. 16–41 *Handbook of Disaster Research*, edited by Havidan Rodriguez, E. L. Quarantelli, and Russell R. Dynes. New York: Springer.

Reeves, Andrew. 2009. Political Disaster: Unilateral Powers, Electoral Incentives, and Presidential Disaster Declarations. *The Journal of Politics* 1(1): 1–10.

Scanlon, Joseph. 1988. Winners and Losers: Some Thoughts about the Political Economy of Disaster. *The International Journal of Mass Emergencies and Disasters* 6(1): 47–63.

Small Business Administration (SBA). 2016. Disaster Planning. Starting & Managing. Available at https://www.sba.gov/managing-business/running-business/emergency-preparedness/disaster-planning, last accessed March 27, 2016.

Smith, Gavin and Dennis Wenger. 2007. Sustainable Disaster Recovery: Operationalizing an Existing Agenda. In *Handbook of Disaster Research*, edited by Havidan Rodriguez, Enrico L. Quarantelli, Russell R. Dynes. New York: Springer.

Stovall, Shane. 2007. Public-Private Partnerships in the 21st Century. Available at http://www.iaem.com/documents/PPPinthe21stCentury.pdf, last accessed March 31, 2016.

Sylves, Richard. 2015. *Disaster Policy & Politics: Emergency Management and Homeland Security, 2nd Edition*. Washington, D.C.: CQ Press.

Sylves, Richard and Zoltan L. Buras. 2009. Presidential Disaster Declarations Decisions, 1953–2003: What Influences Odds of Approval? *State and Local Government Review* 39(1): 3–15.

The White House. 2016. The Cabinet. Available at https://www.whitehouse.gov/administration/cabinet, last accessed March 26, 2016.

U.S. Chamber of Commerce. 2009. Business Leaders Call for Change in Disaster Response Strategies. Available at http://www.uschamber.com/press/releases/2009/january/business-leaders-call-change-disaster-response-strategies, last accessed March 2, 2011.

U.S. Chamber of Commerce. 2011. U.S. Chamber Hails Success of Public-Private Partnerships in Cybersecurity Report. Available at https://www.uschamber.com/press-release/us-chamber-hails-success-public-private-partnerships-cybersecurity-report, last assessed April 4, 2016.

U.S. Chamber of Commerce. 2014. 4th National Conference on Building Resilience through Public-Private Partnerships. Available at https://www.uschamber.com/event/4th-national-conference-building-resilience-through-public-private-partnerships, last accessed April 4, 2016.

U.S. Government Accountability Office. 2008. *Hurricane Katrina: Continuing Debris Removal and Disposal Issues*. Washington, D.C.: U.S. Government Accountability Office.

Veysey, Sarah. 2016. Insured Losses from Natural Disasters Hit 6-year Low. Business Insurance. Available at http://www.businessinsurance.com/article/20160113/NEWS06/160119925/insured-losses-from-natural-disasters-hit-6-year-low-at-35-billion?tags=|64|76|83|302, last accessed March 27, 2016.

Waugh, William. 2005. The Disaster That Was Katrina. *Natural Hazards Observer*. Available at http://www.colorado.edu/hazards/o/archives/2005/nov05/nov05d1.html, last accessed January 25, 2011.

Waugh, William. 2006. The Political Costs of Failure in the Katrina and Rita Disasters. *The Annals of the American Academy of Political and Social Science* 604(10): 10–25.

Waugh, William and Gregory Streib. 2006. Collaboration and Leadership for Effective Emergency Management. *Public Administration Review* (December): 131–140.

Webb, Gary R., Kathleen J. Tierney, and James M. Dahlhamer. 2000. Businesses and Disasters: Empirical Patterns and Unanswered Questions. *Natural Hazards Review* 1(2): 83–90.

Webb, Gary R., Kathleen J. Tierney, and James M. Dahlhamer. 2002. Predicting Long-Term Business Recovery from Disaster: A Comparison of the Loma Prieta Earthquake and Hurricane Andrew. *Environmental Hazards* 4: 45–58.

Wendling, Cécile. 2010. Explaining the Emergence of Different European Union Crisis and Emergency Management Structures. *Journal of Contingencies and Crisis Management* 18(2): 74–82.

Wright, James D., Peter H. Rossi, Sonia R. Wright, and Eleanor Weber-Burdin. 1979. *After the Clean-Up: Long-Range Effects of Natural Disasters*. Beverly Hills, CA: Sage.

Chapter **11**

International and Humanitarian Disaster Relief

Objectives

Upon completing this chapter, readers will be able to:

- Define culture and understand why cultural sensitivity increases the effectiveness of international disaster relief.
- Identify the key components of culture including language, values, symbols, and norms.
- Illustrate the different kinds of disasters that affect international sectors, such as pandemics, famines, droughts, or conflicts.
- Understand the differences between disasters of consensus and disasters of conflict.
- Distinguish between culturally relevant and ethnocentric ways of delivering aid.
- Walk through the basic steps of humanitarian logistic delivery.
- Identify and offer alternatives to inappropriate relief efforts.
- Discuss ways to empower local stakeholders in an international relief effort.
- Understand and describe best practices for refugee assistance and resettlement.

Key Terms

- Cultural diversity
- Cultural relativity
- DART (USAID Disaster Assistance Response Team)
- Empowerment
- Ethnic community-based organization (ECBO)
- Ethnocentrism
- FEDs (famines, epidemics, drought)
- Humanitarian logistics
- Hyogo framework
- Integration
- Norms
- Refugee
- Refugee resettlement
- Sendai framework
- Smart compassion
- Strength based approach
- Values

11.1 Introduction

In this chapter, we will discuss how disasters that occur outside of the United States may differ substantially from those we experience inside this nation. While familiar threats exist such as earthquakes, volcanoes, or floods, different kinds of threats also appear. One example comes from the acronym "FEDs" that stands for famines, epidemics, and droughts. While the United States is not immune from such threats, other nations may fare significantly worse. The 2014 Ebola outbreak in West Africa serves as one example, with thousands dying compared to one death in the United States. Conflicts also represent a different kind of disaster, one that can generate massive humanitarian crises as people flee war or genocide. Disaster relief organizations play an important role in such events.

How people and organizations offer aid matters. Sending high heels to Mexico after an earthquake does not work. Neither does sending the wrong kind of boat to Indian fishermen after a tsunami. Relief flights may clog small airports in developing nations, while medical teams and nutritional supplies are diverted. Used clothing and expired medications will pile up and impede distribution points. All of these and similar situations have happened, over and over, in previous disasters. We must be sure to offer aid tied to what is needed and will be used, rather than what may be inappropriate or thwart aid delivery systems. To be effective, international and humanitarian aid must be organized, partnered, and appropriate to relieve suffering.

The 2015 Nepal earthquake serves as one recent example. A 7.8 magnitude earthquake devastated the nation on April 25, occurring about 77 kilometers from Nepal's capital of Kathmandu. Initial rescue and media efforts focused on the capital where significant damage occurred—while more remote villages lay flattened with relief organizations unable to reach them via devastated roadways. Close to 8000 people perished with an additional 16,392 suffering from various injuries. The earthquake devastated one quarter of a million homes with an equal number sustaining damage. Tribhuvan International Airport in Kathmandu represented the only way to enter Nepal by air. Its small size limited the number of aircraft that could land, unload, refuel, and depart. On May 5, The USAID Disaster Assistance Response Team (DART) was supplemented with the U.S. Air Force Contingency Response Group (CRG) and the Nepal government to manage airport operations (see Photo 11.1).

A similar situation occurred in 2010 when Haiti suffered a massive earthquake. Losing nearly 300,000 people in the event, Haiti's capital city of Port-au-Prince sustained damage to its waterport and airports. Debris had to be removed from the harbor and docks repaired before water-based crafts could deliver aid or hospital ships could arrive. The United States provided support at the beleaguered airport, which had to divert arriving relief flights to the Dominican Republic or back to the U.S. Traffic on roads leading across the border between Haiti and the Dominican Republic backed up due to rubble and traffic congestion.

Another important difference also matters. Quarantelli (1986) first distinguished between two kinds of disasters, which he termed disasters of consensus and disasters of conflict. To this point in the present chapter and throughout much of the book, we have discussed disasters of consensus—including natural disasters like earthquakes or wildfires. Such events typically elicit worldwide compassion and generosity, in a massive and collective effort to provide relief.

PHOTO 11.1 USAID Disaster Assistance Response Team (DART) lands in Nepal to help with the 2015 earthquake. (Courtesy of USAID /Natalie Hawwa.)

Disasters of conflict may be more challenging to distinguish clearly. Some technological events, such as the Bhopal chemical spill in India (1984), occurred because of human negligence. While clearly a disaster, conflict understandably erupted around the event as survivors and officials sought compensation and culpable parties. Similarly, terrorism represents a disaster of conflict where the intentional act is designed to cause great harm in support of a particular cause or ideology. Recent attacks on the Westgate Mall in Nairobi, the airport and subway in Brussels, and a park in Pakistan caused horrendous loss of life, psychological trauma, devastating injuries, and economic losses.

Nonetheless, both types of disasters require similar kinds of organizational responses to alleviate human suffering (see Box 11.1 and Figure 11.1). To broaden our understanding of the range of disasters that require international humanitarian relief, this chapter includes content on what we can do to help those affected by conflicts of various sorts with a particular emphasis on refugees. This section is written by Dr. Jennifer Mincin, a scholar with significant experience in both disasters and international humanitarian relief and refugee resettlement.

BOX 11.1   UNITED NATIONS AID DELIVERY

The United Nations has organized what it calls "clusters" to deliver aid effectively (see Figure 11.1). A cluster is a collection of humanitarian organizations that works on a particular area of concern under the U.N. Office for the Coordination of Humanitarian Affairs (OCHA). Clusters, not unlike the U.S. based Emergency Support Function approach include:

- Emergency shelter
- Camp management and coordination
- Health
- Protection
- Food security
- Emergency telecommunication
- Early recovery
- Education
- Sanitation, water and hygiene
- Logistics
- Nutrition

Similar to the ESF structure you are familiar with from previous chapters, each cluster has a coordinating agency. Health, for example, is coordinated through the World Health Organization (WHO). Sanitation, water, and hygiene is managed by UNICEF which also handles nutrition. In disaster sites, a Humanitarian Coordinator (HC) leads operations designed to be "principled, timely, effective and efficient" (see OCHA, n.d.). Coordination is considered "vital" when a disaster occurs.

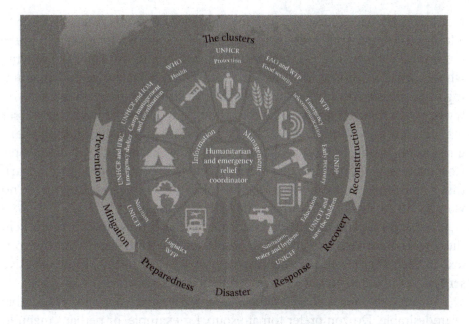

FIGURE 11.1   The United Nations cluster approach to disaster management.

In summary, to deliver international and humanitarian aid more effectively, those who seek to help must learn about the challenges of disasters along with how to work with other cultures, governments, and partnerships to deliver appropriate aid when disasters occur.

11.2 Best Practices for Working Internationally

When people get hurt, we certainly want to help. Providing help may be particularly challenging, though, across national borders and in cultures that differ from our own. In this section, we read about how to work within a diverse set of cultures. Sections that follow address inappropriate relief efforts as well as best practices for relief efforts.

11.2.1 Cultural Understanding and Awareness

To work effectively in other cultures, you have to know that culture—otherwise relief efforts may not work or could go awry. Culture is defined as a design for living that influences how and where people live, work, and interact. Culture includes language, symbols, values, and norms that people share. To start, the way people interact verbally and nonverbally represent the core of a culture's language system. We may bow our head when meeting an elder or shake their hand (or not), depending on what cultural interaction requires. Languages may also use formal words to address someone or to adopt a more informal way of interacting. In Spanish, for example, there are several ways to address people both formally and informally. Knowing which form to use is critical to your success when meeting and interacting in a Spanish-speaking region. People also simply appreciate it when you try to speak their language. Be aware though, that formal language classes may not teach local expressions so it's important to consider taking a language class locally. In Costa Rica, for example, you wouldn't just call people Costariqueños—you would call them "Ticos." And you would quickly learn that a common expression is *no te preocupes* that translates roughly to "no worries" in Australia or "chill" in the United States.

When people suffer from disaster, one of the things we can do to help them feel comforted is to approach and interact with them within the context of their own, familiar and comfortable ways of living. To be effective servants of disaster survivors, we need to be students of their cultures.

To illustrate, culturally based values characterize what is considered desirable or undesirable. Do you prefer tomato soup, for example, or perhaps menudo which is made from the stomach lining of sheep or cattle? Is it appropriate for you to wear shorts and a tank top or does your culture consider it appropriate to be more modest? Values also influence norms, which are defined as behavioral guidelines or rules for how to act (Sumner 1906). Norms include mores (pronounced more-ays) which represent critically important behaviors such as protection of women and children from human trafficking after a disaster (Phillips and Jenkins 2016; Rees, Pittaway, and Bartolomei 2005). Folkways are another type of norm and serve as behavioral guidelines like customs. How we shake hands or make eye contact stems from our folkways. Do you squeeze someone's hand or do a fist bump? Do you look someone directly in the eye or just past their earlobe? Knowing these folkways will enable you to succeed as they demonstrate respect for other cultures. Not knowing these folkways, or choosing not to demonstrate respect, can result in social distancing, ostracism, or denial of entry to an area in need.

Think also, that these examples demonstrate ways to personally interact. Culturally based awareness means understanding how a design for living influences organizations, the way they are arranged, and how people behave inside those organizations. Even the way in which people choose to arrange a room, auditorium, or grassy meadow for a meeting is culturally influenced. Rules, regulations, and policies are all influenced by culture, so "doing business" in another country, including disaster relief, means understanding how and why people do things the way they do and respectfully working within their culture.

Two behaviors represent divergent paths that an individual or their organization can take when working in another culture. These two concepts, ethnocentrism and cultural relativism, depict how people may interact in other cultures. An ethnocentric response situates your behavior within your own cultural beliefs and values. When we act out of an ethnocentric frame of reference, we make judgments about other people's cultural values and norms. By turning up our nose at other people's cuisine, we offend them and implicitly tell them we do not value them, their food, or their hospitality. In many cultures, food is the way that people get to know us. If you don't like grasscutter, for example, you might want to re-think where you do your volunteer or humanitarian work—or perhaps you could just learn to enjoy eating rats. Ethnocentrism also influences the way that we understand and use time. In the United States, people cram activities into a long, busy day of work. In other nations, though, time is spent interacting with others or addressing priorities in a way different from our own. In 2016, Spain began to discuss altering the work day to eliminate the afternoon siesta. Such a change would mean ending the work day around 6 rather than later in the evening, altering a tradition in place for centuries. The siesta tradition existed to deal with afternoon temperatures, but counter arguments say that eliminating the siesta might increase family time. In past disasters, people and organizations have attempted to enter disaster zones using *ethnocentric* assumptions about what they should do, where they should operate, and how they should deliver aid. This usually does not work. Countries that use siestas, for example, might be puzzling to others who work intense days with few breaks.

Indeed, behaving in nonethnocentric ways can facilitate disaster relief. As an example, survivors may not use donated clothing because it is not culturally appropriate, because religious beliefs require other clothing, or because the local climate requires other clothing for the work they have to do. Bhutan, for example, has embraced traditional clothing to symbolize their relationship to their culture. Bhutanese men wear the "gho" rather than more Western attire, in a deliberate attempt to hang on to traditional culture. Muslims may opt for a traditional shalwar qamiz, which is worn by both men and women out of religious beliefs tied to modesty. Indeed, personal appearance is tied to one's way of living. Amish men shave their beards in a particular fashion. Hassidic Jews wear sidelocks (called payot or peyes) based on commands from the Torah.

Working from a *culturally relative* perspective means that you have done your homework to understand what will work in the local disaster. Doing so starts from first researching the culture in which you will work or volunteer. Such an understanding emanates most effectively from people who grew up in that culture. You may find them in your own community, perhaps studying at the local university, or within a community organization. It is also wise to take classes in both language and culture to enhance your ability to enter another country in a manner that is culturally relative and likely to influence your success. Seek out electives in the social sciences, particularly sociology and anthropology, to deepen your understanding of other cultures.

11.2.2 Inappropriate Relief Efforts

When people are hurt and need the right things at the right time in the right place—we need to do the right thing. Though our hearts go out to those affected by disaster, we should stop first and think: what would be the most helpful? On what am I basing this assumption? By now, you know that many times the wrong kinds of donations are gathered up and sent to a disaster site, often causing unanticipated problems. Volunteers and staff must redirect their time to manage overwhelming and unnecessary items. Though people intend well, sending personal prescriptions, inappropriate clothing for a climate or culture, or an item that works in your locale can hinder response efforts. Think also, about the challenges of actually getting items to a damaged location. Earthquakes damage runways and roads and tumble debris along delivery routes. Flooding takes out bridges. Tsunamis destroy port facilities. Volcanoes clog airspaces with ash. The disaster itself may have made it extremely difficult to send and deliver relief items (see Box 11.2).

11.2.3 Appropriate Relief Efforts

After the 2010 Haiti earthquake, the U.S. Agency for International Development (USAID) issued a set of recommendations to guide humanitarian contributions (www.usaid.gov). Summarized, they include these principles:

- Listen to what locals are asking for. Organizations should be careful to send exactly what is needed and be able to deliver the requested item in coordination with area resources and transportation arteries.
- Encourage purchase of local commodities to restart the economy and encourage recovery.
- Delivered relief supplies should be appropriate for local conditions including climate, culture, and languages. When needed, technical training should be offered. Provided items should be sustainable through local supplies or sustained delivery of needed components.

After the 2015 Nepal earthquake, these same principles applied. In addition, USAID recommended making a monetary donation to a reputable humanitarian organization. By practicing "smart compassion" donors can generate more effective relief. USAID's Center for International Disaster Information (USAID/CIDI) provides an online toolkit toward such ends (see resources section). Also within USAID, the Office of Foreign Disaster Assistance (OFDA) sends experts and aid to over 50 countries annually (USAID 2016, see Photo 11.2). OFDA's DARTs rely on technical experts and caches of emergency relief supplies throughout the world to respond quickly and appropriately. In recent years, USAID DARTs have worked on

BOX 11.2 HUMANITARIAN LOGISTICS

Delivering aid to disaster-stricken countries can be particularly challenging. The 1985 Mexico City earthquake damaged the main airport as did the 2010 Haiti earthquake and the 2015 Nepal earthquake. In addition to the airport, Haiti's capital of Port-au-Prince also sustained damage. Travel into Haiti from the adjacent nation of the Dominican Republic became difficult as relief convoys clogged roads. Overland routes of Nepal became problematic as landslides blocked passage. When the airports opened, donations piled up as those managing deliveries faced considerable challenges transferring material goods to areas in need. Imagine the challenges of multiple sites, which is what happened in 2004 when a tsunami damaged thirteen nations spread over a massive area (Kovács and Spens 2007).

The problem of humanitarian logistics is therefore a well-known one, made even more difficult because of the inundation of inappropriate donations. One strategy that is used is sorting materials into High Priority (HP) items that survivors can use right away. Other materials fall into Low Priority (LP) items that could be used during the recovery if storage exists—or into the Non Priority (NP) items that are essentially useless (Holguín-Veras, et al. 2012). The essential problem is one called material convergence, a problem discussed in previous chapters. What happens is that well-meaning people send unnecessary items and cause congestion that those in the affected areas have to deal with (Holguín-Veras et al. 2014). The delivery of donated goods is not the only challenge—as many affected nations will not have experienced personnel to manage the inundation or warehouses in which to store LP items or the infrastructure to transport material goods (Kovács and Spens 2009).

The United Nations cluster approach mentioned in this chapter includes logistics support under the Office for the Coordination of Humanitarian Affairs. The logistics cluster includes:

- Prepositioned equipment between coordinating agencies and the private sector.
- Managing relationships between agencies including airport-handling teams.
- Providing nonroof items appropriately including materials from the United Nations Humanitarian Response Depot.
- Working in advance to deal with customs/entry of goods issues.
- Mapping and managing emergency stockpiles worldwide.

The U.N. Humanitarian Response Depot is located in six sites: Italy, United Arab Emirates, Ghana, Panama, Malaysia, and Spain. The purpose is to enable agencies involved in emergency relief to access and rapidly deliver

(*Continued*)

BOX 11.2 (*Continued*)   HUMANITARIAN LOGISTICS

necessary items by basing the depots worldwide and close to airports and waterways (see below):

Above image: available from visit http://www.unhrd.org/page/our-depots), last accessed April 19, 2016.

For more, visit OCHA Logistics Support at http://www.unocha.org/what-we-do/coordination-tools/logistics-support/overview, last accessed April 19, 2016. The U.N. Humanitarian Response Depot can be viewed at http://www.unhrd.org/, last accessed April 19, 2016.

PHOTO 11.2   USAID efforts in Nepal with Save the Children, May 2015. (Photo courtesy of USAID.)

the Syrian conflict and refugee problem, Ebola, the Nepal earthquake, a typhoon in Burma and more.

Appropriate relief guidelines ensure that staff and volunteers in the damaged area will receive exactly what they need. More importantly, the influx of contributions will not undermine the locally struggling economy. The contributions will also be understandable as they will be written in languages or symbols that are understood by all. After the Haiti earthquake, for example, starving residents threw away nutrition bars stamped with the current date. Survivors incorrectly assumed that the bars had expired and feared they might be harmful. Humanitarian aid must be effective, rather than mire relief efforts or extend suffering.

BOX 11.3   SMART COMPASSION

Repurposing Ideas

- Hold a garage sale or bazaar and donate the proceeds.
- Donate items to local charities and shelters.
- Save inappropriate donations to use in a presentation or campaign for the right donations.
- Donate bottled water to shelters and sports teams.
- Auction items online.
- Host a lottery or silent auction of the items and donate the proceeds.
- Offer a benefit dinner from canned goods and donate the financial proceeds.
- Give donated toys to a local day care or recreational facility.
- Turn empty bottles into bird feeders or plastic bottle terrariums.
- Use old clothes for a relief car wash and donate money raised.

Fundraising Ideas

- Hold a fundraising walk or run.
- Host a rummage sale.
- Create a cultural event and charge admission.
- Sell t-shirts and send the money to a worthwhile organization.
- Show a movie at a local venue or your own backyard and request donations to view it.
- Start a cake walk and auction off the goodies.
- Sponsor an international food festival and donate proceeds.
- Launch a card game tournament or a dance and music festival.
- Put people into pretend jail and make them raise money to get out.
- Have a local restaurant agree to donate a percentage of revenue on a given night.
- Offer a pancake or breakfast event and sell tickets.

Source: USAID CIDI

Typically, money is the best contribution. Money can be used locally to help the economy and buy exactly what is needed (for ideas, see Box 11.3). Donated funds can be transferred electronically and instantaneously. Longer-term recovery efforts may allow you and relief organizations to expand beyond financial contributions. Should the above conditions be met, USAID recommends that material relief should be managed through these conditions (www.usaid.gov):

- Send exactly what is desired with the requested characteristics, quality, and quantities.
- Package and label items specifically for the entry requirements in a particular location.

- Be sure that advance and confirmed transport and delivery plans are in place.
- Be sure the receiving organization has volunteers available to offload, sort, organize, and deliver donations.

Outsiders who use an ethnocentric perspective assume their technologies and solutions will solve problems. Such an approach does not work and "greater attention needs to be paid to non-Western knowledge and local environmental practices" (Bankoff 2004, p. 35).

Another common problem that undermines humanitarian aid and post-disaster programs comes from a lack of adequate planning. One of the most significant problems concerns poor conceptualization of projects, a problem that usually stems from lack of involving local people. Ineffective programs also bring in outsiders to "fix" things rather than provide local training, jobs and loans. But developing capacity so must be done carefully and thoughtfully. Throwing money at people without a process and program in place will not be effective. Cuny (1983, 1994) identified four common program models that operate in disaster relief situations. The "quick and dirty" program sends relief materials with minimal input from locals. The "firefighting" model puts out the fire but does not have a long-term impact on future events. The "development through disaster" model uses the post-disaster time period to integrate development opportunities. But the final option that Cuny terms "planting the seed" offers disaster relief through a slower, development-focused process that is highly participatory.

11.2.4 Empowering Locals

Outsiders tend to assume that, particularly in international situations, people require extensive aid. In most situations, local residents can provide useful guidance for what is helpful, where to get it, and the contexts in which relief supplies can or cannot be delivered. Local residents know and understand their own cultures, the local language, and the customs that are important and where the impacts are the most significant. After a cyclone, for example, road signs may be down and transportation arteries disrupted. We need local residents to navigate the area, find alternate routes, and identify locations in need.

Local residents also understand how people need to interact, connect, and communicate. In temporary shelters, such as huts or tents, it is more difficult to move what is already set up—usually in sequential rows. People are generally assigned into the next available tent. Though doing so seems expedient, it can undermine important social networks and relationships that help people survive socially, psychologically and even economically. People in some South American communities, for example, are accustomed to having homes surround a central courtyard where they visit, share food and mind each other's children. Understandably, the first thing that families and friends usually do is to rearrange shelter cots into areas that allow them to talk, monitor children, and feel secure.

How can we work best with local residents (see Box 11.4)? Whether they are in our own country or in another country, we start by empowering

---

BOX 11.4   BEST PRACTICES FOR POST-DISASTER HOUSING EFFORTS IN INTERNATIONAL SETTINGS

It would seem that people would just want shelter, any shelter, after a disaster happens. And, for a while, they do. But as people transition out of temporary locations, they also want to return to familiar locales, be close to work, and live in a familiar setting. Challenges erupt with outsiders lack an understanding of the local context and local needs. Nongovernmental organizations, for example, may have received extensive amounts of funding to help those shown via worldwide media as displaced and suffering. Those same NGOs may rush in to set up alternative housing, perhaps in response to clear and present needs but also perhaps in response to donor intent. However, it is clear that for post-disaster housing to be adopted, survivors have to be part of the decision-making process (United Nations 1982; Fordham et al. 2013).

Local people know best what works for them, borne out of experience and intergenerational, often culturally and environmentally situated knowledge (Prober, O'Connor and Walsh 2011). Conversely, responding organizations have been known to not include local people even with very basic consultations over locations and housing design (Raju 2013; Davidson et al. 2007). Failure to do so can undermine people's re-integration into their social networks, their proximity to livelihoods, and their personal comfort in the new home. Culture matters as well, with some cultures prescribing the kinds of work that people do. Areas within India, for example, involve women in decision-making over local construction as part of their assigned roles, something that NGOs ignored after the 2004 tsunami. Houses also lacked adjustment to prevailing winds, creating sweltering interiors quite distinct from predisaster dwellings (Barenstein 2006). A similar outcome resulted in Sri Lanka after the same event, when donors funded homes that failed to provide familiar kitchens, bathrooms, and spaces for fishing gear (Karunsaena and Rameezdeen 2014).

The most important lesson learned, then, is to involve and empower those who will need post-disaster housing in the decision-making process. Ideally, doing so will involve stakeholders in more than just consultation but truly consider what they need economically, culturally, and environmentally. Survivors can even be involved in managing projects or in post-disaster construction as a way to help those who have lost their jobs. In short, effective post-disaster housing does not build for survivors—it builds with survivors.

people. Empowerment means that we ask people what they think is needed most, where it is needed, and the best way to deliver aid. Strategies for empowering people can include:

- Finding the leaders of predisaster organizations and convening a task force or long-term recovery committee.
- Allowing those leaders to elect a chairperson(s) they know and trust.
- Paying these leaders for their time because they may well have been affected by the disaster too.
- Enabling local leadership with technologies that enhance communication with the outside.
- Holding meetings in the local language.
- Honoring local customs such as how to structure a meeting, what type of organization works best, and how local leaders prefer to interact. A top down structure may not be as effective as a collaborative, consensus-building model, or a structure consistent with the local culture and context.
- Insuring that people have a voice at planning, response, and recovery meetings. This is particularly important for under-represented groups within the affected area particularly women, racial and ethnic minorities, the elderly, and people with disabilities.
- Turning off your personal microphone so that locals have a chance to speak or sign.

In *Working with Women at Risk*, Elaine Enarson et al. (2003), developed a workbook useful beyond its emphasis on women. The workbook (in English or Spanish) walks a local working group through identifying local hazards. In an example of how important local knowledge is, participants at one workshop discovered that a previously hidden hazard in the Dominican Republic came from deadly electrical power surges in local kitchens. As a local effort designed to identify risks and provide solutions, the power surge issue came to the forefront because local women interviewed local women.

Empowering local residents means that local knowledge rises up and influences relief and recovery efforts. By reaching out to and empowering local residents, it is possible to identify exactly what is needed and to avoid inappropriate contributions. Less time is wasted. More people are helped. Empowering locals also makes your work or volunteering more effective.

Whether compelled to migrate by natural disaster or human means, people who leave regions devastated by drought or conflict require similar kinds of support. We now turn to this aspect of international humanitarian relief.

11.3 Best Practices for Refugee Resettlement Services (Dr. Jenny Mincin)

Refugees have been forced out of their homes, communities, and countries because of significant threat to their lives. They often have fled with little more than the clothes on their backs and what they could carry in bags. Within the refugee population, certain people may be especially vulnerable. These include women and girls (whom are often subjected to gender-based violence and denied education in certain cultures and contexts), people with disabilities including physical and mental disabilities (who are often stigmatized and "forgotten"), children and youth (as they will go through major transitions as they start school in a new country and can be at an increased risk for teasing and bullying) and LGBTQ populations (who may have their lives threatened if "found out"). There should be services to specifically address the needs of the most vulnerable populations as they slowly integrate and build a new life. Creating safe havens for women and girls who have had to endure violence, offering programs to refugee youth to build confidence and thwart the potential of getting involved with gangs, and empowering refugees with disabilities to learn English and gain employment will enable all refugees to increase wellbeing and integration. It is important to recognize the most vulnerable refugees and have staff that have expertise in these issues and programs that target these special needs.

Currently, some countries accept refugees and provide services to them including the United States as well as Canada, Australia, Germany, and other European countries. Of these countries, the United States is a leader in that it accepts more refugees than any other country offering official resettlement programs (Patrick 2004). The goal of refugee resettlement, regardless of which country a refugee goes, is self-sufficiency. Self-sufficiency can include early and long-term employment, financial understanding (such as knowing financial management), the ability to advocate for oneself, self-reliance, independence from government assistance, health and wellness, and services for children and youth, women and girls (Mincin 2012).

This section briefly outlines examples of best practices for refugee resettlement. Best practices include: core, or basic, initial services; early and long-term employment; language proficiency; health and mental health services; meeting the needs of the most vulnerable refugees; and integration. In addition, this section discusses the strength-based approach to refugee resettlement and the importance of program evaluation.

Key components to refugee resettlement incorporate core services such as safe and decent housing, food, general case management services, access to initial health screens, basic employment, and English language services. These services are generally offered in most programs, though programs vary greatly from county to country. Regardless, they are recognized as necessary, basic services to any refugee arriving in their new homeland and community. These are considered basic and immediate services, not long-term services. It is important to note that a goal of refugee resettlement is integration into the new country and community the refugee has newly arrived. The core services are meant to provide a "soft landing," but practitioners working with refugees should also engage in longer-term services.

In order for refugees to attain basic self-sufficiency, early employment is critical. While some practitioners know this to be true, employment in and of itself can be a positive force in a person's general mental and physical well-being. Studies have shown that prolonged periods of time without employment can lead to depression, anxiety, and diminished physical health, including an increase in alcohol/substance abuse, diabetes, and heart problems (Bartley 1994; ISED 2007). One recent study that examined the effects of employment on refugees and immigrants indicated similar findings: employment can assist refugees and immigrants with community integration, enhance English-language capacity, and have a positive effect on mental and physical health (Codell et al. 2011; Potocky-Tripodi 2007; Yakushko et al. 2008).

11.3.1 Employment

Employment plays an important role in an individual's sense of well-being, security, and self-determination (Akabas and Kurzman 2005; Carreon, 2011). One main aspect to being employed as a refugee is English-language proficiency (Carreon 2011; Levinson, 2002; Pine and Drachman 2005). There is an inherent tension between the desire to work and English language acquisition. An issue for consideration is how taking a job soon after arrival sometimes does slow down English acquisition, which in turn compromises the integration process. Refugees, as individuals and as unique groups, report that they integrate at different rates based on their experiences and background. Regardless, there is little doubt that employment can boost self-esteem, create purpose, and drive hope.

Employment not only provides refugees the opportunity to feel self-reliant, but it can expedite deeper integration into the community. However, finding employment while taking ESL classes and adjusting to a new life in a new country can be daunting tasks; practitioners need to be aware of these competing priorities when working with newly arrived refugees.

11.3.2 Home-Country Language Proficiency

Whether being resettled in the United States, Australia, or Germany, it is critical that newly arrived refugees acquire the language skills of their new country they will now call home. Many programs offer language classes. While some refugees can learn English, for example, by working and integrating into the community, gaining a better command of the language of their new country is important to the longer-term success of full integration. English skills and employment are key factors to successful integration. *Integration occurs on multiple pathways* (language acquisition, economic opportunity, civic participation, citizenship, health access, housing, etc.) and involves multiple sectors of a community, such as government agencies, schools, libraries, ethnic community based organizations (ECBOs), employers, faith-based organizations, advocacy groups, health care providers, and other organizations (ISED 2011). An example can be seen within the U.S. resettlement system. Learning to speak English is the most important indicator of and basis for integration in the United States (ISED 2011). Learning English is identified with a refugees' ability to gain employment and participate in the community more fully (ISED 2011).

11.3.3 Integration

The importance of integration is considered a component of resettlement and integral to employability of refugees (HHS 2008; ORR 2008). Integration should be considered in two distinct ways: integration into the community and integration of services delivered to refugees. A main indicator that a refugee is integrated into a community is his or her ability to successfully navigate the many different and diverse systems of their new home country (Gasper 2007; McGillivray 2007; Mincin 2012; Saleebey 1996). In addition, refugees should be linked to social network supports including religious, cultural, educational, and political institutions (HHS 2008). Practitioners need to be cognizant of the types of experiences, traditions, ethnic and religious beliefs, and dimensions of who they are as individuals and a part of a community (Wurzer and Bragin 2009). This multidimensional approach still allows for the assessment and treatment of specific problems, such as depression, but allows for a more solution-oriented approach and treats the refugee as a whole person.

11.3.4 Health and Mental Health Services

Understanding the impact of health and mental health on the lives of refugees is critical to resettlement (ISED 2011). Refugees are coming from different situations; some have been languishing in camps (the Somali in Dadab refugee camp or Karen in the Thailand Camps), others are coming directly from combat zones (Iraqis, Syrians). With each circumstance from which a refugee comes, health and mental health issues may need to be addressed. Without a sense of psychological wellness and feeling healthy, it becomes very challenging to maintain employment, provide for families, function in school, and rebound from potentially significant trauma.

Medical conditions can range from chronic, such as diabetes, to life threatening, such as cancer or kidney failure. Upon arriving at their new location, each refugee should go through an initial physical health screening. In addition, refugees should be tested for communicable diseases such as tuberculosis. Certain conditions, with proper medical treatment, can significantly improve a refugee's health and overall well-being. If a refugee has diabetes, he or she may have suffered in the camps. However, with medications, changes in diet and access to education for self-improvement, diabetes can become a manageable, albeit chronic, illness that one can live with.

The mental health needs of refugees also vary and can include trauma-related symptoms that can be alleviated over time with proper support to more chronic illnesses such as depression and anxiety. Chronic mental illness can be treated with proper medications, self-help supports, and counseling. It is critical that mental health services are offered in a culturally appropriate manner and in the preferred language of the refugee. In addition, psychosocial programs, such as community gardening and youth art classes can provide healing, support, and hope as refugees embark on their new life. Service providers should build in proper health and mental health screenings and referrals into all aspects of case management.

11.3.5 Utilizing the Strengths-Based Approach to Working with Refugees

The strengths-based approach, like integration, takes the prior information a refugee brings with him or her as a part of the full intake process. Therefore, information on where the refugee has been; what he or she has been exposed to and survived, known, or understood; chronic ailments; family dimensions and dynamics; and the political and social structure of the homeland all come into relevance (Ryan et al. 2008). The strengths-based approach, or strengths perspective (Saleebey 1996) differs from a more diagnostic model and is an emerging field within the practice of social work and beyond (Mattaini and Lowery 2007). The strengths-based approach developed as a technique in working with people with severe mental health conditions and has since grown to work with other vulnerable populations such as the elderly, youth at-risk, and even communities (Saleebey 1996). It is also closely aligned with resilience, wellness, integration, and psychosocial approaches.

While practitioners should rely on evidence-based practice, there is also a balance with fully understanding the perspectives, experiences, and strengths that each individual brings to the healing process. Refugees typically have endured a lot of suffering. Understanding how they have managed to survive the suffering may give insightful clues as to how to build further resilience, to understand which evidence-based practices maybe most applicable, and to determine which programs and services may be most useful (Mincin 2012). Increasingly, the strengths-based approach (explicitly and interpretively) and psychosocial programming are being used in the refugee community (Fong 2004; Grigg-Saito et al. 2007; Halcon et al. 2007; Scheinfeld, Walla, and Langendorf 1997; Walsh 2003; Yohani 2008). Best practices are shared among professionals and advocates, as are guidance documents.

Using the strengths-based and community participation approach, Grigg-Saito et al. (2007) studied community health education among Cambodian refugees living in Lowell, MA. The study focused on health disparities, specifically diabetes and cardiovascular diseases in the Southeast Asian community. At the time of the study, Lowell had the second-largest population of Cambodian refugees who survived the genocide under the hands of the Khmer Rouge. According to the researchers: "despite the resulting needs of this refugee community, the strength and resilience evident in daily interactions and in the stories of survival and success from both Cambodian employees and program participants led to inclusion of strengths-based approaches to address health promotion in this community" (p. 416). Seven focus groups were conducted with 141 total participants. During the first phase of the study, every effort was made to understand the culture, experiences, attitudes, and religion of Cambodians (Grigg-Saito et al. 2007). Eighty-five percent of people aged 50 and older in the community were Buddhists and used a nearby community temple. In addition, many Cambodians in Lowell did not have high rates of literacy in any language since the Khmer Rouge had closed schools. Outreach needed to consist of door-to-door; peer support; Elder Council; and media, audio, and other appropriate tools. The goal of this study was to increase participation of Cambodians with cardiovascular disease and diabetes in the healthcare system: "the number of Cambodian patients accessing heath care at LCHC/Metta Health Center increased from zero in 2000 to 4,033 registered patients by the end of 2005, and the number with a primary or secondary diagnosis of diabetes grew from 23 in 2001 to 703 registered patients by the end of 2005" (p. 422). The authors of the study asserted that using a strengths-based approach in health promotion in the Cambodian refugee community was a "viable approach." In this case, including elders, community, and religious organizations, and understanding the culture and attitudes of Cambodians allowed healthcare providers and educators to understand the strengths of individuals and the community.

Finally, those involved in refugee resettlement should also take the time to study their efforts and results. A fair amount of research exists on program evaluation and its benefits for service delivery and programmatic growth (Mattaini 2007). Although many scholarly articles have noted that there are barriers to practice-based research and program evaluation such as funding, resources, and lack of agency commitment (Chen 1980; Donaldson 2007; Mattaini 2007; Weiss 1998), the benefits of integrating evaluation methods can strengthen programming and increase the potential for positive client outcomes (Wade and Neuman 2007). For example, refugee resettlement social services in the United States have gone largely unevaluated. In other countries, such as Canada and Australia, they evaluate programs on regular basis, though it varies from one place to another depending on the program model. Moving toward program evaluation and evidence-based practice can generate benefits for clients and programs. Any agency or organization providing services to refugees should incorporate basic program evaluation into key programs such as employment and self-sufficiency, integration, health, and mental health services (Mincin 2012). Ultimately, though, whether a disaster of conflict or of consensus, the goal is to reduce the overall risks that imperil people and cause suffering and displacement.

11.4 Disaster Risk Reduction

Whether a disaster of conflict or a disaster of consensus, a number of goals exist to move vulnerable people and communities toward a safer future. Since the early 1990s, efforts have been underway globally, such as the International Decade for Natural Disaster Reduction, which was followed by the International Strategy for Disaster Reduction. Such efforts have continued.

Among the more influential has been what is called the "Hyogo" Framework that arose out of a 2005 conference in Hyogo, Japan. With an eye on 2015 as a timeframe to promote more global resilience against disasters, The Hyogo Framework focused on "the substantial reduction of disaster losses, in lives and in the social, economic, and environmental assets of communities and countries" (Hyogo Framework, p. 5, see Resources Section for link). To do so, conference attendees concentrated on integrating disaster risk reduction into development policies, with an effort to reduce vulnerability in high risk areas. The full range of the life cycle of emergency management was considered as well, with efforts to focus on preparedness and mitigation across a multi-hazard context. To do so, attendees prompted actors and agencies to build capacity at the community level—the idea of empowerment so stressed in this chapter—as a way to leverage local resources and knowledge. Within that local context, diversity should be embraced and considered including gender, age, and other historic vulnerabilities. The desired outcome? A culture of prevention designed to reduce casualties and expedite recovery.

In March 2015, the Sendai Framework for Disaster Risk Reduction was adopted by United Nations Member States at the UN World Conference on Disaster Risk Reduction in Sendai, Japan (see Figure 11.2). The Sendai

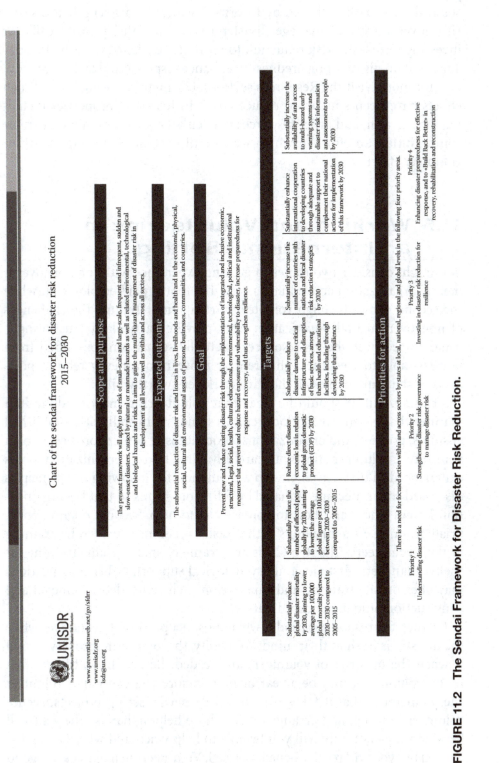

Chart of the sendai framework for disaster risk reduction 2015–2030

UNISDR
The United Nations Office for Disaster Risk Reduction

www.preventionweb.net/go/sfdrr
www.unisdr.org
isdr@un.org

Scope and purpose

The present framework will apply to the risk of small-scale and large-scale, frequent and infrequent, sudden and slow-onset disasters, caused by natural or manmade hazards as well as related environmental, technological and biological hazards and risks. It aims to guide the multi-hazard management of disaster risk in development at all levels as well as within and across all sectors.

Expected outcome

The substantial reduction of disaster risk and losses in lives, livelihoods and health and in the economic, physical, social, cultural and environmental assets of persons, businesses, communities, and countries.

Goal

Prevent new and reduce existing disaster risk through the implementation of integrated and inclusive economic, structural, legal, social, health, cultural, educational, environmental, technological, political and institutional measures that prevent and reduce hazard exposure and vulnerability to disaster, increase preparedness for response and recovery, and thus strengthen resilience.

Targets

Substantially reduce global disaster mortality by 2030, aiming to lower the average per 100,000 global mortality between 2020–2030 compared to 2005–2015	Substantially reduce the number of affected people globally by 2030, aiming to lower the average global figure per 100,000 between 2020–2030 compared to 2005–2015	Reduce direct disaster economic loss in relation to global gross domestic product (GDP) by 2030	Substantially reduce disaster damage to critical infrastructure and disruption of basic services, among them health and educational facilities, including through developing their resilience by 2030	Substantially increase the number of countries with national and local disaster risk reduction strategies by 2020	Substantially enhance international cooperation to developing countries through adequate and sustainable support to complement their national actions for implementation of this framework by 2030

Substantially increase the availability of and access to multi-hazard early warning systems and disaster risk information and assessments to people by 2030

Priorities for action

There is a need for focused action within and across sectors by states at local, national, regional and global levels in the following four priority areas.

Priority 1	Priority 2	Priority 3	Priority 4
Understanding disaster risk	Strengthening disaster risk governance to manage disaster risk	Investing in disaster risk reduction for resilience	Enhancing disaster preparedness for effective response, and to «Build Back Better» in recovery, rehabilitation and reconstruction

FIGURE 11.2   The Sendai Framework for Disaster Risk Reduction.

Framework is designed to move those involved through the year 2030. Four priorities for action undergird efforts to reduce risks. Priority 1 is to understand disaster risk, followed by Priority 2 which is to strengthen disaster risk governance and manage disaster risks. The third priority calls for investing in disaster risk reduction to promote resilience with the Priority 4 focused on disaster preparedness to enhance response and facilitate recovery (for more, visit the Resources section). Ultimately, the goals of all such efforts have been similar: to reduce losses in lives and properties including jobs, health, and other resources particularly within highly vulnerable communities, an effort in which we can all participate through work or volunteer effort.

11.5 Working and Volunteering in an International Setting

You might consider two routes to gaining experience within a nongovernmental organization active in disasters. The first is paid employment while the second comes through volunteer participation. Though the challenges of nongovernmental organization work may be particularly frustrating—usually need overwhelms resources—actually seeing someone lifted from poverty, able to feed their children, or move into a newly rebuilt, post-disaster structure makes all the hard work very worthwhile.

At this point, it should be clear that volunteering must be done in a manner that is sensitive to local cultures and fits in well with established customs, policies, and organizational procedures. It is therefore best to plan your future volunteer efforts out carefully. First, find an organization that is experienced in disaster relief with a reputation for following the principles discussed so far. Become affiliated by filling out forms so that the organization knows where and how to contact you to help. Second, obtain appropriate training. Organizations with disaster missions usually offer training to their volunteers. The Red Cross, for example, offers specific training for shelter managers, first aid, and psychological support. Other organizations may offer on-site training and supervision such as for debris removal and construction or logistics coordination.

Further, the response period is when most people want to volunteer while the disaster is fresh in their minds. In reality, the long-term recovery period is when the majority of volunteers are needed. Be patient and know that if you volunteer it may be a year or more before you can join a volunteer site. Remember that it takes time to assess needs, set up projects, secure volunteer housing, and arrange to feed those helping hands. The wait will be worth it as not only will you be able to help when and where it is most needed but you will receive benefits as well. Volunteering makes us feel good about ourselves while enriching our understanding of the people who we serve (Thoits and Hewitt 2001).

Another route might be to secure an internship that can be volunteer or paid. The USAID, for example, provides both (see resources section). Work for interns can vary from conducting research and drafting documents to supporting meetings, participating in discussions with various federal agencies, or helping with information about USAID.

International career positions can vary widely from straightforward emergency response operations to the behind-the-scenes work of finances or human resources. USAID, for example, hires foreign service officers who respond to crises and humanitarian emergencies. Their work may include some of the more routine work of developing programs, creating partnerships, and engaging in planning efforts—and then transition swiftly into emergency work when disasters occur.

A good example of the diversity in emergency management jobs comes from the International Rescue Committee. Their emergency response team may include those tasked with ensuring safe water and food supplies, sanitation, medical care, or logistics. Depending on the circumstances, a staff member might work on children's issues or with those affected by sexual violence. Clearly, combining a major in emergency management with a minor in social services, psychology, sociology, gerontology, health care and other areas could make a job applicant more attractive to a prospective employer.

Other organizations, like UNICEF or OXFAM, may hire people to work full-time or for disaster-specific events. The United Nations (see link in resources section) includes an array of options to consider. They advertise for logisticians, for example, to manage deployment sites. Humanitarian workers coordinate critical, life-saving relief operations when disaster strikes. Others are needed in public information, conference management, internal security and safety, and with technology, economic development, and legal assistance—yes, all of these areas may be needed during humanitarian crises. Your future career in emergency management at the international level has a broad set of opportunities.

Summary

Cultural sensitivity is the most important principle to lay behind international humanitarian work. Without a culturally relative framework, those trying to help may find themselves ineffective, frustrated, and offensive. Understanding another people's design for living, their culture, leads to more appropriate relief efforts. One of the more important strategies is to work with locally affected people rather than on their behalf. Empowering those who have been affected to offer recommendations and participate in their own recovery is considered a best practice. Disasters of consensus (for example, most natural disasters) or disasters of conflict (genocide, terrorism) can be addressed similarly in terms of how we respond to and set up aid for those affected. A higher degree of programming, though, may be needed for refugees driven out of familiar contexts, away from livelihoods, traumatized by events, and distanced from their social networks.

When a refugee arrives in a new country, providing the necessary services to assist the refugee in settling, gaining employment, and ultimately integrating into the community will make for an overall more positive experience as they become fully participating citizens. In this chapter, we briefly discussed some key approaches to both services as well as practice-based models to incorporate into resettlement services. Tangible services that can go a long way toward creating a sense of security and wellbeing include employment, mental health, and psychosocial support for adults and children, targeted services for more vulnerable refugees (such as women and girls, refugees with disabilities, or refugees who have serious medical conditions), secure and safe housing, and education (for adults and children and youth). However, ensuring the refugee is a part of their own healing, integration, and resettlement is arguably the most important component.

As discussed, refugees taking ownership of their own resettlement process, building upon the resilient skills they already have, and incorporating their hopes and dreams will empower them in real and tangible ways and assist them in building more skills to cope with and navigate their new life. Healing from trauma involves active participation from the client. Refugee resettlement is no exception. Refugees bring a wealth of knowledge to their own process and, indeed, to the community they now call home. Refugees become engaged, functioning, and positive forces in communities brings richness in culture, perspectives, and strong work ethic.

Discussion Questions

1. Distinguish between disasters of conflict and disasters of consensus. Do you see differences in how organizations respond to each?

2. Define and give examples of cultural relativism and ethnocentrism from your own culture. How have others misunderstood or judged your way of living? How has that impacted how people think of people like you and your culture?

3. If you were going to organize a donations drive for an international area impacted by a disaster, how would you do that? What are the evidence-based best practices for doing so?

4. What key programs and efforts should be in place to receive and support refugees from disasters of conflict or disasters of consensus?

5. Organize a panel in your class and trace the history of international efforts to reduce risks and promote resilience. Why is there such a focus on development? Research the ideas of Hyogo and Sendai further (see resources section) and find out more to share on your panel.

Resources

- USAID CIDI Toolkit for Smart Compassion donations http://www.cidi.org/media/usaid-cidi-toolkit/#.VVJMFMtOUdU, last accessed May 12, 2015.
- Bragin (2005) developed a model, the Community Participatory Evaluation Tool (CPET, see resources section for a link), to assist humanitarian organizations on providing services specifically for children. A practical guide, the CPET espouses a holistic system that uses the evaluation tool within the individual, family and community. Community engagement and partnerships with local communities groups also are supported by Bragin, Prabhu, and Czarnocha (2007). You can download the Community Participatory Evaluation Tool (CPET) here: http://www.ourmediaourselves.com/archives/31pdf/03_24%20Bragin%20.pdf
- The Hyogo Framework can be viewed at http://www.unisdr.org/2005/wcdr/intergover/official-doc/L-docs/Hyogo-framework-for-action-english.pdf, last accessed April 19, 2016.
- The Sendai Framework for Disaster Risk Reduction can be viewed at http://www.preventionweb.net/files/44983_sendaiframeworksimplifiedchart.pdf, last accessed April 19, 2016.
- USAID student internships can be viewed at https://www.usaid.gov/work-usaid/careers/student-internships), last accessed April 20, 2016.
- The United Nations provides information on careers at https://careers.un.org/lbw/Home.aspx, last accessed April 20, 2016.

Co-Author Biography

Dr. Jennifer (Jenny) Mincin has over 20 years of experience in the government, nongovernmental, and academic sectors both nationally and internationally. Jenny is a specialist in disaster human services and humanitarian crisis

Dr. Jenny Mincin

work, refugees, vulnerable and special needs populations, mental health and resiliency, and community rebuilding/recovery. She has worked for the City of New York, International Rescue Committee, and the Federal Emergency Management Agency among others. Jenny is currently Assistant Professor at SUNY Empire State College in Community and Human Services. She has taught as an Adjunct Professor at Hunter College (CUNY) in the Human Rights Program and Fordham University's Center for Nonprofit Leaders. Jenny has a PhD in Social Welfare Policy and a Masters of Philosophy in Social Welfare Policy from the Graduate Center CUNY. She also has an MPA from Columbia University School of International and Public Affairs and received her BA from Barnard College/Columbia University in Religion and Environmental Science.

References and Recommended Readings

Akabas, Sheila and Paul Kurzman. 2005. *Work and the Workplace.* New York: Columbia University Press.

Bankoff, Greg. 2004. The Historical Geography of Disaster; Vulnerability and Local Knowledge. pp. 25–36 in *Mapping Vulnerability: Disasters, Development and People,* edited by G. Bankoff, G. Frerks and D. Hilhorst. Sterling, VA: Earthscan.

Barenstein, Jennifer. 2006. Challenges and Risks in Post-Tsunami Housing Reconstruction in Tamil Nadu. *Humanitarian Exchange* 33: 39–40.

Bragin, Martha. 2005. The Community Participatory Evaluation Tool for Psychosocial Programs: A Guide to Implementation. *Intervention: International Journal of Mental Health, Psychosocial Work and Counseling in Areas of Armed Conflict* 3(1): 3–24.

Bragin, Martha, Vrunda Prabhu, and Bronislaw Czarnocha. 2005. Mathematics, Psychosocial Work and Human Rights: A Unique Partnership between Technical Consultants and Community Organizers in India. Los Angeles, CA: National Child Traumatic Stress Network.

Codell, Jonathan D., Robert D. Hill, Dan J. Woltz, and Paul A. Gore, Jr. 2011. Predicting Meaningful Employment for Refugees: The Influence of Personal Characteristics and Developmental Factors on Employment Status and Hourly Wages. *International Journal of Advanced Counseling* 33: 216–224.

Cuny, Frederick. 1983. *Disasters and Development*. Dallas, TX: Intertech Press.

Cuny, Frederick and Richard B. Hill. 1999. *Famine, Conflict and Response: A Basic Guide*. West Hartford, CT: Kumarian Press.

Davidson, Colin, Cassidy Johnson, Gonzalo Lizarralde, Nese Dikmen, and Alicia Sliwinski. 2006. Truth and Myths about Community Participation in Post-Disaster Housing projects. *Habitat International* 31(1): 100–115.

Donaldson, Stewart I. 2007. *Program Theory-driven Evaluation Science: Strategies and Applications*. Mahwah, NJ: Erlbaum.

Enarson, Elaine, Lourdes Meyreles, Marta González, Betty Hearn Morrow, Audrey Mullings, and Judith Soares. 2003. *Working with Women at Risk: Practical Guidelines For Assessing Local Disaster Risk*. Miami, FL: International Hurricane Center, Florida International University. Available at http://www.ihrc.fiu.edu/lssr/working-withwomen.pdf, last accessed January 4, 2010.

Fong, Rowena. 2004. *Culturally Competent Practice with Immigrant and Refugee Children and Families*. New York: The Guildford Press.

Fordham, Maureen, William Lovekamp, Deborah S. K. Thomas, and Brenda D. Phillips. 2013. Introduction to Social Vulnerability. pp. 1–32 in *Social Vulnerability to Disasters*, 2nd edition, edited by Deborah S. K. Thomas et al. Boca Raton, FL: CRC Press.

Gasper, Des. 2007. Human Well-Being: Concepts and Conceptualizations. pp. 23–65 in *Human Well-being Concept and Measure*, edited by Mark McGillivray. Hampshire, England: Palgrave McMillian.

Grigg-Saito, Dorcas, Sheila Och, Sidney Liang, Robin Toof, and Linda Silka. 2007. Building on the Strengths of a Cambodian Refugee Community through Community-based Outreach. *Health Promotion Practice* 9(4): 415–425.

Halcón, Linda L., Cheryl L. Robertson, Karen A. Monsen, and Cindi C. Claypatch. 2007. A Theoretical Framework for Using Health Realization to Reduce Stress and Improve Coping in Refugee Communities. *Journal of Holistic Nursing* 25(3): 186–194.

Holguín-Veras, José, Miguel Jaller, Luk Van Wassenhove, Noel Pérez, and Tricia Wachtendorf. 2012. On the Unique Features of Post-disaster Humanitarian Logistics. *Journal of Operations Management* 30(7/8): 494–506.

Holguín-Veras, José, Miguel Jaller, Luk Van Wassenhove, Noel Pérez, and Tricia Wachtendorf. 2014. Material Convergence: Important and Understudied Disaster Phenomenon. *Natural Hazards Review* 15: 1–12.

Karunasena, Gayani and Raufdeen Rameezdeen. 2014. Post-Disaster Housing Reconstruction: Comparative Study of Donor vs. Owner-driven Approaches. *International Journal of Disaster Resilience in the Built Environment* 1(2): 173–191.

Kovács, Gyöngyi and Karen M. Spens. 2007. Humanitarian Logistics in Disaster Relief Operations. *International Journal of Physical Distribution and Logistics Management* 37(2): 99–114.

Kovács, Gyöngyi and Karen M. Spens. 2009. Identifying Challenges in Humanitarian Logistics. *International Journal of Physical Distribution and Logistics Management* 39(6): 506–528.

Mattaini, Mark A. and Christine Lowery. 2007. Foundations of Social Work. pp. 3–30 in *The Foundations of Social Work Practice: A Graduate Text*, 4th edition, Mark Mattani, and Christine Lowery, Washington, D.C.: NASW Press.

McGillivray, Mark. 2007. Human Well-Being: Issues, Concepts, and Measures. pp. 1–23 in *Human Well-Being Concept and Measure*, edited by Mark. McGillivray. Hampshire, England: Palgrave McMillian.

National Council on Disability. 2009. *Effective Emergency Management: Making Improvements for Communities and People with Disabilities*. Washington, D.C.: National Council on Disability.

Office for the Coordination of Humanitarian Affairs (OCHA). No date. Leadership. Available at http://www.unocha.org/what-we-do/coordination/leadership/overview, last accessed April 19, 2016.

Patrick, Erin. 2004. The U.S. Refugee Resettlement Program. *Migration Policy Institute* (MPI). Retrieved from http://www.migrationinformation.org/feature/display.cfm?ID=229, last accessed April 25, 2016.

Phillips, Brenda and Pamela Jenkins. 2016. Gender-based Violence and Disasters: South Asia in Comparative Perspective. In *Gender, Women and Disasters: Survival, Security and Development*, edited by Linda Racioppi and Swarna Prajnya. Abingdon: Routledge.

Pine, Barbara and Diane Drachman. 2005. Effective Child Welfare Practice with Immigrant and Refugee Children and Their Families. *Child Welfare League of America* 5: 537–562.

Potocky-Tripodi, Miriam. 2001. Micro and Macro Determinants of Refugee Economic Status. *Journal of Social Service Research* 27: 33–60.

Potocky-Tripodi, Miriam. 2003. Refugee Economic Adaptation: Theory, Evidence, and Implications for Policy and Practice. *Journal of Social Service Research* 30: 63–91.

Quarantelli, E. L. 1986. What should We Study? Questions and Suggestions for Researchers about the Concept of Disasters. Preliminary Paper #119, Disaster Research Center, University of Delaware. Available at http://udspace.udel.edu/handle/19716/492, last accessed April 18, 2016.

Raju, Emmanuel. 2013. Housing Reconstruction in Disaster Recovery: A Study of Fishing Communities Post-tsunami in Chennai, India. *PLOS Currents Disasters*. Available at http://currents.plos.org/disasters/article/housing-reconstruction-in-disaster-recovery-a-study-of-fishing-communities-post-tsunami-in-chennai-india/, last accessed January 5, 2006.

Rees, Susan, Eileen Pittaway, and Linda Bartolomei. 2005. Waves of Violence in Post-Tsunami Sri Lanka. *Australasian Journal of Disaster and Trauma Studies* 2. Available at http://www.massey.ac.nz/~trauma/issues/2005-2/rees.htm, last accessed February 24, 2011.

Saleebey, Dennis. 1996. The Strength Perspective in Social Work Practice: Extensions and Cautions. *Social Work* 41(3): 296–305.

Sumner, William. G. 1906. *Folkways*. New York: Ginn.

Sutton, Jeanette. 2003. A Complex Organizational Adaptation to the World Trade Center Disaster. In *Beyond September 11th*, edited by J. Monday. Available at http://www.colorado.edu/hazards/publications/sp/sp39/sept11book_ch16_sutton.pdf, last accessed December 31, 2010.

Thoits, P. and L. Hewitt. 2001. Volunteer Work and Well-Being. *Journal of Health and Social Behavior* 42(2): 115–121.

USAID. 2016. Office of U.S. Foreign Disaster Assistance. Available at https://www.usaid.gov/who-we-are/organization/bureaus/bureau-democracy-conflict-and-humanitarian-assistance/office-us, last accessed April 18, 2016.

Wade, Kathleen and Karen Neuman. 2007. Practice-Based Research: Changing the Professional Culture and Language of Social Work. *Social Work Health Care* 44(4): 49–64.

Walsh, Froma. 2003. *Normal Family Process: Growing Diversity and Growing Complexity*, 3rd edition. New York: The Guildford Press.

Weiss, Carol. H. 1998. *Evaluation*, 2nd edition. New Jersey: Prentice Hall.

Würzer, Janine and Bragin, Martha. 2009. Integrating the Psychosocial Dimension in Women's Empowerment Programming: A guide for CARE Country Offices. Vienna: CARE Austria.

Yakushko, Oksana, Megan Watson, and Sarah Thompson. 2008. Stress and Coping in the Lives of Recent Immigrants and Refugees: Considerations for Counseling. *International Journal for the Advancement of Counseling* 30(3): 167.

Yohani, Sophie. C. 2008. Creating an Ecology of Hope: Arts-Based Interventions with Refugee Children. *Child and Adolescent Social Work Journal* 25: 309–323.

Chapter **12**

The Next Generation of Emergency Managers

Objectives

Upon completing this chapter, readers should be able to:

- Discuss the future of the profession of emergency management.
- Identify personnel needs within emergency management including representation from the diverse set of people across a given nation.
- Articulate reasons for why continuing professional development is essential in this field.
- Conduct and compare institutions offering degrees in emergency management including distance education options.
- Outline and illustrate central ethical principles for the practice of emergency management.
- Know where to look for career opportunities and job openings.

Key Terms

- Certified Emergency Manager
- Discipline
- Education
- Ethics
- Glass ceiling
- LGBTQ

- Mentor
- Scholar practitioner
- Training
- Tribal management
- Whole community

12.1 Introduction

Dr. Bill Anderson, former chairman of the Disasters Roundtable of the National Academies (advisers to the nation on science, engineering, and medicine) once convened academics and practitioners to speak on "The Emergency Manager of the Future" (Hite 2003). After discussing desirable characteristics, the Disaster Roundtable summarized their recommendations for the future emergency manager as an individual:

- Capable of identifying societal trends surrounding population dynamics, organizational configurations, the social and physical environment and evolving technology.
- With a broadly-based set of knowledge across the social and physical sciences "including criminal justice, seismology, public administration, and community planning, to name a few."
- Who uses an all-hazards approach for "effective mitigation/prevention, preparedness, and response and recovery efforts."
- Who builds collaborative relationships between researchers and practitioners.
- Who integrates technology and research in the practice of emergency management.

In short, emergency management is a people profession in many ways (Drabek 1987). We have to be convincing enough so that people at risk will take action. We need to work with a wide array of partners to create effective plans. And, we need to build respect and support from many agencies and officials to succeed in a disaster and its aftermath. To do that, future emergency managers need to develop not only professional but also social skills (Drabek 1987). Indeed, networking turns out to be one of the most important skills for emergency managers, in order to generate working relationships with multiple stakeholders across a broad and diverse community. Getting to know and work with locally elected officials, who make important decisions in a disaster, will also pay off.

Networking is also important within professional emergency management circles including attending workshops, training, and conferences. Organizations such as the National Emergency Management Agency (NEMA) and the International Association of Emergency Managers (IAEM) provide opportunities to network as well as to work toward program accreditation and professional certification. Certification confirms that individuals meet specific experience, training, and educational requirements through a process of testing and documentation. As individuals and programs garner these credentials, salaries and respect for emergency managers will likely increase.

You are this next generation spoken of by the National Academies, the most respected scholarly institution in the United States. And the future for your career in this field looks promising. It is our hope that this book has inspired you to consider the profession of emergency management and to continue your journey through additional courses and degrees. This chapter provides an overview of the promising future career that you may have in emergency management and offers guidance for a diverse set of readers to pursue.

12.2 Reflecting Our Population

Historically, civil defense and emergency management has been dominated by military veterans, the majority of whom have been male. That has been changing, yet very little has been studied in terms of how historically underrepresented populations have fared in the field of emergency management. In this section, we review what is known about the routes and experiences taken by women, racial and ethnic minorities, people with disabilities, and LGBTQ populations into the profession. Encouraging a diverse workforce emerges as an important action to take so that we bring insights, expertise, and networks into the profession—to link to those historically most vulnerable in a disaster context. Through a diversified workforce, we enhance our abilities to reach out to and connect with at risk populations. Understanding the experiences that people face matters, and by diversifying the workforce we are more able to incorporate the range of potential experiences that people will go through in a disaster. Gender serves as one example, with women being at higher risk for domestic violence or human trafficking—although a major concern is certainly safety and security, women also bring valuable capacities, insights, and resources into emergency management.

12.2.1 Women

Historically, the profession of emergency management has been a male-dominated field although that has been changing dramatically, from firefighting to emergency management (see Box 12.1). One study conducted in

BOX 12.1 BREAKING THE GLASS CEILING

Barbara R. Russo, PhD, Emergency Management Coordinator and Adjunct Faculty, Public Policy Leadership, University of Mississippi.

Barbara R. Russo, PhD earned her doctorate in fire and emergency management administration from Oklahoma State University. She is a 19-year veteran of the fire service, having served as both a volunteer and career professional, most recently as the Division Chief of Training and Standards for the City of Jacksonville (NC) Fire Department (2009–2012).

In March of 2016 she was named the first Emergency Management Coordinator for the University of Mississippi. Prior to arriving at Ole Miss, she served as the head of the Fire and Emergency Services Administration bachelor's degree program at Fayetteville State University (NC) where she was also an Assistant Professor of Fire & Emergency Services Administration. She led the program to FESHE Recognition through the United States Fire Administration in the spring of 2014.

Russo became a leader in online education with the North Carolina Community College System, spearheading the development of Wayne Community College's (Goldsboro) emergency management degree program followed by the state's first online delivery of fire certification training courses through the community colleges.

It was through her doctoral research that the discovery of a glass ceiling existing at the rank of captain for women in the fire service led to her being sought out as an expert on the advancement of women in the fire service. She has also identified a number of obstacles that female firefighters

(Continued)

BOX 12.1 (*Continued*)   BREAKING THE GLASS CEILING

state hinder their ability to advance through the ranks as well as strategies that some have used successfully to break down barriers. She continues to advocate on behalf of women in the fire service through her lectures and presentations as she shares her research and solutions with today's fire leaders as well as future leaders who can make a difference on how diversity can finally be achieved in a profession long resistant to change.

She has had the privilege of presenting at the 2015 Virginia Fire and Rescue Conference, International Association of Women in the Fire & Emergency Services 2015 Leadership Conference, and 2015 Fire-Rescue International as well as at numerous fire academies throughout the state of North Carolina.

Her advice includes:

- Continue to train and obtain a formal education, even if on your own time and expense.
- Work toward helping change organizational culture, not simply remain quiet about it—educate others.
- Define a promotional plan and strategy from the beginning, if unattainable at current department find one that will allow for advancement.

Today, at Ole Miss, she is laying the framework and foundation for comprehensive emergency management at the university, and is building and fostering a relationship between the practice of emergency management and the University's Clinical Disaster Research Center. Together, the two will help strengthen and build a more disaster resilient university.

Sources: The glass ceiling is a term used to describe the invisible barrier that seems to prevent women from moving up in the ranks. *See* Phillips, B. and B. Russo. 2012. "Gender and Disasters: Needed Basic and Applied Research." *Emergency Management Review*, Vol. 1, Issue 1; Russo, B. 2013. *Women Firefighters' Strategies for Advancement In The Fire Service: Breaking Down Barriers In Gender-Based Occupations,* Ph.D. Dissertation, Fire and Emergency Management Program, Oklahoma State University, Oklahoma.

California after the 1989 Loma Prieta earthquake did look at the experiences of women in the field of emergency management (Phillips 1990). Women who participated in the survey indicated that several factors prompted their success. One factor stemmed from having the credentials necessary to enter and participate in the field, a condition that several deemed particularly relevant in a profession where the vast majority of professionals were male. A second factor arose from experience in the field. Similar to what Drabek (1987)

BOX 12.2 EMERGENCY MANAGERS: ORIGINALLY LOCAL PIONEERS, NOW GLOBAL PROFESSIONAL LEADERS

Kay C. Goss, CEM®. Former Associate FEMA Director for President Clinton.

This is a most exciting time to be an emergency manager. During the 33 years I have been working in the field of emergency management, I have seen many changes. Just to point to a few:

- There were few professional meetings; now there are professional emergency management meetings everyday.
- For many years, I was the only woman in the room at those professional meetings, whether they were in community, state, regional, or national meetings. Now, sometimes half.
- Only a few emergency managers were professional emergency managers. Most were older members of the communities. Now, new college graduates with degrees in emergency management are populating many positions.
- There were very few women in professional positions at FEMA, state and local emergency management offices. The same was true of fire service, law enforcement, and emergency medical services. Now, the long-time, highly successful Chief of Police for Washington, DC, is a woman.

(Continued)

BOX 12.2 (*Continued*)   EMERGENCY MANAGERS: ORIGINALLY LOCAL PIONEERS, NOW GLOBAL PROFESSIONAL LEADERS

- There were only a handful of academic programs offering degrees and certificates. Now, there are over 300, with another 100 under development.
- Most of the discussions, plans, and procedures were geared locally and limited in their vision to response; now preparedness, mitigation, and recovery are included, and prevention and protection have been added more recently.
- Tribal communities had very complicated processes for disaster declarations. We changed that, first with preparedness working directly with the tribal communities and then with response, and now the Stafford Act has been amended to provide that tribal communities go directly to FEMA and the White House for declarations and assistance, for recovery.

Much of my emergency management work has been seeking diversity, inclusion, holistic approaches, global outreach, and collaboration. We have pushed hard for professional participation in development and application of standards, including the Emergency Management Accreditation Program (EMAP) and the NFPA 1600 Standard for Emergency Management and Business Continuity. We have supported certifications, such as the International Association of Emergency Managers' Certified Emergency Manager® (CEM®). Additionally, accreditation has been gaining in support for higher education programs in emergency management degree programs, as with other professions, a crucial part of building our profession.

The FEMA Higher Education Program has been profoundly effective in facilitating numerous academic programs that have a vital role in building the profession; these programs continue to come on board on average of about one a month for the 21 years since we launched it in 1994. Many such programs are under development around the country and around the world. In the beginning of the higher education program for emergency management degrees and certificates, the faculty were composed of practitioners with Master's degrees or with extensive experience, and a few which combined these attributes. Now, professors are increasingly and often Ph.Ds. in related fields. Eventually, the faculties will be populated with Ph.Ds. in emergency management.

International interest and engagement in emergency management has escalated through the years. During my first year at FEMA, we hosted 400 high level public officials from various countries. By the time I left, we were hosting 1,000 such visitors each year. That international interest and engagement continues to increase across the board and around the world.

(*Continued*)

> ### BOX 12.2 (*Continued*)   EMERGENCY MANAGERS: ORIGINALLY LOCAL PIONEERS, NOW GLOBAL PROFESSIONAL LEADERS
>
> Our urban search and rescue teams are global ambassadors, with remarkable responses and recoveries. Our participation in the NATO Civil Emergency Planning Committee and the United Nations Development Programs are extremely important. Emergency management is rather non-controversial and provides a common ground for many global conversations, collaborations, and cooperation. Numerous nations are creating FEMA-like agencies to make predisaster plans, manage resources during disasters, and provide local, regional, and national leadership for recoveries and other environmental challenges. The increasing number and size of natural and human-induced disasters requires it.
>
> The private and nonprofit sectors are increasingly stepping up to recognize the importance of emergency planning and management, as well as business continuity. Additionally, technology has supported these evolutionary changes in the profession and facilitated the communication and collaboration among practitioners, academicians, students, officials, and the public, beyond anyone's imagination when I entered this arena, those 33 years ago!
>
> In short, the future of our exciting profession is unlimited. There is a compelling need to have this profession open to the whole of the community and I am happy to report that it now is! We have challenges ahead, we are better equipped than ever to meet those, and the best is yet to come, with more women, tribal members, African Americans, Hispanics, and young people joining forces with those special pioneers who have been "in the trenches" for awhile.

indicated, getting to know others and demonstrate competence mattered. Ten years after the Loma Prieta study, Wilson (1999) reported that little had changed to integrate women more fully into the field. It was not until the 1990s, under the Clinton administration, that a woman reached the second-highest post in the United States, FEMA Associate Director Kay Goss (see Box 12.2). Under the Obama Administration, Janet Napolitano became the highest-ranking woman in emergency management when she assumed directorship of the U.S. Department of Homeland Security.

Internationally, women's expertise has been underused in disaster situations despite the disproportionate impact of such events on women and children (Noel 1998). Good examples stem from major international disasters where the experiences of women, girls, and children have not been sufficiently considered. The 2015 earthquake that damaged Nepal pushed thousands of people into makeshift shelters, which quickly became dangerous for women and children. In need of privacy and hygiene facilities, aid agencies such as the United Nations funded safe spaces to reduce gender-based violence (Phillips and Jenkins 2016; UNFPA 2015).

Experts have called for fuller integration of women into the practice of emergency management, with the assumption that their experiences and perspectives can generate insights conducive to improving disaster response and recovery (Enarson and Morrow 1998). At present, about 33% of all the students in emergency management programs are female (Cwiak 2014). Further demographic breakdowns are not yet available but it is clear that the increasing presence of women and a more diverse set of emergency management students is well underway.

12.2.2 Racial and Ethnic Minorities and Tribal Nations

Little is known about the entry and career mobility of racial and ethnic minorities in the field of emergency management. What is clear is that disasters disproportionately affect people of color and that integration of a diverse workforce is necessary to reflect the full range of cultures and backgrounds which influence how we prepare for, respond to and recover from disasters. Insights into vulnerable populations can reduce impacts, such as understanding why disproportionate numbers of older, African American men died during hurricane Katrina (Sharkey 2007). Similarly, people within newly-arriving immigrant groups or those who speak languages other than English may be at particular risk when warnings fail to consider their perspectives. Not understanding ways of speaking or interacting can also undermine efforts to provide preparedness information, inspire mitigation measures, or facilitate recovery when disaster happens.

Tribes and First Nation groups worldwide also have struggled to become part of the emergency management picture. Yet their tribal lands and cultural resources sustain serious damage in disaster events. Along the U.S. Gulf Coast, for example, hurricanes, oil spills and coastal erosion have decimated existing tribes by destroying homes, undermining abilities to engage in sustainable livelihoods, and scattering families to disparate areas. The United States, similar to many other nations, respects federally recognized tribes as sovereign partners in emergency management planning and practice. However, dozens of tribes remain outside that planning parameter because they have not yet secured legal status as a federally recognized tribe. In all cases, emergency management agencies must work with tribal leaders and emergency managers to form meaningful partnerships. Understanding cultures that maintain particular ways of life, though, requires insight that may not be part of the body of knowledge that an emergency manager has obtained.

To counter this, FEMA has launched efforts to work with federally recognized tribes as part of ongoing planning, coordination, and collaboration. FEMA and DHS policy promote consultation, partnership, and meaningful dialogue with American Indian and Alaska Native Tribal governments (FEMA 2013). The Tribal Emergency Management Association (iTEMA, with the "i" meaning Indian, indigenous, inter-Tribal, information, innovative, inclusive and an "eye" to the future) in the United States has also been formed. iTEMA pursues collaborative and multidisciplinary approaches to the life cycle of emergency management. The association organizes training, a conference, and support for its members (see http://itema.org/about/, last accessed April 22, 2016).

12.2.3 People with Disabilities

The inability to meet disaster needs associated with disability has led to lawsuits and strong recommendations after mall evacuations failed to include people with disabilities, shelter accommodations (National Organization on Disability 2005), and accessible temporary housing post-Katrina (*Brou v. FEMA*). Similar to the argument about gendered emergency management practice, it is assumed that involving people with disabilities in every aspect of planning, preparedness, response and recovery will improve outcomes for citizens with disabilities (National Council on Disability 2009).

FEMA's Office of Disability Integration and Coordination embraces the idea of the Whole Community as discussed in this textbook, where everyone should be part of not only preparing for a disaster but part of the team of people who make that possible. First established in 2010, the Office has worked diligently to add disability integration specialists into Regional Incident Management Assistance Teams, deliver guidance about including people with disabilities in FEMA-funded initiatives, create Certified Deaf Interpreter positions, and deploy disability integration specialists to dozens of disasters. The institutionalization of the Office is clear—as is the commitment of FEMA to ensure that disability issues and concerns become routinized as part of overall emergency management. Toward that end, FEMA has supplemented regional disability integration specialists with 70 disability integration experts who travel to events including 25 certified sign language interpreters and five certified deaf interpreters. Their work is supplemented by advisory groups with significant levels of representation from people associated with disability services and advocacy organizations (see link in resources section).

12.2.4 LGBTQ Populations

Certainly, the last decade has been extraordinary in pushing forward the rights of lesbian, gay, bisexual, transgender, and queer (LGBTQ) people. Though limited studies have been done on the experiences and needs of LGBTQ populations during disasters and none on the career paths of people who are LGBTQ, we are certainly poised at a point where such information can accumulate and have an impact. Studies find, for example, that lack of consideration of LGBTQ disaster survivors leads to familial separation, exposure and subsequent discrimination in shelters and post-disaster recovery opportunities, and trauma (Balgos, Gaillard, and Sanz 2012; D'Ooge 2008; Eads 2002; Stukes 2013).

Opportunities exist for LGBTQ individuals to move into emergency management with protections under the law. The federal government, for example, supports the employment rights of all people. According to the U.S. Equal Employment Opportunity Commission (see link in resources), Title VII protects LGBTQ applicants and employees from discrimination and bias. Court decisions and Commission work have secured policy changes and money for those who have experienced discrimination such as not being hired due to being LGBTQ, being fired after a gender transition, being denied access to a restroom because of gender identity, losing a promotion due to being LGBTQ, or being harassed. One federal court decision, *Glenn v. Brumby*, found that the plaintiff experienced discrimination during a gender transition. The EEOC has also established a work group to support further its work on LGBTQ protections against discrimination. The Executive Branch has also taken action toward greater equality for LGBTQ workers. Operating from an assumption that people should be judged only from their "ability to get the job done," President Obama signed Executive Order 13672 prohibiting federal contractors from discrimination including sexual orientation and gender identity (see link in resources section).

One route into fields that manage crises and emergencies has always been internships. USAID, for example, offers a one-year internship in Washington D.C., in their LGBTQ office. To secure the internship, students must hold U.S. citizenship and a 3.0 GPA as part of good academic standing. As with other federal positions, applicants must be able to acquire and sustain a security clearance. Project work might include research, meeting and special event support, writing documents, working on social media and more. As background, USAID recommends international studies, computer science, foreign languages, gender studies, LGBTQ studies, logistics, social services, and policy studies among other fields.

12.3 Becoming a Professional Emergency Manager

As a student in this course, it is up to you to secure a broad range of knowledge, practical experience, interpersonal skills, research capabilities, and much more. It is also up to you to exercise the highest level of professionalism by embracing evidence-based best practices as laid out in this text—and in decades of disaster research. In this section, we discuss the value of acquiring more knowledge, finding a mentor, and securing internships, scholarships, training, exercise and drill experience, and the value of attending conferences and workshops.

After having read this book, you should clearly understand that many factors influence how an evacuation should be conducted. For example, who needs to be evacuated? What resources do they have for doing so—or what do they lack? How can emergency managers, community organizations and officials make up for any evacuation deficits the public may experience—and plan accordingly? What population groups exist and where are they located? Why are they vulnerable? How should I geographically cite the locations of various populations and with which overlays—transportation arteries? Community organizations with accessible vans? Pet shelters? All of the above? [*Yes!*]

To ask good questions and find relevant research, you will also need to know the lexicon—the vocabulary—of the field. This book serves as an introduction to concepts and practices used in the field though it is only the start of your learning journey. Terms change and definitions vary across the disciplines that influence the practice of emergency management. You will need to remain professionally committed to lifelong learning to remain current. As explained in the chapter on recovery, the term itself carries multiple connotations depending on whether you are in construction, social work, or a long-term recovery planning team. Because content for the multi-disciplinary field of emergency management is scattered across many journals, you will also have to understand variations in terms across the disciplines and become proficient at searching out useful information. Firefighters, for example, conceptualize recovery as retrieval of remains or items damaged in a fire. Psychologists view recovery as the result of an intentional, interactive process between therapist and patient. These very different conceptualizations will influence how you search for information. As another example, you may be able to find studies on protective action by searching for that term—or you may need to look for shelter-in-place, evacuation, or duck-and-cover. You must become a scholar-practitioner, someone who searches carefully for research to inform their practice.

As you learned in the chapter on research methods, a number of scientific journals exist to help answer your questions. Staying current can be as simple as having electronic tables of contents delivered to your inbox so that you can identify articles of interest. Memberships in scholarly organizations also help you stay connected to researchers who produce that body of knowledge and even work with them to identify and study critical questions for the field.

Stay tied into critical networks and professional associations as well. The Gender and Disaster Network (www.gdnonline.org) serves as one vehicle to help you stay informed on important topics. After major disasters, researchers and practitioners offer advice on human trafficking, nutrition, medical care, and more. Their work reflects an effort made real through the life of dedicated practitioner Mary Fran Myers (see Box 12.3). Ms. Myers, an experienced floodplain manager, moved on to work as associate director of the Natural Hazards Research and Applications Information Center (www.colorado.edu/hazards).

BOX 12.3   BRIDGING RESEARCH AND PRACTICE: THE LIFE OF MARY FRAN MYERS

The Mary Fran Myers Award, established in 2002 by the Gender and Disaster Network, recognizes that vulnerability to disasters and mass emergencies is influenced by social, cultural, and economic structures that marginalize women and girls. Research-based practice that reduces women's and girl's loss of life, injuries, and property can make a difference. The goal of the Gender and Disaster Network is to promote and encourage such an integration of research and practice.

Mary Fran Myers, Co-Director of the Natural Hazards Center at the University of Colorado at Boulder received the Award in 2002 before her untimely death in 2004. The Mary Fran Myers Award was so-named in order to recognize her sustained efforts to launch a worldwide network among disaster professionals for advancing women's careers and for promoting research on gender issues in disaster research in emergency management and higher education. A scholarship fund also exists to bring underrepresented individuals to the annual Natural Hazards Conference that she so stalwartly supported during her life.

For more information and a list of subsequent award winners, visit http://www.gdnonline.org/mfm_award.php. For a partial list of research that her life inspired, visit http://www.colorado.edu/hazards/research/qr/. *Source:* adapted from http://www.gdnonline.org/mfm_award.php, with permission.

At the Hazards Center, Ms. Myers connected researchers and practitioners through conferences, writing opportunities, and grant funding. For her work, the Gender and Disaster Network established the Mary Fran Myers Award for those who connect research with practice in an effort to reduce suffering. The award alternates annually between developed and developing nations to promote equity. Seeking out those who work to bridge the gap between research and practice is worthwhile. Another funding source, the Mary Fran Myers scholarship provides funds to travel to the annual Hazards Conference in Colorado—one that you may one day receive (see https://hazards.colorado.edu/awards/myers-scholarship, last accessed April 24, 2016).

12.3.1 Finding a Mentor

Relationships matter in this profession. By building strong and effective relationships, you can lay a foundation to work well with others during crises. Perhaps the most important relationship that you can build comes from selecting a mentor in the field. A mentor is defined as someone who guides, advises, and encourages you as you enter and move through the profession. A mentor can identify pitfalls and problems, offer solutions, and be there to listen to your questions. Mentors are not people who tell you what and how to do something, they are a trusted individual who can listen as well as offer advice. Your concerns are their concerns and your professional development reflects their abilities to direct your path.

Choose wisely when selecting a mentor and consider several people to provide you with good guidance. While someone with political pull or connections might lure you and should be respected, you want a mentor who has your best interests at heart—not their own political career. Choose someone with a career path similar to the one that you want who has good people skills and the time to spend with you. How do you find such a person? Attend conferences, join committees, serve on task forces and get to know people (see Box 12.4). Your willingness to step up and serve will garner the attention of prospective mentors, open them up to serving in such a role, and build your resume and networks at the same time. It is likely that a mentor will emerge over time as you begin to get to know people in the profession.

BOX 12.4 MY EMERGENCY MANAGEMENT JOURNEY

DeeDee Bennett, PhD, Assistant Professor of Emergency Services Program, School of Public Administration, University of Nebraska at Omaha.

I am a true interdisciplinary researcher. I have a Bachelor's in Electrical Engineering and a Master's in Public Policy from Georgia Institute of Technology, as well as a PhD in Fire and Emergency Management from Oklahoma State University. My research is three-fold, focused on the practice of emergency management, the advancement of new technology, and the inclusion of underserved populations. I seek to answer: *Can advanced technologies be leveraged to minimize disaster vulnerability among underserved populations?* I analyze this broad question from technical, social, and policy implementation perspectives.

My road to emergency management was very much a winding path that was refined by first-class mentorship. After undergrad, I was a unique research engineer tasked with bridging the divide between potential research sponsors and talented young engineers by explaining potential applications relevant to the interests of private industry, both domestic and abroad. Simultaneously, I was recruited to assist legal teams on export control and

(Continued)

BOX 12.4 (*Continued*)   MY EMERGENCY MANAGEMENT JOURNEY

technical patents, which became especially important after 9/11. I was intrigued; I realized I wanted to know more about the policy considerations for these new and novel technology designs. I decided to return to school part-time for a degree in public policy focused on technology.

During my studies, I met a fantastic mentor, Dr. Helena Mitchell, who led me to research on emergency communications and people with disabilities, later becoming my master's thesis advisor. By the time I completed my degree, I also had my first published article in the *International Journal of Emergency Management* and my first conference presentation. As luck would have it, I met another fantastic mentor and future dissertation advisor, Dr. Brenda Phillips, at that very same conference. She introduced me to the burgeoning academic discipline of emergency management and persuaded me to apply to the Oklahoma State University PhD program. Within a year of meeting Dr. Phillips, I was in Stillwater, Oklahoma pursuing a new career.

Currently, I am an Assistant Professor at the University of Nebraska at Omaha, where I hope to pass on the gift of exceptional mentorship. I teach Introduction to Emergency Management, Disaster Response and Recovery, Disasters and Socially Vulnerable Populations, and Inter-, Intra- and Cross Sector Collaboration.

One recent effort to provide mentoring comes from the William Averette Anderson Fund. Dr. Bill Anderson, a graduate of The Ohio State University, served as a graduate research assistant to Russell Dynes and E.L. Quarantelli (whose work you have been reading in this book). Dr. Anderson went on to serve at the National Science Foundation, guiding and funding much of the disaster research in the United States that has informed this text. His career included serving at the World Bank and then the U.S. National Academies. His prestigious career included a focus on the "next generation" of scholars and practitioners, particularly historically under-represented people. Those he mentored supported the development of a scholarship fund in his memory. Recipients have come from a wide array of disciplines (sociology, planning, geography, public health, disaster science, geoscience and international disaster management) and institutions (University of Delaware, University of South Carolina, Florida International University, Alabama A&M University, University of Iowa, Texas A&M University, see Photo 12.1). Participating students benefit from a Mentor Network of professionals in the field. Mentors are matched to a mentee with similar interests and goals and have monthly meetings to assist with their professional development (see resource section).

12.3.2 Internships

Emergency management graduates often moan about the wording in job announcements, particularly the part that requires experience.

PHOTO 12.1   Recipients of the William Averette Anderson Fund attend a professional development workshop at the University of Nebraska Omaha. (Photo courtesy of the William Averette Anderson Fund.)

Understandably, a community would not want just anyone writing emergency plans or deciding when and how to issue a warning. While courses and degrees do separate you from the pack of resumes on someone's desk—experience serves as an additional qualifier. But how to acquire experience? Throughout this text we have pointed out opportunities for volunteer service. Another form of volunteerism, although sometimes paid, comes through internships. An intern serves in an office of emergency management (or similar location) and supports the professional staff. Activities can range from administrative support to operational aspects depending on the location and need. Increasingly, agencies are offering internship opportunities for academic credit although some may offer salary or transportation support (see Box 12.5).

Academic advisors may be able to secure internships for academic credit, so be sure to visit with yours if you are still in school. You may also be able to secure an internship on your own by contacting an emergency management agency. Many list internships on their websites along with deadlines and requirements. Some may be very competitive but usually offer the best opportunities for learning in jurisdictions with challenging issues. You may want to also seek out opportunities—or even present yourself as such—to a local business or agency that could benefit from your emergency management knowledge. If you do secure an internship on your own and are still in college, though, be sure to ask for academic credit that will look good on a transcript as well as your resume.

12.3.3 Fellowships and Scholarships

A number of opportunities afford you the chance to gain additional experience and even funding during an academic career. In the United States, The National Science Foundation has funded a number of Research Experiences for Undergraduates Sites (REUs) for groups of students as well as individual REUs for individual researchers. An REU site brings students in from across

BOX 12.5

Michael C. Fleming, C.E.M., Joint Emergency Management Coordinator, Cook County, Illinois.

Michael Fleming is the Joint Emergency Management Coordinator for a collection of municipalities in northwest Cook County, Illinois. As the Joint Emergency Management Coordinator Mick collaborates with departments to develop regional plans and response structures. Prior to working as the Joint Coordinator Mick was the Emergency Services Planner in Yolo County, California, which also functioned as a regional emergency management agency. As a student, he held positions as a research and teaching assistant at Oklahoma State University, Interned with the McHenry County, IL Emergency Management Agency as well as worked for Wheels Inc. as a Business Continuity Planner.

When I was growing up, I knew I wanted to pursue a career where I would have the opportunity to help people. I started my education unsure of my end goal. I took classes in fire science, emergency medicine, and criminal justice. Through my studies, I discovered the field of emergency management, a discipline that was dedicated to not only response but also recovery, mitigation, and planning. The tenets of emergency management spoke to my personal values and to the career goals I hoped to one day embody. I enrolled in an emergency management bachelor's degree at Western Illinois University where I was exposed to a wide range of disaster-related studies. While pursuing my degree, I took every opportunity I was offered from internships with local government emergency management agencies

(Continued)

BOX 12.5 (*Continued*)

to opportunities with private business continuity companies. When I graduated, I decided to continue my education and pursue a master's degree from Oklahoma State University, which provided me with an invaluable scientific basis for how the public and emergency managers make certain decisions. Although the time and effort it took to become an emergency manager was substantial, the return is humbling. I have responded to immense floods and terrifying wildfires, assisted people to rebuild their lives and communities, reduced the likelihood of disasters through mitigation efforts, and improved planning through collaboration. The education I pursued helps me with each new challenge I face. As the disasters continue to grow in size and complexity, so too will need for highly educated emergency managers.

---

the nation to learn how to conduct research. Opportunities to apply are advertised widely at conferences, on websites, and through special announcements. The National Science Foundation has funded students in engineering, meteorology, computer science, geography and sociology among other disciplines—many of them focused on careers that generate research useful to the field of emergency management. The Disaster Research Center at the University of Delaware has offered an REU site for social science students interested in research careers (visit http://www.udel.edu/DRC/REU/REU.html). Prospective REU students compete to earn a funded slot. They live at the University for the summer while being instructed on how to conduct disaster research. Students work with a mentor from their home institution to design and carry out a research project. Their funding includes opportunities to travel to and present at professional conferences. Also in the United States, the Department of Homeland Security has funded students as DHS-STEM Scholarship awardees. DHS awards recipients complete tuition and fees along with a monthly stipend to support their education toward a career in homeland security (including disaster management).

12.3.4 Training

Many organizations and jurisdictions offer continual training, which is skill specific and usually occurs over a short time period like CPR training. Depending on local hazards, you may be able to take a variety of classes from your emergency management agency (local or state) or an agency like the American Red Cross or your state Medical Reserve Corps. FEMA sponsors independent study courses that can be taken for certification. Their sequences include a Professional Development Series that is listed in many of their job announcements (visit their site at http://training.fema.gov/IS/crslist.asp). FEMA also brings emergency managers into their campus in

Emmittsburg, Maryland for more intensive workshops and classes (for a listing see http://training.fema.gov/EMICourses/).

Training is important for any professional to keep up to date on current trends in the field. For example, after NIMS became a foundation for disaster response, DHS, state emergency management offices and others offered NIMS training. You can now take individual courses from the FEMA Independent Study program on each of the ESFs. Staying current in the field is critically important to career development. Once you complete the free, online courses, and pass the exam, you will earn a certificate that can be listed on a resume and attached to job applications.

12.3.5 Exercises and Drills

Most jurisdictions plan out some type of exercise or drill ranging from table top walk-throughs of emergency operations plans to full-scale exercises where people enact specific roles and decide what to do given certain scenarios. By being trained, credentialed, and a known member of a local emergency management agency or organization, you can participate or may be allowed to observe. Take these opportunities to gain insight into how partners work together to address a threat event, the challenges they encounter, and the strategies they use to overcome them.

Increasingly, we are seeing opportunities for students to participate in exercises. A recent event held in Columbus, Ohio, for example, involved hundreds of students as walk-through participants in a pandemic exercise. They walked through the various stations in a Point of Distribution or POD, where people may have to go to secure treatments during a pandemic. Participating gives you the opportunity to observe how PODs operate and exposes you to the widespread effort needed to take care of people in such an event.

12.3.6 Conferences, Workshops

People build networks by working together, typically across organizations. Another way to build networks is to attend conferences and workshops in the field. A wide range of such events occur routinely so you will have many options from which you can select. Most states have emergency management organizations that host annual events and often co-host special workshops or training at regular intervals. You may want to look for other relevant events, like the Ohio Safety Congress & Expo where you can find information on a wide array of appropriate content including hazardous materials, working with construction companies and utilities, worker safety, business continuity, and more.

A number of organizations also host conferences on an annual basis, such as the Natural Hazards Workshop offered through the University of Colorado at Boulder or the National Hurricane Conference. Regional FEMA offices sponsor workshops on various topics as do FEMA, DHS, and other federal agencies tasked with emergency management roles. Joining distribution lists serves as the best way to keep informed on upcoming conferences. The IAEM (www.iaem.org), the Natural Hazards Center (www.colorado.edu/hazards) and others disseminate information routinely on conferences and workshops.

12.4 Pursuing Your Degree and Beyond

Increasingly, emergency management jobs require at a minimum a bachelor's degree. Finding the right program is important as considerable variation can exist across colleges and universities. In this section, you will learn more about how to select an undergraduate and graduate degree program. Just as described earlier in the mentoring section, choosing the right academic degree program is critically important. The knowledge base of the faculty along with the professional networks they offer and those that you will build among your peers can launch or expand on your career in the field. You are pursuing an education tied to your discipline—which means that you should make a concerted effort to acquire a body of knowledge. Education is thus different from training, where you learn a specific skill usually in a short amount of time.

12.4.1 FEMA Higher Education Program

A major effort to enhance the professionalization of emergency management came through the development of the FEMA Higher Education Program. Here, a focus evolved on the development of associate, bachelor, and master degrees in emergency management along with academic certificate programs. With the support of FEMA Director James Lee Witt, Associate Director Kay Goss, and FEMA's Emergency Management Institute Director John McKay, Wayne Blanchard organized the first FEMA Higher Education meeting in June 1998. A main goal of this program was to establish some type of emergency management program in all 50 states. At the time, only one bachelor degree program in emergency management existed at The University of North Texas along with a related bachelor's program at Thomas Edison University. About 40 people, primarily representatives of universities thinking about starting a program, attended the meeting.

Today, over 500 people attend the annual meeting to listen to peer-review selected presentations, interact with colleagues, and network. Nearly 200 different types of emergency management programs exist worldwide, and almost all U.S. states have some type of emergency management program.

Certainly, the FEMA Higher Education Program has played a pivotal role with the emergence of emergency management degree programs and the continuing professionalization of the field.

Describing the impact of the Higher Education Program in 2009, Blanchard (2011) made the following comments:

> In the fourteen years since 1994 the EM Hi-Ed Program has helped foster growth in the higher education community to include more than 150 emergency management programs and expanded the reach of emergency management higher education into the practitioner community. Approximately 10,000 students are enrolled in these programs and another 20,000 annually take courses within these programs. Our experience with Emergency Management Higher Education over the past decade leads to the following three general observations:

> - Approximately one dozen new programs appear annually.
> - Established programs become successful in attracting students.
> - Students who graduate attract employers and secure careers in the field.

12.4.2 Undergraduate Degree Programs

Undergraduate programs produce students with a bachelor degree or potentially a minor or certificate in emergency management, homeland security, or related fields. Given your career interests, though, you may want to consider a fuller range of degree options including public health (see Box 12.6), law enforcement, social services, policy analysis, engineering, sociology, aviation, or international studies.

Many students select degree programs out of loyalty to a particular institution, family tradition, or cost. There are other factors to consider though. First, determine how long the program has been in existence. Is this a well-established program or is it new? While both have merit, established programs likely have a record of their alumni on their website—look at the kinds of jobs they now hold.

Next, examine the credentials of faculty members. First, do they have a degree appropriate to the field? You will want to have faculty with content knowledge on the discipline—defined as a substantive body of knowledge tied to a particular profession (Phillips 2015). Because emergency management as a discipline is relatively new most faculty will hold degrees in the social sciences or related areas. Look at their research interests that should reflect content similar to the chapter headings in this textbook. Such listings on a curriculum vitae (CV) indicate the faculty member actively conducts research in the field and is recognized by their colleagues as an expert. Next,

BOX 12.6 HEALTH AND DISASTER MANAGEMENT— AND A ROUTE TO DIRECTING THE MINISTRY

Sarah Stuart-Black, Director, Ministry of Civil Defence and Emergency Management, New Zealand.

Sarah Stuart-Black, originally qualified in New Zealand in 1993 as a registered comprehensive nurse, practicing in public, private and commercial nursing roles both in New Zealand and the England. She returned to University in England in 1997, where she graduated with a first class BSc (Hons) Development and Health in Disaster Management and a Masters by Research in Disaster Management.

Sarah joined the Ministry of Civil Defence & Emergency Management in July 2003 and has held a number of roles in the Ministry since then. She was appointed Director of the Ministry of Civil Defence & Emergency Management in December 2014. Prior to joining the Ministry, she worked for the Department of Health in London as a Regional Health Emergency Planning Advisor. The role had a specific focus on increasing preparedness and response capability of National Health Service organizations in London and providing a regional health response to emergencies affecting London. Prior to this role, she worked for the West Midlands Fire Service.

Sarah has been involved in a variety of operational activities within New Zealand and England, as well as events in Ethiopia, Niue and the Solomon Islands. She has been a member of the United Nations Disaster Assessment & Coordination Team for the last 9 years and has represented New Zealand at a variety of international forums, bilateral, regional and global meetings, exercises and forums.

(Continued)

look at the list of courses that the faculty members teach. Are they teaching within their area of expertise or experience? Then, look at the kind of service work, consulting, and practical experience they list on their CV—or, if they do not list that content, contact them and ask. In many programs, a combination of research with practical application is highly desirable.

Another consideration is the program's content. Approximately one-third focus on the public sector, particularly government service (Cwiak 2014). The private sector serves as the main concentration in 5% of all programs. Most pursue a combination of public, private, and humanitarian/voluntary sectors though an emphasis on the public sector is the most common.

The curriculum is important to consider too. Traditionally, emergency management degrees organize around the phases of disaster but may deviate. The University of Nebraska-Omaha does so, but also offers a number of concentrations that allow students to pursue specific interests like gerontology or public health as well as a concentration in Tribal Management. Take the time to look at course syllabi and consider at the readings and requirements? How will that content help you to acquire knowledge and prepare you for an emergency management career? Do the courses provide a broad range of knowledge so that you can have a wide array of knowledge and career options? What about content areas that are standard in a discipline—do the courses reflect time spent to teach you about the history of the field, the concepts and theories that drive understanding, and the methods needed to accumulate and critique information (Phillips 2005, 2015)?

Consider also the faculty: do they teach full-time in the program, part-time, or just occasionally? Some programs cobble together faculty from across the institution to create a program. Would you want a program with dedicated faculty or those scattered across the disciplines? There are pros and cons for each viewpoint. Involving an array of faculty brings you into contact with the multi-disciplinary body of knowledge that you need to succeed. You will want to count on the core faculty for advising and mentoring so look for such people when considering an institution in which you want to place your career. But, you also want faculty dedicated to the profession you want to enter. Ideally, an academic program will offer a hardy core of scholarly professionals as well as faculty with expertise in specific subjects including specialized instructors working in the field. Typically called adjunct faculty, they represent the practitioner community which is important to emergency management.

Because of the limited number of institutions with a full major in emergency management, it is likely that you will need to consider another discipline with a minor or concentration in emergency management. The majority of students moving into emergency management with a social science focus usually choose sociology or geography. Depending on your interests though, you may want to consider other disciplines. If you are interested in helping survivors for example, psychology and social work represent possible choices. For those interested in public service, a degree in political science or public administration may suffice. Students anticipating a future in the private sector would be wise to take business, management, health care, or hospitality courses. Criminal justice, forensics, and computer sciences allow you to map out a prospective career in homeland security. Pandemic planning requires expertise in medical health care delivery systems along with emergency management. You may even wish to specialize in areas that require knowledge tied to specific populations such as disability studies, Native Americans, or gerontology. Even journalism majors may want to consider emergency management minors given that they will cover a range of crises and disasters. Preparing for and responding to hazardous materials events requires knowledge of chemical, radiological, nuclear, and biological hazards. In short, supplement emergency management with a strong set of general education courses, a minor, and a foreign language to enhance your abilities to communicate information, interact with other cultures, and build community partnerships.

12.4.3 Graduate Programs

Similar concerns should drive your inquiries about a graduate degree but far more intensely. The critical feature of any graduate program should be the existence of highly qualified faculty who engage in research, know the profession, understand and contribute to informed practice, and have an established record as a solid mentor. Their CVs should demonstrate a continuing commitment to an area of expertise in which you hold an interest. Students who have graduated under their supervision should have secured employment and contributed to the field as professionals.

At the master's level you may be able to choose between a terminal or professional degree or a more traditional graduate degree. The first results in completing your education with a master's degree in the field and moving into practice upon graduation. The program curriculum should reflect that practitioner orientation but again should be squarely situated in an understanding of the empirical research, relevant policies, and established practices. Although you might not write a master's thesis, you should still graduate with skills for program assessment, community-based surveys, and an ability to read disaster research.

The more traditional master's degree moves the student through acquiring abilities to answer research questions critical to the field. The goal of many such programs is to enable the student to move into a doctorate-level program. To do so, you should have a strong background in a relevant area with a degree naming that discipline (e.g., sociology, geography, psychology, and emergency management). Your credentials to enter a doctorate-level program should be exceptionally strong as such a program will tax your energies and capacities while simultaneously raising your level of knowledge so that you become an expert and a researcher in the field.

A concern relevant to many students in the field stems from their personal situation. Many nontraditional or older students attempt to earn a graduate degree while working part or full-time in the field. Doing so can be challenging as disasters do not respect the academic schedule and you do have to go to work. However, nontraditional students often make up the majority of those matriculated in graduate programs and bring a valued sense of realism to the content and course discussion. Choosing to pursue a graduate degree can lead an individual into a new career path and upward career mobility. Prospective students should look at the institution offering the degree and speak with faculty to ascertain their level of support and understanding about nontraditional students. You will want to feel both mentored and supported, so look for an institution's success in doing so with nontraditional students.

Finally, an increasing number of institutions offer online courses or degrees. If you choose such a program, be sure to look at several aspects. First, how much experience do the faculty members have in offering distance courses? Do they hold certifications in online teaching? Have they published their approaches to distance education (Neal 2004; Phillips 2004, 2015)? Second, how do those programs offer online content? Education works most effectively when people have the chance to exchange views, ask questions, and actively interrogate the assigned reading. Choose a platform that allows for exchange between yourself, the professor, and the other students. Features that allow you to do so foster a collaborative learning environment that benefits *you*. Look for programs that use chat rooms, online video conferencing, video instruction, e-mail, and social media. Assess the program's potential delivery of that content and desired interaction by how rapidly and *thoughtfully* your future professor responds to an e-mail inquiry. Ask for an online videoconference to see how effective they are at using the technology and how well they communicate with you—prior to expending thousands of dollars in tuition. After all, you do want a really great job and career, right?

12.5 Where Will the Jobs Be?

In 2014, the median salary in the United States for emergency managers was $64,360 per year or $30.94 per hour (U.S. Bureau of Labor Statistics 2015). Though the positions that created that median salary ranged from entry-level to director-level, the typical entry-level education required a bachelor's degree and 5 years of experience in a related occupation. Salaries also differed by sector, with university, school, state, local, and private salaries averaging $84,640; professional, scientific, and technical at $77,720; hospitals at $75,420; local government at $58,020, and state government at $54,820. The number of jobs listed as emergency management directors included 10,600 in the United States, with an expected increase of 700 more positions between 2014 and 2024. The job outlook was said to grow at an average rate of 6% although retirements were expected to provide additional opportunities.

You may want to start with an internships to gain experience, or perhaps with a volunteer position. Think also about temporary jobs. FEMA, for example, has a cadre of on-call reservists who typically work on specific projects. That limited work could last from 2 to 4 years, though, and lead to full-time employment. FEMA Corps, established in 2012, may provide a particularly interesting route into a range of areas and professions. Specifically focused on those from 18 to 24 years of age, FEMA Corps members register for a 10 month term of service in order to gain experience and serve in a disaster context. FEMA Corps accepts 1,600 individuals to participate (see https://careers.fema.gov/fema-corps, last accessed April 21, 2016). Please see the resources for links to additional potential job openings.

12.6 Commitment to an Ethical Practice of Emergency Management

We end this chapter, and this book, by embracing ethical principles in emergency management. Defined ethics means that we act out of certain shared principles designed to promote good over bad. Several sets of ethical principles have evolved within the practice of emergency management. The International Association of Emergency Management, for example, established a Code of Ethics and Professional Conduct (see Boxes 12.7 and 12.8). Their codes and conduct expectations link into their certification

BOX 12.7   ETHICAL BEHAVIOR

The International Association of Emergency Managers (IAEM) has established a Code of Ethics to guide the work and to enhance professionalism of those working in the field. Focused on the principles of respect, commitment and professionalism, IAEM (2010, verbatim) members hold to certain values and ethical standards:

- **Respect**: Professional respect for supervising officials, colleagues, associates, and most importantly, for the people we serve is the standard for Certified Emergency Managers and Associate Emergency Managers. We comply with all laws and regulations applicable to our purpose and position, and responsibly and impartially apply them to all concerned. We respect fiscal resources by evaluating organizational decisions to provide the best service or product at a minimal cost without sacrificing quality. Honest differences of opinion are not a sign of disrespect; deliberately rude conduct or attacking a person's motives or integrity is a sign of disrespect.
- **Commitment**: Certified Emergency Managers and Associate Emergency Managers commit themselves to promoting decisions that engender trust in those we serve. We commit to continuous improvement by fairly administering the affairs of our positions, by fostering honest and trustworthy relationships, and by striving for accuracy and clarity in what we say or write. We commit to enhancing stewardship of resources and the caliber of service we deliver while striving to improve the quality of life in the community we serve.
- **Professionalism**: IAEM is an organization that actively promotes professionalism to ensure public confidence in Emergency Management. Our reputations are built on the faithful discharge of those duties. Our professionalism was founded on Education, Safety and Protection of Life and Property.
- **Ethics**: Certified Emergency Managers and Associate Emergency Managers promise to be professional and ethical by following these guidelines:

  - Fostering excellence in disaster/emergency management by keeping abreast of pertinent issues;
  - Enhancing individual performance by attention to continuing education and technology;
  - Practicing integrity and honesty in matters dealing with the public and one's peers and employer;
  - Avoiding conflict of interests resulting in personal gain or advantage at the expense of the public, one's peers and employer;

(Continued)

BOX 12.7 (*Continued*)   ETHICAL BEHAVIOR

- Conserving and protecting resources through effective use of funds, accurate assessment of potential hazards, and timely decision making;
- Maintaining confidentiality of privileged information; and
- Promoting public awareness toward and understanding of emergency preparedness and public protection.

- **Integrity:** The CEM Commission requires all candidates for and those awarded the CEM/AEM certification(s) to at all times maintain the highest standards of academic and professional integrity. IAEM considers academic and professional integrity to be an essential component to the emergency management profession. A violation of professional integrity is any action or attempted action that may result in creating an unfair advantage for the candidate.

Source: IAEM Code of Ethics, http://iaem.com/page.cfm?p= certification/cem-code-of-ethics, last accessed May 8, 2015.

BOX 12.8   BECOMING A CERTIFIED EMERGENCY MANAGER

Susamma Chacko-Seeley, M.P.A., C.E.M.

In 2007, I started a Master's degree in Emergency and Disaster Management and I went to my first International Association of Emergency Managers (IAEM) Annual Conference. During this conference, I was exposed to many new aspects including the Certified Emergency Manager (CEM) Program. After the conference, I became a member of IAEM. For a new member just starting a degree, pursuing the CEM designation seemed

(Continued)

BOX 12.8 (*Continued*)   BECOMING A CERTIFIED EMERGENCY MANAGER

a daunting task. Once I finished my degree and spent more time in the field doing the work of an emergency manager, attaining my CEM would become extremely valuable and professionally significant. As the only nationally and internationally recognized professional certification for individual emergency managers, achieving the CEM designation indicates than one possesses a certain level of education, experience, knowledge, training, work history, and most importantly, contributions to the field.

Although I had my degree in hand, I chose to wait until 2014 to apply for the CEM in order to gain more experience in the field to understand the true impact of our work. Our field is one where we make many decisions for people and communities and ethical decision making is vital. Given this, I understood a degree alone was insufficient to guide ethical decisions. In fact, since the CEM program requires a certain level of experience in order to achieve the designation, it ensures that individual emergency managers are exposed to varying situations and people, including volunteer or pro bono work that furthers the profession. It is during these opportunities where I realized that working to achieve the CEM designation actually ensured the experience I gained enhanced the framework provided by the degree. For more information about this program, one can go to the IAEM website (www.iaem.com) and click on the *Certification* tab.

process in an effort to ensure consistency. At its heart is the understanding that emergency managers must gain and retain public trust and confidence.

Ethical principles result from a shared commitment to a profession and the people served by that profession. As mentioned earlier in this chapter, emergency management is a people profession so an emphasis on interpersonal communication and relationships is central to being an effective emergency manager. It is likely that you will learn much of this from your faculty mentors who tend to be very supportive in the discipline of emergency management. As stated by Dr. Carol Cwiak at North Dakota State University in her annual address to the FEMA Higher Education Symposium (2014): "the emergency management higher education community continues its forward movement in a collaborative and committed manner with the heartwarming collegiality that is its hallmark."

Your own journey has just begun and we wish you well as you move into the profession of emergency management. May you make a *difference*.

Summary

This chapter provides an overview of opportunities for those intent on joining the next generation of emergency management professionals. The next generation cadre of colleagues will be more diverse than ever in the history of the field, as an appropriate reflection of the people they will serve. Becoming a professional in this field will require lifelong learning, through internships, training, and more educational opportunities. Never stop learning and always commit to immersing yourself in moments that will provide you with enrichment and growth. Find a mentor and learn from his or her guidance, wisdom, and mistakes. Pursue experience through internships, training, volunteerism, and temporary assignments. Hold fast to ethical principles and commit to earning and keeping the public trust that emergency managers need to inspire people to prepare for and be resilient to disasters and hazards they will encounter.

Discussion Questions

1. Where have you seen growth in the diversification of the emergency management workforce? What additional growth needs to take place so that emergency management reflects the population they serve?

2. Where can you find job listings in this field in order to pursue a career in emergency management?

3. What are the qualities that you should look for in a mentor? How can you secure and cultivate a meaningful and professional relationship with a mentor?

4. What lifelong opportunities to continue with your education are possible?

5. Based on the ethical principles laid out in this chapter, describe the kind of person you plan to be once you become an emergency manager.

6. How do you plan to help the next generation of emergency managers once you become established in your career?

Resources

- LGBTQ protections at the U.S. federal level, available at https://www.eeoc.gov/eeoc/newsroom/wysk/enforcement_protections_lgbt_workers.cfm, last accessed April 21, 2016.
- Executive Order 13672, available at https://www.gpo.gov/fdsys/pkg/FR-2014-07-23/pdf/2014-17522.pdf, last accessed April 21, 2016.

- Disability Integration Specialists, FEMA, available at https://www.gpo.gov/fdsys/pkg/FR-2014-07-23/pdf/2014-17522.pdf, last accessed April 21, 2016.
- JOB and CAREER sites, last accessed April 21, 2016): (1) United Nations Careers, available at https://careers.un.org/lbw/Home.aspx; (2) Federal Jobs, https://www.usajobs.gov/; (3) https://careers.fema.gov/; (4) U.S. Department of Homeland Security, https://www.dhs.gov/topic/homeland-security-jobs; (5) Gender and Disaster Network, http://www.gdnonline.org/jobs.php.
- William Averette Anderson Fund for African–American and other minority groups in disaster studies, http://billandersonfund.org/. For their mentee guide, visit http://billandersonfund.org/wp-content/uploads/2016/03/Bill-Anderson-Fund-Mentee-Guide.pdf.
- Gender and Disaster Network, www.gdnonline.org.
- Tribal Emergency Management independent study courses at FEMA include IS-318: Mitigation Planning for Local and Tribal Communities/ (http://training.fema.gov/is/courseoverview.aspx?code=IS-318).
- FEMA Higher Education list of institutions offering emergency management courses and degrees, https://www.training.fema.gov/hiedu/collegelist/.
- IAEM Certification, http://www.iaem.com/page.cfm?p=certification/intro.
- IAEM Code of Ethics, http://www.iaem.com/page.cfm?p=certification/cem-code-of-ethics-intro.

References and Recommended Readings

Balgos, Benigno, J. C. Gaillard, and Kristinne Sanz. 2012. The Warias of Indonesia in Disaster Risk Reduction: The Case of the 2010 Mt Merapi Eruption in Indonesia. *Gender & Development* 20(2): 337–348.

Blanchard, Wayne. 2011. FEMA Emergency Management Higher Education Program Description: Background, Mission, Current Status and Future Planning. Emmitsburg, MD: FEMA, Department of Homeland Security.

Cwiak, Carol. 2014. *Emergency Management Higher Education Today: The 2014 FEMA Higher Education Program Survey.* Presented at the FEMA Higher Education Symposium, Emmittsburg, Maryland.

D'Ooge, Charlotte. 2008. "Queer Katrina: Gender and Sexual Orientation Matters in the Aftermath of the Disaster." pp. 22–24 in *Katrina and the Women of New Orleans,* edited by Beth Willinger. New Orleans: Newcomb College Center for Research on Women, Tulane University.

Drabek, Thomas E. 1987. *The Professional Emergency Manager: Structures and Strategies for Success.* Boulder, CO: Institute of Behavioral Science.

Eads, Marci. 2002. Marginalized Groups in Times of Crisis: Identity, Needs, and Response. Quick Response Report #152. Boulder, CO: Natural Hazards Research and Applications Information Center, University of Colorado. Available at http://www.colorado.edu/hazards/qr/qr152/qr152.html, last accessed May 22, 2011.

Federal Emergency Management Agency. 2013. External Affairs Policy FP 305-111-1. Available at http://www.fema.gov/media-library-data/1390937322352-9e3dd0a0db-27685aed208a3c70c55220/FEMA%20Tribal%20Policy%20-%20Jan%202014.pdf, last accessed April 22, 2016.

Hite, Monique C. 2003. *The Emergency Manager of the Future: Summary of a Workshop.* June 13, 2003, Washington, D.C. A Summary presented to the Disasters Roundtable, The National Academies. Washington, D.C.

National Council on Disability. 2009. *Effective Emergency Management: Making Improvements for Communities and People with Disabilities.* Washington, D.C.: National Council on Disability. Available at www.ncd.gov, last accessed December 21, 2010.

Neal, David M. 2004. Teaching Introduction to Disaster Management: A Comparison of Classroom and Virtual Environments. *International Journal of Mass Emergencies and Disasters* 22(1): 103–116.

Noel, Gloria. 1998. The Role of Women in Health-Related Aspects of Emergency Management: A Caribbean Perspective. pp. 213–223 in *Thee Gendered Terrain of Disaster: Through Women's Eyes,* edited by Elaine Enarson and Betty Hearn Morrow. Westport, CT: Praeger.

Phillips, Brenda D. 1990. Gender as a Variable in Emergency Response. pp. 84–90 in *The Loma Prieta Earthquake: Studies of Short-Term Impacts,* edited by Robert Bolin. Boulder, CO: University of Colorado Institute of Behavioral Science.

Phillips, Brenda D. 2004. Using Online Tools to Foster Holistic, Participatory Recovery: An Educational Approach. pp. 270–277 in *Proceedings of the Recovery Symposium.* New Zealand: Ministry of Civil Defense and Emergency Management.

Phillips, Brenda D. 2005. Disasters as a Discipline: The Status of Emergency Management Education in the U.S. *International Journal of Mass Emergencies and Disasters* 23(1): 85–110.

Phillips, Brenda D. 2015. "Disasters by Discipline Revisited: A Ten-Year Retrospective and a Look Ahead." Keynote Speech, FEMA Higher Education Symposium, Emmittsburg, MD.

Phillips, Brenda and Pamela Jenkins. 2016. Gender-based Violence and Disasters: South Asia in Comparative Perspective. In *Gender, Women and Disasters: Survival, Security and Development,* eds. Linda Racioppi and Swarna Prajnya. Abingdon: Routledge.

Sharkey, Peter. 2007. Survival and Death in New Orleans. *Journal of Black Studies* 37(4): 482–501.

Stukes, Patricia. 2013. Gay Christian Service: Exploring Social Vulnerability and Capacity Building of Lesbian, Gay, Bisexual, Transgender, and Intersex Identified Individuals and Organizational Advocacy in Two Post Katrina Disaster Environments. Doctoral Dissertation, Department of Sociology, Texas Woman's University, Texas.

UNFPA. 2015. News on the earthquake in Nepal, overview. Available at http://www.unfpa.org/emergencies/earthquake-nepal, last accessed January 6, 2016.

U.S. Bureau of Labor Statistics. 2015. Occupational Outlook Handbook: Emergency Management Directors. Available at http://www.bls.gov/ooh/management/emergency-management-directors.htm, last accessed April 21, 2016.

Wilson, Jennifer. 1999. Professionalization and Gender in Local Emergency Management. *International Journal of Mass Emergencies and Disasters* 17(1): 111–22.

Appendices

TABLE A.1 The Enhanced Fujita Scale (EF-Scale)

	Fujita Scale		Derived EF Scale		Operational EF Scale	
F Number	Fastest 1/4-mile (mph)	3 Second Gust (mph)	EF Number	3 Second Gust (mph)	EF Number	3 Second Gust (mph)
0	40–72	45–78	0	65–85	0	65–85
1	73–112	79–117	1	86–109	1	86–110
2	113–157	118–161	2	110–137	2	111–135
3	158–207	162–209	3	138–167	3	136–165
4	208–260	210–261	4	168–199	4	166–200
5	261–318	262–317	5	200–234	5	Over 200

Source: National Oceanic and Atmospheric Administration, 2007, see http://www.spc.noaa.gov/faq/tornado/ef-scale.html, last accessed February 1, 2016.

TABLE A.2 The Saffir–Simpson Hurricane Scale

Category	Winds	Effects
One	74–95 mph	No real damage to building structures. Damage primarily to unanchored mobile homes, shrubbery and trees. Also, some coastal road flooding and minor pier damage.
Two	96–110 mph	Some roofing material, door and window damage to buildings. Considerable damage to vegetation, mobile homes and piers. Coastal and low-lying escape routes flood 2–4 hours before arrival of center. Small craft in unprotected anchorages break moorings.
Three	111–130 mph	Some structural damage to small residences and utility buildings with a minor amount of curtainwall failures. Mobile homes are destroyed. Flooding near the coast destroys smaller structures with larger structures damaged by floating debris. Terrain continuously lower than 5 feet ASL may be flooded inland 8 miles or more.
Four	131–155 mph	More extensive curtainwall failures with some complete roof structure failure on small residences. Major erosion of beach. Major damage to lower floors of structures near the shore. Terrain continuously lower than 10 feet ASL may be flooded requiring massive evacuation of residential areas inland as far as 6 miles.
Five	greater than 155 mph	Complete roof failure of many residences and industrial buildings. Some complete building failures with small utility buildings blown over or away. Major damage to lower floors of all structures located less than 15 feet ASL and within 500 yards of the shoreline. Massive evacuation of residential areas on low ground within 5 to 10 miles of the shoreline may be required.

Source: National Oceanic and Atmospheric Administration, n.d.a; http://www.aoml.noaa.gov/general/lib/laescae.html, last accessed February 3, 2016.

TABLE A.3 Modified Mercalli Earthquake Scale (Verbatim)

I. Not felt except by a very few under especially favorable conditions.

II. Felt only by a few persons at rest, especially on upper floors of buildings.

III. Felt quite noticeably by persons indoors, especially on upper floors of buildings. Many people do not recognize it as an earthquake. Standing motor cars may rock slightly. Vibrations similar to the passing of a truck. Duration estimated.

IV. Felt indoors by many, outdoors by few during the day. At night, some awakened. Dishes, windows, doors disturbed; walls make cracking sound. Sensation like heavy truck striking building. Standing motor cars rocked noticeably.

V. Felt by nearly everyone; many awakened. Some dishes, windows broken. Unstable objects overturned. Pendulum clocks may stop.

VI. Felt by all, many frightened. Some heavy furniture moved; a few instances of fallen plaster. Damage slight.

VII. Damage negligible in buildings of good design and construction; slight to moderate in well-built ordinary structures; considerable damage in poorly built or badly designed structures; some chimneys broken.

VIII. Damage slight in specially designed structures; considerable damage in ordinary substantial buildings with partial collapse. Damage great in poorly built structures. Fall of chimneys, factory stacks, columns, monuments, walls. Heavy furniture overturned.

IX. Damage considerable in specially designed structures; well-designed frame structures thrown out of plumb. Damage great in substantial buildings, with partial collapse. Buildings shifted off foundations.

X. Some well-built wooden structures destroyed; most masonry and frame structures destroyed with foundations. Rails bent.

XI. Few, if any (masonry) structures remain standing. Bridges destroyed. Rails bent greatly.

XII. Damage total. Lines of sight and level are distorted. Objects thrown into the air.

Source: U.S. Geological Survey, 2009. http://earthquake.usgs.gov/learn/topics/mercalli.php, last accessed February 3, 2016.

NOAA Space Weather Scales

Category		Effect	Physical measure	Average frequency (1 cycle = 11 years)
Scale	Descriptor	Duration of event will influence severity of effects	Kp values* determined every 3 hours	Number of storm events when Kp level was met; (number of storm days)
Geomagnetic Storms				
G 5	Extreme	Power systems: widespread voltage control problems and protective system problems can occur, some grid systems may experience complete collapse or blackouts. Transformers may experience damage. Spacecraft operations: may experience extensive surface charging, problems with orientation, uplink/downlink and tracking satellites. Other systems: pipeline currents can reach hundreds of amps, HF (high frequency) radio propagation may be impossible in many areas for one to two days, satellite navigation may be degraded for days, low-frequency radio navigation can be out for hours, and aurora has been seen as low as Florida and southern Texas (typically 40° geomagnetic lat.).**	Kp = 9	4 per cycle (4 days per cycle)
G 4	Severe	Power systems: possible widespread voltage control problems and some protective systems will mistakenly trip out key assets from the grid. Spacecraft operations: may experience surface charging and tracking problems, corrections may be needed for orientation problems. Other systems: induced pipeline currents affect preventive measures, HF radio propagation sporadic, satellite navigation degraded for hours, low-frequency radio navigation disrupted, and aurora has been seen as low as Alabama and northern California (typically 45° geomagnetic lat.).**	Kp = 8	100 per cycle (60 days per cycle)
G 3	Strong	Power systems: voltage corrections may be required, false alarms triggered on some protection devices. Spacecraft operations: surface charging may occur on satellite components, drag may increase on low-Earth-orbit satellites, and corrections may be needed for orientation problems. Other systems: intermittent satellite navigation and low-frequency radio navigation problems may occur, HF radio may be intermittent, and aurora has been seen as low as Illinois and Oregon (typically 50° geomagnetic lat.).**	Kp = 7	200 per cycle (130 days per cycle)
G 2	Moderate	Power systems: high-latitude power systems may experience voltage alarms, long-duration storms may cause transformer damage. Spacecraft operations: corrective actions to orientation may be required by ground control; possible changes in drag affect orbit predictions. Other systems: HF radio propagation can fade at higher latitudes, and aurora has been seen as low as New York and Idaho (typically 55° geomagnetic lat.).**	Kp = 6	600 per cycle (360 days per cycle)
G 1	Minor	Power systems: weak power grid fluctuations can occur. Spacecraft operations: minor impact on satellite operations possible. Other systems: migratory animals are affected at this and higher levels; aurora is commonly visible at high latitudes (northern Michigan and Maine).**	Kp = 5	1700 per cycle (900 days per cycle)

* Based on this measure, but other physical measures are also considered.

** For specific locations around the globe, use geomagnetic latitude to determine likely sightings (see www.swpc.noaa.gov/Aurora).

(Continued)

FIGURE A.1   NOAA Space Weather Scales: Geomagnetic storms.

NOAA Space Weather Scales

Category		Effect	Physical measure	Average frequency (1 cycle = 11 years)
Scale	Descriptor	Duration of event will influence severity of effects		
Solar Radiation Storms			Flux level of $\geq$ 10 MeV particles (ions)*	Number of events when flux level was met**
S 5	Extreme	Biological: unavoidable high radiation hazard to astronauts on EVA (extra-vehicular activity); passengers and crew in high-flying aircraft at high latitudes may be exposed to radiation risk.*** Satellite operations: satellites may be rendered useless, memory impacts can cause loss of control, may cause serious noise in image data, star-trackers may be unable to locate sources; permanent damage to solar panels possible. Other systems: complete blackout of HF (high frequency) communications possible through the polar regions, and position errors make navigation operations extremely difficult.	10^5	Fewer than 1 per cycle
S 4	Severe	Biological: unavoidable radiation hazard to astronauts on EVA; passengers and crew in high-flying aircraft at high latitudes may be exposed to radiation risk.*** Satellite operations: may experience memory device problems and noise on imaging systems; star-tracker problems may cause orientation problems, and solar panel efficiency can be degraded. Other systems: blackout of HF radio communications through the polar regions and increased navigation errors over several days are likely.	10^4	3 per cycle
S 3	Strong	Biological: radiation hazard avoidance recommended for astronauts on EVA; passengers and crew in high-flying aircraft at high latitudes may be exposed to radiation risk.*** Satellite operations: single-event upsets, noise in imaging systems, and slight reduction of efficiency in solar panel are likely. Other systems: degraded HF radio propagation through the polar regions and navigation position errors likely.	10^3	10 per cycle
S 2	Moderate	Biological: passengers and crew in high-flying aircraft at high latitudes may be exposed to elevated radiation risk.*** Satellite operations: infrequent single-event upsets possible. Other systems: effects on HF propagation through the polar regions, and navigation at polar cap locations possibly affected.	10^2	25 per cycle
S 1	Minor	Biological: none. Satellite operations: none. Other systems: minor impacts on HF radio in the polar regions.	10	50 per cycle

*   Flux levels are 5 minute averages. Flux in particles s^{-1}ster^{-1}cm^{-2}. Based on this measure, but other physical measures are also considered.
** These events can last more than one day.
*** High energy particle (>100 MeV) are a better indicator of radiation risk to passenger and crews. Pregnant women are particularly susceptible.

(Continued)

FIGURE A.1 (Continued)   NOAA Space Weather Scales: Solar radiation storms.

NOAA Space Weather Scales

Category		Effect	Physical measure	Average frequency (1 cycle = 11 years)
Scale	Descriptor	Duration of event will influence severity of effects	GOES X-ray peak brightness by class and by flux[*]	Number of events when flux level was met; (number of storm days)
Radio Blackouts				
R 5	Extreme	HF Radio: Complete HF (high frequency[**]) radio blackout on the entire sunlit side of the Earth lasting for a number of hours. This results in no HF radio contact with mariners and en route aviators in this sector. Navigation: Low-frequency navigation signals used by maritime and general aviation systems experience outages on the sunlit side of the Earth for many hours, causing loss in positioning. Increased satellite navigation errors in positioning for several hours on the sunlit side of Earth, which may spread into the night side.	X20 (2×10^{-3})	Fewer than 1 per cycle
R 4	Severe	HF Radio: HF radio communication blackout on most of the sunlit side of Earth for one to two hours. HF radio contact lost during this time. Navigation: Outages of low-frequency navigation signals cause increased error in positioning for one to two hours. Minor disruptions of satellite navigation possible on the sunlit side of Earth.	X10 (10^{-3})	8 per cycle (8 days per cycle)
R 3	Strong	HF Radio: Wide area blackout of HF radio communication, loss of radio contact for about an hour on sunlit side of Earth. Navigation: Low-frequency navigation signals degraded for about an hour.	X1 (10^{-4})	175 per cycle (140 days per cycle)
R 2	Moderate	HF Radio: Limited blackout of HF radio communication on sunlit side of the Earth, loss of radio contact for tens of minutes. Navigation: Degradation of low-frequency navigation signals for tens of minutes.	M5 (5×10^{-5})	350 per cycle (300 days per cycle)
R 1	Minor	HF Radio: Weak or minor degradation of HF radio communication on sunlit side of the Earth, occasional loss of radio contact. Navigation: Low-frequency navigation signals degraded for brief intervals.	M1 (10^{-5})	2000 per cycle (950 days per cycle)

* Flux, measured in the 0.1–0.8 nm range, in $W \cdot m^{-2}$. Based on this measure, but other physical measures are also considered.
** Other frequencies may also be affected by these conditions.
URI: *www.swpc.noaa.gov/NOAAscales*

April 7, 2011

FIGURE A.1 (Continued) NOAA Space Weather Scales: Radio blackouts.

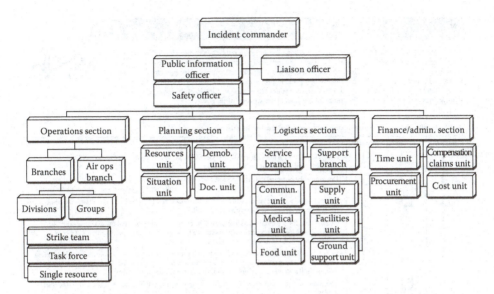

- **Command staff:** The command staff consists of the public information officer, safety officer, and Liaison officer. They report directly to the incident commander.

- **Section:** The organization level having functional responsibility for primary segments of incident management (operations, planning, logistics, finance/administration). The section level is organizationally between branch and incident commander.

- **Branch:** That organizational level having functional, geographical, or jurisdictional responsibility for major parts of the incident operations. The branch level is organizationally between section and division/group in the operations section, and between section and units in the logistics section. Branches are identified by the use of roman numerals, by function, or by jurisdictional name.

- **Division:** That organizational level having responsibility for operations within a defined geographic area. The division level is organizationally between the strike team and the branch.

- **Group:** Groups are established to divide the incident into functional areas of operation. Groups are located between branches (when activated) and resources in the operations section.

- **Unit:** That organization element having functional responsibility for a specific incident planning, logistics, or finance/administration activity.

- **Task force:** A group of resources with common communications and a leader that may be pre-established and sent to an incident, or formed at an incident.

- **Strike team:** Specified combinations of the same kind and type of resources, with common communications and a leader.

- **Single resource:** An individual piece of equipment and its personnel complement, or an established crew or team of individuals with an identified work supervisor that can be used on an incident.

FIGURE A.2   The organizational structure of the Incident Command System (ICS).

FAITH-BASED & COMMUNITY ORGANIZATIONS PANDEMIC IFLUENZA PREPAREDNESS CHECKLIST

The collaboration of Faith-Based and Community Organizations with public health agencies will be essential in protecting the public's health and safety if and when an influenza pandemic occurs. This checklist provides guidance for religious organizations (churches, synagogues, mosques, temples, etc.), social service agencies that are faith-based, and community organizations in developing and improving influenza pandemic response and preparedness plans. Many of the points suggested here can improve your organization's ability to protect your community during emergencies in general. You can find more information at www.pandemicflu.gov.

1. Plan for the impact of a pandemic on your organization and its mission:

Completed	In progress	Not started	
☐	☐	☐	Assign key staff with the authority to develop, maintain, and act upon an influenza pandemic preparedness and response plan.
☐	☐	☐	Determine the potential impact of a pandemic on your organization's usual activities and services. Plan for situations likely to require increasing, decreasing, or altering the services your organization delivers.
☐	☐	☐	Determine the potential impact of a pandemic on outside resources that your organization depends on to deliver its services (e.g., supplies and travel).
☐	☐	☐	Outline what the organizational structure will be during an emergency and revise periodically. The outline should identify key contacts with multiple back-ups, role and responsibilities, and who is supposed to report to whom.
☐	☐	☐	Identify and train essential staff (including full-time, part-time and unpaid or volunteer staff) needed to carry on your organization's work during a pandemic. Include back up plans, cross-train staff in other jobs so that if staff are sick, others are ready to come in to carry on the work.
☐	☐	☐	Test your response and preparedness plan using an exercise or drill, and review and revise your plan as needed.

2. Communicate with and educate your staff, members, and persons in the communities that you serve:

Completed	In progress	Not started	
☐	☐	☐	Find up-to-date, reliable pandemic information and other public health advisories from state and local health departments, emergency management agencies, and CDC. Make this information available to your organization and others.
☐	☐	☐	Distribute materials with basic information about pandemic influenza: signs and symptoms, how it is spread, ways to protect yourself and your family (e.g., respiratory hygiene and cough etiquette), family preparedness plans, and how to care for ill persons at home.
☐	☐	☐	When appropriate, include basic information about pandemic influenza in public meetings (e.g., sermons, classes, trainings, small group meetings, and announcements).
☐	☐	☐	Share information about your pandemic preparedness and response plan with staff, members, and persons in the communities that you serve.
☐	☐	☐	Develop tools to communicate information about pandemic status and your organization's actions. This might include websites, flyers, local newspaper announcements, pre-recorded widely distributed phone messages, and others.
☐	☐	☐	Consider your organization's unique contribution to addressing rumors, misinformation, fear, and anxiety.
☐	☐	☐	Advise staff, members, and persons in the communities you serve to follow information provided by public health authorities--state and local health departments, emergency management agencies, and CDC.
☐	☐	☐	Ensure that what you communicate is appropriate for the cultures, languages and reading levels of your staff, members, and persons in the communities that you serve.

continued

January 9, 2006
Version 1.1

CDC
SAFER·HEALTHIER·PEOPLE™

FIGURE A.3 Pandemic influenza preparedness checklist. (Data from http://www. flu.gov/planning-preparedness/community/faithbaseedcommunitychecklist.pdf, last accessed February 9, 2016.) *(Continued)*

3. Plan for the impact of a pandemic on your staff, members, and the communities that you serve:

Completed	In progress	Not started	
☐	☐	☐	Plan for staff absences during a pandemic due to personal and/or family illnesses, quarantines, and school, business, and public transportation closures. Staff may include full-time, part-time, and volunteer personnel.
☐	☐	☐	Work with local health authorities to encourage yearly influenza vaccination for staff, members, and persons in the communities that you serve.
☐	☐	☐	Evaluate access to mental health and social services during a pandemic for your staff, members, and persons in the communities that you serve; improve access to these services as needed.
☐	☐	☐	Identify persons with special needs (e.g., elderly, disabled and limited English speakers) and be sure to include their needs in your response and preparedness plan. Establish relationships with them in advance so they will expect and trust your presence during a crisis.

4. Set up policies to follow during a pandemic:

Completed	In progress	Not started	
☐	☐	☐	Set up policies for non-penalized staff leave for personal illness or care for sick family members during a pandemic.
☐	☐	☐	Set up mandatory sick-leave policies for staff suspected to be ill, or who become ill at the worksite. Employees should remain at home until their symptoms resolve and they are physically ready to return to duty (Know how to check up-to-date CDC recommendations).
☐ ☐	☐ ☐	☐ ☐	Set up policies for flexible work hours and working from home.
			Evaluate your organization's usual activities and services (including rites and religious practices if applicable) to identify those that may facilitate virus spread from person to person. Set up policies to modify these activities to prevent the spread of pandemic influenza (e.g., guidance for respiratory hygiene and cough etiquette, and instructions for persons with influenza symptoms to stay home rather than visit in person.)
☐	☐	☐	Follow CDC travel recommendations during an influenza pandemic. Recommendations may include restricting travel to affected domestic and international sites, recalling non-essential staff working in or near an affected site when an outbreak begins, and distributing health information to persons who are returning from affected areas.
☐	☐	☐	Set procedures for activating your organization's response plan when an influenza pandemic is declared by public health authorities and altering your organization's operations accordingly.

5. Allocate resources to protect your staff, members, and persons in the communities that you serve during a pandemic:

Completed	In progress	Not started	
☐	☐	☐	Determine the amount of supplies needed to promote respiratory hygiene and cough etiquette and how they will be obtained.
☐	☐	☐	Consider focusing your organization's efforts during a pandemic to providing services that are most needed during the emergency (e.g., mental/spiritual health or social services).

6. Coordinate with external organizations and help your community:

Completed	In progress	Not started	
☐	☐	☐	Understand the roles of federal, state, and local public health agencies and emergency responders and what to expect and what not to expect from each in the event of a pandemic.
☐	☐	☐	Work with local and/or state public health agencies, emergency responders, local healthcare facilities and insurers to understand their plans and what they can provide, share about your preparedness and response plan and what your organization is able to contribute, and take part in their planning. Assign a point of contact to maximize communication between your organization and your state and local public health systems.
☐	☐	☐	Coordinate with emergency responders and local healthcare facilities to improve availability of medical advice and timely/urgent healthcare services and treatment for your staff, members, and persons in the communities that you serve.
☐	☐	☐	Share what you've learned from developing your preparedness and response plan with other Faith-Based and Community Organizations to improve community response efforts.
☐	☐	☐	Work together with other Faith-Based and Community Organizationsin your local area and through networks (e.g., denominations and associations) to help your communities prepare for pandemic influenza.

FIGURE A.3 (Continued)   Pandemic influenza preparedness checklist. (Data from http://www.flu.gov/planning-preparedness/community/faithbaseedcommunity-checklist.pdf, last accessed February 9, 2016.)

Index